CONTEMPORARY
Hispanic
Biography

CONTEMPORARY
Hispanic
Biography

Profiles from the International Hispanic Community

Volume I

Ashyia N. Henderson, Project Editor

GALE®

THOMSON

™

GALE

Detroit • New York • San Diego • San Francisco • Cleveland • New Haven, Conn. • Waterville, Maine • London • Munich

THOMSON

GALE

Contemporary Hispanic Biography, Volume 1

Project Editor
Ashyia N. Henderson

Editorial
Jennifer M. York, Ralph Zerbonia

Permissions
Maria Franklin, Margaret Chamberlain

Manufacturing
Dorothy Maki, Rhonda Williams

Compositition and Prepress
Mary Beth Trimper, Gary Leach

Imaging and Multimedia Content
Barbara Yarrow, Kelly A. Quin, Leitha
Etheridge-Sims, David G. Oblender, Lezlie
Light, Randy Bassett, Robert Duncan,
Dan Newell

ISBN 0-7876-6538-X

Printed in the United States of America
10 9 8 7 6 5 4 3 2 1

Contemporary Hispanic Biography
Advisory Board

Contents

Introduction ix

Photo Credits xi

Cumulative Nationality Index 223

Cumulative Occupation Index 225

Cumulative Subject Index 227

Cumulative Name Index 231

Introduction

Contemporary Hispanic Biography provides informative biographical profiles of the important and influential persons of Latino heritage who form the international Hispanic community: men and women who have changed today's world and are shaping tomorrow's. *Contemporary Hispanic Biography* covers persons of various nationalities in a wide variety of fields, including architecture, art, business, dance, education, fashion, film, industry, journalism, law, literature, medicine, music, politics and government, publishing, religion, science and technology, social issues, sports, television, theater, and others. In addition to in-depth coverage of names found in today s headlines, *Contemporary Hispanic Biography* provides coverage of selected individuals from earlier in this century whose influence continues to impact on contemporary life. *Contemporary Hispanic Biography* also provides coverage of important and influential persons who are not yet household names and are therefore likely to be ignored by other biographical reference series. Each volume also includes listee updates on names previously appearing in CHB.

Designed for Quick Research and Interesting Reading

- *Attractive page design* incorporates textual subheads, making it easy to find the information you re looking for.

- *Easy-to-locate data sections* provide quick access to vital personal statistics, career informa- tion, major awards, and mailing addresses, when available.

- *Informative biographical essays* trace the subject s personal and professional life with the kind of in-depth analysis you need.

- *To further enhance your appreciation* of the subject, most entries include photographic portraits.

- *Sources for additional information* direct the user to selected books, magazines, and news-papers where more information on the individuals can be obtained.

Helpful Indexes Make It Easy to Find the Information You Need

Contemporary Hispanic Biography includes cumulative Nationality, Occupation, Subject, and Name indexes that make it easy to locate entries in a variety of useful ways.

Available in Electronic Formats

On-line. *Contemporary Hispanic Biography* is available on-line through Gale Group's Biography Resource Center. For more information, call (800) 877-GALE.

Disclaimer

Contemporary Hispanic Biography uses and lists websites as sources and some of these websites may be obsolete.

We Welcome Your Suggestions

The editors welcome your comments and suggestions for enhancing and improving **Contemporary Hispanic Biography.** If you would like to suggest persons for inclusion in the series, please submit these names to the editors. Mail comments or suggestions to:

The Editor
Contemporary Hispanic Biography
Gale Group
27500 Drake Rd.
Farmington Hills, MI 48331-3535
Phone: (800) 347-4253

Photo Credits

by Bruno Bebert. AP/Wide World Photos. ***Valdez, Luis,*** photograph. Courtesy of Luis Valdez. ***Vargas Llosa, Mario,*** photograph. Courtesy of Jerry Bauer. ***Velásquez, Nydia,*** photograph. AP/Wide World Photos. ***Welch, Raquel,*** photograph by Mark Lennihan. AP/Wide World Photos.

Arnoldo Alemán

1946—

Nicaraguan legislator and former leader

After the people of Nicaragua had endured years of political conflict and sometimes civil war brought to them by the succession of autocratic right-wing and revolutionary left-wing governments under which they had lived for decades, they hoped in the 1990s for stability and for the strengthening of democratic institutions. With Arnoldo Alemán, who served as Nicaragua's president from 1996 until 2002, they got some of both—after a fashion. A fierce opponent of the leftist Sandinista regime that ruled Nicaragua in the 1980s, Alemán as president emerged as a dealmaker who shared power with the Sandinistas even though he had personally suffered considerable hardship as a result of programs they enacted. His dealmaking tendencies had a less savory side, however; observers accused Alemán of partaking in the graft and corruption that had long plagued Nicaragua and was largely to blame for its status as the second-poorest country (ahead of only Haiti) in the Western Hemisphere.

Alemán (whose full name is José Arnold Alemán Lacayo) was born on January 23, 1946, in the Nicaraguan capital of Managua. As quoted in the *New York Times,* he described his family as having "roots in the soil," as "united, simple, hard-working, honest and Christian." That description, however, fails to communicate some aspects of Alemán's family background; his father was a lawyer who was an associate of the 1970s Nicaraguan strongman Anastasio Somoza and served as Somoza's minister of education for a time. The family owned a coffee plantation south of Managua.

Following his father into the legal profession, Alemán earned a law degree from the National Autonomous University in León, Nicaragua in 1967. From then until 1979, he was a practicing lawyer in Managua; his clients were banks, agriculture concerns, and large businesses. He married and fathered four children. In 1979 the Somoza regime was overthrown by the Sandinistas and their leader Daniel Ortega. Alemán's employer at the time, an investment firm, was nationalized, and shortly afterward Alemán was arrested on suspicion counter-revolutionary activity. He spent nine months in prison.

After his release, rather than going into exile like many other Nicaraguans connected with the Somoza government, Alemán remained in Managua and decided to resist the Sandinistas' efforts to transform Nicaragua into a socialist state. He emerged as a leader in several groups that worked to resist Sandinista land redistribution schemes: he became president of the Coffee Growers Association of Managua from 1983 to 1986, president of the national Coffee Growers Union from 1986 to 1990, and vice-president of the National Farmers Union. During this period, Alemán also established ties with the anticommunist Cuban exile community in Miami, Florida.

In 1989 the Sandinistas arrested Alemán once again, seizing the family coffee plantation and sentencing Alemán to seven years in prison. After his arrest his wife was diagnosed with brain cancer, and the government refused to permit Alemán to visit her before she died. Released after the Sandinstas suffered an electoral loss in 1990, Alemán now felt compelled to enter the public sphere. "That was a very painful time for me, but it made me determined that my children should not grow up under a totalitarian system," Alemán was quoted as saying in the *New York Times.* "That is what finally pushed me into politics."

After winning a seat on the Managua city council, he was elected mayor of Managua that year, defeating his Sandinsta rival. He promptly set about erasing reminders of Sandinista rule; the letters FSLN (the Spanish initials for the Sandinista political party) painted on a hillside overlooking the city he ordered changed to FIN, in Spanish "the end." Alemán gained popularity with

Managua's poor through a group of public-works projects that included the rehabilitation of a waterfront park destroyed in the 1972 Nicaraguan earthquake. He set his sights on national office, building a small political party into a national force by packing the city government with allies and by freely dispensing aid dollars that came in from the U.S. government and from Miami's Cuban exiles.

Charges of kickbacks and the misuse of municipal funds were aired, but Nicaraguans contrasted Alemán's accomplishments with the malaise of a national government beset by infighting between recalcitrant Sandinistas and new president Violeta Chamorro. By 1994 Alemán's party, the Liberal Constitutionalist Party, had won several regional elections, and two years later he forged an alliance of right-wing parties and emerged as the chief conservative candidate running against Sandinista leader Ortega, who was attempting to regain the presidency.

Given Alemán's family ties to the Somoza regime and his status as a member of Nicaragua's landholding elite, some observers feared that an Alemán victory would mean a return to the days of rightist authoritarian rule. The Sandinistas did their best to further this impression, but they underestimated Alemán's personal appeal and popularity among ordinary Nicaraguans. Dubbed "Gordoman" ("Fatman") after a cartoonist lampooned his rotund stature, Alemán happily adopted the label and used it in his campaign materials. Former U.S. president Jimmy Carter, in Nicaragua to observe the elections, called Alemán "a very exuberant sort of guy who bubbles forth."

In the national elections held in October of 1996, Alemán defeated Ortega by a 51-to-38-percent margin, taking power in Nicaragua's first peaceful transition from one elected civilian leader to another in over 100 years. The country's national assembly remained closely divided, however, and Alemán, quoted in the New Orleans *Times-Picayune* as saying that "the culture of death has left nothing but pain, tears and grief in our country," moved to include Sandinista figures in his government. By 2000, in fact, he had worked out a deal with the Sandinistas that ensconsed them and his own Liberal Constitutionalists as a virtual two-party monopoly in Nicaraguan politics. The fact that the Sandinistas still wielded considerable influence in the country's armed forces may have played a role in his decision.

Alemán took visible anticorrpution measure at the beginning of his term, such as requiring full financial disclosure from Cabinet ministers. He worked with international lenders to gain relief from Nicaragua's crushing foreign debt, and was perhaps best known for his leadership of the recovery effort that followed the devastation wreaked by Hurricane Mitch in 1998. Among Nicaraguans sensitive to the role corruption had played in engendering the country's endemic poverty, however, he encountered criticism; one poll taken in 2000 found him with an approval rating of only 26 percent, although others found him with solid majority support. One damaging revelation was that from the time of Alemán's election to Managua's city council until his victory in the presidential election, the worth of his personal assets had increased from $26,118 to $993,015. He owned eight late-model cars at the completion of his mayoral term.

As a result, Alemán chose to step aside from the 2001 elections in favor of a fellow Liberal Constitutionalist party member, Enrique Bolanos, whose political history in many ways resembled Alemán's own. Bolanos defeated a now pro-American Daniel Ortega once again and took office in January of 2002, promising to investigate corruption in the Alemán government. But Alemán had already been chosen as head of the country's national assembly. For better or worse, he seemed a linchpin of a new order in Nicaragua—a desirable thing for many in a country that had known a great deal of disorder.

Sources

Periodicals

Financial Times (London, England), December 16, 1999, p. World News-8; May 30, 2000, p. World News-4; January 23, 2001, p. World News-3.
Los Angeles Times, October 27, 1996, p. M2; January 26, 1997, p. M3; February 27, 1999, p. A3; September 12, 1999, p. A2.
NACLA Report on the Americas, September-October 1996, p. 6.
New York Times, October 23, 1996, p. A3; March 12, 2002, p. A8.
Times-Picayune (New Orleans, Louisiana), March 9, 1997, p. A30.

On-line

Current Leaders of Nations, Gale Group, 1999. Reproduced in *Biography Resource Center,* Gale, 2001 (http://www.galenet.com/servlet/BioRC).

—James M. Manheim

Isabel Allende

1942—

Novelist

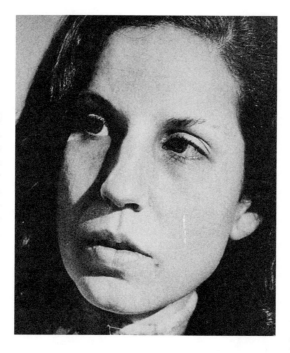

One of the most popular and widely acclaimed writers in the Western Hemisphere, the Chilean novelist Isabel Allende has been hailed as the creator of a distinctively female voice within the largely male-dominated Latin American literary tradition. In a series of best-selling novels written in the last decades of the twentieth century, Allende mixed elements of Latin American "magical realism" with strands drawn from the social upheavals that had occurred through Latin America's turbulent history—some of which she had personally experienced. A popular touch, perhaps shaped by the romance novels Allende edited as a young journalist in Chile, propelled her work to wide popularity in the United States after the release of her stunning 1982 debut, *The House of the Spirits,* in English translation.

The daughter of a Chilean diplomat, Isabel Allende was born in Lima, Peru, on August 2, 1942. Her parents divorced when she was young, and she was raised in the Chilean capital of Santiago. Well-educated in private schools, Allende traveled the world with her mother and her new stepfather, another member of Chile's diplomatic corps. As a young woman Allende worked for a United Nations office in Santiago as a secretary; she married an engi-

neer, Miguel Frias, when she was 20.

Worked as Advice Columnist

Gradually Allende began to gravitate toward a writing career. She held a variety of positions with magazines and publishing houses in Santiago between 1967 and 1974, one of them as an advice columnist with a magazine called *Paula,* and also worked as a television interview host and as a movie newsreel editor. Allende's life was turned upside down, however, by national events; Chilean president Salvador Allende, who was her uncle and godfather, was overthrown and assassinated in a 1973 coup backed by the United States, which objected to the Allende government's socialist reforms. After the coup, Allende said in a *Publishers Weekly* interview quoted in *Contemporary Authors,* "I realized that everything was possible—that violence was a dimension that was always around you."

Allende and her family fled Chile for Venezuela, where she wrote for the newspaper *El Nacional.* But less work came her way than in her native country, and she found herself with a lot of time on her hands for thought. She used it to take stock of her own life and of

At a Glance . . .

Born August 2, 1942, in Lima, Peru; raised in Chile; daughter of Tomàs Allende, a Chilean diplomat, and Francisca Llona Barros Allende; married Miguel Frias, an engineer, 1962 (divorced, 1987); married William Gordon, a lawyer, 1988; children: Paula (deceased), Nicolas. *Education:* Graduated from a private high school in Santiago, Chile.

Career: Secretary, United Nations Food and Agricultural Organization, Santiago, Chile, 1959-65; worked as journalist and advice columnist, *Paula* and *Mampato* magazines, Santiago, 1967-74; television interviewer, Santiago, 1970-75; writer for movie newsreels, 1973-75; journalist, *El Nacional,* Caracas, Venezuela, 1975-84; published debut novel, *The House of the Spirits,* 1982 (English trans. 1985); guest lecturer and writing instructor at various U.S. institutions, 1980s and 1990s.

Addresses: *Agent*—Carmen Balcells, Diagonal 580, Barcelona 21, Spain.

the history of her own culture. One of the fruits of her reflections was a long and ultimately unmailed letter she wrote to her ailing grandfather in Chile, surveying the long and complicated history of her own family. That letter, fictionalized and heavily elaborated, grew into Allende's first novel, *The House of the Spirits (La casa de los espíritus).*

Like Colombian author Gabriel García Marquez's *One Hundred Years of Solitude,* to which it has often been compared, *The House of the Spirits* is a complex family saga that spans several generations. Its main characters are a traditional patriarch, Esteban Trueba, who becomes estranged from his wife, Clara, and later from his activist daughter, Alba. The book includes so-called magical realist devices—supernatural or unexplainable events, such as salt and pepper shakers that move around a dining room table of their own accord. As the novel moves toward the present, though, South America's recent political history comes to the fore and the storytelling becomes more conventionally realistic. Alba, who is revealed as the story's narrator, is seized by the military after a right-wing coup.

Based Novel on Pinochet Dictatorship

Although *The House of the Spirits* took place in an unnamed country, Allende's second novel, *Of Love and Shadows (De amor y de sombra,)* was specifically situated in Chile during the Pinochet dictatorship. It tells the story of two journalists who are forced into exile after investigating a military-sponsored murder of a young woman who has seemingly miraculous powers that have allowed her to defy their commands. Drawn on actual events, the novel combined magical realism with scenes of Latin American life in much the same way as *The House of the Spirits,* but seemed more closely identified with Allende's own career.

The House of the Spirits was translated into English in 1985 (it was made into a film in 1994), and began to gain wide attention in the United States; translated into other languages as well, it became a best seller in several European countries. Allende won several new-author awards and was brought to the United States for a promotional tour as *Of Love and Shadows* was released. After giving a reading in San Jose, California, Allende met a U.S. lawyer, William Gordon; the two later married, and Allende continues to make her home in northern California.

Allende remained steadily productive through the 1990s, experimenting with new forms and settings and consistently holding the interests of critics who, even if they did not give Allende universal acclaim, kept her in the literary limelight. Allende's novel *Eva Luna* and its successor volume of short fiction *The Stories of Eva Luna (Los cuentos de Eva Luna)* feature a South American writer who becomes involved with an Austrian immigrant who is the son of a former Nazi (many Nazis fled to South America after World War II). Her 1993 novel *The Infinite Plan (El plan infinito),* however, was set in her adopted country, with a male, Anglo-American central figure who grows up in a poor, mainly Hispanic neighborhood in Los Angeles. *Paula* (1995) was a nonfiction work about the death of Allende's daughter, and in 1997 Allende published *Aphrodite: A Memoir of the Senses (Afrodite: Recetas, cuentos y otros afrodisiacos),* an unusual mixture of autobiography, essays, and cookbook.

Novels Link United States and Latin America

Returning to the epic sweep of her debut in the late 1990s, however, seemed to bring Allende back to the roots of her creative impulses. Her novels *Daughter of Fortune (Hija de la fortuna,* 1999) and *Portrait in Sepia (Retrato in sepia,* 2001) featured characters who had appeared or been mentioned in *The House of the Spirits,* once again structuring her stories to encompass the experiences of several generations, and this time capturing the cultural interchange that has linked the western United States with Latin American countries. *Publishers Weekly* noted that "Allende expands her geographical boundaries in this sprawling, engrossing historical novel flavored by four cultures—English, Chilean, Chinese and American—and set during the 1849 California Gold Rush."

Daughter of Fortune landed on best-seller lists and brought Allende an important marker of popular U.S. acceptance and a virtual guarantee of substantial future sales—it was named as a pick title by the nationwide book club headed by talk-show host Oprah Winfrey. Allende became the first Hispanic author Winfrey had selected. Continuing to create new examples in her series of strong female characters, Isabel Allende remains in the process of redefining, for the general U.S. reading public as well as for Spanish-language readers, the image of Latin American fiction.

Selected writings

The House of the Spirits, 1982 (English trans. 1985).
Of Love and Shadows, 1984 (English trans. 1987).
Eva Luna, 1988.
Stories of Eva Luna, 1990 (English trans. 1991).
The Infinite Plan, 1993.
Paula, 1995 (nonfiction).
Aphrodite: A Memoir of the Senses, 1997 (English trans. 1998).
Daughter of Fortune, 1999.
Portrait in Sepia, 2001.

Sources

Books

Dictionary of Hispanic Biography, Gale, 1996.
Feminist Writers, St. James, 1996.

Periodicals

People, April 20, 1998, p 47.
Publishers Weekly, August 23, 1999, p. 41; February 21, 2000, p. 20; July 16, 2001, p. 164.

On-line

Contemporary Authors Online. The Gale Group, 2001. Reproduced in *Biography Resource Center.* Farmington Hills, MI: The Gale Group. 2001. (http://www.galenet.com/servlet/BioRC).

—James M. Manheim

Pedro Almodóvar

1951—

Filmmaker

As notorious as he is notable, Pedro Almodóvar, long Spain's reigning king of film, has taken center stage as one of the world's most successful and original directors. His art, borne out of a childhood of bleak villages and Catholic repression, took shape during "la movida," Spain's cultural revolution that followed the fall of General Francisco Franco, the country's fascist dictator who ruled for 36 years. Even as he progressed from short films made with a hand-held Super 8 camera to Academy Award-winning features, Almodóvar has maintained a distinctive style: surreal sets awash in ultra-bright colors; ferociously independent characters that don't push the limits of convention but barrel through them; and outrageous storylines rampant with sexuality, hedonism, humor, and kitsch. He was once quoted in *Film Comment* as saying, "for the individual [passion] is undeniably the only motor that gives sense to life." It is also, undeniably, the motor that drives Almodóvar. Despite the eccentricities, his films still somehow manage to be familiar enough to stir the heart of his audience. This is Almodóvar's magic.

Pedro Almodóvar Caballero was born on September 25, 1951 in Calzada de Calatrava, a small dusty village in southwestern Spain. On www.express.co.uk Almodóvar is quoted as describing his birth town as "a land so hard where there was no understanding of colour. Maybe that is why I use so many colours in my films." His father, Antonio Almodóvar, worked at a gas station. On the side he made wine which he sold to supplement the family's meager income. His mother, Francisca Caballero, was a homemaker who ruled her house with an iron fist. Almodóvar suffered the possessiveness of his mother along with two older sisters, María Jesús and Antonia, and a younger brother, Agustín. Her dominance would come to influence Almodóvar's work. "As a result of having seen my mother fight it out always, it's the women who end up running life in my films," he told *Vanity Fair*.

Escaped Abuse Through Films

When he was eight years old, Almodóvar and his family moved to a small rural village in the cold mountainous region of Extremadura in Eastern Spain. There, under pressure from his mother, Almodóvar taught local children how to read. By ten, his intelligence had earned him a scholarship to an all boys Catholic school. It was much less than a blessing. At the school his spirit

At a Glance . . .

Born September 25, 1951, Calzada de Calatrava, Spain; son of Antonio Almodóvar, a gas station attendant and Francisca Caballero, a homemaker. *Religion:* raised Catholic.

Career: Director, writer, and producer of films. Administrator, Telefonica, Madrid, Spain, 1970-1980; singer, Almodóvar and McNamara, 1980s; actor, Los Goliardos, 1980s; writer and columnist as Patty Diphusa, La Luna, 1980s.

Awards: Silver Toucan for the Best Director, Rio de Janeiro, 1987; New Generation Award Association of Critics of Los Angeles, 1987; Award of the Association of Theater Critics of New York, 1988; Orson Welles Award, Best Director, Foreign Language Film, 1989; Silver Ribbon Award, Best Director, Italy, 1989; David di Donatello Award, Best Director Rome, 1989; National Award of Cinematic Art, Spain, 1989; Best Director, Festival of Gramado, Brazil, 1992; César, France, 1993; the decoration of Arts and Humanities, French Ministry of Education and the Arts, 1995; Gold Medal for Merit in the Fine Arts, Spanish Government, 1998; honorary César, France, 1999. Best Director, Cannes Film Festival, 1999; Best Movie of the Year, San Sebastian Film Festival, Spain, 1999; Best European Film of the Year, European Film Awards, 1999; Best European Director, European Film Awards, 1999; Golden Globe, Best Foreign Language Film, 2000; Seven Goyas, including the Premio Goya, Best Director, 2000; César, Best Foreign Language Film, France, 2000; Guldbagge Award, Best Foreign Language Film, Sweden, 2000; Academy Award, Best Foreign Language Film, 2000; BAFTA Award, Best Foreign Language Film, 2000; David Lean Award, Best Director, 2000; Premio Sant Jordi de Cinematografía, 2000; German Movie Award, Best Foreign-Language Film, 2000. Honorary Doctorate, University of Castilla-La Mancha, Spain, 2001.

Addresses: *Home*—Madrid, Spain. *Office*—El Deseo, SA, C/Francisco Navacerrado, 24, 28028, Madrid, Spain, (34) (91) 724-8199, eldeseo@eldeseo.es.

was dampened by the repressive moral strictures imposed by the church and his trust was broken by a priest who sexually abused him. He told *Time* that his Catholic education was "full of hypocrisy," concluding, "you can't learn by being terrorized." He found his escape at a movie theater not far from the school. "[There] I reconciliated myself with the world, my world," he is quoted on www.express.co.uk.

Barely seventeen, Almodóvar moved to Madrid on his own. He wanted to make movies, but it was 1968 and because Franco was still in power, Spain's official School of Cinematic Arts was shuttered. Almodóvar would have to learn filmmaking on his own. Without money, he settled for a variety of odd jobs from making crafts to selling used items at flea markets. When he landed an administrative position at the state-run telephone company, he finally earned enough money to buy a small Super 8 camera. During the day he was part of Spain's burgeoning middle class. According to his biography on www.almodovarlandia.com, this social class with "[i]ts dramas and its misery … was a goldmine," for Almodóvar's future works.

At night Almodóvar found another goldmine of inspiration in the Madrid movement of the early 1980s known as "la movida," literally the action. Almodóvar described that time to *Newsweek International.* "It was an explosion of life, the rebirth of joie de vivre, the younger generation seeking pleasure as its immediate objective, the legitimacy of all political choices and the loss of fear of the police." Almodóvar, the country boy from rural Spain, was at the center of the action. Wielding his Super 8 he made short films with titles like "Two Whores or a Love Story that ends in Marriage" and "Sex Comes, Sex Goes." These films reveled in sexuality—a complete antithesis to the repressive morality imposed by Franco. He also brought homosexuality, including his own, out of the closet and into the Spanish consciousness. When not filming, the prolific Almodóvar wrote a sham autobiography under the pseudonym Patty Diphusa, international porn star. In Spanish, patidifusa means "flabbergasted." He also performed in drag in a wildly popular underground punk band, acted with an avant garde theater group, and wrote screenplays that would later become his films.

Broke Taboos with Early Films

In 1980 Almodovar released his first feature film, *Pepi, Luci, Bom, and Other Girls on the Heap.* Shot on weekends and vacations, it took over a year and a half to make. Its screening at the San Sebastian Film Festival, Spain's answer to Cannes and Sundance, elicited shock and disgust from mainstream audiences. With wild antics and oversexed characters, Almodóvar's first film foreshadowed his work to come. In 1982's *Labyrinth of Passion,* a sex-crazed bisexual pop star who hates the sun, the gay son of an emperor, and a young victim of incest and rape, seek pleasure and freedom in Madrid. 1983's *Dark Habits* is set in a convent of lesbian, drug-using nuns. This film brought Almodovar international exposure when it was screened at film festivals in Venice and Miami. Back home, his films got his mother exposure too. According to *www.express.co.uk,* "the neighbours complained to her every time Pedro made a film, which was seen as controversial amongst the Calatrava neighbours." His mother didn't get involved in the controversy, quite simply, by refusing to see any of his films. Still, she remained supportive of her son and even appeared in four of his movies.

In 1984 Almodóvar struck box-office fame in Spain when *What Have I Done to Deserve This?* became one of the top grossing films of the year. Again quirky characters and plots abound including a glue-sniffing housewife who murders her husband with a ham bone. Just for fun there is a subplot involving a scheme to forge Hitler's diaries and a promiscuous son who has affairs with his classmate's fathers. Two years later he repeated this success with *Matador.* Its campy mix of sex, murder, bullfighting, and religious repression garnered Almodovar cult status in international film circles. The film also found art house success in the United States.

In 1987, along with his brother Agustín, Almodóvar started his own film company, El Deseo. The following year, with the release of *Women on the Verge of a Nervous Breakdown,* he earned his greatest success to date. The film brought Almodóvar's distinctive style to the masses. Drenched in primary colors, it centers on a strong ensemble of female actors led by Almodóvar's then muse, Carmen Maura. She plays a pregnant Madrid soap opera actress whose married lover dumps her by answering machine. Through her ensuing loneliness, she manages to befriend her lover's ex-wife, the son she didn't know her lover had, and his fiancée. Along the way, they are joined by two police officers and everyone partakes of a drug-laced gazpacho.

Wacky, irreverent, and a bit absurd, *Women on the Verge* nonetheless manages to touch on themes close to the hearts of women everywhere—love, loss, loneliness. It helped establish Almodóvar as a women's director. A 1999 article in *Time* he was described as, "the man who loves women, who understands them, who writes women's roles that any actress would die or kill for." Almodóvar explained, " ... I do prefer to work with women. Maybe that's because when I was young, I was surrounded by strong women, real fighters. This was in La Mancha, a very machista and conservative region. There, the man is a king sitting on his throne. And the women are like the prime minister; they are the ones who govern the house, resolve the problems." Spanish women are thankful to Almodóvar for bringing this out in his films. Penelope Cruz, one of Almodóvar's regular actors, told *Time International,* "When Pedro shoots, everybody wants to see ... especially these 40-year-old women—they cried when they saw him. They'd come up to him in tears and tell him how much he's changed their lives." *Women on the Verge* changed his life too. The film received over 50 awards internationally including the Oscar nomination for Best Foreign Language Film. In Hollywood, where the bottom line is always the dollar, Almodóvar also proved his merit as a moneymaker. The movie earned $2.5 million dollars in the first ten weeks of its U.S. release becoming North America's most financially successful foreign language film.

Showed No Stop To His Creativity

The 1990s ushered in a slew of Almodóvar hits *Tie Me Up! Tie Me Down!* debuted in 1990, *High Heels* in 1991, *Kika* in 1993, *The Flower of My Secret* in 1995, and *Live Flesh* in 1997. His style had matured with his characters showing more restraint, despite plots as crazy as anything Almodóvar had created earlier including a disgruntled daughter who marries her mother's ex-lover, a mental patient who kidnaps a porn star in the hopes that she will fall in love with him, and a man in love with a prostitute who is sent to jail for shooting a police officer who turns out to be the prostitute's husband. Almodóvar told *Time* the source of these wild tales. "Cinema you can learn by yourself," he told *Time.* "But the stories must come from inside you. When I am writing something, I have the feeling that I am really reading something, and that I have to keep on writing to find out what is going to happen next." What happened next is that the stories that he had created and made into films reaped dozens of prestigious film awards and created a new genre of filmmaking—the Almodóvar style.

In 2001 Almodóvar reached the height of his career with the critically and popularly acclaimed film, *All About My Mother.* Again the plot is delightfully complex and the characters endearingly eccentric. A mother loses her teenage son in a car accident following a play. She then goes off in search of the boy's father, a transvestite prostitute who has impregnated a young nun and infected her with HIV. Through her mourning, the mother pulls together an unlikely sorority including the young nun, the actress who had starred in the play she had seen with her son before the accident, the actress's drug addicted lesbian lover, and a philosophical transsexual. They are the quintessential abnormal family that is the norm of Almodóvar's films. Yet, with his deft touch, the characters speak to the audience, sharing the themes of family, life, loss, love, and friendship. It is a story anyone can relate to even if there is nary a transsexual in their life. The film also spoke to international film critics. *All About My Mother* earned nearly 100 awards. It was the star at Cannes, San Sebastian, and countless other film festivals. It gained best film and best director awards at the French Cesar's, Britain's Academy of Film and Television Awards, the Goya's, and in the ultimate film acclaim, scored the Academy Award for Best Foreign Language Film.

Following his Oscar win, Almodóvar received the congratulations of King Juan Carlos of Spain and Spain's prime minister, Jose Maria Aznar. However, for a man who despite his kinky films is a firm believer in home, family, and country, he wanted to return to the village of his parents to share his prize. With Oscar in hand, Almodóvar was hailed by the villagers who once derided his films. "This is not Calzada de Calatrava, this is Pedro Almodóvar's town," one woman was quoted on www.express.co.uk.

In 2002 Almodóvar began work on *Speak to Her,* a film centering on the friendship between a female bullfighter and a ballerina. He already has completed the script for his following movie, *Bad Education.* He is also flirting with the idea of making an English-language film. When at 17 he fled his rural roots for the country's urban capital, it was with "the intention of becoming Madrid's most modern person," he told *Vanity Fair.* With dozens of films to his credit, hundreds of awards, and numerous books and film courses devoted to his body of work, Almodóvar has not only become Madrid's most modern person, he has become one of the world's most modern icons.

Selected filmography

Pepi, Luci, Bom y Otra Chicas del Monton (Pepi, Luci, Bom and Other Girls on the Heap), 1980.
Laberinto del Pasiones (Labyrinth of Passion), 1982.
Entre Tinieblas (Dark Habits), 1983.
Que He Hecho Yo a Para Mercerer Esto (What Have I Done to Deserve This?), 1984.
Matador, 1985.

Ley del Deseo, (The Law of Desire)), 1987.
Mujeres al Borde de un Ataque de Nervios (Women on the Verge of a Nervous Breakdown), 1988.
Atame! (Tie Me Up! Tie Me Down!), 1989.
Tacones Lejanos (High Heels), 1991.
Kika, 1993.
La Flore de mi Secreto (The Flower of My Secret), 1995.
Carne Tremula (Live Flesh), 1997.
Todo Sobre Mi Madre (All About My Mother), 1999.

Sources

Periodicals

The Economist, April 1, 2000, p. 48.
Film Comment, November/December, 1988, p.13.
GQ, November 1989, p. 104.
Interview, April 1996, p. 48.
Newsweek International, May 8, 2000, p. 21.
Time, January 30, 1989, p. 68; November 15, 1999, p.100.
Time International, December 13, 1999, p. 48.
Vanity Fair, April 1999, p.182.
Washington Post, June 30, p. G1.

On-line

http://www.almodovarlandia.com
http://www.clubcultura.com/clubcine/clubcineastas/almodovar/eng/
http://www.express.in2home.co.uk/almodovar.htm
http://www.hollywood.com/celebs/bio/celeb/3465 22
http://www.spainview.com/

—Candace LaBalle

Alicia Alonso

1921—

Dancer, choreographer, ballet director, dance instructor

Cuba is known for Castro, Cuban cigars, and communism. But thanks to the tenacity and talent of Alicia Alonso, it is also a world-renowned center for ballet. When Alonso was born in the early 1920s there was no ballet school or professional company in Cuba. Instead she traveled to New York City, Russia, Spain, and Monte Carlo to dance, eventually becoming arguably the most popular and admired ballerina in the 20th Century. Despite a lifelong struggle with failing vision and the political machinations that have defined post-revolutionary Cuba, Alonso returned to her beloved land and founded the Ballet Nacional de Cuba and created the island's first dance school. She has been lauded as a hero by her countrymen and as a visionary by dance aficionados worldwide. At the age of eight, when she took her first dance lesson, she recalled to www.spainalive.com, "I knew that I was going to love it more than anything in my life." That love has propelled her through six decades of dance.

Born Alicia Ernestina de la Caridad del Cobre Martinez Hoya on December 21, 1921 (though some sources say it was 1917), Alonso was the youngest of four children. Her father, Antonio Martinez, was an officer in the Cuban army and her mother, Ernestina Hoya,

was a homemaker. This was pre-revolutionary Cuba and the family enjoyed a comfortable lifestyle in a moneyed section of Havana. Alonso began dancing at a very young age. "When I was little, I'd move around whenever I heard music, maybe like Isadora Duncan, because I didn't know what dancing was. I dreamed of having long hair, so I'd dance around with towels on my head, pretending it was my hair streaming out behind me," she told www.culturekiosque.com. Her first dance training occurred during her father's year-long military assignment in Spain. Her Spanish grandfather suggested she learn the local dance, so Alonso studied flamenco and even learned to play the castanets. At eight years old, she returned with her family to Cuba and took her first ballet lesson at the Sociedad Pro-Arte Musical school in Havana. At ten she made her first stage appearance in a production of *Sleeping Beauty* dancing as Alicia Martinez.

At fifteen Alonso married fellow dancer Fernando Alonso and adopted the stage name of Alicia Alonso. In 1937 the young couple moved to New York City to continue their dance training. Alonso danced at the School of American Ballet with some of the best private teachers of classical ballet in the world. She recalled in

At a Glance . . .

Born Alicia Ernestina de la Caridad del Cobre Martinez Hoya in Havana, Cuba on December 21, 1921; daughter of Antonio Martinez, a military officer, and Ernestina Hoyo, a homemaker; married Fernando Alonso, 1937, later divorced; one daughter, Laura Alonso; remarried Pedro Simon, 1975. *Education:* Studied dance at Sociedad Pro-Arte Musical, Havana, Cuba and the School of American Ballet, New York, NY.

Career: Ballet Caravan, soloist, 1939-40; American Ballet Theater, New York, prima ballerina, 1940-41, 1943-48, 1950-55, 1958-59; Ballet Nacional de Cuba, founder, principal dancer, artistic director, 1959; Gran Teatro de la Habana, Cuba, general director, 1981; Ballet Russe de Monte Carlo, guest artist, 1955-59; guest artist with the following: Paris Opera, Bolshoi Theater, Moscow, Kirov Ballet, St. Petersburg, Royal Danish Ballet, Les Grandes Ballets Canadiens, Ballet du XXe Siécle; performed until early 1990s.

Memberships: World Council for Peace, 1974-; vice president, National Union of Cuban Writers and Artists; Advisory Council, Ministry of Culture, Cuba.

Awards: Annual Award, *Dance Magazine,* 1958; Workers Award, Democratic Republic of Vietnam, 1964; Anna Pavlova Prize, Dance University of Paris, 1966; Grand Prix de la Ville de Paris, 1966, 1970; Medal of the Gran Teatro Liceo de Barcelona, 1971; Honorary Doctorate of Arts, University of Havana, 1973; Ana Betancourt Award, Women's Foundation of Cuba, 1974; National Hero of Labor, Cuban Workers' Union, 1976; Felix Varela Award, Cuba, 1981; Honorary Doctorate of Arts, Art Institute of Cuba, 1987; Great Honour Award, Japan, 1991; Heroine of Labour of the Republic of Cuba, 1998; Honorary Ambassador of Cuba, 2002.

Address: *Office—* Ballet Nacional de Cuba, Calzada 510, Vedado, Havana, 4, Cuba.

Lady in 1938 and *Stars in Your Eyes* the following year. In 1939 her ballet training bore success when she was made a soloist with the American Ballet Caravan, later to become the New York City Ballet. Then in 1941 she joined the Ballet Theater (later the American Ballet Theater) as a ballerina. There she was tapped for high profile solos and it seemed her career was on the verge of flourishing.

Late in 1941 Alonso began to have troubles with her vision. She was diagnosed with detached retinas in both eyes and became temporarily blind. Three surgeries to restore her vision left her confined to bed for nearly a year unable to even to turn her head, much less practice her art. Doctors told her that her dance career was over. However, as she lay prostrate, heavy bandages around her eyes, she continued to practice in her head, going over and over the movements of great ballets such as *Giselle.* By the time her eyes had healed, she knew *Giselle* by heart. With her love of dance still burning, she transferred that knowledge to her body. She later explained the connection between brain and body to Chicago's *Art Beat,* " ... this is a career where you must exercise everyday, almost to the extreme. You cannot stop working, not only your body, but your brain." Her body quickly caught up and Alonso soon returned to New York City to rejoin the Ballet Theater.

In 1943 Alonso received the break of her career when she was appointed to dance the lead role in *Giselle.* An article on the website for Radio Progreso describes how this came about: "The company's first ballerina, Alicia Markova, who would dance the title role, was suddenly taken ill. The theater is sold out and a full house is expected. The impresario does not want to close the show and asks all the dancers, one by one, who wants to substitute Markova. All refuse. There's only one week for opening night and practically no time to learn the part. It's Alonso's turn to answer. She had dreamed of that moment, of the opportunity to perform *Giselle.* She agrees and learns the part in seven days, rehearsing by day and performing other ballets every evening. Her feet are bleeding, but a week after she makes her debut as *Giselle.*" Her performance was widely acclaimed. The *New York Times* hailed it as "one of the most distinguished performances of the season." Throughout her illustrious career she would dance and produce *Giselle* hundreds of times, becoming nearly synonymous with the role. She would perform the role for three more years with the Ballet Theater before being appointed to the position of principal dancer.

Having always harbored a deep love for and commitment to her homeland, Alonso decided in 1948 to return to Cuba and there founded the Ballet Alicia Alonso with her husband as general director. As there were few decent ballet schools in Cuba, the ranks of her company were filled by non-Cubans. To remedy this she opened the Alicia Alonso Academy of Ballet in Havana and began to train legions of dancers. How-

an interview with www.culturekiosque.com, "I was like a sponge, so eager to learn from all of them." However, her first professional performance was not as a ballerina but as a chorus girl in musicals including *Great* ever, in 1956 the political situation in Cuba was becoming increasingly unstable and the government pulled funding from her school and company. Alonso closed shop and moved to Monte Carlo as a guest artist with the Ballet Russe.

In 1957, in an unprecedented nod to her international fame as a renowned dancer, Alonso received an invitation to perform in the Soviet Union. The cold war was in full swing and no Western dancer had before been asked to cross over the Iron Curtain. Alonso performed in Moscow, St. Petersburg, and Kiev, dancing with both the famed Bolshoi and Kirov ballets. In 1958 Alonso was awarded the prestigious annual award from *Dance* magazine. It was just one of many major awards her dancing would garner. Over the next decade, Alonso performed as a guest artist with companies throughout the world and danced under the top choreographers of the era including George Balanchine and Anges de Mille. Balanchine created *Theme and Variations,* a ballet just for Alonso and her then partner, the great dancer Igor Youskevitch. Alonso and Youskevitch were widely considered the Ginger Rogers and Fred Astaire of ballet. Alonso also mounted her own productions during this time, including her famed rendition of *Giselle* for the Paris Opera. Her amazing performances are even more incredible when viewed in light of her faltering eyesight. Despite the success of her earlier operations, her vision continued to deteriorate. She was determined to keep her handicap from the audience not wanting it to color their perception of her work. "The difficulty was in dancing with partners, knowing where to find them without my eyes on the stage. They sometimes used special lighting effects to guide me. But the biggest difficulty was always coming off the stage, trying to find the wings and the curtain drops," Alonso recalled to www.spainalive.com.

After the Cuban Revolution of 1959 and the ascension of Fidel Castro to power, Alonso chose once again to return to her dear Cuba and reopen her ballet company and school. With political and financial support from Castro's government, the Ballet Nacional de Cuba was borne. In addition, Alonso put considerable energy in the creation of a national ballet school and training program. Under the communist regime no child was to be denied access to education. Following the Russian style, Alonso and her corps of teachers would travel throughout Cuba to find talented youth and then fund and manage their training. "I go all over the island, to every one of the tiny mountain villages to find children who want to dance. We play music and then choose those who have the best physique and bone structure," she told www.culturekiosque.com.

A network of regional dance schools eventually emerged and with it a corps of talented dancers. Manuel Legris, principal dancer with the Paris Opera Ballet, was quoted on www.culturekiosque.com as saying, "The Cuban school is exceptional. I meet Cuban dancers all the time ... and they all have this astonishing technique allied artistry and style." Dancers from Alonso's school have also made an indelible mark on international dance competitions. Varna, the most prestigious ballet competition in the world has awarded medals to more Cuban dancers than any other nationality in its thirty year history. The style that Alonso's protégés embrace was borne out of Alonso's commitment to both technique and artistry. "Technique has progressed so much today, there's a temptation to dance everything the same unless the dancer understands and masters the meaning of style," Alonso told www.culturekiosque.com. "Dancers must transmit an emotion, or the classics will just become meaningless. In the Ballet of Cuba, we are trying to produce artists who respect the purity of the original work rather than just brilliant technicians."

Despite her international fame, Alonso and her dance company found themselves barred from performing in the United States for nearly two decades. Despite having once been the principal ballerina of the American Ballet Theater, Alonso's alignment with Castro prevented her from even being allowed on U.S. soil. Finally, in 1971 the company was invited to embark upon a North American tour. Though she was in her fifties and nearly blind, her performances garnered accolades. "In some respects the physical command is not so certain as it was years ago, but [Alonso] is now a far better dancer than she was" wrote a reviewer from the *New York Times*. "The nuances and grace notes that distinguish great classic dancing from the superbly accomplished are now very evident, and her musical phrasing is as individual as ever."

In 1972 Alonso underwent another operation on her sight allowing her to continue performing. She danced throughout the 1970s and 1980s as a guest performer with the most prestigious ballet companies in the world and also with her Ballet Nacional de Cuba. During this time she also divorced Alonso and married Pedro Simon, a writer and lawyer. By the 1990s, Alonso, nearing seventy years of age, was still performing as the principal dancer of the Havana-based ballet, despite the fact that her vision was once again deteriorating. In January of 1990, as part of the celebration of the fiftieth anniversary of the American Ballet Theater, Alonso danced part of *Swan Lake* at the Metropolitan Opera House. She was the only founding member still dancing and her performance drew a rousing ovation. Though her age was obviously taking a toll on her performance, a reviewer in the New Leader noted that her technique "gave the ballet a glow that was missing from every performance by ABT's young beauties in their spanking new Swan Lake last spring."

A few years later while on tour with the Ballet Nacional de Cuba she decided to finally hang up her ballet slippers and retired from dancing. "I found myself on a tour in Italy with my own creation *Farfalia* which means butterfly. I began to think how short the lives of butterflies really are. I was dancing the role of the butterfly then and when I finished my season in Italy I knew that that was it," she told www.spainalive.com. "I didn't programme myself to dance anymore. My decision had come to me as softly as that." Though she left performing, she did not leave center stage and continued to choreograph for the company even as her eyesight finally left her. She explained to the *Seattle Times* how she accomplished this. "I put it in my mind. I listen to the music, then I explain it to my wonderful maitres des ballets (ballet masters)."

In 1998 Alonso received Cuba's highest civil decoration, the title of "Heroine of Labour of the Republic of Cuba." It was a great honor for a woman who had remained committed to her country through adversity even as artists of all ranks were fleeing. Then in 2002 she was named honorary Ambassador on the occasion of her 70th anniversary of dancing. She deferred this honor to her country saying, "this magical island, despite its small size has made and continues to make great history as an example of culture, valor, and heroism." On the international front, ballets around the world continue to be inspired by her work. In 2001 the Ballet Nacional de Cuba launched a production entitled *La Magia de Alonso* which toured extensively to rave reviews. In one of her oft-repeated sentiments, Alonso told *Art Beat,* "Dance to me is life itself." It is a life she has lived long and well, leaving a legacy not only for the

Cuban dancers that will dance in her footsteps, but for millions of fans worldwide. She summed up her career best to www.spainalive.com. "I have lived well. I have achieved a lot. I am aware that I have made history. I planted a seed which grew into a tree and the fruits have been exported all over the world."

Sources

Periodicals

New Leader, March 5, 1990.
New York Times, November 3, 1943; June 21, 1971.
Saturday Review, January 6, 1979.
Seattle Times, February 18, 1999.
World Press Review, April, 1982.

On-line

Art Beat, www.networkchicago.com/artbeat/alonso.htm
www.culturekiosque.com/dance/Features/rhecuba.htm
www.rprogreso.com/RPWeekly011702/art011702.htm
www.spainalive.com/spain/people

—Candace LaBalle

Julia Alvarez

1950—

Author

Dominican author Julia Alvarez has given voice to the themes of displacement, alienation, and search for identity in her poetry and fiction. Thrown into a foreign language and culture as a child, Alvarez found refuge in books and writing. She discovered through words she could build her own worlds that both revealed and transcended the meaning of her life. Alvarez became a nationally acclaimed author in 1991 at the age of 41 with the publication of her first novel, *How the García Girls Lost Their Accent.* Her writings include four novels, two collections of poetry, a book of essays, and two children's stories.

From Latina to "Gringa"

Although Alvarez was born in New York City on March 27, 1950, soon after her birth her parents returned to their native home of the Dominican Republic, where her father, a doctor, ran a local hospital. The second of four sisters, she was reared close to her mother's family, amidst a slew of cousins, aunts, uncles, and maids. When Alvarez was ten years old, her father became actively involved in the underground coalition poised to overthrow dictator Rafael Leonidas Trujillo

Molina. As a result, the police set up surveillance on their home and Alvarez's father was warned by an American agent that his arrest was imminent. To avoid this fate the family fled the country.

Their destination was New York, where Alvarez's father had secured a fellowship at a hospital. For Alvarez, the mystique of the United States loomed large in her ten-year-old mind. "All my childhood I had dressed like an American, eaten American foods, and befriended American children," Alvarez told *American Scholar.* "I had gone to an American school and spent most of the day speaking and reading English. At night, my prayers were full of blond hair and blue eyes and snow.… All my childhood I had longed for this moment of arrival. And here I was, an American girl, coming home at last."

Once the plane landed in New York, Alvarez's storybook image of life in the United States was quickly shattered by the harsh realities of life as an immigrant. Uprooted from her culture, her native language, and extended family, Alvarez, once a vivacious child who made friends easily, became introverted. Her father took her to a library, and Alvarez discovered her love for the written word. "Back home, I had been a very

At a Glance . . .

Born on March 27, 1950, in New York, NY. *Education:* Connecticut College, 1968–69; Middlebury College, B.A., 1971; Syracuse University, M.A., 1975.

Career: KY Arts Commission, writer-in-residence, 1975–77; California State Coll. (Fresno) and Coll. of the Sequoias, Visalia, CA, English instructor, 1977; DE Arts Council, writer-in-residence, 1978; NEA, writer-in-residence, Fayetteville, NC, 1978; Phillips Andover Academy, Andover, MA, English instr., 1979–81; Univ. of VT, English Dept., visit- ing assistant prof., 1981–83; George Washington Univ., Jenny McKean Moore Visiting Writer, 1984–85; Univ. of IL, asst. prof., 1985–88; Middlebury Coll., asst. prof., 1988–96, professor, 1996–98, writer-in-resi- dence, 1998–.

Membership: Academy of American Poets; the Associated Writing Programs; Poets & Writers; the Latin American Writers' Institute.

Awards: Benjamin T. Marshall Poetry Prize, Connecticut Coll., 1968, 1969; The Acad. of Amer. Poetry Prize, Syracuse Univ., 1974; La Reina Press, Creative Writing Award, poetry, 1982; Third Woman Press Award, first prize, 1986; General Electric Foundation Award for Younger Writers, 1986; PEN Syndicated Fiction Prize, 1987; Notable Book, *New York Times Book Review,* 1991; PEN Oakland/Jose- phine Miles Award; Notable Book, ALA, 1992, 1994; Book of the Month Club choice, 1994; National Book Critics' Award finalist in fiction, 1995; *In The Time of Butterflies* chosen as one of the Best Books for Young Adults, Young Adult Lib. Services Assn. and ALA, 1995; Reader's Choice Award, "Coco Stop," 1994; Amer. Poetry Review's Jessica Nobel-Maxwell Poetry Prize, 1995; Literature Leadership Award, Do- minico-American Soc. of Queens, Inc., 1998; Semana Cultural y Festival Dominicano (Boston), Woman of the Year, 2000; *Latina Magazine,* Woman of the Year, 2000.

Addresses: *Office*—English Department, Munroe Hall 111, Middlebury College, Middlebury, VT 05753. (802) 443-5276. *Agent*—Susan Bergholtz Literary Services, 17 West 10th St., No. 5, New York, NY 10011-8769.

poor student, a tomboy, and a troublemaker, so my father was eager to encourage this new trend in [me]," she told *Library Journal.* Books became her new home. She explained to *Frontera Magazine,* "Coming to this country I discovered books, I discovered that it was a way to enter into a portable homeland that you could carry around in your head. You didn't have to suffer what was going on around you. I found in books a place to go."

At the age of 13 Alvarez left home to attend boarding school. Already an avid reader, she realized her desire to write after an English teacher gave her class a writing assignment, asking them to write an essay about themselves. What began as homework turned into self-discovery. Years later Alvarez reflected that it was her feelings of alienation and displacement that pushed her toward a life as an author. She is fond of quoting exiled Polish poet Czeslow Milosz, who said, "Language is the only homeland." By the time she had reached high school, Alvarez knew with certainty that she wanted to become a writer.

Student, Itinerant Poet, and Teacher

In 1967 Alvarez enrolled at Connecticut College. "I grew up in that generation of women thinking I would keep house. Especially with my Latino background, I wasn't even expected to go to college," she told *Publishers Weekly.* "I had never been raised to have a public voice." Yet the appeal of writing outweighed her cultural and family heritage, and under the tutelage of encouraging teachers, Alvarez began to take her writing seriously. For her efforts she won the Benjamin T. Marshall Prize in poetry at Connecticut College in 1968 and again in 1969. After attending the Breadloaf Writers' Conference at Middlebury College in Vermont, she transferred to the school. In 1971 she was awarded the Creative Writing Prize, and in the same year earned her B.A. from Middlebury, graduating with highest honors. With her confidence growing, Alvarez enrolled at Syracuse University to pursue graduate studies. In 1974 she won the American Academy of Poetry Prize; the following year she was awarded a M.A. in creative writing.

After her graduation, Alvarez became something of an itinerant poet, writer, teacher, and lecturer, claiming 15 different addresses over the next 13 years. From 1975 to 1977 she served with the Kentucky Arts Commission as one of three poets in the state's poetry-in-the-schools programs. In 1978 she was involved with pilot projects funded by the National Endowment for the Arts: a bilingual program in Delaware and a senior citizen program in North Carolina. Alvarez enjoyed her years of travel. She told *Publishers Weekly,* "I felt like the [Walt] Whitman poem where he travels throughout the country and now will do nothing but listen. I was listening. I was seeing the inside of so many places and so many people, from the Mennonites of Southern Kentucky to the people of Appalachia.... I was a migrant poet. I would go anywhere."

In 1979 she began her career as a teacher of English and creative writing. After two years as an instructor at Phillips Andover Academy in Massachusetts, Alvarez joined the faculty at the University of Vermont in1981. In 1984 she moved to George Washington University, where she served the year as the Jenny McKean Moore Visiting Writer. In 1985 she became an English professor at the University of Illinois. During the winter of 1988 she served as the resident writer in an artists' colony in the Dominican Republic. In the same year she returned to her alma mater, Middlebury College as an assistant professor of English. She was awarded tenure in 1991 and named full professor in 1996. Two years later, she remitted her professorship to become the college's writer-in-residence, which allows her to continue to teach creative writing on a part-time basis and advise Latino students and English majors.

Poet and Author

In 1984 Alvarez published her first collection of poetry, *Homecoming,* featuring a 33-sonnet sequence entitled "33." The poem, which fills nearly have the book, is exercise in self-examination carried out by Alvarez, who at the age of 33, found herself confronting middle age with no permanent home, no family of her own, and no specific career plan. The poems in *Homecoming* often focus on the search for love and the pain of failed relationships, with such verse offerings as "Are we all ill with acute loneliness,/chronic patients trying to recover/the will to love?" In the section entitled "Housekeeping," Alvarez delves into the meaning found in mundane daily tasks, such as folding clothes, sweeping, washing windows, and making bread. In 1996 Alvarez published an expanded edition, *Homecoming: New and Collected Poems,* this time featuring 46 sonnets to match her age at the time.

In 1991 she published her first novel, *How the García Girls Lost Their Accents.* In many ways a fictional account of Alvarez's own experiences, the book is a series of 15 interrelated stories about a family from the Dominican Republic who immigrates to the United States. Like Alvarez's family, the García family consists of four sisters, Carla, Sandra, Yolanda, and Sofía. The story, which covers a 33-year span, examines the struggles of the girls-turned-women as they attempt to reestablish their identity after leaving their privileged social standing in the Dominican Republic to forge new lives as immigrants in the United States. Alvarez received high praise for *How the García Girls Lost Their Accent;* Ilan Stavans in *Commonweal* referred to it as a "delightful novel, a tour de force that holds a unique place in the context of the ethnic literature from which it emerges."

In 1994 Alvarez published her second novel, *In the Time of the Butterflies,* a 300-page fictional account of the lives of three sisters, Patria, Minerva, and Maria Terese (Mate) Mirabal, who were assassinated in 1960 during the last days of the Trujillo dictatorship, just four months after Alvarez and her family had fled the country. Revered for their martyrdom, they are known in the Dominican Republic as *las mariposas,* meaning the butterflies, which served as their code name during the resistance. Upon its publication, Kay Pritchett noted in *World Literature Today,* "With *In the Time of the Butterflies* a superb, heartrending story, Julia Alvarez has again displayed her fine talent as a novelist. Especially noteworthy is her ability to maintain an equilibrium between the political and the human, the tragic and the lyrical. What we remember most is not the harshness of the times but the Butterflies themselves, along with a delicious flavor of their homeland." In 1999 Showtime produced the film version of *In the Time of the Butterflies.*

The Other Side/El Otro Lado, Alvarez's second collection of poems, was published in 1995. The poems, organized into five sections, lyrically follow Alvarez through her journeys as a Latina immigrant. She begins with the poem "Bilingual Sestina," an account of leaving the Dominican Republic to enter a new land of strange language and cultural. Alvarez ends the collection having come full circle back to her native land in the title poem "The Other Side/El Otro Lado," in which she writes, "There is nothing left to cry for,/ nothing left but the story/of our family's grand adventure/from one language to another." This collection of poems introduced Alvarez's poetry to many readers who had only previously known her fiction.

Alvarez's third novel, *¡Yo!,* published in 1997, is a continuation and an elaboration of the life of Yolanda from *How the García Girls Lost Their Accent.* Whereas the other sisters have made peace with their lives as Dominican-Americans, Yolanda still feels torn between two cultures. Her life in the United States has taught her independence and assertiveness, which made her a female oddity in her native land. Yet despite her failings, Alvarez leaves room in her tale for Yolanda to seek redemption and find wisdom.

Something to Declare, published in 1998, is a nonfiction accounting of Alvarez's personal experiences of both alienation and assimilation as a "hyphenated American," along with a rendering of her life as a writer and teacher. In a *People Weekly* review, Laurie Jamison wrote, "A likable storyteller, [Alvarez] also writes with candor and humor about her picky eating habits, her decision not to have children and her vagabond life as a writer and teacher." Alvarez titled her book *Something to Declare* after having decided that most questions posed to her by her readers can be summed up as "Do you have anything more to declare?' These 24 autobiographical stories are her response.

Alvarez returned to historical fiction in *In the Name of Salomé,* published in 2000. The novel, which covers more than 100 years, tells the story of Salomé Urena de Henriquez, the nineteenth-century poet laureate of the Dominican Republic, and her daughter, Camila Henriquez Urena. Salomé, who is considered a national hero because of her patriotic and revolutionary poems, died of tuberculosis when her daughter was three years old. Struggled with her mother's death, Camila was taught by her aunt to end her prayers with the irreverent yet comforting saying, "In the name of the Father, the Son, and my Mother, Salomé." *Publishers Weekly* referred to it as "one of the most moving political novels of the past half century."

Children's Books

After *In the Name of Salomé,* Alvarez's next two literary efforts were children's books. In 2000 she published *The Secret Footprints,* which was geared for children from ages four to seven and based on a traditional Dominican fable. In 2001 Alvarez published *How Tia Lola Came to Stay.* Written for children from ages 9 to 12, the book tells the story of nine-year-old Miguel, who struggles to adjust to his mother's divorce and subsequent move from New York to Vermont. Life is turned on end yet again when Miguel's colorful aunt, Tia Lola, comes from the Dominican Republic to stay with the family.

Much of Alvarez's writings come from her personal experiences of alienation, marginalization, and the need for self-discovery. "People think that we write because we know things," she explained to Jean Charbonneau of the *Denver Post.* "But we write because we want to find things out, in the way that stories only can help us understand, without giving any real answers, but with all their richness, in a way that facts and figures don't do it." Alvarez has struck a common chord, not only among Latinos, but also with a larger audience that find much to contemplate and learn from homelands that Alvarez creates with words.

Selected Writings

Novels

How the García Girls Lost Their Accents, Algonquin Books of Chapel Hill, 1991.
In the Time of the Butterflies, Algonquin Books of Chapel Hill, 1994.
¡Yo!, Algonquin Books of Chapel Hill, 1996.

In the Name of Salomé, Algonquin Books of Chapel Hill, 2000.

Poetry

Homecoming, Grove Press (New York, NY), 1984, revised edition, Dutton, 1995.
The Other Side/El Otro Lado, Dutton, 1995.
Seven Trees, Kat Ran Press, 1999.

Other

Something to Declare (essays), Algonquin Books of Chapel Hill, 1998.
The Secret Footprints (children's picture book), illustrations by Fabian Negrin, Knopf, 2000.
How Tia Lola Come to Stay (young adult), Knopf, 2001.

Sources

Books

Authors and Artists for Young Adults. Gale Research, 2001.
Dictionary of Hispanic Biography. Gale Research, 1996.

Periodicals

Americas, January/February 2001.
Commonweal, April 10, 1992.
Denver Post, July 9, 2000.
Library Journal, August 1998; September 1999; May 2000; September 2000.
The Progressive, July 1995.
Publishers Weekly, April 5, 1991; July 11, 1994; April 24, 1995; March 18, 1996; October 14, 1996; December 16, 1996; July 13, 1998; September 21, 1998; May 15, 2000; August 14, 2000; February 26, 2001.
World Literature Today, autumn 1995; autumn 1997; winter 2001.

On-line

Contemporary Authors Online, www.galenet.com/servlet/BioRC
Frontera Magazine, www.fronteramag.com/issue5/Alvarez
Middlebury College, www.middlebury.edu/~english/faculty.html

—Kari Bethel

Janeth Arcain

1969—

Professional basketball player

South American players are rare in professional basketball, whose practitioners from outside the sport's U.S. homeland tend to come from Europe or Africa. But Houston Comets guard Janeth Arcain, a veteran Brazilian player, emerged as a Women's National Basketball Association (WNBA) star in 2000. Arcain's rise to prominence was a study in persistence; after several years as a participant but not a leader of the Comets's WNBA dynasty, Arcain made the most of her moment in the spotlight.

Janeth Arcain was born in Sao Paulo, Brazil, on April 11, 1969. Arcain and her younger brother, Danilo, suffered after their parents separated when Janeth was six years old, and she turned to sports as a youngster. Arcain played volleyball and the Brazilian national sport of soccer for a time, but the 1983 basketball world championships, held in Sao Paulo, caught her attention. Within a couple of years she was hooked, and by 1986 she was playing on a South American championship team.

Won Olympic Silver Medal

Excelling in international competition, Arcain was a member of Brazil's Pan American Games teams in 1987, winning a silver medal, and in 1991, taking home a gold medal. She played for Brazil's Olympic team in 1992 and experienced her greatest thrill up to that time when she returned in 1996 and Brazil won the Olympic silver medal. "It's the first Olympic medal Brazil ever won [in basketball]," Arcain told the *Houston Chronicle*. "Mine is hanging in the office at my home."

Arcain played eight seasons of professional basketball in Brazil, six for the Polti team, and two for one called Leite Moca. Essentially, she dominated the league. She has been named the Brazilian Most Valuable Player every year she has been active, and was the league's top scorer in 1995 and 1996. She rented an apartment on Rio de Janeiro's magnificent beachfront. Arcain's Brazilian career continued even after she came to the U.S. and began playing for the Comets—a transition that presented special challenges. Even the ball in Brazilian play is a slightly different size from that in the American game. And when she came to the United States in 1997, she spoke very little English, although she was fluent in Spanish in addition to her native Portuguese.

Most important, Arcain as a WNBA player was just one of a multitude of talented players. Chosen 12th in the WNBA expansion draft, she was obviously a player for whom the Comets had high expectations. "Back in Brazil, they look for me to score," Arcain told the *Houston Chronicle*. "I average about 26 or 27 points a game." In Arcain's first season with the Comets, playing the position of small forward, she averaged 10.7 points per game—and that was her top performance until the 2001 season.

Benched as Comets Star Returned

Arcain started every game but one in the 1997 season, ranking second in the WNBA in free-throw percentage and turning in an especially strong performance in the postseason playoffs. The 1997 campaign would mark the first of an amazing four consecutive championships for the Comets, but Arcain's role changed in subsequent seasons as forward Sheryl Swoopes, Arcain's nemesis in Brazil's 1996 Olympic final loss to the United States, returned to the Comets's lineup after a pregnancy leave. Arcain found herself in an unfamiliar spot—on the bench.

"Yeah, it affects me," Arcain admitted to the *Chronicle*. "All players like to play. To us, it's good to play 40 minutes. But on our team, we have a lot of great players." The situation was especially frustrating for a woman whose identity was so wrapped up in the game of basketball. Arcain thrived on recognition and attention from fans. "All my friends tell me, 'You should be tired of that. Everybody recognizes you. You should be

scared to go outside,'" Arcain told the *Chronicle*. "But no, I like that. If I stopped doing that, probably I would die, because this is my life. Basketball is my life. It's what I like to do."

Indeed Arcain continued playing in Brazil, putting her on virtually a year-round schedule. She often missed part of the preseason Comets's training camp—which wasn't a problem in terms of physical conditioning, but it did impede her ability to quickly fit in with the flow of her teammates' game in Houston. The challenge for Arcain, and for Houston coach Van Chancellor, was to develop her abilities anew so that she could fit into a variety of roles on the court. An experiment in putting Arcain in the play-making point guard position was disappointing, but Arcain persevered, rather than adopting the play-me-or-trade-me attitude that other players might have.

Broadened Her Skills

Arcain averaged twenty minutes per game in the 1998 season, scoring 6.5 points per game, and there were signs that she was beginning to develop a new all-around game. "If there was an award in this league for Sixth Man, it would have to be Janeth," Chancellor told the *Chronicle*. Over the next few seasons, Arcain developed a reputation as a quiet pillar of the Comets squad, as a player who often came off the bench at crucial moments or scored a game-winning point, yet was often upstaged by her flashier teammates. Through it all, Arcain rededicated herself to the mastery of new skills and to a spirit of teamwork. By the end of the 2000 season, in which she averaged 8.4 points per game, Arcain was appearing more and more often in the position of point guard.

Finally, in 2001, Arcain returned to the starting lineup, and all the pieces fell into place. "Until this year, I've just waited for my time," she told the *Chronicle*. "There were times when I wasn't so happy here. But I always told myself that this is my job, this is what I have chosen to do." Arcain gained her own coterie of fans in Houston, experienced the excitement of playing in the WNBA All-Star Game, and scored a career-high 29 points in a July game against the Utah Starzz. At the season's end she was named the league's Most Improved Player and was selected for the All-WNBA first team, picking up a $10,000 check for the honor.

She was the fourth-leading scorer in the league with 18.5 points per game and ranked seventh in steals; she was noted as a fine defensive player overall. Arcain planned to retire from basketball after playing one more time for Brazil in the 2004 Olympics. In the meantime, American basketball fans seemed likely to find greater and greater enjoyment in her efforts on the court.

Sources

Periodicals

Houston Chronicle, June 9, 1997, p. Sports-7; July 12, 1997, p. Sports-8; July 6, 1998, p. Sports-1; August 1, 1998, p. Sports-1; May 27, 2000, p. Sports-2; June 12, 2000, p. Sports-7; June 23, 2000, p. Sports-6; July 1, 2000, p. Sports-1; May 22, 2001, p. Sports-9; June 2, 2001, p. Sports-4; June 23, 2001, p. Sports-1; July 16, 2001, p. Sports-1; August 19, 2001, p. Sports-4; August 31, 2001, p. Sports-14.

USA Today, July 16, 2001, p. C3.

On-line

http://www.wnba.com.

—James Manheim

Jose Maria Aznar

1953—

Prime Minister of Spain

Jose Maria Aznar Lopez was born in Madrid, Spain on February 25, 1953 to a middle class family with political ties to General Francisco Franco's ultra-conservative dictatorship. Aznar's father and one of his grandfathers both held posts in the dictator's government. His family also included several notable conservative journalists, one of whom wrote a history of the Spanish Civil War from Franco's very unpopular viewpoint. Thus the Spanish public's perception of Aznar's brand of conservatism as related to the conservatism of Franco was more than just speculation. Aznar attended college at Madrid's Complutense University where he earned a law degree. Following graduation he obtained work as a government tax inspector, a position he held through the death of Franco in 1975 and well into the first wave of the democratization of Spain.

Entered Conservative Politics

Aznar began his political career in the Alianza Popular (Popular Alliance), Spain's leading conservative political party. In 1979 he assumed the position of secretary general of the party's wing in the Logrono region of Spain. In 1982 he was elected Secretary General of the national party. He held this position for five years.

Concurrently he served as an elected congressional representative for the region of Castile-Leon, a post he also held for five years. During this time, Aznar became a vocal proponent for a political shift towards the center for the party, which had been renamed Partido Popular (Popular Party). His goal was to distance the right wing party from the politics of Franco. He also pushed the party to appeal to more women and young voters.

The 1980s were a time of massive change culturally and socially for Spain. It was also a time of extreme financial instability. In addition to one of the highest unemployment rates in Europe, Spain also lagged under the remnants of the welfare state that had been institutionalized by Franco. Citizens expected to have their needs taken care of by the state despite a financial environment that made this impossible. Aznar promoted conservative fiscal and economic policies to combat these problems.

Assumed National Political Role

Despite a public persona widely described as dull, Aznar moved towards greater political roles. "Aznar

At a Glance . . .

Born February 25, 1953, Madrid, Spain; married to Ana Botella, three children. *Education*:Law Degree, Complutense University, Madrid. *Religion*: Catholic.

Career: Politician. Tax inspector, 1970s and 1980s; general secretary, Alianza Popular, Logrono region of Spain, 1979; general secretary, Alianza Popular, 1982-1987; congressional representative, Spanish Parliament, 1982-1987; elected president, Partido Popular, 1991; Prime Minister of Spain, 1996–.

Address:*Office*—Partido Popular, C/ Genova 13, 28004 Madrid, Spain; *Residence*—Presidential Palace, Moncloa, Madrid, Spain.

has always been considered somewhat colorless and lacking in charisma," noted www.spainview.com. Partido Popular, unfazed by his dourness, elected Aznar as the president of the party. Though Aznar had already done much to revamp the conservative party, steering it free of any lingering Francoist elements, the party failed miserably in the first national elections under Aznar's leadership. The incumbent Socialist party which had assumed control of the presidency and congress did so under the leadership of the charismatic Felipe Gonzalez. Spain, still smiting from Franco's ultra-conservative dictatorship, were not yet ready to elect a conservative prime minister, especially a lackluster taxman whose family included members of Franco's government.

Four years later, in 1993, the Socialists won again, however by a much narrower margin. The Partido Popular gained a large portion of congressional seats, just twenty short of a majority. Support for Gonzalez's government had began to erode in the late 1980s and early 1990s when a rash of scandals surfaced. Involving some of the highest members of government and their family members, the scandals—both financial and criminal—were serious enough to force Gonzalez to call for early national elections. Even before the first scandals were made public, Aznar had already begun to vocally promote the need for clean government.

With the support of over 99% of Partido Popular members, Aznar embarked on a vigorous campaign to become prime minister in 1996. Capitalizing on the vulnerability of the ruling party, one of Aznar's campaign tenets was the eradication of corruption in government. He also managed to turn his own subdued personality into a plus by declaring that "Spain has had enough charisma," as quoted in *The Economist*. The

implication was that the time had arrived to get serious and tackle the country's financial and social woes. Who better to do the job than a tax inspector? The voters agreed and in a historic election, Aznar was elected Prime Minister. According to www.cnn.com, "[The election] was only the second time in 60 years that power passed from one elected party to another."

Despite Aznar's victory, the Partido Popular did not gain a majority of congressional seats. Rural voters, government workers, and those old enough to remember the terror of Franco's regime chose to vote for the incumbent Socialists. The idea of a conservative party in power reminded them too much of Franco's dictatorship. However, young voters and women voters, as well as Spain's new burgeoning middle class, were forward thinking in their vote. They chose to vote for the future of Spain, not in fear of the past. They would become Aznar's most important constituents.

Following his election, Aznar began to institute reforms designed to "cut back the bloated government bureaucracy, balance the budget, root out corruption, and crack down on Basque terrorism," according to www.cnn.com. Another goal of the new prime minister was to further Spain's role in the European Union (EU), and specifically, to improve the economy sufficiently enough to meet the European Union's standards for inclusion in the single European monetary system of the Euro. At the time, both Spanish and foreign economists, openly declared that it would be impossible for the Spanish economy to improve enough to qualify for the first round of the Euro in 2001. Aznar didn't listen to the pundits and Spain met the EU standards just two years after his election. *The Economist* noted, "[Aznar] managed to confound Europe's doubting bankers by getting Spain to ride the first wave of single-currency surfers." What he lacked in personal style and charm, he made up for with economic reform. "He sets about the job with a seriousness and single-mindedness that have suited the moment," *The Economist* noted.

Steered Spain to Success

During his first four-year term as prime minister, Aznar made many astonishing gains. Unemployment, at an appalling 23% when he entered office, was reduced to 15%—still dismal, but a marked improvement. According to *Europe,* he did this "by generating 1.8 million jobs, more than were created in the rest of the other European Union nations combined." He also saw Spain's economic growth inch up to an average of 3.5% per year of his term. The previous rate was about 2%. He accomplished these economic leaps while slowly making steps to dismantle Spain's welfare state—a system near to the hearts of Spanish stalwarts. "He has continued to liberalise, while maintaining a remarkable degree of social peace," wrote *The Economist*. Another change Aznar made was the inclusion of women in some of the highest levels of the government. For a country that barely 30 years ago did not allow women to open their own bank account, Aznar's appointment of four women to his Cabinet is no less than radical. He also continued to court voters too young to remember the days of Franco.

For Spain, a country still self-conscious of its authoritarian past, its Civil War, and its history of economic instability, Aznar's achievements were a much-needed boost for the Spanish ego. An article in *The Economist* declared, "Spain under Mr. Aznar is riding high. It is a confident, modern-minded country that fights its corner in the European Union with vigour and effectiveness. Politically stable, economically prosperous, it is gaining respect in the world." Aznar also gained respect and in the 2000 elections the Partido Popular enjoyed a landslide, gaining a majority of the congressional seats and assuring Aznar another four years as prime minister. "The Spanish people have generously renewed and widened their confidence in us," Aznar was quoted in *Europe,* "and the attitude of this government is to be open to dialogue with all political and social forces because everyone wants to see Spain progress."

Tormented by Terrorism

However, Aznar's tenure has not been without problems. The biggest of those being ongoing terrorism by a group of separatists from the Basque region of Spain, near the French border. The group, operating under the acronym ETA, uses bombings and assassinations as the means of obtaining their goal—secession from Spain or at the least regional autonomy. Excluding a 15 month ceasefire, ETA has been very active during Aznar's rule. One week in July of 2000 there were three separate bombings—in the Basque region and in the capital of Madrid. Businessmen, politicians, and military leaders have all been murdered by ETA during Aznar's first term. In 1999, during the ceasefire, Aznar's government opened up talks with ETA's political wing for the first time in ten years. The dialogue ended in a stalemate. The separatists continued to demand a referendum on what they call "self-determination" while Aznar clung unwaveringly to the Spanish constitution, which declares that Spain remain whole.

As Aznar entered his second term, ETA's commitment to terrorism showed no sign of stopping. Aznar refused to commence new dialogues until all violence stopped and has pursued military means to fight the terrorists. Some critics complained that this refusal to negotiate with ETA or their political wing is a mistake. Aznar remained unmoved. Without delving into specifics, Aznar told Larry King during a November 2001 taping of *Larry King Live,* "I must point out that terrorists will be eradicated. And terrorists will be brought to justice before the courts."

Shortly into Aznar's second term as prime minister, Spain will assume the presidency of the European Union. The high profile position will allow Aznar the chance to further Spain's prominence in the EU and implement changes he sees as necessary for the success of the EU. These include the improvement of the infrastructure of transport between member nations— especially rail and air travel; the opening of energy markets for member countries; the full integration of the EU's various financial markets; free movement of labor, allowing workers greater mobility and support to work in other member nations; and a standardized educational system across the borders. These are lofty goals for the burgeoning Union and in pursuing them Aznar will face stiff opposition from other member states. Yet for the former taxman who—against all odds—brought conservatism and fiscal responsibility back to Spain, they may just be obtainable.

Sources

Periodicals

The Economist, February 3, 1996, p44; December 5, 1998, p62; March 11, 2000, p23; August 12, 2000, p45; June 30, 2001, p4.
Europe, May 2000, p22; December 2001, p28.

On-line

www.cnn.com/resources/newsmakers/world/europe /aznar.html
Eurowatch, April 15, 1996, www.csis.oirg/html/euro 1.html
www.la-moncloa.es
Transcript of *Larry King Live* interview, November 2001, www.spainemb.org/novedades/Aznar/cnnb. htm
www.spainview.com/Aznar.html

—Candace LaBalle

Hugo Bánzer Suárez

1926—

Politician

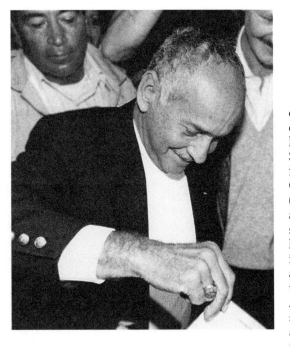

Ailing Bolivian president Hugo Bánzer Suárez resigned in August of 2001 after a long and sometimes controversial political career. A top military officer who engineered a 1971 coup, Bánzer led Bolivia through seven years of harsh military rule. Nearly twenty years after yet another military coup forced him from office—and after Bolivia had implemented sweeping democratic reforms—Bánzer was elected president. Over the next four years, he won praise for allowing Bolivia's progress toward a full democracy to flourish. Diagnosed with cancer at age 76, Bánzer resigned from office for the second time and his Vice President, Jorge Quiroga Ramírez, was named to succeed him. The handover continued Bolivia's relatively recent tradition in peaceful transitions of political power.

Long Military Career

Bánzer was born in 1926 into a Spanish ranching family. They lived in Concepción, in the largely agrarian Santa Cruz province. He was sent to La Paz, Bolivia's largest city, for schooling, and then entered the Bolivian Army Military College. He became a cavalry lieutenant in the army upon graduation, and enjoyed a successful military career for a number of years. Postwar-era involvement in South American political affairs on the part of the U.S. Central Intelligence Agency (CIA), brought Bánzer to the attention of American "advisors" interested in keeping leftist movements from gaining ground on the continent, and he was invited to attend the U.S. Army School of the Americas in Panama. He also studied at the Armored Cavalry School in Ft. Hood, Texas in 1960, and at the School of the Americas in Ft. Benning, Georgia.

Bánzer served as Bolivia's minister of education from 1964 to 1966, but his first cabinet post also came at the onset of a period of notorious political instability in the country: 16 governments came and went over the next 19 years. "Some lasted only days, even hours," explained a report in the *Economist*. "Vociferous working-class and peasant movements gave the generals all the excuse they needed to overthrow left-wing civilian governments, often with American encouragement, as part of a struggle against communism." Bánzer was named as Bolivia's military attaché in Washington, D.C. in the 1960s, a prestigious post. Returning home in 1969, he was named commander of the military school of the Bolivian Army. The

At a Glance . . .

Born May 10, 1926, in Concepción, Santa Cruz, Bolivia; married; Yolanda Prada; children: five. *Education:* Earned degrees from Bolivian Army Military College, Military School of Argentine Republic, U.S. Army School of the Americas (Panama), Armored Cavalry School (Ft. Hood, TX), 1960, School of High Command of the Bolivian Army, School of the Americas (Ft. Benning, GA), School of National Superior Studies of Bolivia. *Politics:* National Democratic Action Party, Bolivia. *Military Service:* Joined Bolivian Army; made commander of Fourth Cavalry Regiment; served as military attaché, Bolivian Embassy to the United States, 1960s; commander-in-chief, Armed Forces of Bolivia; commander, military school of the Bolivian Army after 1969; chief of intelligence dept. of the Bolivian Army; also served as chief of high command, departmental commander division, and military professor.

Career: Bolivian minister of education, 1964-66; became president of Bolivia in a military coup, 1971, left office, 1978; served as Bolivia's ambassador to Argentina, 1978-97; National Democratic Action Party, Bolivia, founder, 1979, and chair; president, Political Council of the Patriotic Alliance, 1989; elected president, 1997, retired, August 2001.

Awards: Recipient, gold medal of Mayor's Office of Sucre, Bolivia; gold medal of the Ret. Magistery; Guerrilleros Lanza medal; El Condor de los Andes award, government of Bolivia; Army Merit medal, United States military; also decorated by the governments of Argentina, Brazil, Colombia, Ecuador, Panama, Paraguay, Peru, Uruguay, and Venezuela.

following year, he was exiled after a coup by General Juan José Torres; in response, he planned his own successful military takeover, which occurred on August 22, 1971.

Bánzer's seven-year regime was one of the longest in Bolivian history; since becoming a nation in 1825, power had changed hands, often by coup, nearly 200 times. His rule was marked by typical hallmarks of repression amongst South American autocracies: universities were closed, the press was controlled, and political parties had little power. Furthermore, human-rights abuses occurred; 15,000 were arrested, and

19,000 were forced to flee. Bánzer was also accused of allowing the drug-trafficking trade to flourish in order to bolster Bolivia's economy after exports from one main crop, cotton, diminished. Bolivia suffers a statistical honor as the poorest nation in South America. Once part of the Spanish Empire and a thriving center of the tin mining trade, it is home to a majority of Amerindians, comprising half of its population of 8 million, who are mostly of Quechua and Aymara ethnicity. About 30 percent of Bolivians are mestizo, or mixed heritage, while families of European descent, like Bánzer's, make up the remaining 15 percent of the populace. Rich in resources, it is landlocked and lacks a large infrastructure because of mountainous Andes terrain and jungle topography. Its neighbors are Brazil, Paraguay, Chile, and Peru, each of which has also endured its own political or economic woes in the modern era.

During the 1970s Bolivia under Bánzer became one of the world's largest suppliers of cocaine on the illegal international market; the drug is made from plants grown for centuries by Quechua and Aymara farmers. In 1975, his private secretary was found to be carrying a large amount of cocaine at the Montreal airport, and Bánzer's son-in-law was also found in possession of the drug. Yet perhaps the most notorious incident of Bánzer's military regime was a crackdown on a peasant rebellion in the Cochabamba Valley in 1974. Fighter planes and armored vehicles dispersed crowds gathered to protest price increases, and 200 died—and none among that number were military personnel. It came to be known as the "massacre of the valley." Bánzer also worried some for forging political ties with General Augusto Pinochet Ugarte, who became ruler of Chile in a bloody 1973 coup. The two countries had warred in 1883 over a section of the Pacific coastline, and Chile emerged victorious. Bánzer unsuccessfully tried to regain the territory in a 1976 summit on the border, and the two generals famously embraced for press photographers.

Ousted from Office

Still, Bánzer's 1971-78 rule ushered in a period of stability for Bolivia. His economic policies stabilized the economy, and the country enjoyed short-term benefits from U.S. foreign aid and high oil prices. But when the economy began to falter, protesters went on hunger strikes, and there were widespread calls for democratic elections. Bánzer complied and held elections in 1978, in which he did not run but instead backed a general. That candidate, Juan Pereda, won, but Bánzer's government declared the election fraudulent, and nullified the vote. In response, Pereda led a coup that ousted Bánzer.

Bánzer served as Bolivia's ambassador to Argentina from 1978 to 1997, but also moved toward the political mainstream soon after his ouster. He formed the National Democratic Action Party of Bolivia (ADN)

in 1979, and he ran for election in every presidential contest after a constitutional government was restored in 1982. Though he failed to win, candidates of his ADN party usually took a number of seats in the Bolivian Congress. The party made peace with workers and peasants, and forged coalitions with the other leading political groups, such as Nationalist Revolutionary Movement (MNR). That alliance gave Bánzer and his party control of the country's economic policy for four years between 1989 and 1993.

Later in the 1990s, Bolivia began to enact some free-market reforms under a new president, Gonzalo Sanchez de Lozada. This involved selling off parts of large state-run utilities to private investors. Public sentiment was opposed to some of these economic policies, for the reforms seemed to benefit only a small, elite class of Bolivians and foreign investors. The country remained desperately impoverished: two out of three Bolivians still lived below the poverty level, the annual average income was just $800, 20 percent of adults were illiterate, and one child in three in the rural and mountain areas suffered from malnutrition.

Bánzer was elected in 1997—although not by a popular vote. He and the ADN took a thin majority of the votes, besting MNR candidate Juan Carlos Duran, former president Jaime Paz Zamora, and Ivo Kuljis, a millionaire from the agrarian center of Bolivia. Bolivia's constitution specifies that a presidential candidate must win over half the popular vote, or the election will then be decided by Congress. Amidst some worries from international observers about the return of a former dictator, Bánzer was approved by Congress and was sworn in for his five-year term on Bolivia's Independence Day, August 6.

A New Era

Bánzer's four years in office proved to be something of a surprise for his detractors. Instead of reviving the harsh autocratic rule of his earlier presidency, he worked to ensure progress on human-rights laws, and championed a reform of the judiciary with a new criminal-law procedure code. He strengthened ties to the United States, and complied with American and United Nations strategies to eliminate Bolivia's drug trade. This move—which sometimes involved paramilitary raids on Aymara or Quechua coca farms, whose families had been growing the plant for centuries—was an unpopular strategy in the countryside. The resulting decline in the coca trade brought economic hardship and ensuing violence.

Bánzer's presidency was marred by his prior association with Pinochet. In October of 1998, Pinochet was arrested in London, and a judge in Spain ordered him extradited there to stand trial for human-rights abuses stemming from his presidency. Pinochet was eventually returned to Chile and placed under house arrest. but

the Spanish legal case presented evidence that linked Bánzer to Chile's infamous "Operation Condor" in the 1970s. This was an attempt by Chilean military intelligence to eliminate political threats to the Pinochet regime, which was said to have been supported by the CIA. Allegedly Bánzer and leaders of Argentina, Chile, Paraguay and Uruguay agreed to return political refugees to their home countries—where they were usually harassed and often imprisoned; some died in custody.

Bánzer denied any knowledge of Operation Condor and asserted that the charges were baseless, according to a report in the *Economist*. He claimed instead "that he is the victim of an international socialist conspiracy to defame him," the magazine reported. "In off-the-cuff remarks, he also blamed certain unnamed European governments for providing shelter to these supposed far-left libellers." Bánzer was criticized both at home and abroad for these statements, which were viewed as a setback for progress on human-rights issues in the country. Some members of Bolivia's Congress had been part of that younger generation in South America targeted by Operation Condor, and had even been jailed during Bánzer's own regime.

On a more positive note, Bánzer backed down when protests in Cochabamba Valley once again threatened to turn deadly. A plan to privatize the water system and build a dam there would have yielded increased water charges for residents, and protests in April of 2000 grew into a road blockade. Bánzer sent in army troops, and protesters fought back, setting fire to government vehicles. Anti-government sentiment across Bolivia gathered force, and there were several strikes, including one by its police force. As a result, Bánzer's government was forced to make some concessions, and the dam project was canceled.

Resigned Due to Poor Health

In 2001 Bánzer read a statement before Congress that called for further constitutional amendments to change the country's electoral system, making it fully democratic. His 50-point plan was viewed, however, as a concession and stop-gap measure in the face of a growing movement for further reform. As a report in the *Economist* noted, the backdown of Bánzer's government the previous year in the Cochabamba Valley protests inspired "new political movements—formed to lobby for water rights, more power for indigenous Indians, or stronger measures against corruption" to challenge the government on other fronts. "Many people want a broad referendum on how the country should be governed," the *Economist* article continued, "and there are even demands for a constituent assembly."

Bánzer's days in office were limited, however: he had been diagnosed with lung and liver cancer. He went to the United States for treatment in July of 2001, and received chemotherapy at the esteemed Walter Reed Army Medical Center in Washington, D.C. He returned to La Paz and resigned his office on August 6, 2001. His vice president, Jorge Quiroga Ramírez, took over to complete the remainder of the term. *Telegraph* correspondent Jeremy McDermott quoted Bánzer as saying when he arrived back in the country, "I want Bolivians to remember me simply as the sower of realities, not illusions."

Sources

Books

Current Leaders of Nations, Gale, 1998.

Periodicals

Dallas Morning News, August 2, 2001.
Economist, July 1, 1989; June 5, 1993; May 31, 1997; August 9, 1997; November 7, 1998; February 27, 1999; April 15, 2000; February 24, 2001.
Independent (London, England), July 22, 1998.
New York Times, March 14, 1999.
Oil Daily, July 10, 2001; July 30, 2001.
Telegraph (U.K.), August 7, 2001.
Washington Post, July 28, 2001.
World Press Review, June 2000.

—Carol Brennan

Fernando Cardoso

1931—

Sociologist, politician

Fernando Henrique Cardoso became the first reelected president of Brazil, based on the strides he made in modernizing the nation. During his terms, he emphasized economic reform, privatization, foreign investment, and funding for social services and education, and did so without a hint of the corruption that had plagued Brazil's former leaders. He is best known for his economic policies that succeeded in halting the chronic hyperinflation that plagued the country. The inflation rate in 1994 was 50 percent a month; by 1998, Cardoso had reduced it to three percent per year, but was facing criticism for his austere economic reforms. He also introduced a new stable currency, the *plano real*. Under Cardoso's leadership, Brazil has become the largest developing-world trading partner of the United States. Trained as a political sociologist, Cardoso sympathized with left-wing politics as a student and professor, and spent the late 1960s and 1970s blacklisted by the nation's former military-dictatorship government.

Cardoso was born on June 18, 1931 in Rio de Janeiro. His father, Leoncio, and grandfather were both military generals. During his time as an officer in the Brazilian army, Leoncio Cardoso was imprisoned briefly for his involvement in a democratic revolt, though he retired as brigadier general. Leoncio Cardoso was happy to see his son pursue sociology and academia rather than follow in his military footsteps. The president has kept much about his early life private, though it is known he studied sociology at the University of Sao Paulo, Brazil and earned his doctorate in 1961. As a young professor, he was part of a Marx study group. Though the group analyzed the social and political theories of Karl Marx, Cardoso maintains that he "was never a Marxist in an ideological sense," wrote Cardoso biographer and sociology professor Ted Goertzel after an interview located online at Goertzel's homepage.

Leftist President Joao Goulart was overthrown in a military coup in 1964, and Brazil came under power of a military dictatorship. Cardoso fled to Chile to avoid the fate of other distinguished liberal academics throughout the country, who had been forced to retire or even were tortured and imprisoned. He remained in exile in Santiago from 1964 to 1967 as a professor at the Latin American Institute for Economic and Social Planning, and spent the next two years at the University of Paris at Nanterre. During his years in exile, Cardoso continued his research into the relationship between developing countries and the West. He also

At a Glance . . .

Born Fernando Henrique Cardoso on June 18, 1931 in Rio de Janeiro, Brazil. married to Ruth Correa Leite Cardoso (an anthropologist); three children. *Education:* University of Sao Paulo, Brazil, doctorate, sociology, 1961. *Politics:* Brazilian Social Democratic Party.

Career: Sociologist, politician. Professor of developmental sociology, Latin American Institute for Economic and Social Planning, Santiago, Chile, 1964-67; co-wrote book, *Dependency and Development in Latin America;* professor of sociological theory, University of Paris-Nanterre, 1967; professor of political science, University of Sao Paulo, 1968; professor at Stanford University, Cambridge University, University of Paris, c. 1969-78; ran for Senate on Brazilian Democratic Movement ticket, 1978; associate director of studies, Institute for Higher Studies in Social Sciences, Paris, and University of California; Brazilian Senator, 1983-93; foreign minister, 1993; finance minister, 1993-94; president of Brazil, 1995-.

Awards: Grand Cross of the Order of Rio Branco; Grand Cross of the Order of Merit of Portugal; named a chevalier in the French Legion of Honor.

Addresses: *Office*—Gabinete do Presidente, Palacio do Planalto, Praca dos Tres Poderes, 70150 Brasilia, D.F., Brazil.

earned a distinguished reputation in the field of sociology after publication of the book *Dependency and Development,* which he co-authored, and which "revolutionized thinking in the field," according to Goertzel.

Blacklisted From Teaching

Upon his return to Brazil at the end of 1968, Cardoso taught political science for a short time at his alma mater, the University of Sao Paulo. In 1969 he was arrested, banned from teaching at any Brazilian university, and his political and civil rights were suspended. Cardoso and his fellow liberals and intellectuals then formed a social science think tank called the Brazilian Analysis and Planning Center (also known as the Brazilian Center for Analysis and Research, and Cebrap). Rather than shrinking into the background,

he became known as one of the most prominent members of the left-wing opposition. The group's Sao Paulo headquarters were bombed in 1975 by right-wing terrorists. Cardoso was summoned to military police headquarters, where he was blindfolded and interrogated about a meeting he had had in Mexico City with a leading Belgian intellectual. When his blindfold was removed, he witnessed a man being tortured.

After twenty years of successive military rulers who drove the country's inflation rate out of control, a general election re-instituted a direct-election system. In 1986 Cardoso won a Senatorial seat for Sao Paulo. In his first days in politics, Cardoso's colleagues were impressed at his high level of intelligence. He brought an unusual level of intellect from his academic days into his inspired Senate speeches. In his first speech, he quoted form the works of German sociologist Max Weber, which proposed the need to attempt the impossible to achieve the possible. In 1988, he co-founded the moderately-leftist Brazilian Social Democratic Party.

Brazil's President Fernando Collor de Mello was impeached for corruption in 1992 and was replaced by Itamar Franco. President Franco appointed Cardoso Foreign Minister, in part because of his established intellectual and political reputation and in part because he is multi-lingual. (In addition to his native Portuguese, he speaks English, French, and Spanish.) In May of 1993, Cardoso was shocked to hear that Franco had appointed him Finance Minister. He called Franco to complain, but Franco told him "the public response has been excellent," according to an excerpt from Cardoso's biography located online at *Brazzil* magazine. Cardoso tempted fate by taking the position. It seemed a hopeless assignment for a sociologist after the long line of economists that had failed to halt inflation. Cardoso put together a team of the country's leading economists, but ignored the advice of those who told him it was impossible to draw back inflation before the end of Franco's term.

Introduced the New Plano Real

Cardoso's plan was rooted in the use of a currency which was continually readjusted to the U.S. dollar. The *plano real* was introduced in 1994, during his last year as finance minister. According to an excerpt from Goertzel's biography of Cardoso, Cardoso recognized the immediate effect of the real on his nation. "The society got tired of inflation," the president told Goertzel. "There came a point when they were fed up with it. At that point, we needed something to close the circuit. That was the *plano real.* We took a chance on it, and we won because the country understood. It was fantastic. Within a week, everyone knew what it meant." Once Brazil had a hard currency system, Cardoso exuded optimism for Brazil's future and for the fundamental reforms that would be necessary to achieve it. The nation responded by electing him president in October of 1994.

Cardoso triumphed in the election over his more charismatic opponent, Labor Party candidate Luis Ignacio da Silva. Brazilian voters could understand Cardoso's plans—in fact, they already had already been put into action. Brazil's business leaders overlooked Cardoso's liberal politics and education in Marxism and gave him their support, mainly because he had already proven his understanding of Brazil's complex economic problems and his preparedness to deal with them. While some of some leaders associated with the former military regimes found reasons to support him, so did many leftists, who felt his socialist convictions were still intact. Cardoso considers his "strong personality," bold vision for Brazil's future, and motivational and decision-making skills among the qualities that voters twice elected him for, according his interview with Ted Goertzel. Some Brazilians liken Cardoso's wife, anthropologist Ruth Correa Leite, to Eleanor Roosevelt, former first lady of the United States. The couple has three adult children and several grandchildren.

Cardoso continued his regimen to get Brazil's economy back on track. He privatized some industries and was active in attracting foreign trade to the nation, which had previously avoided foreign imports. Cardoso's policies benefitted the poorest Brazilians the most, bringing service-industry wages up. Because they had to pay an increased cost for services, the middle class felt the greatest pinch. In 1994 the inflation rate was 50 percent per month; by 1998, Cardoso had reduced it to three percent per year. Brazil became South America's cornerstone trade market—billions of dollars in foreign trade and investment poured into the nation. In fewer than four years, Cardoso had made great strides toward stabilizing the nation. So well-liked was Cardoso that voters improved an amendment to the Brazilian constitution that allowed him to serve a second term as president. This second victory was not as easy for Cardoso as his first election was.

Crumbling World Markets Threatened Brazil

In 1997 Asian stock markets crashed and shook Brazil's economy. In response, Cardoso subjected Brazil to austere financial reforms that included spending cuts and tax increases to reduce the nation's budget deficit and to secure international loans. Unemployment rose, as did inflation. Though his motivation was to secure the economy, the strict reforms were not popular with voters. Then Russia's government defaulted on its foreign debts, which damaged confidence throughout Latin America, and investors began pulling their money out of Brazil. Before the election, Cardoso began negotiations for an economic bailout with the International Monetary Fund (IMF), the international agency designed to stabilize the world economy. Despite the downturn, In Cardoso became Brazil's first president to be reelected to a second term.

After the election, Brazil accepted a $41.5-billion aid package from the IMF to secure its economy. The deal required that legislation be introduced in Brazil to restructure Brazil's tax and social security systems and further reduce government spending. Cardoso devalued the real in January of 1999 in hopes of lowering the cost of Brazilian exports, making products more attractive in overseas markets and increasing Brazil's incoming cash flow. Unfortunately, the real's value continued to slide.

For as many issues as he has tackled successfully, Cardoso is often cited for what many consider his shortcomings. "Cardoso may have done too good a job of containing the crisis," suggested one *Business Week* writer in an article published in October of 1999. In addition to his tenuous hold on Brazil's economy, "critical intellectuals" found his administration too predictable, according to Goertzel. Leftists complained that he had not solved more of the nation's ills, including poverty, destruction of the Amazon rainforests and other environmental damage, murders of street children by police death squads, and displacement and extermination of indigenous tribes. His approval ratings plummeted.

The corruption Brazilians had come to associate with politics before Cardoso once again appeared when scandal involving a number of questionable legislators threatened his administration. It was not suggested that Cardoso himself was involved. In a speech, Cardoso accused his political opponents of "pretending that we're taking away social rights, when we're trying to do away with abuses of privilege," according to *Business Week* in October of 1999. Because he is prevented from running for a third term, the best Cardoso can hope for is that a candidate of his choosing will carry on his legacy, though voters may opt for a candidate with an entirely different approach.

Sources

Periodicals

Business Week, January 25, 1999, p. 38; October 11, 1999, p. 64; May 21, 2001, p. 29.
Economist, October 10, 1998, p. 16; March 27, 1999, p. 3; July 29, 2000, p. 35; January 6, 2001, p. 1; September 15, 2001; September 29, 2001.

On-line

Brazzil magazine, http://www.brazzil.com/blaaug99.htm (February 20, 2002).
Christian Science Monitor online, http://www.csmonitor.com/durable/1999/01/04/p7s2.htm (February 20, 2002).

Current Leaders of Nations, Gale Group, 1999. Reproduced in *Biography Resource Center,* The Gale Group, 2001 http://galenet.galegroup.com/servlet /BioRC (February 20, 2002).

Encyclopedia Britannica, http://www.britannica.com (February 27, 2002).

Encyclopedia of World Biography Supplement, Vol. 18, Gale Research, 1998. Reproduced in *Biography Resource Center,* The Gale Group, 2001 http:// galenet.galegroup.com/servlet/BioRC (February 20, 2002).

Ted Goertzel's Homepage, http://www.crab.rutgers. edu/~goertzel/fhcpres.htm (February 21, 2002).

—Brenna Sanchez

Ana Castillo

1953—

Novelist, poet, and essayist

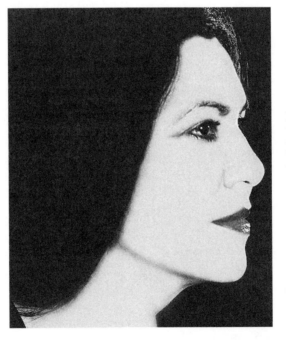

Emerging from the ferment of radical Chicano thought that shaped her ideas as a student in the 1970s, Ana Castillo was long known as a writer who was vigorously critical of the dominant Anglo-American mainstream and who worked to create alternative visions of what American society could become. "I was a Chicana protest poet, a complete renegade—and I continue to write that way," Castillo told *Publishers Weekly*. Yet by the beginning of the 21st century, Castillo's sheer gift for storytelling had brought her a substantial popular readership. Leaving the academic world, where she had made a living for much of her adult life, Castillo began to write full-time in the 1990s.

That storytelling bent, Castillo has said, had roots in her Mexican-American family background. Castillo was born in Chicago on June 15, 1953; her parents came to Chicago from the southwestern U.S. "I've written since I was very little," Castillo told *Melus*. "I wrote poetry and wrote stories and drew on whatever I could, painted on whatever I could—anything, any piece of paper that was around." Nevertheless, her parents did not encourage her creative impulses, steering her toward a common path at the time for verbally inclined young Latinas— she was sent to secretarial school. "I'm

a lousy typist and I've always had this aversion to authority, so I knew that I wouldn't get far in that atmosphere" she told *Melus*.

Became Disillusioned with Art Studies

Instead, Castillo enrolled in junior college and then at Northern Illinois University, scrambling to finance her classes through a combination of grants and various jobs. At first she studied art, but became discouraged in courses that did little to encourage her unique perspective. She had more luck with poetry, giving a reading of her own poems when she was 20 and seeing her first poems published before she graduated from Northern Illinois in 1975. Nevertheless, she went on for a Master's degree at the University of Chicago not in fine arts, but in Latin American studies. After her initial negative experiences as an art student, Castillo has always been leery of writing classes and fiction workshops.

Already as an undergraduate, Castillo had adopted a radical political outlook and had come to a strong consciousness of her own identity as a subject of dual oppression—as a woman and as a Mexican American. In an essay in her book *Massacre of the Dreamers:*

At a Glance . . .

Born June 15, 1953, in Chicago, IL; daughter of Raymond and Rachel Rocha Castillo; children: Marcel Ramon Herrera. *Education:* Northern Illinois University, B.A., 1975; University of Chicago, M.A., 1979; University of Bremen (Germany), Ph.D., 1991.

Career: Instructor in Ethnic Studies, Santa Rosa Junior College, Santa Rosa, CA, 1975; writer-in-residence, Illinois Arts Council, 1977; history lecturer, Northwestern University,1980-81; Urban Gateways of Chicago, poet-in-residence, 1980-81; instructor in women's studies, San Francisco State University, 1986-87; G California State University at Chico, visiting professor of creative writing and fiction, 1988-89; instructor, Department of English, University of New Mexico, 1989, 1991-92; professor of creative writing, Mount Holyoke College, 1994; published story "Juan in a Million" in *USA Today,* 1997.

Selected awards: American Book Award, Before Columbus Foundation, 1986, for *The Mixquiahuala Letters;* California Arts Council fellowship for fiction, 1989; National Endowment for the Arts fellowship for poetry, 1990, 1995.

Addresses: *Home*—Chicago, IL; *Agent*—c/o Susan Bergholz, 17 W. 10th St. #5, New York, NY 10011.

dedicated the novel to Cortázar in tribute. *The Mixquiahuala Letters* was published by the small Bilingual Review Press in Tempe, Arizona.

Inspired by Telenovelas

Castillo's second novel, *Sapogonia,* was also published by Bilingual Review, but the giant Doubleday/Anchor publishing house acquired the rights to both books after the success of Castillo's next book, *So Far from God* (1993), which was published by another major firm, W.W. Norton. *So Far from God,* seen by some as taking its structure from the popular Latin American *telenovela* television soap operas, was a kaleidoscopic story of the experiences of a Latin American matriarch and her four daughters. Incorporating folklore, magical episodes, recipes, and vivid scenes of Mexican-Amerian life, the book brought Castillo a new level of fame.

Although she had earned a living through a series of academic appointments (and finished a Ph.D. degree at the University of Bremen in Germany in 1991), Castillo now began to write full-time. One new fruit of her labors was the story collection *Loverboys* (1996), which was generally positively reviewed and dealt with a large variety of romantic and erotic relationships, heterosexual and homosexual. *Massacre of the Dreamers* (the title refers to an episode from Mexico's pre-Columbian history) was based on materials from her Ph.D. thesis, but incorporated unusual creative elements within the essay form. Castillo also edited several collections of writings by other Latin American authors, one of them dealing with the Virgin of Guadalupe. Castillo has renounced the Catholic religion, but, she told *Melus* in 1997, "Catholicism is embedded in our culture, in our psyche."

Story Published in USA Today

That same year, Castillo wrote a story called "Juan in a Million" that was published in that most mainstream of American print outlets, the Sunday-newspaper insert *USA Weekend.* Castillo herself would not agree, however, that her writing has moved in a mainstream direction; an enthusiastic promoter of a community of Latina writers, she believes that the growth in the field of Latin American women's writing as a whole has allowed alternative viewpoints to gain wider exposure. She continued to enjoy wide success with the novel *Peel My Love Like an Onion* (1999), which was set in Chicago's gypsy community and told the story of a handicapped flamenco dancer, and with a collection of her poetry, *I Ask the Impossible,* published in 2001.

Essays on Xicanisma, Castillo argued that she has "much more in common with an Algerian woman" than with a Mexican man. Now she began to read voraciously, encountering the works of the Latin American "magical realist" school and of African American female writers such as Toni Morrison (herself influenced by magical realism). She published a "chapbook," a small, self-published volume of poetry called *Otro Canto,* in 1977, and wrote and published several other books of poetry. One of them, *The Invitation* (1981) was published with the help of a grant from the Playboy Foundation.

Castillo began her first novel, *The Mixquiahuala Letters,* when she was 23, and it was finally published in 1986. The novel is cast in the form of a series of letters between two Latina friends: Teresa, a poet in California, and Alicia, an artist in New York City. Like the 1963 novel *Hopscotch* by the Argentine writer Julio Cortázar, Castillo's novel requires the reader to choose between one of several possible orderings of the material. Castillo arrived at the idea independently, but

Castillo rejects the term "Hispanic" in favor of "Latina" or "Chicana," arguing that the first of these terms signifies a determination to become assimilated into mainstream American society. She herself coined the term "Xicanisma," ("Chican-isma") to denote a specifically Mexican-American brand of feminism that aimed toward a new vision of society untouched by male-dominated, European-derived social structures. As Castillo put it in a *Mester* interview quoted in *Feminist Writers,* "[I]t's not about assimilation, it's really about looking for ways for us to survive as people." Considered one of the most prominent American writers of Latin descent by 2002, Ana Castillo remained a prolific and energetic communicator of an idealistic stance that sought to right the injustices of American history.

Selected writings

Zero Makes Me Hungry (poetry), Scott, Foresman, 1975.
i close my eyes (to see) (poetry), Washington State University Press, 1976.
Otro canto (poetry), Alternativa Publications, ca. 1977.
Clark Street Counts (play), produced 1983.
Women Are Not Roses, Arte Publico, 1984.
The Mixquiahuala Letters (novel), 1986.
My Father Was a Toltec: Poems, West End Press, 1988, reprinted as *My Father Was a Toltec and Selected Poems 1973-1988,* Norton, 1995.
Sapogonia: An Anti-Romance in 3/8 Meter (novel), Bilingual Press, 1990.
So Far from God (novel), Norton (New York City), 1993.
Massacre of the Dreamers: Essays on Xicanisma, University of New Mexico Press, 1994.

Loverboys (stories), W. W. Norton, 1996.
Peel My Love Like an Onion (novel), 1999.
I Ask the Impossible (poems), Doubleday, 2001.

Sources

Books

Contemporary Women Poets, St. James, 1998.
Dictionary of Hispanic Biography, Gale, 1996.
Feminist Writers, St. James, 1996.

Periodicals

Library Journal, October 15, 2000, p. 53; January 1, 2001, p. 111.
MELUS, Fall 1997, p. 133.
Publishers Weekly, August 12, 1996, p. 59.
The Review of Contemporary Fiction, Spring 1997, p. 201.

On-line

Contemporary Authors Online. The Gale Group, 2001. Reproduced in *Biography Resource Center.* Farmington Hills, MI: The Gale Group. 2001. (http://www.galenet.com/servlet/BioRC).

—James M. Manheim

Fidel Castro

1927—

President

Fidel Castro has ruled Cuba since his revolutionary forces overthrew dictator Fulgencia Batista in 1959. He introduced agriculture, medical, and education reforms to improve the quality of life for poor Cubans during the 1960s, but was criticized for suspending elections. His socialist philosophy and close ties to the Soviet Union led to tensions with the United States, reaching a pinnacle during the Cuban Missile Crisis of 1962. During the late 1950s and early 1960s United States trade embargos greatly impacted the Cuban economy, leading Castro to rely on the Soviet Union and Eastern Europe as primary trading partners. Castro also attempted to cast himself upon the world stage by exporting Cuba's socialist revolution to Latin America and Africa during the 1960s, 1970s, and 1980s.

The end of the Cold War in the late 1980s, along with a reduction in Soviet support, led to drastic changes in Cuba. The collapse of the economy between 1989-1993 persuaded Castro to introduce market-oriented reforms, and to seek investment from Canada, Britain, and Spain. The United States, meanwhile, maintained its embargo and continues to call for democratic reforms in Cuba. "Castro, perhaps as much as any major

political figure of this century," wrote Peter G. Bourne in *Fidel: a Biography of Fidel Castro,* "could simultaneously raise to fever pitch feelings of love, hatred, loyalty, reverence, and contempt."

Born into Privilege

Fidel Alejandro Castro Ruz was born on August 13, 1927 near the village of Brián in the Oriente Province. His father, Angel Castro, came from the Galacia region of northwest Spain in the 1890s and performed contract work for the United Fruit Company. He eventually accumulated 2,000 acres of land, leashed another 25,000 acres, and became a wealthy farmer. Angel Castro married a schoolteacher named Maria Louisa Argote and they had two children, Lidia and Pedro Emilio. He later married Lina Ruz González and they had seven children: Angela, Ramón, Fidel, Juana, Raúl, Emma, and Augustina.

Although Fidel Castro grew up in privilege, he was influenced by the poverty of his municipality. In *Cuba: or, the Pursuit of Freedom,* Hugh Thomas wrote, "Castro's early impressions and ambitions were mostly therefore formed by conditions in Oriente province, the most savage part of Cuba, where gun-law often reigned; the area where the U.S. influence was stron-

At a Glance . . .

Born Fidel Alejandro Castro Ruz on August 13, 1927, in Mayarí region of the Oriente Province, Cuba; married Mirta Díaz-Balart (divorced); children: Fidelito; married Dalia Soto del Valle; children: Angel, Antonio, Alejandro, Alexis, and Alex; other children: Alina Fernandez Revuelta. *Education:* University of Havana, studied law, 1945-50.

Career: Azpiazu, Castro y Rosendo, lawyer, 1950-52; Prime Minister, 1959-76; Council of State president, Council of Ministers chairman, 1976–.

Awards: Order of the White Lion.

Adresses: Cuban Interests Section, 2639 16th Street NW, Washington, DC 20009; Cuban Consulate, 2630 16th St, NW, Washington, DC 20009.

gest and most brutally exercised; where the doctors, teachers, dentists and indeed all social professions were least numerous in proportion to the population." His hero from youth was a national leader named José Martí who had died in 1895 fighting for Cuban independence. "As the island's greatest thinker and patriotic hero," wrote Tad Szulc in *Fidel: a Critical Portrait,* "Martí was always Castro's role model ... "

Castro attended the French Marists brothers' La Salle school in Santiago and at nine enrolled in Colegio Dolores boys' school. In 1941 he entered Belén College, an exclusive high school in Havana and Bourn noted, "From the moment Fidel arrived at the school, he was spotted by the fathers as a boy with exceptional talent and leadership potential." He became active in sports and won a prize for Cuba's best all-round school athlete in 1943-44.

Castro became interested in politics while studying law at the University of Havana in the mid-1940s. He took part in abortive invasion of the Dominican Republic in summer of 1947, designed to overthrow dictator Rafael Trujillo. When the expedition was called off, Castro escaped in a small boat that overturned. Thomas wrote, "he swam, carrying an Argentinian submachine gun and a pistol, across the Bay of Nipe, known to be infested with sharks ... " In February of 1948, Castro mobilized a mass protest against the invasion by the police of university autonomy, and in April, he traveled to Bogotá as a member of the student congress and became involved in the street violence that erupted during the Ninth Inter-American Conference.

Rejected Batista's Dictatorship

Castro married Mirta Díaz-Balart on October 10, 1948, and in 1949, Fidel Castro Diaz-Balart, or Fidelito, was born. Castro received a doctorate in law in 1950 and worked for the law firm of Azpiazu, Castro y Rosendo. He also became involved in politics, joining the Party of the Cuban People (Ortodoxos) in 1947. Many believed that the party's leader, Eduardo Chibás, would win the presidential election in 1952, but he surprised his followers by committing suicide on live radio on August 5, 1951. Castro became a candidate for Congress in 1952, but the elections were called off when former president Fulgencio Batista staged a coup on March 10, 1952. Bourne noted, "It was a moment of despair for those who thought that through the elections and the idealism of the Ortodoxo Party Cuba was finally going to end fifty years of turmoil and become a tranquil democratic country. No one was more angered than Fidel, who saw his hopes for a political career dashed."

Castro openly challenged Batista by submitting a petition to the Court of Constitutional Guarantees, accusing the dictator of violating the Constitution of 1940. When the petition was rejected, Castro gathered a small band of opposition forces and planned an armed insurrection. With 150 men, mostly factory workers, agriculture workers, and shop assistants, he attacked the Moncada military barracks in Santiago de Cuba, hoping to stir an uprising in Oriente Province. The armed assault ended in disaster. Nearly half of the participants were captured, tortured, and then killed, while Castro and his brother Raúl were arrested.

During his trial in September of 1953, Castro made a speech justifying his actions, but he also added political elements calling for land reform, civil liberties, and rural improvements. The speech later appeared in a pamphlet that circulated secretly. Castro lost his plea and was sentenced to 15 years in prison. In 1953, while in jail, Mirta Castro was granted a divorce. On May of 1955, after only a year and a half in prison, Castro, his brother Raúl, and 18 followers left the Isle of Pines under the amnesty law.

Instigated Revolution

In July of 1955, Castro and a small number of followers regrouped in Mexico. They called themselves the 26th of July Movement in memory of the attack on the Moncada barracks. In November of 1955, Castro met Ernesto "Che" Guevara, a doctor who enrolled in his army. When the small rebel force returned to Cuba aboard the yacht, Granma, they were attacked and a third of their forces decimated. The remaining rebels reassembled in the Sierra Maestra, located in the southern most part of Cuba. Within six months, Castro had won over the local peasants with promises of land reform; within a year, the 26th of July Movement controlled the Sierra Maestra region. "For two years, he and his small band stayed in the rough mountains of the Sierra Maestra," wrote Georgie Anne Geyer in *World and I,* "hiding from the army, engaging in occasional ambushes, but above all writing with their lives the new mythology of the Cuban revolution."

The revolution began in earnest when Castro called a strike over the radio on April 9, 1958 and many dissidents were killed in the street. In May Batista launched a major attack on Sierra Maestra. Thomas wrote, "For weeks it was impossible to know what was going on." While the rebels were greatly outnumbered, ill-trained government troops suffered a series of defeats. This pattern continued throughout 1958, climaxing when Guevara attacked a government train column in December and achieved a decisive victory. On New Years, Batista fled Cuba to the Dominican Republic. A general strike was called to show support for the rebels and the Cuban army surrendered. Castro arrived in the capital on January 8, 1959.

Cubans were excited about the revolution, but also anxious because of their new leader's lack of political experience. 1,500 laws were passed during the first year, increasing pay, decreasing rents, and forming state farms that offered steady employment. The Agrarian Reform Act confiscated land from anyone with an estate over 1,000 acres. Bourne noted, "In the eyes of the masses, the revolution had already led to the redistribution of some land, a reduction in the cost of essential services, the elimination of corruption, and the promise for the first time of education, health care, and steady employment." A massive literacy campaign sent 250,000 volunteers into rural areas, eventually achieving a 94 percent rate. Hundreds of medical clinics and hospitals were built in the countryside, raising the average Cuban life expectancy to 76 years. Schools and universities were erected, and postgraduate education was free.

Other actions were controversial. Revolutionary tribunals sent political enemies to firing squads and elections were suspended. Castro nationalized oil refineries, sugar mills, and utilities, most belonging to American companies. In retaliation, the United States canceled sugar purchases completely in October of 1960 and prohibited all exports to Cuba except food and medical supplies. Eisenhower recalled the United States' Cuban ambassador in January of 1961 and suspended diplomatic relations.

Clashed With United States

When John Kennedy became president in 1961, the United States attempted to remove Castro from power with an inland invasion of Cuba. Emily Hatchwell and Simon Calder wrote in *Cuba In Focus: a Guide to the People, Politics and Culture,* "Political considerations aside, the Bay of Pigs attack was a shambles from its very inception. The idea that the people of Cuba would rise up against Castro following an invasion showed a complete lack of understanding of the situation on the island." Within 48 hours, the United States operation had been defeated. Castro's success at repelling the invasion made him very popular.

In 1962 Castro requested military aid from Russia because he believed the United States was planning another assault. More than 40 nuclear missiles arrived in Cuba before the Kennedy administration realized what had happened. On October 22, Kennedy ordered a blockade of Russian ships carrying arms to Cuba and issued an ultimatum: remove the missiles from Cuba or face the possibility of nuclear war. Russian leader Khrushchev agreed to withdraw the weapons, but only if the United States pledged not to invade Cuba. Kennedy agreed. Cuba became further isolated in 1962 when the Organization of American States (OAS) suspended Cuba's membership and two years later, suspended all diplomatic and trade ties. Only Mexico refused to join the boycott.

During the 1960s, 60,000 political prisoners crowded Cuban jails. Homosexuals, artists, intellectuals, and former friends of Castro's were also imprisoned. Hatchwell and Calder noted, "Anyone who was not with the Revolution was by definition against it. Trade unions were disbanded and the media came under direct government control." Castro also attempted to export the revolution by supporting communist rebels in a dozen other countries. Cubans fought in the Angolan Civil War, helped Ethiopia defend itself against Somalia, and aided guerilla movements in South and Central America, including the Sandinistas in Nicaragua.

Political repression and lack of economic opportunity led many Cubans to seek asylum in the United States. During 1980 Castro opened the port of Mariel near Havana, allowing 120,000 Cubans to flee. Another 30,000 left in 1994.

Enlisted New Economic Reforms

Castro suffered many setbacks during the 1990s, primarily due to the collapse of the Soviet Union and the reduction of Russian aid. In 1996 the United States passed the Helms-Burton Act, tightening the embargo by attempting to impose penalties on other countries that traded with Cuba. Reductions in Russian oil left many Cuban factories inoperative. There was a shortage of electricity, and bicycles became the primary mode of transportation in cities like Havana. Many farmers were forced to replace their tractors with oxen, while a deficiency of farm products required Cubans to stand in line to receive a single load of bread.

Despite such difficulties, Castro remained in power. He has, however, made a number of concessions toward market economies during the 1990s, leading to a greater emphasis on tourism. He also encouraged investment from Spain, Mexico, France, and Canada. Cuba also softened its rhetoric against the United States. In November of 2001, Cuba received $30 million in humanitarian aid from American companies after a hurricane devastated the island. The *Economist* noted, "Foreign diplomats speculate that Cuba, facing great economic difficulties, has the desire, and may have an opportunity, to improve relations." Castro, however, has shown no intention of instituting the one reform most requested by American critics: democracy. After over 40 years as Cuba's leader, he appears determined to maintain the status quo. Hatchwell and Calder summarized, "It is difficult to imagine Fidel Castro standing down; any subsequent leader would be hard pushed to command any authority as long as he was still alive."

Selected Writings

Playa Girón: A Victory of the People, Editorial en Marcha, 1961.
History Will Absolve Me, Carol Publishing Group, 1961.
Revolutionary Struggle, MIT Press, 1972.
In Defense of Socialism, Pathfinder Press, 1989.

Selected Speeches of Fidel Castro, Pathfinder Press, 1992.
Fidel Castro Reader, Ocean Press, 2002.

Sources

Books

Bourne, Peter G., *Fidel: a Biography of Fidel Castro,* Dodd, Mead & Company, 1986, pp. 14, 26, 64, 195.
Calder, Simon, and Hatchwell, Emily, *Cuba In Focus: a Guide to the People, Politics and Culture,* Interlink Books, 1999, pp. 15, 19, 38.
Szulc, Tad, *Fidel: a Critical Portrait,* William Morrow and Company, 1986, p. 14.
Thomas, Hugh, *Cuba: or, The Pursuit of Freedom,* Da Capo Press, 1998, pp. 808, 809, 812, 996.

Periodicals

Economist (US), January 26, 2002.
World and I, May 2001, p. 265.

On-line

Biography Resource Center, Gale, 2002, http://www.galenet.com/servlet/BioRC.

—Ronnie D. Lankford, Jr.

Ida Castro

1953—

Public official, lawyer

Ida Castro rose through the ranks of the U.S. Department of Labor before being named the first Latina to head the U.S. Equal Employment Opportunity Commission in 1998. Over the course of her three years as the agency's leader, Castro implemented numerous changes and initiatives that improved its ability to provide quality services to the public. She was then appointed as secretary of personnel for the state of New Jersey.

Castro was born in 1953 in New York City. Her father, Ezequiel, was a restaurant worker, and her mother, Aurora, was a garment worker. Although she was born in New York, Castro spent much of her childhood in Hato Rey, a suburb of San Juan, Puerto Rico. As a first-grader in the Bronx, Castro was struck by the prejudice and bigotry surrounding her when a teacher instructed Castro that she was not to translate some classroom instructions to another student who spoke only Spanish. Years later, remembering the teacher's disgust as she referred to the student as a "spic," a racial slur for a Hispanic, Castro would be motivated to do what she could to defend the rights of all.

After receiving her bachelor of arts degree from the University of Puerto Rico, Castro attended Rutgers University in New Jersey, where she earned both an M.A. in labor studies and a J.D. In 1973 she accomplished one of her many "firsts" when, at the age of 20, she became the first woman and youngest person to serve on the city cabinet of Carolina, Puerto Rico, assuming the role as the director of Manpower. In 1976 she joined the faculty of Rutgers Labor Education Center at the Institute for Management and Labor Relations. She established another first when she became the first Hispanic woman to be tenured as an associate professor at the Institute.

Along with her career as a professor at the Institute for Management and Labor, Castro also served in various positions as an employment and labor law attorney. She was senior counsel for legal affairs for the Health and Hospital Corporation in New York, the largest U.S. municipal health care system; director of labor relations and special counsel to the president at Hostos Community College, associated with City University of New York; associate counsel at Eisner, Ley, Pollack, and Ratner; and associate counsel at Giblin and Giblin. In 1989 she became the first Hispanic woman to serve as deputy campaign manager of a successful mayoral campaign in New York City, helping Democrat David

At a Glance . . .

Born in 1950 in New York,NY; children: one daughter. *Education:* University of Puerto Rico, B.A.; Rutgers University M.A., J.D. *Politics:* Democrat.

Career: Assistant professor, Labor Education Center, Institute for Management and Labor Relations, Rutgers University, 1976–88; Director of Labor Relations and Special counsel to the president, Hostos Community College, New York, 1988–94; Deputy Assistant Secretary and Director of the Office of Workers' Compensation Programs, U.S. Department of Labor, 1994–96; Acting Director of the Women's Bureau, U.S. Department of Labor, 1996–98; Chair, Equal Employment Opportunity Commission, 1998–01; Senior Advisor and Director, Women's Vote Center, Democratic National Committee, 2002–.

Awards: Saint Joseph College, Doctor of Human Letters, Honoris Causa, Class of 2000; Outstanding Public Service Award, Rutgers School of Law; Outstanding Leadership Award, Puerto Rican Legal and Education Fund; 2000 Lifetime Achievement Award, National Puerto Rican Coalition; Legal Services Award, Mexican American Legal Defense and Educational Fund; Dream of Equality Award, Asian Americans for Equality; and Rutgers University Hall of Distinguished Alumni Award, 1999.

Address: *Office*—Democratic National Committee, 430 S. Capitol St. SE, Washington, DC 20003, (202) 863-3000.

Dinkins to become mayor of New York City. Three years later, in 1992, Castro served as deputy campaign manager for Nydia Velásquez of New York in her first successful bid to become a U.S. congresswoman. More firsts came when Castro founded the first Hispanic women's group in New Jersey and when the governor of New Jersey appointed her as the first Hispanic woman to serve on the New Jersey Commission on the Status of Women.

In 1994 Castro joined the U.S. Department of Labor as deputy assistant secretary of the Office of Workers' Compensation Program in the Employment Standards, becoming the first woman to be named Director of that office. She was later named acting deputy solicitor of the Labor Department. In 1996 Castro was selected to head the U.S. Department of Labor's Women's Bureau

as the agency's acting director. The Women's Bureau was formed by Congress in 1920 to promote the welfare of working women. Upon entering the office, Castro vowed to promote the rights of wage-earning women, focusing increased attention on older women, very young women, and women of color. During her two year tenure as Acting Director, Castro is credited with the development of an agency web site, improving and expanding outreach to women, and developing relations with small and medium sized businesses.

In 1998 Castro fulfilled her greatest "first" when she was named the director of the U.S. Equal Employment Opportunity Commission (EEOC), the first Latina to serve in this capacity. Castro was nominated by President Clinton on April 2, 1998, and received unanimous confirmation from the U.S. Senate on October 21, 1998. Two days later she was sworn in. The EEOC was created by Congress as a result of Title VII of the Civil Rights Act of 1964. The agency fulfills its role by enforcing and promoting equal employment opportunities regardless of race, color, age, sex, religious faith, national origin, or disability by means of education, arbitration, and litigation.

Upon joining the EEOC as its new leader, Castro focused on the challenges presented by the internal disarray of the agency. In an interview with *HR Magazine*, Castro noted, "Probably my greatest challenge is turning the agency around internally. The agency has experienced more than 20 years of resource starvation. We have issues of staff allocations, training, and professional development. We also have issues relating to technology, where the agency is far behind the private sector." Using increased funding from Congress, Castro started the process of upgrading the technology throughout the EEOC offices. She pushed for increased training and better communication among staff.

Castro's goal in improving her agency internally was twofold. First, she strongly believes that well trained and well prepared staff will understand the mission of the EEOC and strive to fulfill it. Second, by cleaning house internally, Castro wanted to present a more positive image of the EEOC to the public. Prior to Castro's term as director the EEOC had come under public criticism for its use of "racial testers." In such cases the EEOC would perform a sting operation on a company by sending in two people, employed by the EEOC and equipped with fake resumes, to apply for a job, with one person being notable by racial identity. The goal was to expose companies that used unfair and illegal hiring practices, which had the companies screaming entrapment. The use of testers was suspended but the public relations damage was left for Castro to attempt to clean up.

Castro remained at the head of the EEOC for three years. During that time, she was credited with reducing the backlog of discrimination charges by 23 percent.

She also decreased the average processing time of complaints from approximately ten to six months. As a result of her outreach efforts, assistance was expanded to underserved communities and a new field office was opened in San Juan to serve Puerto Rico and the Virgin Islands. She is also credited with the development of the National Mediation Program, a highly successful program through which employers and employees can avoid litigation by using EEOC or private mediators. Part of the success of the program is due to Castro's added stress on upgrading the agency's litigation services, thereby motivating employers to find alternative solutions to the problems.

In August of 2001, Castro stepped down as head of the EEOC. According to an EEOC press release, Castro said of her departure: "I am very proud of the tremendous progress EEOC has made, such as slashing the backlog of charges, implementing the National Mediation Program, establishing a comprehensive enforcement strategy to ensure a fair and efficient process, and improving customer services." After departing the EEOC, Castro joined the Democratic National Committee (DNC) as a senior advisor and director of the DNC Women's Vote Center. The Women's Vote Center was established in June of 2001 as a special initiative to educate, engage, and mobilize women voters for Democratic candidates. DNC Chairman Terry McAuliffe commented in a DNC press release, "I am proud to welcome a woman of Ms. Castro's caliber to lead this incredibly important initiative. Her strategic vision, proven leadership, impressive record of accomplishments and strong commitment to women's issues make her the perfect choice to direct the Women's Vote Center." In the fall of 2001, Castro was appointed as the personnel director for the state of New Jersey.

Despite her impressive career as the achiever of so many "firsts," Castro remains dubious about this honor.

In an interview with Kuliva Wilburn of IMDiversity.com, she noted, "In terms of being the first, I've been the first on several occasions. I should probably say it with greater pride, except that I'm always concerned when I'm the first in anything. It just reminds me in how late in coming that it is.... I would certainly like to see our society reach a point where saying the first of anything is no longer of relevance, because we are in every place —as women, as Latinas, as Blacks, as Asian-Pacific Americans, whatever group. I think, regrettably, that we've got a long way to go in that regard and that being said I will try to do my best to open those doors for everyone."

Sources

Periodicals

The Star Ledger, (New Jersey), April 23, 2002.

On-line

Democratic National Committee, http://www.dnc. org
Rutgers University, http://rutgers.edu
Pricewaterhouse Cooper's Endowment for the Business of Government Profiles in Leadership, http:// endowment.pwcglobal.com/radio/castro_bio.asp
HR Magazine, February 1999, http://www.shrm.org /hrmagazine/articles/0299castro.htm
U.S. Department of Labor, Women's Bureau, http:// www.dol.gov/opa/media/press/wb/wb96103.htm
U.S. Department of State, The President's Interagency Council on Women, http://www.secretary. state.gov/www/picw/acwbio_castro.html
Women's Village, IMDiversity.com, http://www.im diversity.com/villages/woman/village_woman.asp
http://www.state.nj.us/personnel/commissioner.htm

—Kari Bethel

Hugo Chávez

1954—

President

The charismatic Hugo Chávez, elected president of Venezuela in 1998, is sometimes described by political pundits as Latin America's most controversial leader after Fidel Castro. Chávez has set this mineral– and resource-rich South American nation on a course of political, economic, and social reform he describes as a "Third Way" between a socialist and a free-market economy. In 2002, Chávez faced growing national discontent as his promised economic betterments were not forthcoming.

Childhood in Farming Village

Hugo Chávez Frias was born July 28, 1954, in Sabaneta, a small farming town in Venezuela's western state of Barinas. Both parents were teachers, and they struggled to make ends meet, as Chávez recalled in an interview with Lally Weymouth of *Newsweek*. "I had to go with my father in the wee hours of the morning to help him fish to be able to eat. I sold sweets that my grandmother baked in the public square to have money to buy shoes and notebooks." Such a situation was not uncommon for much of Venezuela's population. Crude oil was a steady export out of Venezuela by 1930, but political and economic power remained in the hands of a small group of wealthy landowners and industrialists. For much of the twentieth century, *caudillos,* or military dictators, ruled from Caracas, its capital.

Chávez was a standout baseball player as a teen, a talent that helped gain him entry into the country's elite military academy. From there he joined the army and advanced through its ranks to head an elite paratrooper unit. Rankled by the corruption among the officer class—bribery and payoffs had become common currency at nearly all levels of Venezuelan life—Chávez formed a secret anti-corruption organization in the late 1980s with other disgruntled officers. He captured international attention on February 4, 1992, when he commanded a force of 12,000 troops in a coup against President Carlos Andrés Pérez. The insurrection was suppressed, "but not before Chávez, in an unforgettable televised jeremiad, denounced the moral and economic rot at the heart of that once-so-hopeful republic. He became an immediate hero," wrote Benjamin Moser in *Newsweek International*. For leading the coup, he was sentenced to prison.

The notoriously corrupt Pérez regime eventually fell byitself through the impeachment process. Years later,

Chávez explained his reasoning behind his bid for power. "Here was a country full of gold, oil, iron, aluminum, water and fertile lands, yet 80 percent of the population was living in poverty," he told Joseph Contreras in *Newsweek International*. Released from jail in 1994, he became active in the political organization that he and other soldiers had founded, the Bolivarian Revolutionary Movement.

Became Legitimate Political Threat

Venezuela is one of the world's major exporters of oil. The country daily sends 1.5 million barrels to the United States alone. Still, the nation of 23 million has suffered under a moribund economy, with high rates of inflation and unemployment. By 1998, Venezuela, under President Rafael Caldera Rodríguez, was still suffering from a long-term recession. The country struggled to make its foreign debt payments when barrel prices on the world market fell. Venezuela also had a bloated public sector; nearly one in every three employed Venezuelans held a government job. Corruption continued: even middle-ranking government officials enjoyed such perks as chauffeurs for themselves and families. Tax evasion was widespread. There were estimates that 80 percent of customs revenues went uncollected because of bribery at the ports and borders.

Chávez formed the Polo Patriotico (Patriotic Pole), a coalition of 14 small parties, and decided to make a bid for the presidency under the banner of a "Fifth Republic Movement." His 1998 campaign tapped into the national mood of discontent and won widespread support. He promised great changes should he be elected, foremost among them an end to corruption. Concerning the powerful Petroleos de Venezuela (PDVSA), or state-run oil company, he pledged to give it less financial support and make it more accountable. He called for a constituent assembly, and charged the country's past leaders and long-entrenched political organizations with selling the country's oil, gas, and mineral resources off to foreign investors. They alone profited from such deals, Chávez asserted, while the majority of ordinary Venezuelans did not. His speeches were sprinkled with quotes from Christ and Simón Bolívar, the hero of Venezuela's independence movement, but his opponents charged him with demagoguery. Chávez told *Time International* in November of 1998 that his foes were justified in smearing his name. "There's an offensive against us—painting me as Hitler or Mussolini, a crazed assassin," Chávez told reporters. "What they're really scared of is losing all that they're used to robbing from this country."

Chávez's supporters ranged from the poor to the left to the conservative business community in Caracas. He was called "El Comandante," and those who gathered for his political rallies often sported the trademark of his Fifth Republic Movement, a red parachutist's beret. In polling on December 6, 1998, he was elected with 56 percent of the vote to become the youngest president in Venezuelan history. He immediately began fulfilling his pledge to reform Venezuela entirely. In July of 1999, a constitutional assembly met and drastically reduced the powers of Congress. The assembly also began a process of judicial reform to rid the court system of corruption. Chávez also purged the Customs Service, and revenues at the country's major seaport, Puerto Cabello, doubled.

Chávez's promised new constitution was drafted and put to voters in a referendum on December 15, 1999. It was approved by 71 percent of voters. The changes were sweeping: Venezuela officially changed its name to the "Bolivarian Republic of Venezuela," stipends were granted for stay-at-home mothers, and university education became free. The power of Venezuela's political parties was also dramatically slashed. For this, Chávez was accused of decimating the country's democratic institutions, but he explained in an interview with *Time* that his goal was to bring "moral" as well as "electoral" power to Venezuelans. "Moral power is a restructuring of offices that already exist—the comptroller general and the prosecutor general," Chávez stated. "These institutions are supposed to be independent, but they're used for political purposes. They're appointed by Congress and serve as a shelter for corruption."

Re-Elected with Larger Majority

Venezuela's new constitution called for elections in 2000. Chávez won a sound 60 percent of the vote. He was a charismatic leader, and citizens regularly pressed "wish letters" into his hands during public appearances. Tales circulated that Chávez had interceded to help many in personal or financial crises. His weekly radio call-in program, *Alo Presidente,* offered him a chance to solve problems, dispense wisdom, and explain his government's policies.

At times, Chávez's foreign policy worried Washington, for the United States was dependent on Venezuelan oil and interested in maintaining good relations. Chávez spurned an offer of ships and Army Corps of Engineers personnel after 1999 floods killed several thousand, and he refused to allow anti-drug flights over Venezuelan territory. As Chávez told *Newsweek*'s Weymouth, "what would be the opinion of President Clinton if President Chávez asked for permission to conduct flights over Washington? We cannot violate our sovereignty." He also made visits to Iraq and its president, Saddam Hussein, as well as to Libya and to Cuba. He invited Castro for a state visit, where they played baseball for the press. The Chávez government was also accused of aiding leftist rebels in next-door Colombia. Interviewed by Maria Amparo Lasso for *Newsweek International,* Chávez stated his position clearly. "We do not have a relationship with the guerrillas," he told Lasso. "We decided not to continue the line of previous Venezuelan governments who declared that the guerrillas were the common enemy of Colombia and Venezuela. The guerrillas are not our enemy, unless they attack Venezuela, which has not occurred. What we've done is facilitate the paths for a dialogue to peace."

Since taking office, Chávez has been accused of displaying increasingly dictatorial behavior. In June of 2001, the El Pantaletazo, or "G-String" Scandal erupted. An anonymous mailing to 140 top Venezuelan military officers included women's undergarments and the taunt that they were not macho enough to stage a coup against Chávez. At other times, Chávez charged that Pérez, the former president, now living in Miami, was behind a conspiracy to unseat him.

Chávez provoked a minor diplomatic squabble in the fall of 2001, when he appeared on Venezuelan national television and displayed a photograph of slain Afghan women and children. He linked their deaths to the U.S.-led military effort launched that October. "We must find the terrorists," a report in *NotiSur* quoted him as saying. "But not like this.... Look at these children. These children were alive yesterday. They were eating with their parents and a bomb fell on them." The U.S. ambassador to Venezuela was recalled to Washington.

Significant Land Reform Law

Later that year, Chávez forced 49 economic decrees through the national assembly just before its special legislative powers were slated to expire. The most dramatic of them was a land reform program. Statistics indicated that 70 percent of Venezuela's fertile land was owned by just three percent of the population; moreover, only four percent of arable land was being farmed. In the new Ley de Tierras, unused land would be given to the landless poor. The Ley began with unused government land, but there were worries that private property would be confiscated as well. That and other economic reforms served to increase the emigration of middle-class Venezuelans, who had been relocating to Florida and Spain since Chávez first took office. Even the Vatican representative in Caracas complained, declaring that the Chávez government was becoming too radical.

There was also a mainstream reaction to Chávez's 49 reforms. The country experienced a widespread work stoppage and a series of bank closures on December 10th. Chávez then surprised many by stating he would consider changing some of his more controversial laws to maintain peace in the country. Despite the conciliatory remarks, his approval rating continued to plummet. He made an especial target of *El Nacional,* the independently-owned Caracas daily. Its offices were attacked by a rock-throwing mob of Chávez supporters in January of 2002. The president lost further ground after the incident, widely believed to have been staged by his government. Later that month he lost some of his support in the Asamblea Nacional, when members of the Fifth Republic Movement, irate with his policies, allied with the opposition.

In February of 2002, there were further hints that serious opposition was gathering inside the armed forces, and more than one high-ranking officer began to publicly call for Chávez's resignation. Protests took place in the streets of the capital, mimicking those in Argentina in recent weeks, with women banging pots and pans and denouncing government policies. "In a poor Caracas neighborhood, [Chávez] was greeted not with roses but with bitter protest—a sign that the loathing he inspires in the middle and upper classes had dangerously percolated into even the indigent areas that had once invested such hopes in his revolution," wrote Moser in *Newsweek International.* The *New York Times* stated that the Bush administration had received hints that a coup might be imminent, and an unnamed State Department source said the Venezuelan representative was warned not to subvert the democratic process in the country. A day before, a fourth high-ranking military officer called for Chavez to step down. "Remember that the people are above all else. And our loyalty is to the nation, not with a particular leader," Air Force General Román Gómez Ruiz was quoted as saying in the *New York Times.* "President Chávez, for the good of the country and for love of the armed forces, resign peacefully and take responsibility for your failure." But Chávez gave an interview to the French newspaper, *Le Monde,* and claimed the alleged dissatisfaction among the military was a publicity plot. "Venezuela has a government that was legitimately elected and enjoys popular support," the *New York Times* Chávez told the French paper. "I might even say that it enjoys more popular support than any other country in the American continent."

Chávez is still an avid baseball player and an occasional playwright as well. With his second wife, María Isabel Rodríguez, he has five children.

Sources

Periodicals

Current Leaders of Nations, Gale, 1999.

Periodicals

Business Week, December 13, 1999, p. 34; September 18, 2000, p. 66; May 28, 2001, p. 35.
Commonweal, October 23, 1998, p. 11; February 11, 2000, p. 11.
Cuba News, November 2000, p. 10.
Economist, December 12, 1998, p. 35; February 6, 1999, p. 33; June 5, 1999, p. 33; September 25, 1999, p. 38; February 5, 2000, p. 28; August 5, 2000, p. 35; November 18, 2000, p. 4; December 9, 2000, p. 4; January 20, 2001, p. 4; January 27, 2001, p. 1; March 24, 2001, p. 4; October 27, 2001; February 2, 2002; February 16, 2002.
Editor & Publisher, February 4, 2002, p. 28.
International Economy, May 2001, p. 28.
LatinFinance, July 2000, p. 46.
Latin Trade, November 1999, p. 22.
NACLA Report on the Americas, May 2000, p. 15.
New Republic, June 25, 2001, p. 16.
Newsweek, October 23, 2000 p. 45.
Newsweek International, September 13, 1999, p. 39; October 4, 1999, p. 50; October 4, 1999 p. 52; December 27, 1999, p. 23; February 28, 2000, p. 22; July 31, 2000, p. 21; February 5, 2001, p. 4; August 20, 2001, p. 52; November 12, 2001, p. 49; January 28, 2002, p. 29.
Oil Daily, July 27, 1999; November 30, 2000; January 10, 2001; February 26, 2001; December 11, 2001; February 20, 2002.
New York Times, February 26, 2002.
NotiSur: South American Political and Economic Affairs, September 14, 2001; November 9, 2001; January 18, 2002.
Time, October 9, 2000, p. 70.
Time International, November 23, 1998, p. 26; May 10, 1999, p. 19; August 9, 1999, p. 16; May 29, 2000, p. 26.
U.S. News & World Report, December 21, 1998, p. 40; June 11, 2001, p. 36.

On-line

http://www.mre.gov.ve/Chávezing.htm (February 25, 2002).

—Carol Brennan

Linda Chavez-Thompson

1944—

Labor leader

As the number three person at the American Federation of Labor and Congress Industrial Organizations, better known by the acronym AFL-CIO, Linda Chavez-Thompson is in a powerful position. She can turn the ears of politicians, labor union leaders, and the media. She can also put fear into corporate leaders dead set against unionism. When Chavez-Thompson talks labor, people listen. She is the first woman and the first minority to hold this position. One of eight children born to a second generation Mexican-American family in Texas, Chavez-Thompson left school in ninth grade to pick cotton. She never returned. Instead she learned on the job—analyzing job contracts and legislature, leading strikes, and mediating worker grievances. Lack of formal education did not prevent her from ascending the ranks of labor and becoming not only a role model, but also a powerful force in the reinvigoration of a labor movement that has been waning since the 1950s. Since her appointment to the executive council of the AFL-CIO membership numbers are up. Her message reaches laborers because she is one of them. A garbage worker quoted in *U.S. News and Report* summed up her success, "This little lady knows what hard work is," he said, "and if anybody is going to be able to represent us, she can."

Linda Chavez was born in Lubbock, Texas on August 3, 1944, the granddaughter of Mexican immigrants. Her parents worked as sharecroppers to support their eight children. Like her siblings, Chavez-Thompson began working at an early age to supplement her family's meager income. She was just ten when she began picking cotton for 30 cents an hour in the small town of Lorenzo. A few years later, she was asked by her father to leave school to work for the family full-time while her brothers continued their education. His reasoning was that education was not as important for a girl, since she would eventually marry and become a housewife. In an oft-told anecdote from her childhood, lack of schooling did not prevent Chavez-Thompson from becoming an early labor negotiator. With the backing of her siblings/workers Chavez-Thompson convinced her father that her mother should stay home and care for the house instead of joining them in the fields. The threat that the children would walk off the job was real enough for her father to agree.

At nineteen Chavez married Robert Thompson and took on her hyphenated surname. Following her marriage, she left the cotton fields for cleaning houses and entered the work world of minimum wage. Then in

At a Glance . . .

Born July 28, 1954, in Sabaneta, Barinas, Venezuela; son of schoolteachers; married to María Isabel Rodríguez; children: Rosa Virginia, María Gabriela, Hugo Rafael, Raúl Alfonzo, and Rosa Inés. *Education:* Earned degree from Military Academy of Venezuela, 1975; Simón Bolívar University, graduate degree, international relations *Military Service:* Venezuelan Army; held rank of lieutenant-colonel by 1990; commander of paratrooper unit. *Religion:* Roman Catholic. *Politics:* Bolivarian Revolutionary Movement; Fifth Republic Movement.

Career: Graduated from Military Academy with rank of second lieutenant; joined Venezuelan Army, 1975; jailed for coup attempt, 1992; formed Fifth Republic Movement, political opposition group, c. 1992; elected president of Venezuela, 1998.

Addresses: *Office*— Embassy of Venezuela, 1099 30th St. NW, Washington, DC 20007.

1967, through the help of an uncle, she landed a secretarial position with the Lubbock local of the Laborers' International Union, the same union to which her father belonged. At $1.40 an hour, the pay was barely higher than what she made as a cleaner, but in this position she began to find her calling. As the only bilingual staff member, she soon took on more responsibilities and began to serve as the union representative for the Spanish-speaking membership. Though Texas was a state notorious for its anti-union mindset, Chavez-Thompson embraced her job. "From not even knowing what a union was, Chavez-Thompson soon found herself drafting grievances for workers, then representing them in administrative proceedings. She pored over the rule books and took every organizing course offered," wrote the *U.S. News and World Report.*

In 1971 Chavez-Thompson went to work for the American Federation of State, County and Municipal Employees Union, AFSCME. She began with the Austin Local as an international representative. However, in 1973 she moved to the San Antonio Local 2399 and accepted a less demanding position as an assistant business manager. A mother by this time, she wanted to spend more time with her family. She remained with 2399 over the next twenty years, being appointed executive director in 1977. During this time Chavez-Thompson endured some of the most difficult times of her career. Not only was Texas business hostile to unions and labor organizing, but government em-

ployees—the very workers AFSCME represented—were denied union status under Texas law. "Trying to defend the rights of government workers in Texas was a difficult proposition, because Texas law didn't allow for unions of government workers to be recognized as such. You had to maneuver and 'persuade' state officials," Chavez-Thompson told the *Los Angeles Times.* Persuade she did and many of the states under AFSCME's umbrella saw marked increases in their memberships.

Chavez-Thompson's hard scrabble past also began to emerge during this time as a powerful ally. Not only in her ability to take a hands-on approach, but also because of her first-hand knowledge of what it means to work hard just to stay at the poverty level. "I know what it is to be told the odds are against you," she told *U.S. News and World Report.* In one instance she took up the cause of 33 community college workers who were facing job losses because they spoke about financial abuse by a handful of trustees. Chavez-Thompson took up the battle call and was instrumental in the public ousting of three trustees, which resulted in the workers keeping their jobs. On another occasion a wildcat strike by garbage truck drivers meant that Chavez-Thompson had to provide emergency drivers. She was one of them. For the laborers she represents, Chavez-Thompson has faced arrest many times on picket lines and at protests. She has won many battles, saved jobs, and improved working conditions for untold thousands.

Chavez-Thompson's commitment to labor paid off with her appointment to positions of increasing visibility and responsibility. In 1986, she was elected national vice president of the Labor Council for Latin American Advancement, a branch of the AFL-CIO. Then in 1988 AFSCME appointed her vice president of their seven-state region. Finally, in February of 1995 she took over the executive directorship of the Texas Council 42, AFSCME. In October of the same year Chavez-Thompson made history when she was elected to executive vice president of the AFL-CIO at its annual convention in New York. At the time the 13-million member group was facing many problems. Membership was at an all time low and no funds were being set aside to recruit new members. Also, workers were suspicious of unions as corrupt and felt little desire to join. Those that were union members felt little loyalty to the organizations. Of these problems, Chavez-Thompson told *Report on the Americas,* "We realized that the nature and the seriousness of these problems called not for moderate change, but for drastic change." Though some decried her appointment as merely a gesture for the organization which had become too 'male, pale, and stale,' Chavez-Thompson paid no attention and instead focused on the challenge of solving the problems facing unions and labor.

Chavez-Thompson set about reinvigorating the U.S. labor market by earmarking funds for recruitment.

"We're dedicating 30 percent of our budget to organizing—that was never done before—and we're going to get results," she told *Hispanic.* She also focused recruiting efforts on women and minorities—two groups long underrepresented in unions. Another effort she has undertaken is teaching the importance of organized labor and activism to youth. "We've lost a couple generations of children who don't realize what their parents have done to build the workplace in America. Forty hours a week didn't just come automatically. Overtime didn't come automatically. Labor Day is more than just the last holiday before you go back to school," she told *NEA Today.* Her efforts have yielded success both in increasing membership and in the election of politicians committed to labor issues. "We stopped the hemorrhaging," Chavez-Thompson told *Hispanic,* "but it is still not easy for unions to build up their membership."

One of the most successful initiatives she has implemented in the promotion of unionizing is the enlistment of community groups such as churches, schools, civil rights groups like the NAACP, women's groups, and more. Though unions have traditionally kept their business private, Chavez-Thompson's point is that unions are made of workers who make up the community. "They are voters, parents, neighbors, and members of congregations she wrote in *New Labor Forum.* "We don't want to be considered outsiders because we know that our interests overlap with those of the communities. We want to be considered as part of the communities and as one with the groups that are contributing to improve people's living conditions," Chavez-Thompson told *Report on the Americas.* This approach has been wildly successful in numerous labor disputes, from K-Mart workers in North Carolina trying to obtain their first union contract to cafeteria workers at finance giant Saloman Smith Barney suffering retaliation for forming a union. Community groups recog-

nizing the impact such anti-labor practices have on their community join forces to expose the unfair practices and the bottom-line focused companies back off.

In 1997 Chavez-Thompson was elected to another four-year term as executive vice president of the AFL-CIO and in 2001, Chavez-Thompson was elected president of the Inter-American Regional Organization of Workers ORIT, a group that represents over 45 million workers in North, Central, and South America. Growing up Chavez-Thompson was told repeatedly that a poor Hispanic woman like herself would never make it in American society. Recalling this she told *U.S. News and World Report,* "Well, that did it. I was determined to prove traditional society wrong." Not only did she carve her own success in American society, but in doing so she has paved the way for hundreds of thousands of workers—perhaps millions—to succeed on their own terms with the guarantee of fair treatment and pay for their hard work.

Sources

Periodicals

Hispanic, September 1998, p. 70.
Los Angeles Times, October 27, 1995, p. 1.
NEA Today, May 1997, p. 42.
New Labor Forum, Fall/Winter 1998.
Report on the Americas, July-August 1997, p.52.
U.S. News & World Report, December 25, 1995, p. 95.

On-line

http://www.aflcio.org

—Candace LaBalle

Henry Cisneros

1947—

San Antonio mayor and Cabinet secretary

Henry Cisneros has often been compared with his immediate supervisor for much of the 1990s—U.S. president Bill Clinton. Both men were intelligent, politically skilled, well-educated, and committed not only to the ideal of change but to the nuts-and-bolts challenges of implementing it. And both were irreversibly diverted from their goals by revelations of extramarital sexual relationships. Nevertheless, as Clinton's political career came to an end at the dawn of the 21st century, no one was closing the book on that of Cisneros. He had already rebounded from adversity more than once during a spectacular career that included eight years as mayor of San Antonio, Texas—as the first Hispanic American to lead a major U.S. city.

Cisneros was born in San Antonio on June 11, 1947, in a middle-class neighborhood on the city's predominantly Mexican west side. He was the oldest of five children of a Mexican-American father, a civilian administrator at a U.S. Army base, and a Mexican-expatriate mother, the daughter of a renowned dissident journalist and intellectual. Cisneros's parents spoke Spanish at home but switched to English when their children were born. It was Cisneros's mother, especially, who instilled educational ambitions in her

five children, all of whom graduated from college and two of whom earned Ph.D. degrees. One of those two was Henry, who was a academic star from the beginning.

He breezed through Catholic schools in San Antonio and then enrolled in Texas A&M University, graduating in 1968 with a degree in English. Along the way he won a scholarship to a national student current-events conference, where he began to see the problems of his largely poor and oligarchically run hometown in a new light. Seized with a strong interest in public policy, Cisneros switched to the study of urban planning and administration, earning a master's degree from Harvard University. He had already made inroads into politics, living in Washington, D.C., with his wife and young daughter and working for the National League of Cities. In 1971 Cisneros was honored as a White House Fellow, and by 1975 he had completed his Ph.D. in public administration at George Washington University.

Clearly Cisneros could have pursued a successful career in academia (he turned down a professorship at the Massachusetts Institute of Technology) or in the federal government, but he chose to return to San Antonio to

When he announced his candidacy for mayor in 1980, it was as an independent.

With substantial support from white voters as well as Hispanics, Cisneros was elected mayor in 1981 by a nearly two-to-one margin. Cisneros was an unqualified success as mayor of San Antonio; *Texas Monthly* in 1999 named him its Texas Mayor of the Century, pointing to such achievements as a downtown riverfront redevelopment that drew tourists from far and wide and contending that he had "changed San Antonio's image from a poor and somewhat sleepy town to a culturally and economically vibrant model for the future of urban America." San Antonio's glittering downtown did not come at the expense of its residential neighborhoods; over $200 million was devoted to infrastructure improvements on the west side alone. Cisneros was reelected three times by overwhelming margins, once (in 1983) with 93 percent of the vote.

In 1988, even though his name had been floated several times as a possible contender for national office, Cisneros stunned the political world by announcing his retirement. His reasons were twofold. The official reason given for his withdrawal from politics was a desire to devote more time to the care of his son John Paul, who had been born the previous year with four life-threatening birth defects. Facing huge medical bills, Cisneros also hoped to make more money in private industry. Another motivation, however, was the imminent disclosure of an ongoing extramarital affair between Cisneros and his chief campaign fundraiser, Linda Medlar.

Cisneros founded a financial-management firm in 1989, and his cooperation with his wife in caring for John Paul (who recovered to flourish in school after several major surgeries) brought the two back together. Despite the bad publicity he had faced, Cisneros still retained enough popularity to stimulate talk of a comeback among political observers. With the election of Bill Clinton in 1992, Cisneros was mentioned as a possible replacement for various Texas officials who had ascended to jobs in the new Democratic administration. But Clinton had bigger plans for the ambitious young reformer: he named Cisneros as his new Secretary of Housing and Urban Development (HUD).

Taking office in 1993, Cisneros immediately stirred up new activity in that hidebound government department that had long been associated primarily with grim urban low-income housing projects. He attacked the problems of low-income ghettoization and homelessness with a $70 million plan that would provide housing vouchers enabling low-income Americans to rent living space in the communities of their choice—an idea that brought Cisneros criticism in affluent circles in his native Texas and elsewhere. More generally, Cisneros proved an able advocate for HUD's very existence; the agency was under perennial attack from conservative budget-cutters.

apply the lessons he had learned to the place in which he had grown up. Taking a teaching job at the University of Texas at San Antonio, he ran for city council and became the city's youngest council representative in history when he was elected in 1975 at age 27. Impressing observers immediately with the hands-on energy that would become the hallmark of his political career, Cisneros deftly steered a middle course between the city's conservative Anglo-American power structure and the west side's first stirrings of Latino activism.

The following year, however, the Medlar affair resurfaced. Medlar filed a breach-of-contract suit against Cisneros, claiming that he had agreed to support her until her daughter's college graduation but had then discontinued the monthly payments after joining the Clinton administration. Medlar argued that she had been silenced in order to permit the rehabilitation of Cisneros's political career. "There is a side to Henry that is very narcissistic, that is very much concerned with what is good for Henry Cisneros," she told *People*. Cisneros admitted that he had made the payments to Medlar, saying that he had discontinued them only after being forced to take a pay cut upon returning to public life.

Cisneros had divulged payments of $60,000 during the FBI background check that preceded his appointment as HUD secretary, but Medlar claimed to have received over $200,000—raising the possibility that Cisneros had lied to the FBI. Attorney General Janet Reno launched a probe of Cisneros that ballooned into a five-year investigation costing an estimated $15 million. In 1996 Cisneros took himself out of the running for the HUD post in Clinton's second term. Three years later he pleaded guilty to a single misdemeanor charge, paying a $10,000 fine and avoiding a prison sentence. Cisneros received one of the pardons dispensed by Clinton in the last days of his presidency; although the investigation dragged on into the presidency of George W. Bush, his legal liabilities seemed finally to be coming to an end.

After leaving the Clinton administration, Cisneros served from 1997 to 2000 as president and CEO of the Spanish-language Univision television network. Before long, however, he had returned to his reformer's ways, returning to San Antonio to head a firm that developed affordable housing there and in other American cities. "Home ownership is the way people step into the American dream," Cisneros told the *San Diego Union-Tribune*. "It creates access to the levers of wealth." Still a charismatic speaker much in demand at civic and professional gatherings, Cisneros contin-ued to ponder solutions to the sharp inequities of circumstance that bedeviled American cities even during the 1990s economic boom. It seemed not inconceivable that he would one day return to political office and attempt to implement his ideas once again.

Sources

Books

Gillies, John, *Señor Alcalde: A Biography of Henry Cisneros,* Dillon, 1988.

Periodicals

Broadcasting and Cable, August 14, 2000, p. 49.
Houston Chronicle, February 12, 2002, p. A23.
Insight on the News, September 18, 1995, p. 10; October 4, 1999, p. 6; December 13, 1999, p. 14; February 5, 2001, p. 6.
Newsweek, December 22, 1997, p. 70.
People, April 3, 1995, p. 81.
San Diego Union-Tribune, November 21, 2001, p. B4.
Texas Monthly, Marc h 1993, p. 100; November 1994, p. 5; December 1999, p. 136; July 2000, p. 47; September 2001, p. 184.
U.S. News & World Report, April 7, 1986, p. 32; September 7, 1998, p. 33.
Variety, June 2, 1997, p. 23.

Online

American Decades CD-ROM, Gale, 1998. Reproduced in *Biography Resource Center,* Gale, 2001 (http://www.galenet.com/servlet/BioRC).
Encyclopedia of World Biography, 2nd ed., 17 vols., Gale, 1998. Reproduced in *Biography Resource Center,* Gale, 2001 (http://www.galenet.com/servlet/BioRC).

—James M. Manheim

Sandra Cisneros

1954—

Writer

As the first Hispanic-American to receive a major publishing contract, Sandra Cisneros has provided a voice for she who had had none before, the Hispanic-American woman—or to use Cisneros' favored word—the chicana. "I'm trying to write the stories that haven't been written. I feel like a cartographer. I'm determined to fill a literary void," Cisneros told Jim Sagel of *Publishers Weekly.* In doing so,she speaks out against racism, sexism, poverty, and shame. Growing up a chicana in the poor barrios of Chicago, Cisneros knows these things well. She watched as the women around her gave up and gave in, accepting lives of second class citizenship, beholden to their fathers, their brothers, their husbands, and their priests. This wouldn't be Cisneros's fate. She escaped through language, writing her way out of that future. Along the way she has collected numerous awards and critical acclaim. The woman who proudly proclaimed she is "nobody's mother and nobody's wife," is in fact the greatest caregiver of all. She charts the map that shows chicanas and chicanos, women and wives, sisters and servants, the possibilities of freedom.

Sandra Cisneros was born on December 20, 1954 in a poor neighborhood of Chicago, populated mainly by Hispanic immigrants and hyphenated Americans. Cisneros and her family were of the latter category, Mexican-Americans or Chicanos. Her father, a Mexican native from a family of means had traveled to the United States in search of adventure. A chance visit to Chicago led him to Cisneros's mother, a Mexican-American from a working class family that had lived in the United States for many generations, working mainly on railroads. Love blossomed and Cisneros's father decided to settle in Chicago and raise a family of six boys and one girl. However, "like the tides," Cisneros told *Publishers Weekly* in 1991, they regularly moved back to Mexico to be near her paternal grandmother. And from Mexico back to another barrio of Chicago that looked to the young Cisneros like "France after World War II—empty lots and burned-out buildings," she told *Publishers Weekly.* The moving continued for many years. In "Ghosts and Voices: Writing from Obsession," an article for *The Americas Review,* Cisneros noted that her grandmother's Mexican home was "the only constant in a series of traumatic upheavals."

Escaped Shame Through Books

The invariable movement—pulling up roots, packing boxes, new schools, new beds—took a toll on Cisneros.

At a Glance . . .

Born December 20, 1954 in Chicago, IL; daughter of an upholster and a homemaker, both of Mexican descent; six brothers. *Education:* Loyola University, Chicago, BA, 1976; University of Iowa, MFA, 1978. *Religion:* Catholic.

Career: Writer. Guest professor, California State University, Chico, 1987-88, University of California, Berkeley, 1988, University of California, Irvine, 1990, University of Michigan, Ann Arbor, 1990, University of New Mexico, Albuquerque, 1991; Literary Director, Guadalupe Cultural Arts Center, San Antonio, TX, 1984-85; Artist in Residence, Foundation Michael Karolyi, Vence, France, 1983; College Recruiter and Counselor, Loyola University of Chicago, Chicago, IL, 1981-82; Teacher, Latino Youth Alternative High School, Chicago IL, 1978-80.

Memberships: PEN; Mujeres por la paz (a women's peace group).

Awards: MacArthur Genius Award, 1995; National Endowment for the Arts fellowship, 1982, 1988; American Book Award, Before Columbus Foundation,1985; Paisano Doble Fellowship, 1986; First and second prize in Segundo Concurso Nacional del Cuento Chicano, Lannan Foundation Literary Award, University of Arizona, 1991; Honorary Doctorate of Literature, State University of New York at Purchase, 1993.

Addresses: *Home*—San Antonio, TX.

Though Cisneros attended Catholic schools, the education she received was less than ideal. In an interview for the anthology *Authors and Artists for Young Adults,* she said, "If I had lived up to my teachers' expectations, I'd still be working in a factory." Fortunately Cisneros's parents were firm believers in education, knowing that it was the only way their children could break the bonds of poverty. Library cards were mandatory in the family and Cisneros, without sisters to play with, too shy to make new friends, lost herself in the library's riches. Though she wrote a few poems as a child and served as the editor on her high school's literary magazine, it would not be until graduate school that Cisneros would finally become a writer.

Following high school, Cisneros enrolled in Loyola University, Chicago to pursue a degree in English. In her household, gender stereotypes were strongly upheld. She told *Publishers Weekly* that her "seven fathers," meaning her father and six brothers, expected her to conform to appropriate women's roles. She was to be a caretaker, get married, have children—to be like the other women who "lay their necks on the threshold waiting for the ball and chain," as the child narrator Esperanza described in *The House on Mango Street.* "In retrospect, I'm lucky my father believed daughters were meant for husbands. It meant it didn't matter if I majored in something silly like English," Cisneros later told *Glamour.*

Found Her Voice in Her Past

Cisneros graduated from Loyola in 1976 and was accepted into the University of Iowa's Writers Workshop. At first she felt out of place. "What did I, Sandra Cisneros, know? What could I know? My classmates were from the best schools in the country. They had been bred as fine hothouse flowers. I was a yellow weed among the city's cracks," she recalled to *Publishers Weekly.* In an effort to fit in, she mimicked the writing of famous male authors, her professors, and even fellow students. Cisneros finally found her place during a class discussion of the home as a metaphor for writing. As her well bred classmates talked of long hallways and homey kitchens, she realized that she had no such home in her memory. It was this realization that finally let Cisneros break free. "It was not until this moment when I separated myself, when I considered myself truly distinct, that my writing acquired a voice," she told *Publishers Weekly.* "That's when I decided I would write about something my classmates couldn't write about."

The themes of her childhood—poverty, cultural difference, uprootedness, and male dominance over women's lives—became her topics. "If I were asked what it is I write about, I would have to say I write about those ghosts inside that haunt me, that will not let me sleep, of that which even memory does not like to mention," she later wrote in "Ghosts." The little red bungalow she

She became shy and self-conscious. Already the odd one out as the only sister in a house of brothers, Cisneros found she fit nowhere. So she retreated into books and stories. One of her favorites was *The Little House* by Virginia Lee Burton, a picture book about a little house on a little hill, "where one family lived and grew old and didn't move away," Cisneros wrote in "Ghosts." It was a fantasy that she could never imagine for her own life. Instead, in 1966 her parents scraped together the money for a down payment on a small red bungalow. It sat on a broken down street in a poverty scarred Puerto Rican neighborhood on the north side of Chicago. It was a house Cisneros was ashamed of.

was so ashamed of as a child became the house on Mango Street. People she knew, had laughed at, and feared populated her stories. Her characters were Hispanic-Americans isolated from mainstream America by more than just a hyphen. Peppered with vivid, sensory imagery and Spanish turns of phrase, her work straddled the line between poetry and prose. Cisneros had created a beautiful language with which to share her stories.

After earning her master's degree in 1978, Cisneros returned to Chicago to teach at the Latino Youth Alternative High School for school dropouts. Though her job was demanding she continued to pursue her writing. She began to submit her poems to literary journals and found some success. Locally, she became a regular on the spoken word circuit, performing her work at bars and coffee shops. Her fame spread further when one of her poems was chosen to grace the buses of the Chicago public transport system.

Earned Literary Acclaim and Fame

In 1981 Cisneros took a short-lived administrative position at Loyola and then moved to Cape Cod. The following year Cisneros received the first of two National Endowment for the Arts fellowships. With the award money she left for Europe and three years later, while on the Aegean Sea in Greece, finished the manuscript that would become *The House on Mango Street.* Its 1985 publication was met with accolades and awards. Critics declared her a stunning new voice. Descriptions like sudden jewels filled the stories that made up the book. Her imagery stirred the senses and secured Cisneros a place on literary scene. General audiences devoured the book up and in a nod to the ultimate academic acclaim, *The House on Mango Street* found its way onto university syllabuses, most notably on the required curriculums of Yale and Stanford. The awkward young writer once intimidated by her more learned classmates was now listed prominently on "Required Reading" lists nationwide.

Made up of a series of poetic vignettes, *The House on Mango Street* is narrated by Esperanza, a Mexican-American girl coming of age in a Chicano barrio of Chicago. Not unlike Cisneros herself, Esperanza longs for a stable home. "Not a flat. Not an apartment in back. Not a man's house. Not a daddy's. A house all my own. With my porch and my pillow, my pretty purple petunias." Instead Esperanza has a house that is "small and red with tight steps in front and windows so small you'd think they were holding their breath." Dedicated *a las Mujeres,* or to the Women, the book offers a voice of defiance to the oppressed, sidelined, subservient Hispanic woman. As Esperanza says, "I have begun my own quiet war. Simple. Sure. I am one who leaves the table like a man, without putting back the chair or picking up the plate."

Following the publication of *The House on Mango Street,* Cisneros returned to the United States and accepted a position as an arts administrator in San Antonio, Texas. There, in 1986 she received a Doble-Paisano fellowship. This allowed her the freedom to produce *My Wicked, Wicked Ways,* a book of poetry published in 1987. The poems tell of her European travels, her childhood in Chicago, and the Catholic guilt she feels at being a sexual, uncompromising woman. It also declares freedom for the Hispanic woman. A woman who says, "I've learned two things/To let go/clean as a kite string/and to never wash a man's clothes./These are my rules." By this time, Cisneros had decided to make San Antonio her home. Despite her literary acclaim, she found it difficult to find work. She found herself pasting flyers on street posts and 24-hour stores, trying to drum up enough students for a private workshop. Defeated and depressed, Cisneros left San Antonio for a guest lectureship at California State University in Chico. "I thought I couldn't teach. I found myself becoming suicidal," she told *Publishers Weekly.* Soon after arriving in California, Cisneros was awarded a second NEA fellowship. She promptly moved back to San Antonio and began writing again.

Became First Hispanic-American to Sign with a Major Publisher

Cisneros broke new ground by becoming the first Chicana author to receive the backing of a major publishing house when Random House published *Woman Hollering Creek and Other Stories* in 1991. The collection of stories highlights the lives of Mexican-American women living in the San Antonio area. Again, her work drew critical and popular acclaim. Its publication also helped establish Cisneros financially. No more teaching or posting flyers, Cisneros could now make a living from writing alone.

In 1995 Cisneros achieved what many consider to be the height of artistic success when she was awarded the MacArthur Genius Fellowship. Its $225,000 purse allowed Cisneros to finally realize her childhood dream—a house of her own. She bought a large Victorian home in a historic district of San Antonio that she painted a bright neon purple. The local historic board promptly challenged her color choice saying it was not a historically accurate color. Not one to sit idly by while decisions are made for her, Cisneros clad in purple held news conferences on her lawn. She passed out petitions on purple paper. She declared the color a part of her Mexican heritage and accused the board of bias against Hispanic culture. "We are a people sin papeles ['without papers']!" she was quoted in *Texas Monthly.* "We don't exist. This isn't about my little purple house. It's about the entire Tejano community." In 1997 the board withdrew its objections and Cisneros's purple house stands. There she lives on her own terms, still "nobody's mother and nobody's wife," she makes her life with a small army of pets and a worldwide family of fans. In the last vignette of *The House on Mango Street,* Esperanza promises to go away in order "to come back. For the ones I left behind.

For the ones who cannot [get] Editors check this source., see if word in brackets should be included. out." Cisneros continues to fulfill Esperanza's promise. "I'm looking forward to the books I'll write when I'm 60," she told *Publishers Weekly*. "There's a lot of good writing in the mainstream press that has nothing to say. Chicano writers have a lot to say. The influence of our two languages is profound."

Selected Works

Books

Bad Boys, Mango Publications, 1980.
The House on Mango Street, Arte Publico, 1983.
Antojitos / appetizers, Art Publico Press, 1985.
The Rodrigo Poems, Third Woman Press, 1985.
My Wicked, Wicked Ways, Third Woman Press, 1987.
Woman Hollering Creek and Other Stories, Random House, 1991.
Hairs: Pelitos, Knopf, 1994.
Loose Woman, Knopf, 1994.

Articles

"Ghosts and Voices: Writing from Obsession," *The Americas Review,* Spring 1987.

"Notes to a Young(er) Writer," *The Americas Review,* Spring 1987.

Sources

Books

Authors and Artists for Young Adults, Volume 9, Detroit, Gale Research, 1992.

Periodicals

The Americas Review, Spring 1990, p 64-80.
Glamour, November 1990, p 256-257.
Los Angeles Times, May 7, 1991, p F1.
Publishers Weekly., March 29, 1991, pp. 74-5.
Texas Monthly, Oct 1997, p148-151.

On-line

http://twu.edu/www/twu/library/zumwalt.html
http://voices.cla.umn.edu/authors/ SandraCisneros.html
http://www.english.uiuc.edu/maps/poets/a_f/ cisneros/career.htm
http://www.lasmujeres.com/cisneros.htm

—Candace LaBalle

Bert Corona

1918-2001

Labor organizer

Bert Corona, a longtime leader in Latino civil-rights circles, died in early 2001 after nearly seventy years of public service. Following a career as a union organizer, Corona served for many years as executive director of La Hermandad Mexicana Nacional, a Latino organization in the Los Angeles area that fought on behalf of undocumented Mexicans and other Latinos in the United States. Corona was by all accounts a dedicated and tireless organizer, and often evoked comparisons to César Chávez, the migrant-labor leader. He once contributed an autobiographical essay to *Memories of Chicano History,* edited by Mario Garcia. According to *Progressive,* he stated in *Memories:* "I never planned my life," Corona reflected. "It just happened the way it did. I'm proud that I was able at certain times to help organize a plant or a community group and that these organizations helped people struggle to better their lives."

El Paso Childhood

Corona was born in El Paso, Texas in 1918. Both parents were of a progressive mind: his father Noe had, during the 1910 Mexican Revolution, fought on the side of the Partido Liberal Mexicano. During his military service he met a Chihuahua City woman, Margarita Escápite Salayandía, who ran the local teachers' college. After the Mexican conflict ended, the pair wed in Juárez and then again El Paso. Corona was the second of their children, but Noe Corona was slain in the early 1920s, and Corona and his sister were raised by their mother and maternal grandmother, who had been a physician in Chihuahua City. He attended public schools in El Paso, but during the 1920s children of Mexican heritage were forbidden to speak their language at school, and transgressions against this rule were punished harshly. Margarita Corona objected to such tactics as forcing children to wash their mouths out with soap, and for a time Corona was transferred to a boarding school in Albuquerque, New Mexico.

Corona was a standout basketball player at El Paso High School, and graduated at the age of sixteen. Ineligible to become a college athlete at that age, he played on El Paso community teams until 1936, when he accepted an athletic scholarship to the University of Southern California (USC). He was surprised at the differences between Los Angeles Latinos in 1936 and those back home in El Paso. In Texas Corona had been proud of his Mexican heritage; one day on a Los

Angeles streetcar asked two Mexican-American men for directions in Spanish. They ignored him, but followed him at his exit, and told him that in Los Angeles it was wiser to speak English.

During his time at USC, while studying commercial law, Corona also worked for a drug company. The position with Brunswick Pharmaceutical Company led to a job with the local Longshoremen's Union organizing farm workers in Orange County. The agribusiness in the Southern California region depended on Latino labor, and Corona helped the workers carry out successful strikes for wage increases and fair treatment. He was so enthused by this work that he dropped out of college altogether. He took his next job with the Congress of Industrial Organizations (CIO) as a union organizer, then did similar work on behalf of the United Cannery, Agriculture, Packing and Allied Workers of America. For a time in the 1940s he even served as president of Local 26 of the Longshoremen's Union.

Corona's labor activities drew him into political matters. In 1938 he worked with labor organizer Luisa Moreno to form one of the first nationwide groups of its kind, the League of Spanish-Speaking People. He also organized chapters on behalf of the Community Service Organization and worked with La Asociación Nacional Mexico-Americana (ANMA); through these activities he met César Chávez. By 1960 he had co-founded National Association of Mexican Americans, one of the first Latino political organizations in California, which organized "Viva Kennedy" groups to give Latino voter support to Democratic presidential hopeful John F. Kennedy.

Fought Crackdowns on Undocumented Latinos

But Latinos who were ineligible to vote eventually became Corona's main focus. For many years, the border between the United States and Mexico was a relatively open one; Mexicans were encouraged to cross and provide a temporary work force for the growing agriculture and textile industries in California and southwestern United States. Moreover, many Mexicans believed that the border itself was a moot point, since a large section of the American Southwest had originally belonged to Mexico. During World War II, the U.S. government sponsored a guest-worker program to combat labor shortages in the San Diego area, but later federal officials began actively trying to deport some of them; two San Diego union leaders, Phil and Albert Usquiano, founded La Hermandad Mexicana in 1951 to help fight this.

Corona became active in La Hermandad Mexicana, one of the few Latino organizations to help undocumented aliens. Even Chávez opposed their presence, for undocumented workers had sometimes been used against his own union, the United Farm Workers, as strikebreakers. In 1968 Corona opened a Los Angeles branch of La Hermandad Mexicana, and from there established an auxiliary organization, Centros de Acción Social Autónomo, or Centers for Autonomous (Independent) Social Actions (CASA), that gave undocumented Mexicans and other Latinos help with obtaining housing aid, medical care, and legal advice. Its community centers soon became focal points for neighborhood political action. Corona was adamant in his belief that undocumented immigrants should benefit from the same protections as citizens of the United States or permanent resident aliens. Once inside U.S. borders, Corona often stated, the laws applied to everybody.

CASA was eventually taken over by a more radical student element, and Corona's involvement with the organization ended. Yet by 1976 he had made La Hermandad Mexicana a national organization, with branch offices all over California as well as in Chicago and Washington, D.C. In 1978 he was active in the formation of the Coalition for Fair Immigration Laws and Practices. The Immigration and Naturalization Service (INS) was becoming increasingly hostile in its actions against undocumented aliens in California, and some lawmakers and citizens supported harsher laws and penalties. For many years, Corona and La Hermandad fought proposed legislation that would require employers to ask potential hires for proof of citizenship or residency. It was eventually unsuccessful, for the Immigration Act of 1986 was passed into law, but the Act also included an amnesty program for undocumented aliens who had entered the country before 1982.

Corona and La Hermandad dealt with the new Immigration Act on several fronts. He believed that the amnesty clause unfairly excluded thousands from protection, and tried to find ways to encourage these Latinos to pursue the citizenship process without fear of deportation. He also objected to one of the requirements in the citizenship application process, which forced applicants to prove that they were learning the English language. Hermandad, however, provided English-language classes as well as citizenship courses. It also received federal funds earmarked for such efforts, and buoyed by this, its membership increased dramatically. By 1992, when the federal funding came to an end, Corona's La Hermandad Mexicana Nacional had helped some 160,000 Latinos became citizens. Mario T. Garcia, a history professor at UC-Santa Barbara, told the *Los Angeles Times,* "He [Corona] did what no one else had successfully done—organize undocumented workers."

"Remained Optimistic"

Corona's organization suffered financially after the funding ceased, and took on increasing debt to stay active. Corona was still serving as its executive director when he traveled to Mexico to visit relatives in 2001. He fell ill there and underwent three operations in Leon; he was later transferred to a Los Angeles hospital, where he died on January 15, 2001. He was survived by his second wife, Angelina Casillas, and four children with his first wife, Blanche Taff.

In the *Memories of Chicano History* volume, Corona responded to a question about how history might remember him. "Frankly, I never concerned myself with a place in history," he wrote. "I've been busy organizing and working with others. If my life has meant anything, I would say that it shows that you can organize workers and poor people if you work hard, are persistent, remain optimistic, and reach out to involve as many people as possible."

Sources

Books

Encyclopedia of World Biography, second edition, Gale, 1998.
Profiles of American Labor Unions, second edition, Gale, 1998.

Periodicals

Los Angeles Times, January 17, 2001, p. B10; January 23, 2001, p. B1; March 19, 2001, p. B1.
Progressive, August 2001, p. 26.

—Carol Brennan

Celia Cruz

1924(?)—

Salsa vocalist

Although the Cuban-born music known as salsa, like other forms of Latin jazz and dance music, has been primarily male-dominated, its biggest vocal star is female. Celia Cruz has a powerful voice that transfers the rhythmic energy of salsa into the vocal medium, and she has been a prominent figure in the music since the beginnings of her career in Cuba in the 1950s. Leaving Cuba for the United States after the Castro takeover in 1959, Cruz has become a true legend of Latin American music and something of an emblem of Latin American identity.

The early facts of Cruz's life are somewhat obscure. Always reluctant to discuss her age, Cruz—according to some accounts—was born in Havana, Cuba, on October 21, 1924. Growing up in the city's poor Santo Suárez neighborhood in a household of 14 children (some were her cousins), she stood out because of her singing ability. Cruz won a singing contest called "La hora del té" and with her mother's encouragement began to enter other contests in various parts of Cuba.

Traveled on Streetcar to Contests

Sometimes Cruz would travel to the contests with a cousin named Nenita. "I was very skinny and tiny," she told *Billboard*. "And since the tram cost five cents each way and we didn't have enough money, I'd sit on Nenita's lap, because she was bigger. The drivers knew us and, sometimes, they'd let me sit on the seat beside her, if it was empty. One time, we had no money to return and we walked back. We arrived at 2 a.m."

Cruz's father, however, believed that she should become a teacher, an altogether more common profession for a Cuban woman at the time. She enrolled at the national teachers' college, but dropped out after finding more and more success with her music in live and radio performances. Something of a compromise was reached when she enrolled at Havana's National Conservatory of Music—but there a professor encouraged her to consider a full-time singing career.

Her breakthrough came in 1950 when she became the lead vocalist for a big band called La Sonora Matancera. Bandleader Rogelio Martínez showed faith in Cruz when he continued to feature her despite the protests of fans of the band's previous vocalist, and once again when an American record executive resisted the idea of making a Sonora Matancera disc that featured Cruz, believing the a rumba record with a

At a Glance . . .

Born on October 21, 1924; raised in the Santo Suarez neighborhood, Havana, Cuba; came to the United States in 1960, and became a citizen in 1961; married Pedro Knight, trumpeter, 1962. *Education:* Studied at National Conservatory of Music, Havana, Cuba, 1947-50.

Career: Began singing on Cuban radio in the late 1940s; became lead singer of Cuban big band, La Sonora Matancera, 1950, recording and touring with them until 1965; joined Tito Puente Orchestra,1966; recorded eight albums with Puente; sang the role of Gracia Divina at Carnegie Hall in *Hommy—A Latin Opera* (adaptation of Tommy), 1973; signed to Fania label and performed with Fania All-Stars group, 1970s; appeared in The Mambo Kings Play Songs of Love and *The Perez Family;* has recorded over 50 albums, 20 of which became gold; performed worldwide.

Awards: Grammy Award for Best Tropical Latin Album, 1989, awarded medal by President Bill Clinton from the National Endowment of the Arts, 1994.

Addresses: *Record Company*—Omar Pardillo-Cid, RMM Records, 568 Broadway, Suite 806, New York, NY 10012; *Agent*—Bookings Online Talent Agency, Ltd., 236 West 26th St., Ste. 701, New York, NY 10001.

female vocalist would not sell well. Martínez promised to pay Cruz himself if the recording flopped. It did well in both Cuba and the United States, and Cruz toured widely through Central and North America with La Sonora Matancera in the 1950s.

Group Fled Cuba

At the time of the Communist takeover of Cuba in 1959, the group was slated to tour Mexico; from Mexico, rather than returning to Cuba, they entered the United States and remained there. Cruz herself became a U.S. citizen in 1961. Cuban Communist leader Fidel Castro was furious and barred Cruz from returning to Cuba, enforcing the ban even after Cruz's parents' deaths. Cruz for her part has vowed not to return to Cuba until such time as the Castro regime is deposed. In 1962 she married La Sonora Matancera trumpet player Pedro Knight.

Although Cruz had made numerous recordings with La Sonora Matancera, she experienced little success in the United States in the 1960s. Although she spoke English well she refused to record in the language. Younger Hispanic Americans at the time were gravitating away from big-band dance music and toward rock-and-roll, in both Latin and non-Latin inflections. Cruz's fortunes began to improve when she meshed her talents with those of the musicians and bandleaders who were creating the new music called salsa—chief among them Tito Puente, Johnny Pacheco, and Willie Colón.

Salsa was firmly rooted in Cuban dance traditions, but it was a high-energy new hybrid that incorporated elements of jazz, traditional Afro-Caribbean rhythms, and other forms. It was an ideal medium for the showcasing of Cruz's vocals, for she was both an exciting improviser (she is known for her vocal imitations of instruments in the manner known as "scat" singing in the jazz world), and a singer with the power to stand up to an intense rhythm section. Cruz on stage was a commanding figure whose control over audiences resulted not only from her flamboyant, stage-filling attire, but also from her ability to engage them in call-and-response patterns that spring from salsa's Afro-Cuban roots.

Recorded for Fania Label

In 1973 Cruz appeared in *Hommy,* a Spanish-language adaptation of the Who's rock opera *Tommy.* Her reputation spread both within and beyond the Hispanic community in the 1970s after she signed with the new salsa label Fania and recorded with a cream-of-the-crop lineup, the Fania All-Stars, drawn from its stable of artists. The Fania All-Stars album *Live at Yankee Stadium* (two vols., 1976) documented the power of her performances. Cruz has appeared in several films, including *The Mambo Kings Play Songs of Love* (1992) and *The Perez Family* (1995).

One of Cruz's performance trademarks is a full-throated shout of "Azucar!" (Sugar!); she explained its 1970s origins in a 2000 *Billboard* interview. "I was having dinner at a restaurant in Miami, and when the waiter offered me coffee, he asked me if I took it with or without sugar. I said, 'Chico, you're Cuban. How can you even ask that? With sugar!' And that evening during my show ... I told the audience the story and they laughed. And one day, instead of telling the story, I simply walked down the stairs and shouted 'Azucar!'"

Cruz might be compared with U.S. jazz vocalist Sarah Vaughan in her ability to bring vocal techniques to a primarily instrumental music, but she has a more essentially popular appeal than any jazz singer. Seemingly indestructible vocally, Cruz continued a full schedule of concerts and recordings throughout the 1980s and beyond. She received a Grammy award for theal-bum *Ritmo en el corazón,* recorded with conga player Ray Barretto, in 1990, as well as an honorary doctorate from Yale University.

Still a major star in her own right, Cruz became an inspiration for numerous younger performers (such as Gloria Estefan) in the 1990s; her audience hardly aged along with her. "We've never had to attract these kids," she told *Time*. "They come by themselves. Rock is a strong influence on them, but they still want to know about their roots." For most Hispanic Americans, indeed, Celia Cruz has been and remains a much-loved figure, an icon of Latin culture.

Selected discography

The Winners, Vaya, 1987.
Best, Sony/Globo, 1992, originally issued on Fania Records.
Best, Vol. 2, Sony Discos/Globo, 1994 (more Fania-label music).
Canciones Premiadas, Palladium, 1994.
Irrepetible, UNI/RMM, 1994.
La Tierna Conmovedora Bambolea, Palladium, 1994.
Homenaje a Los Santos, Polydor, 1994.
Celia and Willie, 1994.Vaya.
Cuba's Queen of Rhythm, Palladium, 1995.
Canta Celia Cruz, Palladium, 1995.
Irresistible, Sony Discos/Orfeon, 1995.
Fania All-Stars, Sony Discos, 1997.
La reina de Cuba, International, 1997.
Azucar Negra, UNI/RMM, 1998.
Fiestón Tropical, Orfeon, 1998.
Mi vida es cantar, RMM, 1998.
Tributo a las Orishas, International, 1999.
Celia Cruz and Friends: A Night of Salsa Live, RMM, 2000.
Siempre vivire, Sony, 2000.
On Fire: The Essential Celia Cruz, Manteca, 2000.
La negra tiene tumbao, Sony, 2001.
Recuerdos de Cuba, Orfeon, 2002.
Carnaval de Éxitos, RMM, 2002.
Su Favorita Celia Cruz, Secco.

Reflexiónes De Celia Cruz, Secco.
Bravo Celia Cruz, Tico.
With Tito Puente Cuba y Puerto Rico Son, Tico.
El Quimbo Quimbumbia, Tico.
Alma Con Alma, Tico.
Algo Especial Para Recordar, Tico.
100% Azucar: The Best of Celia, Rhino, 1997.
Cuba's Foremost Rhythm Singer, Secco.
Con Amor: Celia Cruz with La Sonora Matancera, Secco.
La Incomparable Celia and Sonora Matancera, Secco.
Feliz Encuentro, Barbaro.
Nostalgia Tropical, Orfeon.
Celia and Johnny,Vaya.

Sources

Books

Boggs, Vernon W., *Salsiology : Afro-Cuban Music and the Evolution of Salsa in New York City*, Excelsior Music Pub. Co., 1992.
Bossy, Michel-Andre, et al., eds., *Lives & Legacies: Artists, Writers, and Musicians*, Oryx, 2001.
Broughton, Simon, Mark Ellingham, David Muddyman, and Richard Trillo, eds., *World Music: The Rough Guide*, Penguin, 1999.
Contemporary Musicians, volume 22, Gale, 1998.

Periodicals

Billboard, May 21, 1994, p. LM-6; October 28, 2000, p. 50.
Time, July 11, 1988, p. 50.

On-line

http://music.lycos.com
All Music Guide, http://www.allmusic.com

—James M. Manheim

Salvador Dalí

1904—1989

Artist

Surrealism was a European artistic movement that extended into film, fiction, poetry, and other arts in addition to its primary medium of painting. Nevertheless, in the public mind surrealism is identified above all with one towering figure: the Spanish painter Salvador Dalí. With a series of dreamlike works executed in the late 1920s and 1930s (including the landscape filled with drooping watches that has become the surrealist image *par excellence*), Dalí mesmerized not only art enthusiasts but also the general public on both sides of the Atlantic. Even as modern art moved toward increasingly abstract and arcane languages, Dalíremained a public figure for much of his long life.

Born the son of a notary in the Catalan-region town of Figueras (now known by its Catalonian spelling of Figueres) on May 11, 1904, Dalí attended religious schools. From the beginning he had a strong imagination that tended toward the bizarre, and, if his sometimes-suspect autobiographical writings are to be believed, an occasional masochistic streak. As a child, Dalí would sometimes throw himself down a flight of stairs to get his parents' attention. His artistic gifts manifested themselves from the start, and he com-pleted some substantial religious paintings before reaching his tenth birthday.

Dressed in Cape as Student

Admitted to the School of Fine Arts in Madrid in 1921, Dalí stood out from the crowd with outfits that included a cape and an oversized black felt hat. Yet, according to *Time,* his fellow students remembered him as "morbidly sick with timidity." In the 1920s Dalí experimented with many of the strains of European contemporary art of the day. He was expelled from the School of Fine Arts after refusing to take an exam. "I am sorry," he recalled saying (as quoted in *Contemporary Authors*), "but I am infinitely more intelligent than these … professors." In 1928 Dalí made his way to Paris, the center of European modernism at the time, and rapidly developed his wildly distinctive style after he allied himself with the surrealist movement.

Surrealism emphasized not only distortions of reality but also the power of unconscious, specifically sexual drives; the movement drew to some extent on the thinking of the Austrian founder of psychoanalysis, Sigmund Freud. Dalí rapidly became the movement's star attraction, producing canvases that seemed to

At a Glance . . .

Born Salvador Felipe Jacinto Dalí y Domenech in Figueras, Spain, May 11, 1904; died January 23, 1989, in Figueras; married Gala Eluard, 1930. *Education:* Attended Marist Friars School, Figueras, 1914-18; attended San Fernando Academy of Fine Arts, Madrid, Spain, 1921-25. *Religion:* Roman Catholic.

Career: Worked as a book and magazine illustrator, Figueras, 1919-21; painted in Spain, first individual exhibition, Galería Dalmau, Barcelona, Spain, 1925; late 1920s; with Luis Buñuel made international impact with surrealist film *An Andalusian Dog,* 1929; moved to Paris, France, and became connected with surrealist movement, 1930; first U.S. exhibition, Julien Levy Gallery, New York, 1932; lived in Pebble Beach, CA, and New York City during World War II; returned to Spain, 1948; cultivated overtly religious style, late 1940s and 1950s; established Dalí Museum, Figueras, 1973; author of more than 15 books and pamphlets.

mirror the most bizarre depths of his subconscious mind and yet rendering them with a technique that was exquisitely controlled and exact. With friend and fellow surrealist Luis Buñuel, Dalí made a major impact in 1929 with the film *An Andalusian Dog,* a short subject that featured such disturbing images as an eyeball being sliced open with a razor blade. By 1931, Dalí was creating works that have become icons of surrealism; the most famous of them all, the watch-filled landscape entitled *The Persistence of Memory,* was painted that year.

Many art critics consider Dalí's works of the 1930s his best. During that period he merged his surrealist sensibilities with a serious outlook that produced such masterpieces as *Soft Construction with Boiled Beans—Premonition of the Spanish Civil War* (1936); that work, centered on the image of a powerful god tearing itself to pieces, has been compared with Pablo Picasso's Spanish Civil War masterpiece, *Guérnica.* When war did break out, Dalí showed some sympathy with the fascist leadership of dictator Francisco Franco.

Covered Rolls-Royce with Cauliflower

In the meantime, however, the artist was becoming a star. He visited the United States several times and proved a master of publicity, honored by, among other things, a surrealist-themed dance in which a cow carcass stuffed with a horn-type record player was mounted on the wall at one end of the room. He designed department-store windows in New York and even lent his name to a perfume line. Returning to Europe for a time, Dalí intensified his flamboyant ways, driving through Paris in a cauliflower-covered Rolls-Royce and appearing for a lecture in England dressed in a diving suit and leading two Russian wolfhounds on a leash. "The only difference between a madman and myself is that I am not mad," the artist said once in a widely quoted remark.

Dalí spent much of World War II in the United States, living well off the proceeds of his autobiography, *The Secret Life of Salvador Dalí.* The work attracted attention with its portraits of high-society figures, its work with fashion designers including Coco Chanel, and of Dalí's design of the dream sequence in Alfred Hitchcock's film *Spellbound.* With public acclaim, though, came increasing disdain in the art world. Part of that disdain came from Dalí's public success; fellow surrealist André Breton rechristened him with an anagram of his own name, "Avida Dollars."

But Dalí's style itself was growing more and more distant from the abstract modernist art mainstream and changing on its own terms. The artist rededicated himself to Catholicism in the late 1930s, and after the war began to produce canvases that, while they did not renounce surrealist elements, had a grandiose quality that, in the eyes of some observers, tried unsuccessfully to mimic the monumentality of the works of Spain's Old Masters. Dalí moved back to Spain with his wife Gala in 1955. He admitted (as quoted by *Maclean's*) to a "pure, vertical, mystical, gothic love of cash," and turned out huge quantities of prints of his works. Sometimes he simply signed his name to blank sheets onto which copies would be printed later.

Market Plagued by Inauthentic Prints

But the general public never lost its affection for Dalí's works. There was always a market for whatever he produced. Indeed, Dalí collectors in later years have been bedeviled by the large number of fake Dalí prints circulating through the art market—a result, certainly, of Dalí's own lax supervision of the printmaking process, but also of the sheer demand for his work. In later years Dalí painted less, troubled by the symptoms of Parkinson's disease and other ailments. Yet he remained a public figure, attending the construction of a museum devoted to his own works in his hometown of Figueras, and in the 1980s lending his support to a campaign to bring the summer Olympic Games to the Spanish city of Barcelona in 1992.

Dalí died of heart failure on January 23, 1989, and was buried on the grounds of his own museum. As the rigid canons of abstraction have weakened and modern art has become more welcoming to realist and even surrealist elements, there have been signs of an upward trend in Dalí's posthumous reputation. Though the disclosure of the number of ersatz Dalí works and the world recession of the early 1990s hurt prices of Dalí items for a time, the value of his artwork rebounded after several museums held major retrospectives in the 1990s. The city of St. Petersburg, Florida, continued to acquire works for the lavish new Dalí museum it had opened in 1982. For the average art lover, though, there had never been any question of fluctuations in critical opinion: Dalí *was* surrealism.

Sources

Books

Contemporary Artists, St. James, 1996.
International Dictionary of Art and Artists, St. James, 1990.

Periodicals

The Economist (US), December 17, 1988, p. 99; January 28, 1989, p. 88.
Forbes, August 29, 1994, p. 104.
Maclean's, February 6, 1989, p. 58.
The New Republic, October 17, 1994, p. 40.
Time, March 13, 2000, p. 79.

—James M. Manheim

Oscar De La Hoya

1973—

Boxer

Oscar De La Hoya became the "Golden Boy" of boxing with his surprising win of a gold medal in the 1992 Olympic Games. Since then he has captured five boxing titles in five different weight classes, ranking him among boxing's elite. He has often been referred to as the best contemporary American boxer.

Oscar De La Hoya was born on February 4, 1973 in East Los Angeles, California. His parents had immigrated to the United States from Mexico. De La Hoya's family was poor when he was growing up. His father, Joel,Sr., worked as a warehouse clerk for a heating and cooling company and his mother, Cecilia, was a seamstress. De La Hoya had two siblings—an older brother named Joel Jr. and a younger sister, Ceci.

Boxing was a tradition in the De La Hoya family. De La Hoya's paternal grandfather, Vincente, was an amateur featherweight in Durango, Mexico, and his father had a brief professional boxing career in the United States with a 9-3-1 lightweight record. As De La Hoya told *Interview* magazine, "Boxing has been in my blood since I can remember. It comes naturally to me, and I've enjoyed it ever since I started, at the age of six." As a child De La Hoya would join his father and older

brother at the Pico Rivera Sports Arena. The family had assumed that Joel, as the oldest son, would continue the family's boxing tradition. De La Hoya himself admitted that he was an unlikely candidate to become a boxer. "I was a little kid who used to fight a lot in the street—and get beat up," he told *Sports Illustrated.*

Started Boxing at an Early Age

De La Hoya's father put him in the ring for the first time when he was six years old and he won his first match against a neighborhood kid. By the time he was 11 years old he was winning competitions. Soon De La Hoya began to train at the Resurrection Boy's Club Gym with Al Stankie, who had trained another East Los Angeles boxer, Paul Gonzales, to an Olympic Gold medal. De La Hoya's career quickly began to soar. At the age of 15 he won the National Junior Boxing Championship at a weight of 119 pounds and a year later he won the National Golden Gloves title at a weight of 125 pounds.

In 1990 when De La Hoya was only 17 years old, he won the U.S. National Championship in the 125-pound division and he won a gold medal at the

At a Glance . . .

Born Oscar De La Hoya on February 4, 1973, in East Los Angeles, CA; married Millie Corretjer; two children.

Career: Amateur boxer, 1984-92; professional boxer, 1992–; singer, 2000–; businessman, 2001–.

Awards: U.S. National Junior Champion, 1988; 125-pound champion, Golden Gloves competition, 1989; gold medalist, U.S. Olympic Cup, 1990; gold medalist, Goodwill Games, 1990; gold medalist, U.S. National Championships, 1990; gold medalist, USA vs. Olympic Festival, 1991; gold medalist, USA vs. Boxing National Champions, 1991; gold medalist, USA vs. Bulgaria, 1992; gold medalist, USA vs. Hungary, 1992; gold medalist, World Challenge, 1992; gold medalist, Olympic Games, 1992; Junior Lightweight Title and later Lightweight Title, World Boxing Organization, 1994; Lightweight Title, International Boxing Federation, 1995; Super Lightweight Title, World Boxing Council, 1996; Welterweight Title, World Boxing Council, 1997; Junior Middleweight Title, World Boxing Council, 2001; Grammy nomination for *Oscar De La Hoya*, 2001.

Addresses: Golden Boy Promotions, 2102 Business Center Drive, Suite 121, Irvine, CA 92612.

Goodwill Games. He was the youngest U.S. boxer to compete in that event. It was after the Goodwill Games that De La Hoya learned that his mother was dying of cancer. She had wanted to keep her illness a secret until after the Goodwill Games so that her son could focus on his competition. In October 1990 Cecilia died of breast cancer at the age of 38. She had always hoped that her son would win a gold medal at the Olympics and her untimely death gave De La Hoya a concrete goal for the next two years.

Won Olympic Gold

De La Hoya continued his success as an amateur boxer. In 1991 he won the U.S. Amateur Boxing National Championship in the 132-pound division and he was named Boxer of the Year by USA Boxing. During this time De La Hoya changed trainers because of Stankie's problems with alcohol. His next trainer was Robert Alcazar, an ex-boxer who had worked with Joel De La Hoya, Sr.

While he easily made the U.S. Olympic team, De La Hoya was not expected to make it past the first round of Olympic competition. His first opponent was Cuba's Julio Gonzalez, a 27-year-old four-time World Amateur Junior Lightweight champion. De La Hoya won the match in a 7-2 decision, which was considered the biggest boxing upset of the Olympics. His second round match against Korean champion Hong Sung Sik was close, with De La Hoya winning by only one point. De La Hoya also beat Adilson Silva, Dimitrov Tontchev, and finally defeated Marco Rudolph of Germany for the gold medal. De La Hoya was the sentimental favorite of the Games since the media had promoted his story about a son trying to fulfill his dying mother's wish. However, his victory took everyone by surprise. De La Hoya celebrated by carrying the American and Mexican flags around the ring. He told *Los Angeles Magazine*, "The American flag was for my country; the Mexican flag for my heritage." After this accomplishment De La Hoya was nicknamed the "Golden Boy" by the media and that name has stayed with him throughout his career.

Became Knock-Out King

The Olympics was the last event of De La Hoya's amateur career and he ended with an amateur record of 223 wins and 5 losses, with an impressive 153 knock-outs. After the Olympics De La Hoya decided to turn professional. As he told *Sports Illustrated*, "I won the gold for my mom. Now the championship will be for me." On September 4, 1992 De La Hoya signed the richest deal in boxing history for over $1 million with New York agents Robert Mittleman and Steve Nelson. The deal included money for a house for his family in Montebello, quite a step up from the barrio in which he grew up.

De La Hoya's first professional fight was on November 23, 1992 against Lamar Williams. He knocked Williams out in the first round. His next opponent, Cliff Hicks, suffered the same fate in December 1992. In 1993 De La Hoya won nine more fights, mostly with knock-outs. While young boxing professionals often fight less talented opponents in order to improve their record, De La Hoya fought some tough competitors early in his career, including Mexican champion Narciso Valenzuela. Despite his professional and popular success, De La Hoya broke his contract with Mittleman and Nelson in December 1993 after only one year because he wanted more control over his career. Instead he chose to be advised by his father, his cousin Gerardo Salas, and Los Angeles advertising consultant Raynaldo Garza. At the same time De La Hoya signed a three-year deal with promoter Bob Arum, one of the biggest promoters in boxing.

In 1994 and 1995 De La Hoya continued his winning streak. On May 6, 1995 he captured the InternationalBoxing Federation lightweight title against Rafael Ruelas. However, an earlier fight against John John Molina made De La Hoya question his strategy. Even though he won the bout, De La Hoya was disarmed by Molina's style and he felt he needed a more experienced trainer to better prepare him for his matches. In February 1995 De La Hoya replaced family friend Robert Alcazar as his trainer with Jesus "The Professor" Rivero. Rivero's philosophy was to develop the boxer as a whole person, both in and out of the ring. He encouraged De La Hoya to develop his mind by reading literature and listening to classical music.

Capitalized on Golden Boy Image

De La Hoya built his career not only on his professional accomplishments, but also on his popularity with the media. His good looks, rags-to-riches life story, and charming personality made him one of the public's best known and most liked boxers. He was confident, ambitious, and successful. "I want to make history," he told *Sport* magazine, "I want to win seven world championships in seven different weight classes from 130 pounds to 168 pounds." He told *Sports Illustrated for Kids* that his secret for success was the "D formula." "My three D's are dedication, discipline, and desire." De La Hoya capitalized on the "Golden Boy" image in the ring through lucrative deals with HBO to televise his fights. He also cashed in on his success outside of the ring as a spokesperson for Champion athletic shoes, B.U.M. equipment clothing, Levi, John Henry Menswear, and McDonald's, among others.

However, De La Hoya's success has not made him popular with some members of the Hispanic community. In fact, one of his biggest professional successes actually decreased his popularity. In 1996 De La Hoya beat the famous Mexican boxer Julio Cesar Chavez, his boyhood boxing idol, in a bloody battle for the World Boxing Council super lightweight title. Some Hispanics were disenchanted by the Golden Boy's pummeling of a hero. In addition, De La Hoya has been labeled a "sellout" because of his financial success. He moved out of the barrio to a wealthy neighborhood and he spends his free time at country clubs or on the golf course. This has led some to accuse him of abandoning his Mexican-American roots. In 1996 an article in *Esquire* magazine described " the contradictions that define Oscar De La Hoya. He's the pretty boy of an ugly business; a child star spinning in a constellation of has-beens; Mexican by blood, American in his inclinations; barrio by birth, country club by preference." In addition, De La Hoya's personal life generated some negative press. He was engaged a few times, he fathered two children out of wedlock, and he faced a palimony suit by ex-fiancée and former Miss USA Shanna Moakler.

Experienced First Losses in the Ring

Despite controversy outside of the ring, De La Hoya continued to win matches throughout 1997 and 1998. He also added another title to his collection, beating Pernell Whitaker for the World Boxing Council welterweight title on April 12, 1997. However, the Golden Boy's run came to an end in 1999. In a much anticipated match De La Hoya lost the WBC welterweight title to Felix Trinidad on September 18, 1999. Rather than the usual bloodbath, De La Hoya danced around Trinidad in a way that did not impress the judges. "I've proved that I can stand in with anybody, but this time I wanted to put on a boxing show," he told *Sports Illustrated,* "I think I have the boxing lesson of my life." In reality De La Hoya gave up his title. *Sports Illustrated* went on to write, "It was not a fight that Trinidad won; it was a fight that De La Hoya perversely handed over."

De La Hoya recovered from his loss by beating Derrell Coley with a knockout in February of 2000. However, in June of the same year he suffered another loss at the hands of welterweight Shane Mosley. Disappointed by two major losses in less than a year, De La Hoya decided to take a break from boxing to pursue his other passion—singing.

Pursued Other Interests

De La Hoya's musical interests came from his mother who was a ranchera song stylist in Mexico. On October 10, 2000 De La Hoya released his self-titled debut album with EMI Latin. The bilingual collection of love ballads featured the single "Ven a Mi" ("Run to Me"), written by the Bee Gees. "In a way, this album is like me giving something back to my Mexican and Latin roots," De La Hoya told *Billboard* magazine. "But it also had to represent all of America—and not just because I was born here." The album was nominated for a Grammy.

In 2001, at the age of 28, De La Hoya returned to the ring in search of redemption. He won a match against Arturo Gatti and he won the World Boxing Council junior middleweight title from Javier Castillejo. With his victory against Castillejo, De La Hoya became the youngest boxer to win world titles in five weight classes and he joined the ranks of Sugar Ray Leonard and Thomas Hearns for this distinction. In May of 2002 De La Hoya was scheduled to fight Fernando Vargas for the super welterweight title.

De La Hoya's future in boxing is uncertain. Earlier in his career he stated that he could not imagine boxing past the age of 30. However, he would still like to avenge his losses to Trinidad and Mosley. His priorities may also have changed due to his personal life. In October of 2001 De La Hoya married Puerto Rican pop singer Millie Corretjer and moved to Puerto Rico. He also has several other interests outside of the ring. In 2001 De La Hoya established his own boxing promotional company called Golden Boy Promotions. He also founded the Oscar De La Hoya Foundation to sponsor Olympic hopefuls and he is renovating the Resurrection Gym where he trained as a child into the new Oscar De La Hoya Youth Boxing Center. He has also considered going to school to pursue architecture. As he told *Interview* magazine, "I really have a passion for designing." Whatever De La Hoya decides to undertake, if he does it with the passion he's used to box, he'll certainly be successful and exciting to watch.

Selected discography

Oscar De La Hoya (includes "Ven a Mi"), EMI Latin, 2000.

Sources

Periodicals

Billboard, January 8, 2000, p. 41; September 23, 2000, p. 21.
Chicago Tribune, June 24, 2001.
Daily News (New York), February 7, 2002.
Daily News Record, December 18, 1995, p. 3.
Entertainment Weekly, October 3, 2000, p. 80.
Esquire, November, 1996, p. 78.
Forbes, March 22, 1999, p. 220; March 20, 2000, p 240.
Houston Chronicle, December 21, 2001.
Interview, June, 1997, p. 84.
Jet, July 3, 2000, p. 51.
Los Angeles Magazine, March, 1994, p. 74.
Los Angeles Times, November 21, 2001; November 30, 2001; December 2, 2001; February 10, 2002.
Newsweek, September 4, 2000, p. 61; October 23, 2000, p. 78.
New York Times, February 8, 2002, p. D6.
People Weekly, January 20, 1997, p. 93; April 3, 2000, p. 168.
PR Newswire, January 28, 1999; September 2, 1999; July 10, 2000; July 12, 2000; September 12, 2000; September 15, 2000; December 21, 2000; October 8, 2001.
PR Week, January 28, 2002.
Scholastic Choices, January, 2001, p. 4.
Sport, February, 1999, p. 51.
Sports Illustrated, October 21, 1991, p. 66; December 7, 1992, p. 78; December 20, 1993, p. 13; September 22, 1997, p. 42; February 22, 1999, p. 54; March 1, 1999, p. 78; May 31, 1999, p. R27; September 27, 1999, p. 56; March 6, 2000, p. 74; March 13, 2000, p. 52; June 19, 2000, p. 80; June 26, 2000, p. 54; April 2, 2001, p. R2; July 2, 2001, p. R2.
Sports Illustrated for Kids, January, 1997, p. 32.
USA Today, February 14, 2002, p. 4C.

On-line

www.oscardelahoya.com
Latino Sports Legends, www.latinosportslegends.com/Delahoya_Oscar_htm
About.com, boxing.about.com/library/bl_delahoya.htm

—Janet P. Stamatel

Fernando de la Rúa

1937—

Politician, lawyer

The former president of Argentina, Fernando de la Rúa attempted to restore solvency to a nation deep in debt and out of patience with governmental corruption, rampant inflation, and unemployment. Elected late in 1999 by South America's second largest nation, de la Rúa, Argentina's 47th president, applied the negotiation skills he perfected as an attorney, senator, and mayor of Buenos Aires. For a few tranquil months, he appeared to outclass his predecessor, Carlos Menem, in integrity and direction. The return of scandal and disruption to the cabinet and Senate forced de la Rúa to resign.

Joined Union Civica Radical

A native of Cordoba, de la Rúa was born on September 15, 1937, and studied law at the University of Cordoba. After joining the Union Civica Radical (UCR), Argentina's most traditional party at age 26, he took an advisory post in the Ministry of the Interior as one of the youngest members of Dr. Artier Illia's radical government. Later in 1973 he campaigned unsuccessfully for vice president as the running mate of Ricardo Balbín. In 1983 de la Rúa won election to the Senate

from the city of Buenos Aires during the presidency of Juan Perón and survived an era of political chaos that threatened civil war.

De la Rúa came of age politically during the downfall of the Peróns. When Juan Perón died, his wife Isabel —then vice president—supplanted him and became president. She managed to suppress uprisings with a hard-handed right-wing backlash. On March 24, 1976, when a military coup ended her presidency, death squads began engineering the disappearance of thousands of citizens. In the upheaval, de la Rúa lost his senate post. He took his family to safety outside Argentina and, for seven years, taught at universities in Mexico, the United States, and Venezuela.

De la Rúa returned from self-imposed exile in 1983. Late in the decade, at a time when Argentina agonized under a military junta and weathered defeat by Britain in the Falkland Islands war, the mild-mannered attorney campaigned for the presidency. He lost to flamboyant Carlos Saul Menem, a Perónist Party strongman who took office in 1989. De la Rúa was elected to the senate, where he served for six years. In 1996 he was elected mayor of Buenos Aires, one of the largest

At a Glance . . .

Born Fernando de la Rúa on September 15, 1937, in Cordoba, Argentina; married Inés Pertiné; three children. *Education:* law degree from the University of Cordoba. *Politics:* Union Civica Radical Party.

Career: Ministry of Interior, Argentina, adviser, 1963-66; senator, 1973-76; university professor, 1976-83; senator, 1983-89; mayor, Buenos Aires, Argentina, 1996-99; president of Argentina, 1999-01.

urban centers in the Southern Hemisphere. In three years of office, he distinguished himself by expanding the subway, improving street lighting and garbage collection through privatization, and netting a budget surplus.

Ran for President

Boosting de la Rúa's conservative image were blatant profiteering in Menem's cabinet and mounting crime and unemployment while the president partied, entertained the smart set, and kept on the move in his Ferrari and presidential jet. In 1999 de la Rúa defeated Graciela Fernández Meijide in a run-off for candidacy representing the Alianza, a center-left coalition of the UCR and the National Solidarity Front (FREPASO). He toppled Menem, largely on issues that the former president himself raised by arrogant public behavior and a disdain for populist issues. Vying against Eduardo Duhalde, the Justicialist Party contender, de la Rúa surveyed a muddled political scene. He touted his reputation for sobriety and fiscal responsibility and promised to cut discretionary spending, create new jobs, and halt the corruption for which Menem was notorious.

Applying contrast as his campaign strategy, de la Rúa admitted to being an unflashy gardener and chess and golf player. An expert on Argentine law and the author of five texts on legal issues, he pictured himself on TV ads as a boring nine-to-five politician intent on ushering out Menem's good-timing associates. With a plurality of 48.5 percent to Duhalde's 38.1 percent, on October 24, 1999, de la Rúa won the election, ending a decade of the decadent Menemists. Thousands of well-wishers stood outside his Buenos Aires hotel suite and cheered. On December 10, de la Rúa moved his wife, Inés Pertiné, and their three children into Casa Rosada, the presidential residence known as the "pink palace."

At his first-floor office overlooking the Plaza de Mayo, de la Rúa countenanced the imprisonment of the former military dictator's henchmen for kidnapping and selling infants born to political prisoners. He began making immediate improvements in pocketbook issues by lowering fuel costs, highway tolls, and railroad freight prices and by maneuvering through congress more flexibility in labor practices. He faced off against powerful trade unions and curtailed partying and frivolity in high office by selling the presidential jet. By flying on commercial airlines, he set an example for his staff. Most important for the nation's future, he pledged to raise the credit rating as an enticement to foreign investors.

Although analysts of Latin American politics were dubious of de la Rúa's ability to actualize so stringent an austerity plan, he won converts with persuasive dialogue. He methodically replaced dysfunctional department heads and mismanagers and appointed a competent, low-key cabinet, including Foreign Minister Adalberto Rodriguez and Economy Minister Jose Luis Machinea. Lacking a majority, de la Rúa faced an unending realignment of consensus against a pro-Menem senate, supreme court, and General Confederation of Labor, all stacked against the left. On de la Rúa's side stood a workable minority in the Chamber of Deputies and a majority of state governors. Within two months, he was battling tax evaders, dealers in contraband, money launderers, drug lords, and graft takers and making inroads against religious intolerance.

Cracks appeared in the façade with public disclosure of a higher deficit than Menem's economic ministry admitted to. In June of 2000 he blamed Spain's Iberia Airlines for sending into receivership Aerolineas Argentinas, Argentina's carrier. Privatized during the Menem regime in 1991, the company slid rapidly into bankruptcy. De la Rúa also surprised Western Hemisphere watchers by shifting toward a closer alliance with Brazil and Mexico, more dependence on Europe, and less reliance on the United States. He rescinded the policy of supporting the United Nations' peacekeeping forces by refusing to call up Argentina soldiers to combat international crises. Later in 2000 he made a state visit to China's President Jiang Zemin, who reciprocated in April of 2001 to discuss economic, trade, scientific, and technological issues.

Despite de la Rúa's efforts, the economy remained a stubborn obstacle to Argentine progress. On May 31, 2000, 20,000 took to the streets to protest spending cuts. In November of 2000 the International Monetary Fund (IMF) proposed measures to ease edgy financial markets and to halt the ripples of monetary crisis threatening to engulf South America. In a televised speech, to placate fearful international investors, de la Rúa put up a brave front of economic control. The IMF pledged billions to shore up Argentina's failing finances. De la Rúa called in provincial governors and political advisors to study ways to privatize the nation's social security system, reduce the number of civil servants, restructure public health, and rein in tax cheats, who owed a total of $25 billion to public coffers.

De la Rúa's downfall paralleled that of Raul Alfonsin, who had fled the presidency in the wake of looting and mob violence in 1989. On December 13, 2001, a one-day general strike demonstrated a pervasive disgruntlement bordering on national outrage. With the economy shrinking annually at the rate of 11 percent and unemployment approaching 20 percent, critics had had enough of the new president. To circumvent a run on banks, the government limited depositors' withdrawal of cash, generating a shortfall in retail sales. To earn the sympathies of the IMF, De la Rúa and economy minister Domingo Cavallo tried to impose wage cuts and a spartan budget. Without loans to bulk up the treasury against defaulting on $143 billion in foreign debt, the Argentine economy approached collapse. Facing the Perónists, de la Rúa risked his backers' disapproval by conferring with former president Menem while juggling various plans of lowering university staff salaries, confiscating private pensions, delaying state pension checks, dollarizing currency, and restructuring foreign debt.

Abandoned Office

De la Rúa's last days in office were a desperate avoidance of the inevitable. He replaced departing finance secretary Daniel Marx with Miguel Kiguel, but could not deny the seriousness of the October 6th resignation of Vice President Carlos "Chacho" Alvarez, who declared his boss incapable or unwilling to punish senators caught in a bribery scandal. Promotion of scandal-soiled Labor Minister Alberto Flamarique to chief of staff increased rumors of mismanagement and coverup and fears that de la Rúa's rickety coalition would crumble. Flamarique lasted only a day before quitting. President of the Senate Jose Genoud followed within the week, leaving Chief of Intelligence Fernando Santibanez clinging to his post.

A bizarre turn of events ended de la Rúa's chances of restoring public confidence. In mid-December, Ernesto Belli, member of Daughters and Sons for Identity and Justice against Forgetting and Silence (HIJOS), grabbed President de la Rúa on camera during the popular TV show Video Match to dramatize the hopelessness of La Tablada prisoners who dwindled from a fourteen-week hunger strike. As a result de la Rúa reduced life sentences for 71 inmates. The president's public humiliation worsened as a two-week state of siege gripped the nation. Pensioners saw their savings and retirement funds rifled, their real estate devalued.

De la Rúa's approval ratings plummeted 40 points to 30 percent.

Amid mounting chaos that caused hundreds of injuries and 30 deaths, the de la Rúa presidency had little hope of survival. On December 20th, Economy Minister Domingo Cavallo led the rest of the cabinet in tendering letters of resignation. Hours later, de la Rúa abandoned his office. The admitted failures left some 18.3 percent of Argentines unemployed, homelessness mounting, state companies up for sale, and a treasury facing $132 billion in foreign debt. Replacing de la Rúa was Adolfo Rodriguez Saa, the interim president until Argentines went to the polls in March of 2002.

Sources

Books

The Complete Marquis Who's Who, Marquis Who's Who, 2001.

Periodicals

Airline Industry Information, June 22, 2000.
Business Week, November 8, 1999; October 30, 2000.
Economist (US), December 22, 2001.
Forbes, February 18, 2002.
Maclean's, December 31, 2001.
NACLA Report on the Americas, January 2000; January 2001.
U. S. News & World Report, February 28, 2000.
Washington Post, October 27, 1999; October 11, 2000; November 11, 2000; December 22, 2001; January 6, 2002.
World Press Review, January 2000.

On-line

Biography Resource Center Online, Gale Group, 2000.
http://www.lasalle-academy.org/ worldleaders/ site.htm
http://www.presidencia.gov.ar/
http://www.chinaembassy-india.org/eng/9665.html
http://www.socialistinternational.org/9SocAffairs/4-V47/eProfile.html
http://www.guardian.co.uk/argentina/story/ 0,11439,623073,00.html

—Mary Ellen Snodgrass

Cameron Diaz

1972—

Model, actress

"She has an energy, an electricity in her face—a sparkle that is unmistakable," photographer Jeff Dunas is quoted as having said in *People Weekly* about model-turned-actress Cameron Diaz. Diaz is an interesting combination of naiveté and geek—she actually won a belching trophy from Nickelodeon Kids' Choice Awards—mixed with sophistication and beauty. In 1995 she was chosen as one of *Empire* magazine's 100 Sexiest Stars in film history, and in 1998 she was chosen as one of *People* magazine's 50 most beautiful people in the world.

Diaz was born August 30, 1972 in Long Beach, California to a Cuban-American father Emilio, and an Anglo-German mother. She graduated from Long Beach Polytechnic High School in 1990. She did not originally intend to model or act, but instead intended to study zoology. She met an agent at a party and soon she started down the road to stardom. An adventurous and independent woman, Diaz left home at 16 to live and model around the world in such places as Japan, Australia, Mexico, Morocco, and Paris. She was a responsible young woman, but the allurements open to young women away from home were very strong, and

while she was in Australia she almost died from alcohol poisoning.

For about a year after that Diaz went through a rocky time full of rejections and hard work and she finally returned to California when she was 21. While on a shoot for L.A. Gear she met video producer Carlos de la Torre. The two moved in together and their relationship lasted for five years. While in Los Angeles Diaz continued working as a model until she was offered the role of Tina Carlyle in 1994's *The Mask*. She auditioned for a small, three-line role, and was stunned to be offered the female lead opposite Jim Carrey. In 1994 Diaz was also seen in a commercial for Salon Selectives.

After *The Mask*, the world of acting opened for Diaz. She was next seen in such movies as *The Last Supper*, (1995,) *She's the One*, (1996,) *Feeling Minnesota*, (1996,) *Head Above Water*, (1996,) and *Keys to Tulsa*, (1997,) none of which attracted much attention. It was in 1997's *My Best Friend's Wedding*, that Diaz came more prominently into the public eye. Diaz was lauded by critics for her sweet, impetuous performance. *Entertainment Weekly* wrote, "[Diaz's] hilariously humiliating karaoke scene revealed: (1) her voice

At a Glance . . .

Born August 30, 1972 in Long Island, California; daughter of Emilio and Billie Diaz. *Education:* Attended Long Beach Polytechnic High School; studied acting with John Kirby.

Career: Model, 1988-94. Actress, 1994-.

Awards: Blockbuster Entertainment Award, Favorite Supporting Actress-Comedy for *My Best Friend's Wedding,* 1998; American Comedy Award, Funniest Actress in a Motion Picture (Leading Role) for *There's Something About Mary,* 1999; nominated Golden Globe, Best Performance by an Actress in a Motion Picture-Comedy/Musical for *There's Something About Mary,* 1999; MTV Movie Award, Best Female Performance for *There's Something About Mary,* 1999; NY-FCC Award, Best Actress for *There's Something About Mary,* 1999; ShoWest Award, Female Star of Tomorrow, 1999; ALMA Award, Outstanding Actress in a Feature Film for *Any Given Sunday,* 2000; Blockbuster Entertainment Award, Favorite Actress Drama for *Any Given Sunday,* 2000; Blockbuster Entertainment Award, Favorite Actress Comedy for *There's Something About Mary,* 2000; nominated Golden Globe, Best Performance by an Actress in a Supporting Role in a Motion Picture for *Being John Malkovich,* 2000; Blockbuster Entertainment Award, Favorite Action Team (Internet Only) for *Charlie's Angels,* 2001; BSFC Award, Best Supporting Actress for *Vanilla Sky,* 2001; CFCA Award, Best Supporting Actress for *Vanilla Sky,* 2002; nominated Golden Globe, Best Performance by an Actress in a Supporting Role in a Motion Picture for *Vanilla Sky,* 2002; nominated Screen Actor's Guild Award, Outstanding Performance by a Female Actor in a Supporting Role for *Vanilla Sky,* 2002.

Address: *Agent*—Artists Management Group, 9465 Wilshire Blvd. Suite 519, Beverly Hill, CA 90212 (310) 271-9818.

Mary. The New Statesman said of Cameron's character, "Everybody, whatever their role in the plot, is a fool rather than a knave—except for Mary. The California blonde Cameron Diaz portrays her as so drop-dead gorgeous, the only surprise is that the entire male population are not pursuing her." However, according to *People Weekly,* it wasn't her beauty that made Diaz so good in *There's Something About Mary,* but "It's what's beneath that beauty—sporty confidence, absence of attitude, and madcap point of view—that has made Cameron Diaz … Hollywood's sexiest, silliest sweetheart." Also in 1998 Diaz was seen alongside Christian Slater and Jeremy Piven in *Very Bad Things.* In an interview with *People Weekly* Diaz stated that her growing popularity has changed her: "It has toughened me up. I used to be such a nice girl. Now, I'm all calloused and bruised."

In 1999 Diaz was seen in *Being John Malkovich* as a frizzy-haired, sweet pet shop worker whose life was enhanced when she discovered a portal that allowed her to live through the eyes of John Malkovich. Diaz was quoted on the Internet Movie Database as having said of the film, "It's been said that in Hollywood there are only 14 different scripts. Well, this is number 15." It was an odd film, but according to the *Advocate,* "Thanks in no small way to Cameron Diaz and Catherine Keener, the wildly inventive *Being John Malkovich* is a sexy, gender-bending trip." The *Variety* said of Diaz's performance, "While it takes time to recover from the shock of seeing Diaz so dismally plain, with shapeless outfits and a bad perm, the actress again demonstrates her verve and razor-sharp comic skills as she falls for Maxine, is thwarted by her husband, and responds with fierce determination to secure happiness at any price."

Things You Can Tell Just by Looking at Her, (2000,) was Diaz's next film. The film is a collection of five vignettes that are linked by characters and not by story. Also in 2000 Diaz was seen in the TV-to-film remake, *Charlie's Angels.* According to *Variety,* "Of the three women, Diaz is indisputably the dazzler; with her long limbs, beach-blond hair, lagoon-blue eyes, mile-wide smile, and shimmying booty, she all but pops off the screen as if in 3-D, and rarely has a performer conveyed the impression of being so happy to be in a particular movie." And *Entertainment Weekly* said that the film makes "beating the unholy crap out of bad guys as adorable as it is exciting."

Diaz's next project was the 2001 animated film *Shrek.* The film, different from anything Diaz had done before, was an unlikely fairytale that was praised by critics and audiences alike. Besides garnering many rave reviews from critics, Diaz was honored by the Girl Scouts for her portrayal of Princess Fiona. According to *PR Newswire,* "Princess Fiona's example of the meaning of true beauty was hailed by Girl Scouts, who inspired by the film, created a program tie-in to two activity patches for their membership." Diaz's next selection of

was not as pretty as her face, and (2) this was one blond who had more funny than anyone had previously suspected."

With her ability at comedy proven, Diaz next took the part of Mary in 1998's *There's Something About* projects was as far from the comical *Shrek* as possible—her next film was *Vanilla Sky*, (2001,) a mystery starring Diaz, Tom Cruise, and Penelope Cruz. According to *The Roanoke Times*, "Cameron Diaz gives one of her better performances."

The spunky actress returned to her comedic flair with the 2002 film, *The Sweetest Thing*, co-starring Christina Applegate, Thomas Jane, Selma Blair, and Parker Posey. She is set to appear in *Gangs of New York*, a film set in the 1800s in which she plays a prostitute opposite Leonardo di Caprio and Daniel Day-Lewis. She has also signed on to recreate her parts in both *Charlie's Angels 2* and *Shrek 2*. Throughout her acting career, she has been nominated for and won many awards, including ALMA Awards, AFI Film Awards, Boston Society of Film Critics Awards, Golden Globes, MTV Movie Awards, and Screen Actors Guild Awards.

Selected filmography

The Mask, 1994.
The Last Supper, 1995.
She's the One, 1996.
Feeling Minnesota, 1996.
Head Above Water, 1996.
Keys to Tulsa, 1997.
My Best Friend's Wedding, 1997.
There's Something About Mary, 1998.
Very Bad Things, 1998.
Being John Malkovich, 1999.
Things You Can Tell Just by Looking at Her, 2000.
Charlie's Angels, 2000.
Shrek, 2001.
Vanilla Sky, 2001.
The Sweetest Thing, 2002.

Sources

Books

Contemporary Theatre, Film, and Television, Volume 28, Gale Group, 2000.
Notable Hispanic American Women, Book 2, Gale Research, 1998.

Periodicals

Advocate, November 9, 1999.
Boston Herald, November 2, 2001, p. 21.
The Christian Science Monitor, December 14, 2001, p. 15.
Entertainment Weekly, October 31, 1997,p. 12; December 12, 1997, p. 50; December 26, 1997, p. 72; June 26, 1998, p. 24; November 10, 2000; March 30, 2001, p. 50.
Milwaukee Journal Sentinel, January 20, 2002, p. 04.
Newsmakers 1999, Issue 1, Gale Group, 1999.
New Statesman, September 25, 1998, p. 65; July 2, 2001, p. 47.
People Weekly, May 11, 1998, p. 167; October 12, 1998, p. 176; December 28, 1998, p. 52.
PR Newswire, December 15, 2001.
The Roanoke Times (VA) , December 15, 2001, p. 1.
Teen Magazine, June, 1997, p. 54; December, 2001, p. 128.
Time, November 16, 1998, p. 133.
Variety, September 6, 1999, p. 61; January 24, 2000, p. 57; October 30, 2000, p. 21; December 10, 2001, p. 32.

—Catherine Victoria Donaldson

Plácido Domingo

1941—

Opera singer, conductor, administrator

The Spanish-Mexican tenor Plácido Domingo is among the greatest all-around musicians of the last quarter of the twentieth century. With a voice matched only by a very few of his contemporaries, he has sung every major role in the classical operatic repertoire and quite a few more unusual roles. With fellow tenors José Carerras and Luciano Pavarotti he formed the Three Tenors, am ensemble that brought opera to pop fans and attracted the largest audience ever to hear a concert of classical music. Domingo, almost alone among opera singers, has also branched out into conducting and arts administration.

Domingo was born in the Spanish capital of Madrid on January 21, 1941. His parents were both performers in the Spanish musical theater genre called zarzuela, roughly comparable to operetta in the English-speaking world. The family toured Latin America with great success during Domingo's childhood; his mother Pepita became known as the Queen of Zarzuela, and by 1950 the family had settled in Mexico City and taken steps toward forming a zarzuela troupe there. Plácido took piano lessons, dreamed of a conducting career in high school, and performed in his parents' zarzuela productions; in the midst of a chorus that had

a brief solo passage, his fellow choristers, having realized the power of his voice, shoved him forward to sing the solo.

Talented Soccer Goalie

As a young man Domingo also excelled as a soccer goalie, but he elected to embark on a musical career and enrolled at the National Conservatory of Music in Mexico City. He studied both voice (as a baritone at first) and conducting. His musical theater experience led to his first professional roles, one in the Mexican production of the U.S. musical *My Fair Lady* and the other in a 1957 zarzuela production. Domingo's operatic debut came in 1960 with the Mexican National Opera, in Giuseppe Verdi's *Rigoletto*. He served his apprenticeship in the opera world with a two-and-a-half year stint in Israel in the early 1960s, singing in 280 performances (most of them in Hebrew) with that country's national opera company.

By the late 1960s, Domingo was ready to conquer the stages of the world's major opera houses. He joined the New York City Opera in 1965 and quickly impressed critics with his acting skills—sometimes a weak point among conservatory-trained and technique-focused

At a Glance . . .

Born January 21, 1941, in Madrid, Spain; parents were zarzuela (light opera) performers; married Marta Ornelas (a lyric soprano); children: Jose, Plácido, Jr., Alvaro Maurizio. *Education: Attended National Conservatory of Music, Mexico City, Mexico; studied voice and conducting.*

Career: Made debut as baritone in a zarzuela (*Gigantes y cabezudos*), 1957; switched to tenor; joined Mexican National Opera, 1959; made operatic debut, in *Rigoletto,* 1960; performed in first major role, as Alfredo in *La Traviata,* Monterrey, Mexico, 1961; sang with Israel National Opera Company, 1962-65; joined New York City Opera, 1965; performed with Hamburg State Opera, 1967; made debut at Metropolitan Opera House, New York, NY, 1968; debuted at La Scala, Milan, Italy, 1969; performed at Covent Garden, London, U.K., 1971; conducted an opera performance for first time (*La Traviata*) with New York City Opera, New York, NY, 1973; recorded duet with John Denver ("Perhaps Love"), 1981; recorded duet with Jennifer Rush ("Till I Loved You"), 1989; helped found Los Angeles Music Center Opera; first performed with Luciano Pavarotti and José Carreras as The Three Tenors, 1990; starred in film versions of *Carmen, Otello,* and *La Traviata;* founded vocal competition for young singers, 1993; became artistic director of the Washington Opera, Washington, D.C., 1996.

Awards: Grammy Award, Best Latin Pop Performance, 1984; Legion of Honor, France.

Addresses: *Record company*—Columbia/Sony Records: 51 West 52nd Street, New York, NY 10019.

News writer Walter Price. Price pointed to the "burnished, dark color" of Domingo's voice. Through the 1990s Domingo appeared at the Met at least once each season, and his debut there was followed by appearances at the major European opera houses. By the mid-1970s, Domingo was considered one of the top tenors in the world.

Has Memorized Over 30 Roles

Keeping up what seemed to many a grueling schedule of appearances, Domingo displayed an enthusiasm that rarely flagged; he attributed his endurance to the examples of his parents, who had sometimes given two or three performances in a single day. Part of what endeared Domingo to operatic producers was his tremendous knowledge of the operatic repertory. He knows over 30 roles by heart and is familiar with many more, and in one case studied a role on the plane as an emergency substitute at the San Francisco Opera, changing into his costume in a limousine on the way to the opera house.

A new chapter in Domingo's career began in 1972, when he served as orchestra conductor on an album by fellow opera star Sherrill Milnes. Domingo followed that up with a conducting appearance at the New York City Opera (in Verdi's *La Traviata*) during the 1973-1974 season, and since then has been active as a conductor in most of the major opera houses in the United States and Europe. Some observers believed that Domingo was trying to build a place for himself in the world of opera after his singing days ended, an understandable goal in view of the long career fade-out suffered by some operatic vocalists. In Domingo's case, however, conducting came naturally, for he had occasionally conducted performances for his parents' zarzuela company as a young man and had studied conducting in Mexico.

Domingo also branched out in another way in the late 1970s and 1980s: he made forays into popular music, recording duets with pop stars John Denver and Jennifer Rush. Though there was a long history of such efforts by opera stars, these brought the singer some criticism from purists. Another semi-popular project of Domingo's middle age was an effort to promote a rediscovery of the zarzuela music with which he had grown up. Domingo was becoming more and more of a public figure, a status that intensified after his energetic efforts to help victims of Mexico City's disastrous 1985 earthquake. But few could have predicted the success of the move that in the 1990s would make Domingo an instantly recognizable figure in the pop world to a degree that few other classical performers have ever accomplished.

The Three Tenors

United by their common love of soccer, Domingo, Pavarotti, and Spanish tenor José Carreras joined

singers, but second nature to the raised-in-the-theatre Domingo. Throughout his career he would be praised for the depth of his dramatic interpretations, and of all the roles he has performed he is perhaps most identified with Verdi's *Otello,* based on the Shakespeare play *Othello* and making similarly difficult interpretive demands on its star.

Domingo made his most important debut at New York's Metropolitan Opera in 1968, in the opera *Adriana Lecouvreur.* Pavarotti made his own debut there during the same season, which is remembered as "an important one in Met history," according to *Opera* forces for a "Three Tenors" performance at the 1990 World Cup soccer championship in Rome, Italy. The Three Tenors were a blockbuster success, with CD and video releases of the World Cup concerts topping sales charts worldwide. The 1994 concert at Dodger Stadium in Los Angeles (Three Tenors concerts were held every four years in conjunction with the World Cup) was viewed on television by an estimated 1.3 billion people, the all-time largest audience for classical music and one of the most successful televised events of any kind.

Domingo slowed down only slightly in the late 1990s and the first years of the 21st century. He added yet another facet to his all-around participation in musical events when he was named artistic director of the Washington (D.C.) Opera in 1996, and he worked to cultivate the careers of his own successors when he established a competition for young singers in 1992. In the year 2000 he received a Kennedy Center Honor in Washington, D.C. Opera publications around the turn of the century recognized that it would be very difficult to find a successor for this vocally towering, dramatically gifted, and physically compelling singer. Many consider him to have reached the pinnacle of operatic artistry in the late twentieth century.

Selected discography

Romantic Arias, RCA, 1969.
Domingo Conducts Milnes! Milnes Conducts Domingo!, RCA, 1972.
Carmen, London, 1975.
Carmen (soundtrack), RCA, 1984.
Otello, RCA, 1978.
Perhaps Love, CBS, 1981.
Tangos, Pansera/DG, 1981.
Requiem (Andrew Lloyd Webber), Angel, 1985.
Nights at the Opera, CBS, 1986.
Be My Love … An Album of Love, Angel, 1991.
The Broadway I Love, Atlantic, 1991.

(With Paloma San Basilio) *Por Fin Juntos,* Capitol/EMI Latin, 1991.
Canta Para Todos, Capitol/EMI Latin, 1991; reissued, Polygram Latino, 1993.
(With Luciano Pavarotti and José Carreras) *Domingo, Pavarotti, Carreras in Concert With Mehta,* Mobile Fidelity, 1993.
De Mi Alma Latina, Angel, 1994.
Granada: The Greatest Hits of Placido Domingo, Deutsche Grammophon, 1994.
(With Luciano Pavarotti and José Carreras) *The Three Tenors: Paris 1994,* Atlantic, 1994.
(With Luciano Pavarotti and José Carreras) *The Three Tenors: Live 1998,* Atlantic, 1998.
(With Luciano Pavarotti and José Carreras) Romantic Tenors, Atlantic, 2002.

Sources

Books

Contemporary Musicians, volume 20, Gale, 1997.
Dictionary of Hispanic Biography, Gale, 1996.
International Dictionary of Opera, St. James, 1993.
Slonimsky, Nicolas, et al., eds., *Baker's Biographical Dictionary of Music and Musicians,* Schirmer, 2000.

Periodicals

Billboard, November 10, 2001, p. 22.
Opera News, September 13, 1993, p. 8; March 16, 1996, p. 8; July 1997, p. 12; November 1997, p. 71; September 1998, p. 24.
Time, December 28, 1998, p. 180.

On-line

All Classical Guide, http://www.allclassical.com

—James M. Manheim

Laura Esquivel

1951 (?)—

Novelist

Like Water for Chocolate, a unique novel in the form of a cookbook by the Mexican writer Laura Esquivel, became one of the surprise literary hits of the 1990s and spawned one of the most successful foreign-language films of all time in the United States. Esquivel followed up that novel with other works that, if less consistently acclaimed, displayed equal originality. Like her Chilean contemporary Isabel Allende, Esquivel put a feminist twist on the important Latin American literary trend of "magical realism," embedding supernatural elements symbolic of deep forces inside conventionally realistic narratives. With her sense of humor and her winning way of describing family dynamics in *Like Water for Chocolate,* however, Esquivel merged magical realism with a storyteller's common touch.

Born in Mexico City around 1951, Esquivel was the daughter of a telegraph operator—a profession that plays a role in Esquivel's novel *Swift as Desire.* Although many novelists look back on a childhood filled with books, Esquivel gained her narrative sense from stories told to her by her parents, especially her father. "I loved to get sick because he'd come and stay with me

and invent stories with great characters," Esquivel told *Southwest Review.* "A long time ago he bought a reel-to-reel tape recorded and we would spend whole afternoons inventing stories and taping them, with all kinds of interesting sound effects and things." Esquivel also inherited a wealth of cooking lore from her grandmother.

Attracted to 1960s Counterculture

Attending the Escuela Normal de Maestros in Mexico City, a teachers' college, Esquivel worked toward a career in early childhood education. The student counterculture of the late 1960s, which affected Mexico as strongly as it did the United States, left its mark on Esquivel. "I was pretty much a hippie," she told *Southwest Review.* "I was a vegetarian, gypsy-like. I liked to meditate, and it's curious because I was very much attracted to the possibility of change." After college Esquivel became a kindergarten teacher. Her own creative potential was reawakened when she resolved to stage plays with her young students and discovered that few plays in Spanish for young children were available. She solved the problem by writing new ones herself.

Esquivel married a young filmmaker, Alfonso Arau, from whom she took a screenwriting course. Growing more and more interested in drama and film herself, Esquivel wrote scripts for children's television programs in the late 1970s and early 1980s. She penned the screenplay for a film directed by Arau, *Chido One, El taco de oro,* and was nominated for an Ariel award, the Mexican equivalent of the Oscar, for best screenplay in 1985. Esquivel then began work on the novel *Like Water for Chocolate* (*Como agua para chocolate*), which was published in 1989.

Like Water for Chocolate (in Spanish the title connotes a state of approaching the boiling point, of restless ferment or sexual arousal) traces the story of a young woman named Tita de la Garza who has been forbidden by her mother to marry the man she loves, who is betrothed to her older sister. Tita is forced to prepare the wedding cake, and discovers that her tears, which have fallen into the batter, have magical powers—they cause everyone at the wedding party to begin weeping uncontrollably over their own failed love affairs. Food plays a role in all the novel's important plot junctures, and each chapter contains a recipe that both applies to the situation at hand and carries rich over-

tones of folklore. The *Times Literary Supplement* noted approvingly that the reader could enjoy "two books for the price of one: a cookery book and a love story, with a distinctive Hispanic flavour."

Esquivel's novel became a bestseller in Mexico. It was well received after its translation into English and publication in the United States in 1990, but really gained momentum after the 1992 release of the film version, adapted for the screen by Esquivel herself and directed by Arau. The film, which garnered several awards both inside and outside Mexico, spurred sales of the novel that resulted in its translation into more than 30 languages; more than three million copies of the book have been printed worldwide. The film, Esquivel told *Entertainment Weekly,* was a "labor of love between [herself and Arau], like a child almost." Soon after the film's release, however, Esquivel and Arau were divorced. Esquivel later married a dentist, Javier Valdez, whom she has called her twin soul.

Fortified by her regime of meditation (Esquivel was raised Catholic but holds to a blend of indigenous and New Age beliefs) and rising every morning at 5:30 a.m. to write, Esquivel has been prolific in the years since *Like Water for Chocolate* was published. She continued to write film screenplays, and her second novel, *The Law of Love* (*La ley del amor*), was released in the United States in 1996. Less suited to cinematic treatment than *Like Water for Chocolate,* it was equally innovative formally: the book came packaged with a CD of music that ranged from Italian opera to Mexican *danzón* and included a series of 48 cartoon-like illustrations. The novel's plot moved between pre-Columbian Mexico and the 23rd century, depicting a romance and incorporating science-fiction and New Age ideas.

Book Illustrated with Drawings

The same innovative spirit with regard to form was evident in Esquivel's next book, the nonfiction *Between Two Fires* (*Intimas suculencias*), an essay collection, again illustrated with drawings, that ranged from philosophy to culinary meditations in the vein of *Like Water for Chocolate.* A theme running through these writings was Esquivel's idea of the New Man, who "will give equal value to production and reproduction, to reason and emotion, to the intimate and the public, to the material and the spiritual" All of Esquivel's writings have unfolded against a backdrop of the changing relationships between men and women in Mexican society, and the same was true of her 2001 release *Swift as Desire,* (*Tan veloz como el deseo*).

That book, which *Library Journal* called "a welcome improvement over the New Age theme of its not-so-successful predecessor," depicted (as did *Like Water for Chocolate*) a frustrated love affair. Its narrator Lluvia investigates the dissolution of the marriage of her parents after her father, a Maya-descended telegraph operator who can sense the electrical life force present in others, becomes enmeshed in a game of chance that derails his marriage. Clearly Laura Esquivel had many more stories to tell of a changing Mexico in which women were in the process of reconnecting with ancient wisdom.

Selected writings

Como agua para chocolate (novel), Editorial Planeta Mexicana, translated as *Like Water for Chocolate,* Doubleday, 1991.
La ley del amor (novel), translated as *The Law of Love,* Crown, 1996.
Intimas suculencias (essays), translated as *Between Two Fires,* Crown, 2000.
Tan veloz como el deseo (novel), translated as *Swift as Desire,* Crown, 2000.

Sources

Periodicals

Entertainment Weekly, April 23, 1993, p. 23; September 21, 2001, p. 78.
Library Journal, February 1, 1997, p. 126; August 2001, p. S33.
Publishers Weekly, July 22, 1996, p. 225; December 4, 2000, p. 70; July 16, 2001, p. 165.
Southwest Review, Autumn 1994, p. 592.
Times Literary Supplement (London, England) April 16, 1993, p. 22.

On-line

Contemporary Authors Online. The Gale Group, 2001. Reproduced in *Biography Resource Center.* Farmington Hills, MI: The Gale Group. 2001. (http://www.galenet.com/servlet/BioRC).

—James M. Manheim

Gloria Estefan

Singer, songwriter

Gloria Estefan has been entertaining fans since she joined The Miami Latin Boys in the 1970s. She has inspired many people, and helped to bring the Latin sound to the pop genre. She has weathered many storms, but still managed to continue to release platinum-selling record after record.

Estefan was born "Glorita" Fajardo, in Cuba, on September 1, 1957, just two years before Fidel Castro became president of the island nation. Following Castro's ascent to power, Estefan's parents, Jose Manuel Fajardo and his wife, Gloria, fled to Miami with their infant daughter. In Cuba, Jose had been a former volleyball star and policeman, and two years after his arrival in America, he participated as a tank commander in the futile Bay of Pigs invasion of Cuba. He was captured by his cousin, a member of Castro's military, and was jailed for over a year and a half. While Estefan's father was imprisoned, her mother struggled in a strange land to make ends meet. Young Gloria was in first grade when Jose returned from Cuba. Soon thereafter, however, he enlisted in the United States Army, and went on to serve in Vietnam. When he returned to the United States in 1969, Jose was diagnosed with multiple sclerosis, leaving ten-year-old Gloria to take over much of the burden of caring for him as well as her younger sister, Becky, while her

mother worked in the daytime and attended night school.

Gloria managed to maintain excellent grades at Our Lady of Lourdes all-girl high school while caring for her father, but she had no time for a social life. Instead, she found comfort in singing and playing her guitar. Estefan had loved music from a young age; while her father was in Vietnam, she sent him recordings of her singing. He had responded with a letter saying "One day, you're going to be a star." When Gloria was 16, her long role as caretaker was finally over when her father was admitted to the VA hospital. In 1975 she graduated from Lourdes Academy, going on to attend the University of Miami, where she graduated summa cum laude with a B.A. in Psychology in 1978.

Miami Sound Machine

While she was still in college, Gloria was persuaded by her mother to attend a wedding, where a band called the Miami Latin Boys was playing. The band leader, Emilio Estefan, asked Gloria to sing with the band for a few numbers—she received a standing ovation. Soon, Gloria and her cousin, Merci, joined the band, which was quickly renamed the Miami Sound Machine. As the popularity of the band grew, they went from playing small weddings to performing in front of larger crowds and eventually recorded their first album, *Renacer.*

Although Gloria and Emilio maintained a platonic relationship for the first few months of playing in the band together, they eventually began dating, and on September 1, 1978, Gloria's birthday, they were married. In 1980 Estefan gave birth to a son, Nayib. The same year, her father died. Emilio Estefan, sensing the band's potential for stardom, resigned from his job as director of Hispanic marketing at Bacardi in order to manage the band full time, swiftly obtaining a contract for them to record four albums with the Latin Music division of CBS, Discos.

The music of Miami Sound Machine blended sambas with pop and disco influences. Their first albums were in Spanish and were largely unknown to English speakers, but they were very popular with Hispanic American audiences, especially, of course, in Miami. During their early years, the band toured several Latin American countries and had several hit songs in Spanish-speaking countries. In 1984, they released their first English-language album, *Eyes of Innocence,* and scored their first big American hit with "Dr. Beat." The song rose to number ten in the United States and was on the charts in Europe as well.

In 1986 the song "Conga Love" from the album *Primitive Love* became a true crossover breakthrough: it was the first song ever to simultaneously hit the top of Billboard's charts in pop, R&B, Latin, and dance music. The album included both English and Spanish language recordings, and the song itself went on to win the American Music Awards for Best New Pop Artist and Top Pop Singles Artist. Other hits from the album included "Bad Boys," and "Words Get in the Way". This would be the last album on which Emilio Estefan would perform—from this point on, he was full-time manager and producer for the band.

The band's success prompted a move to CBS Epic label, the mainstream music division of CBS. Miami Sound Machine had altered over time, with several changes in band members over the years. The recording studio musicians were often different from the touring concert band members, and musically, dance numbers were interspersed with ballads, featuring Estefan's melodic singing. As Estefan herself rose in popularity, the band changed names yet again to Gloria Estefan and the Miami Sound Machine.

Estefan and the Sound Machine's popularity continued to soar, and they performed to sell-out crowds in large stadiums. Music videos on MTV and VH-1 introduced to band to many more fans. In 1987 the album *Let It Loose* sold four million copies and featured the hit singles "1-2-3," "Anything for You," and "Betcha Say That." Their 1989 album, *Cuts Both Ways,* had only Estefan's name on the cover. She had written seven of the songs and won BMI Songwriter of the year. Estefan was one of the first musicians to recognize that undiluted Cuban music had huge potential among world audiences, and in 1990, she released the Spanish-language single "Oye Mi Canto."

Accident Changed Life

On March 20, 1990, Estefan was on a tour bus near Scranton, Pennsylvania, bound for a concert in Syracuse. The singer was stretched out on a bunk, asleep, while the bus was stopped in traffic backed up behind a jackknifed truck, when a truck plowed into the back of the bus. Estefan was thrown from her bunk and slammed into the middle of the bus, breaking her vertebrae. Emilio and Nayib, who was nine at the time, suffered minor injuries. She was rushed to the Scranton Community Medical Center, where doctors stabilized her back, and then she was flown via helicopter to the Hospital for Joint Diseases Orthopaedic Institute in New York City, where surgeons used titanium rods to align her vertebra and fuse them.

Months of difficult recovery followed, and Estefan underwent endless hours of physical therapy for over a year. At first, she had great difficulty with even simple tasks, such as brushing her teeth, but she persevered against the pain. In an interview with Patti Davis of *Living Fit* magazine, Estefan explained that she continued to strive "Because I had studied psychology. I understand the stages. You have to go through the depression, the crying. Then, at a certain point, I pulled myself up and said, 'Okay, no more. You can't continue this way.' I wasn't going to end up in a wheelchair. I had seen my father confined to a wheelchair; I saw his helplessness and I didn't want that for myself or my family." Estefan feels that her recovery was aided by the love and support of her family and of the thousands of fans who expressed their best wishes for her recovery with a barrage of flowers, gifts, and notes.

Amazingly, she made her first public appearance only six months after the accident, on the Jerry Lewis Labor Day Muscular Dystrophy Telethon, to a standing ovation. She had already started writing songs for her next album, *Into the Light,* and within a year she was on the road, starting on a world concert tour. In 1992 she released a *Greatest Hits* album, which went platinum.

Estefan continued her dedication to presenting Latin music to the mainstream audience: her 1993 album *Mi Tierra* (My Land) was entirely in Spanish and was a tribute to Cuban music of the 1930s and 1940s. It was wildly successful, selling nearly 10 million copies, and won a Grammy award for Best Tropical Latin Album. A string of successes followed, including both Spanish and English language recordings. Estefan was the first performer asked to perform a song in Spanish at the 1995 Grammy Awards, where she also received a Grammy for Best Latin Performance for *Abriendo Puertas* (Opening Doors), a song that was heavily influenced by South American music. She was asked to sing at the Olympic Games in 1996, where she performed her hit song "Reach" to an audience of millions.

In 1998 Estefan performed at the Super Bowl XXXIII half-time show, as well as released the album *Gloria!,* which mixed Cuban and dance music. That same year, she appeared on VH-1 in the *Diva's Live* concert with such performers as Shania Twain and Aretha Franklin. In 2000 she received an Award of Merit at the American Music Awards, and in 2001 she released a hit album titled *Alma Caribena* (Caribbean Soul), which was entirely in Spanish. She also released her second *Greatest Hits* album, which contains a version of "Conga" remixed by her son Nayib. Also in 2001 Gloria and Emilio Estefan also became the first Hispanics to be inducted into the Songwriters Hall of Fame of the National Academy of Popular Music/Songwriters Hall of Fame.

Although she was successful with her music during the early 1990s, the bus accident left Estefan with a lingering health issue. She and Emilio had been trying to have another child with no success; tests showed that her fallopian tube had been injured in the accident. Within a month of surgery to repair the injury, Estefan was pregnant, and daughter Emily was born in October of 1994. Several months later, Gloria and Emilio decided to take a break and went boating in Miami. A small boat tried to jump their wake but crashed into the Estefan's boat. Tragically, the driver, a 29-year-old law student, was sucked under the propellers. Emilio dove into the sea and kept the man's head above water while Gloria called for help from her cell phone, but the young student died. The event prompted Estefan to begin a campaign for boating-safely legislation, and she was instrumental in bringing about the passage of a Florida law requiring young boaters to take safety classes.

Declined Pope's Invitation

Despite leaving Cuba when she was very young, Estefan has remained keenly aware of the political developments in that country. When the Pope was visiting Cuba, Estefan turned down an invitation to sing before him. Explaining her reasons in an interview with the *Miami Herald*, she said, "My going there would have turned a beautiful spiritual thing into a political thing because I thought it was fantastic that the pope was going…. But me going there would have been very political…. I would have asked for permission from the Cuban government, which I'm not about to do, and it just would have been a slap into the face of my father and everything he fought for."

In 2000 Estefan became the focus of media attention in a political context once again as she spoke out in the now-famous Elian Gonzalez case. The six-year-old Gonzalez and his mother had been trying to reach the United States from Cuba when the boat sank, killing young Gonzalez's mother, leaving the boy adrift on a life preserver until he was rescued and brought to Florida. The boy's father and the Cuban government wanted him returned to Cuba. Like many Cuban-

Americans, Estefan believed that Gonzalez should have been allowed to remain in the United States, and she appeared at protests outside the house where the boy was kept, believing that as an immigrant, he had a right to stay in the United States.

Estefan has received criticism for her defense of Peggi McKinley, who was expelled from the Miami-Dade film board after speaking out against the ban on Cuban artists. Estefan's music also reflects her dedication to Cuban rights: her song, "Oye Mi Canto," was written for the Cuban people and contains the words "I want my Cuba free." In addition to her concern about Cuban rights, Estefan and her husband donate a great deal of their wealth towards good causes and charities, and in 1997 they formed the Gloria Estefan Foundation to support charities for disadvantaged youngsters.

In addition to her music, family, and charitable causes, Estefan has also tried her hand at acting, including a part in the 1999 film *Music of the Heart,* which starred Meryl Streep. This was followed by a role in the HBO telemovie, *The Arturo Sandoval Story.* For several years, Estefan has been working on a script based on the book *Many Lives, Many Masters,* and she is producing a movie based on the book *Only Love is Real* for NBC.

In recent years, Estefan has stated that she would like to spend more time with her family, cutting down on public appearances. In 2002, however, she performed again at the Olympic Games, this time at the closing ceremony in Salt Lake City, Utah. Son Nayib, who spent much time as a youngster accompanying his mother on tour, is a DJ in England and husband Emilio continues to expand their music empire.

Estefan has played a pivotal role in popularizing Latin music and paving the way for stars such as Ricky Martin. Martin has recognized his debt to Estefan, praising her "pioneering efforts." Her continuing success is due in part to her ability to meld Latin music with American tastes, and she once stated in an interview with *Time,* " I have the best of both worlds. I have a Cuban heart and an American head. It's a good balance."

Selected discography

Eyes of Innocence, Discos CBS, 1984.
Primitive Love, Epic, 1985.
Let It Loose, Epic, 1987.
Cuts Both Ways, Epic, 1989
Into the Light, Epic, 1991.
Greatest Hits, Epic, 1992.

Mi Tierra, Epic, 1993.
Christmas through Your Eyes, Sony/Epic, 1993.
Hold Me, Thrill Me, Kiss Me, Epic, 1994
Abriendo Puertas, Epic, 1995
Reach, EpicRecords,1996
Don't Let This Moment End, Epic,1998
Greatest Hits, Volume 2, Epic, 2001)
AlmaCaribena, Epic, 2000

Sources

Books

Destefano, Anthony M., *Gloria Estefan : The Pop Superstar from Tragedy to Triumph*, New American Library.

Periodicals

Billboard, Nov 28, 1998, p. 66.
Calgary Sun, November 1, 1999.
Daily Express (U.K), 2000.
Entertainment Weekly Magazine, March 2001.
Entertainment Wire, June 12, 2001.
Horzu, September 8, 1998.
Ladies Home Journal, April 1997, p. 118.
Las Vegas Sun, November 2, 2001.
Living Fit, April 1998.
Miami Herald, September 28, 1997; October 8, 1997; December 20, 1997; May 31, 1998.
People Weekly, August 12, 1996, p. 60.
Time Magazine August 12, 1996.

On-line

American Decades CD-ROM, Gale, 1998, reproduced in Biography Resource Center. Farmington Hills, MI, Gale Group, 2001, http://galenet.gale group.com/servlet/BioRC
Biography Resource Center, Gale, 2002, http:/www. galenet.com/servlet/BioRC
http://immigration.about.com/library/weekly/ aa012400a.htm?terms=Gloria+Estefan
http://members.v3space.com/gloriaestefanlibrary/
http://www.forbes.com/finance/lists/57/2000/ LIR.jhtml?passListId=57&passYear=2000&uni queId=6020&passListType=Person&datatype=Person Gloria Estefan Foundation
http://www.gloriafan.com/bio.html
Vista Magazine, 2001, http://www.spiritualfitnesson line.com

—Ruth Savitz

Patrick Flores

1929—

Roman Catholic archbishop

A respected minister and peacemaker, Archbishop Patrick F. Flores has helped and inspired many people as he rose through the ranks in the Roman Catholic church. His openness to other faiths has put him on a platform alongside Protestant minister Dr. Billy Graham and Lutheran officials mending the hurt caused by the Reformation. Without arousing rancor, Flores stood at the forefront of a move to encourage doctrinal unity among theology professors at Catholic colleges in Texas. Evidencing Flores's abilities as a counselor and minister to the oppressed is his skill on a one-to-one basis that helped him end a hostage situation at his own office.

Mexican-American Roots

Flores required no special training to introduce him to the concerns and needs of immigrant Latinos in Southern Texas. He was born on July 26, 1929, seventh among the nine children of Patrico and Trinidad Fernandez de Flores, Mexican-American immigrants, and migrant farm workers living in Ganado, Texas. Intent on quitting school in the tenth grade, Flores obeyed the urgings of a Catholic bishop and obtained a diploma from Kirwin High School in Galveston, Texas. While sweeping up beer cans and cigarette stubs in a public dance hall in his teens, he decided to make the world cleaner and more liveable by becoming a priest.

Once the decision was made, Flores did not waver in his career goal. After studying at St. Mary's Seminary in La Porte, Texas, and at St. Mary's Seminary in Houston, he took holy vows. Bishop Wendellin Nold ordained Flores on May 26, 1956. As Father Flores, he celebrated his first mass at the Guardian Angel in Pasadena, Texas, before accepting a post in the Houston diocese. At the time, he wanted to serve a parish, but he had no drive to reach the upper levels of officialdom in the American Catholic Church.

Flores began his career at Holy Name Parish, Guardian Angel Parish, then St. Joseph's-St. Stephen's parish as assistant pastor and pastor. An activist from the beginning, he directed the Christian Family Movement and the Bishop's Committee for the Spanish Speaking, a ministry that encouraged bilingual congregations. After Pope John Paul VI named Flores auxiliary to the archbishop of San Antonio in May of 1970, within months, he advanced to interim bishop, becoming the

At a Glance . . .

Born Patrick F. Flores on July 26, 1929, in Ganado, TX. *Education:* Attended St. Mary's Seminary, La Porte, Texas, 1949; divinity degree, St. Mary's Seminary, Houston, TX, 1956. *Religion* Roman Catholic.

Career: Roman Catholic Church, St. Mary' Cathedral, Galveston, TX, ordained priest, 1956; Houston Diocese, assistant pastor and pastor, 1956-1970; Archdiocese of San Antonio, auxiliary to the archbishop and interim archbishop, 1970; Mexican-American Cultural Center, San Antonio, co-founder, 1972; National Hispanic Scholarship Fund, founder, 1976; Diocese of El Paso, TX, bishop, 1978; Archdiocese of San Antonio, TX, archbishop, 1979.

Awards: Medal of freedom Ellis Island medal of honor Statue of Liberty 100th Birthday, 1986; Hispanic Heritage award for leadership, 1986; American Jewish Committee, Human Relations Award, 1995; Salute to Education award, 1995; San Antonio Council fo Churches, San Antonio, Texas, Distinguished Churchman Award, 1995.

Addresses: *Office*—Chancery Office, P. O. Box 28410, 2718 West Woodlawn Avenue, San Antonio, TX, 78228-5124; also, 2600 West Woodlawn Avenue, San Antonio, TX, 78228-5122.

first native Texan to head the state's largest archdiocese and the first Mexican American to attain so powerful a position in the Roman Catholic Church.

Despite a title and ecclesiastical power, Flores's activities continued to center him in humble undertakings. In 1972 he nourished city-wide plans for San Antonio's Mexican-American Cultural Center, for which he served as honorary chairman. He helped form the National Foundation of Mexican American Vocations and the National Hispanic Scholarship Fund. In his twentieth year in the priesthood, he co-founded the "Telethon Navideno" [Nativity Telethon], a charity aiding indigent Latino families.

From Bishop to Archbishop

In 1978 Flores advanced to bishop of the diocese of El Paso, Texas. Within months, his career made an even greater leap after he returned to San Antonio to serve as archbishop of the largest archdiocese in the United States. In Thomas J. Reese's text *Archbishop: Inside the Power Structure of the American Catholic Church*, the author used Flores's rise from parish work to archbishop as an example of "vox populi"—a spontaneous grassroots selection based on parishioners' love and respect. His responsibilities encompassed one million Catholics living in a broad span of territory reaching north from the Texas-Mexico border into the uplands. Among the prickly issues he weathered were charges of a church cover-up in the child molestation scandal involving two diocese priests, Father Xavier Ortiz-Dietz and the Reverend Federico Fernandez.

At home in the archdiocese of San Antonio, Flores does not think of himself as a racial or ethnic role model. Rather, he accepted as his calling a lifetime ministry to people of all cultural backgrounds, particularly the poor fleeing misery in Central America. As a fellow Texan known simply as Patrick or Patricio and nicknamed the "mariachi bishop," he hasn't allowed piety or majesty to overrule his love of celebration, Latino music and dance, and congenial fun. He has cooked benefit breakfasts, fought urban violence, hosted retreats for married couples, and joined "Kiss-a-Pig" contests to support the American Diabetes Foundation. In addition to providing transportation for a parental support group for death-row inmates, he has raised funds to defray utility and medical bills for needy families and to support the San Antonio Battered Women's Shelter.

Flores has displayed a courage and flair in the execution of priestly duties that has cinched his reputation for resolve. He extended hospitality to Pope John Paul II during his 1987 visit to San Antonio by offering a room at the archbishop's residence next door to the chancellery. During a 1997 land-use lawsuit that progressed to the Supreme Court, Flores represented the congregation of Beorne, Texas, in demanding the right to a permit from the city of Beorne to enlarge a church that has been declared an historic property. In his world travels, he has been spokesman for the entire American Catholic Church, a task that attests to the trust he has earned from followers of the faith.

Two public events exemplify Flores's openness toward people of all faiths and his intent to bring Protestants, Catholics, and Jews together in commitment to faith and spirituality. In 1997, before a four-night religious crusade at San Antonio's Alamodome in Hemisfair Park, he supported Dr. Billy Graham's evangelistic mission by taping radio promotions in English and Spanish. In gratitude for the 247, 500 attendees from fifty denominations, many from seventy area Catholic Churches, Graham credited Flores for encouraging the record response among largely Catholic Hispanics, who comprise 60 percent of the city's population. On January 1, 2000, during a joint Catholic-Protestant service at Trinity Lutheran Church in San Antonio, Flores joined Lutheran bishop James Bennett in a public embrace to perpetuate the spirit of the Joint

Declaration on the Doctrine of Justification. The gesture commemorated the abolition of doctrinal condemnations issued by Protestants and Catholics against each other during the Reformation.

Ministered to the Oppressed

At age 70, Flores returned to his background in pastoral counseling to end a potentially deadly situation. On June 28, 2000, Nelson Escolero, a disgruntled Spanish-speaking immigrant from El Salvador, took Flores hostage along with the archdiocese secretary, Myrtle Sanchez. Escolero entered the archbishop's office at the chancery on Woodlawn Avenue and threatened to detonate a hand grenade. One office employee escaped and turned on a silent alarm to police headquarters.

After Escolero ripped out the telephone, Flores had only his faith and experience as a means of ending the situation peacefully. A nine-hour standoff on the third floor of the episcopal residence that involved officers of the police SWAT teams and FBI negotiators as well as the kidnapper's wife and son and 100 onlookers, who stood in 90-degree heat awaiting the victims' fate. Under reasoned counsel from Flores, Escolero relented and released first Sanchez, then the archbishop later. Flores was unharmed, but attendants took the precaution of removing him by stretcher.

Flores publicly forgave the kidnapper and took pity on the man's emotional distress over a passport problem. Flores explained his actions in *America* magazine: "I forgive. In this I have no choice. If I want to be forgiven, I have to forgive." Commentators from the parish noted that one of Flores's strengths as a priest is sympathy for immigrants like Escolero.

Rewards for Character and Trust in Parishioners

Another test of Flores's commitment occurred in 2001 during a renewed campaign to assure that theology teachers at the seven Catholic institutions of higher learning in his archdiocese remained true to the faith. He proposed a loyalty oath affirming intent to teach authentic Catholic doctrine. Typical of Flores's open-mindedness was his presentation of the controversial document. He asked each teacher to make a formal promise, but declined to expel those who refused to sign the oath. Instead, he predicted to doubters that nearly all staff members would follow church teachings. Rich Heffern, writing for *National Catholic Reporter*, disclosed the archbishop's logic: "It's simply a profession of faith, and we make a profession of faith every time we say the Creed at Mass."

Describing his archdiocese, Flores told reporters from the *San Antonio Express* that the city "has the greatest ecumenical spirit I've found anywhere. When I'm with non-Catholic ministers and rabbis, I feel at home with them and they feel at home with me." His numerous outreaches to diverse nationalities and cultures have earned him accolades, in particular for broadcasting Sunday mass from the Cathedral of San Fernando across the Southwest to English- and Spanish-speaking worshippers. In 1995 he won the San Antonio Council of Churches' Distinguished Churchman Award. In addition he received several honorary doctorates and the American Jewish Committee's Human Relations Award. Some church officials have proposed Flores for the position of cardinal, even election to the papacy, a supposition that he humbly disregards as more work than he bargained for.

Sources

Books

The Complete Marquis Who's Who, Marquis Who's Who, 2001.
Dictionary of Hispanic Biography. Detroit: Gale Research, 1996.
McMurtrey, Larry. *The Mariachi Bishop: The Life Story of Patrick Flores.* San Antonio: Corona Publications, 1987.
Reese, Thomas J. *Archbishop: Inside the Power Structure of the American Catholic Church.* San Francisco: Harper & Row, 1989.
Religious Leaders of America, 2nd ed. Farmington Hills, Mich.: Gale Group, 1999.

Periodicals

Albuquerque Journal, April 14, 1999.
America, November 4, 1989; July 15, 2000.
Christianity Today, May 19, 1997, p. 51.
Dayton Daily News, June 29, 2000.
London Independent, June 29, 2000.
Lutheran, January 1, 2000.
National Catholic Reporter, November 1, 1996; March 2, 2001, p. 9.
New York Times, February 2, 1997.
San Antonio Express, March 25, 2000.
San Antonio Light, October 28, 1992.
St. Louis Post-Dispatch, June 29, 2000.
Zenit, June 29, 2000.

On-line

Catholic Church in North America, http://www.rc.net/org/ccita/bishop/bflores.html
http://www.abcnews.go.com/sections/us/DailyNews/texas_hostage000628.html
Biography Resource Center, Farmington Hills, Mich.: The Gale Group. 2001.
http://www.cnn.com/2000/US/06/28/archbishop.threat.03/, June 28, 2000.
AP Online, June 28, 2000.

—Mary Ellen Snodgrass

Vincente Fox

1942—

politician; businessman

On July 2, 2000, Vincente Fox, newly elected president of Mexico, gathered before 100,000 supporters in Mexico City. "The city hadn't seen such jubilation since the pope's visit nearly ten years ago," wrote Dick Reavis in the *Texas Monthly.* Fox's victory was astounding to many because the International Revolutionary Party (PRI) had held the presidency since 1929, often by illegal means. Now, his victory, with 43 percent of the popular vote, would be allowed to stand. "Never before," stated a *New York Times* editorial, "in the memory of living Mexicans has presidential power passed peacefully to an opposition party."

Fox did not plan to become a politician. A businessman from a middle class background, he had risen to chief executive of Coca-Cola de Mexico and later helped his brothers manage the family's 1,100 acre farm in San Francisco del Rincón. Government laws and red tape, however, created hardships for many small business owners during the 1980s and 1990s. His own frustration with the system and encouragement from others led Fox to run for the legislature in 1988, the governorship of Guanajuato in 1991 and 1995, and the presidency in 2000. When President Ernesto Zedillo announced Fox's victory on television, Mexicans cel-

ebrated the changing of the guard. "Fed up with rampant corruption, crime and seemingly intractable poverty," *Maclean's* wrote, "Mexican voters finally said basta (enough) and threw out the world's longest-surviving political dynasty."

Born Into Privilege

Vincente Fox Quesada was born on July 2, 1942 in Mexico City, the second of nine children. His mother, Mercedes Quesada, was born in Spain and immigrated to Mexico as an infant. His father, José Luis Fox, was a prosperous landowner of Irish decent. Fox grew up on his parent's 1,100 acre ranch in San Francisco del Rincón in the Guanajuato region, located in central Mexico. Although he dreamed of becoming a bull-fighter, his parents directed him toward a business education. Fox attended Catholic schools in Mexico, and spent a year at Campion High School in Prairie du Chien, Wisconsin where he learned English.

Although he was born into wealth, the circumstances of Guanajuanto's poor made a lasting impression on Fox. He told Andrew Reding of the *World Policy Journal,* "all my friends were poor; I went to their humble homes to eat and sleep, and be friends, some-

At a Glance . . .

Born Vincente Fox Quesada, July 2, 1942, in Mexico City, Mexico; son of Mercedes Quesada (a homemaker) and José Luis Fox (a rancher); married Lillian de la Concha, 1975, divorced 1991; children: two daughters, Ana Cristina and Paulina, and two sons, Vincente and Rodrigo, all adopted; married Martha Sahagun, 2001. *Education:* Universidad Iberoamericana, Mexico, bachelor's degree in business administration, 1964; Harvard University School of Business, M.B.A., 1974.

Career: Coca-Cola de Mexico, route salesman, 1964-71, transferred to headquarters in Mexico City, worked in marketing; 1971, chief executive, Mexico, 1975-79; returned to Guanajuato to manage family boot manufacturing and vegetable exporting business with brothers, 1980-88; served one term in the Mexican legislature, 1988-91; elected governor of Guanajuato, 1995; elected president of Mexico, 2000.

Awards: Civic Man of the Year, Alianza Civica (Civic Alliance), 1991.

Adresses: *Office*—Grupo Fox, Venustiano Carranza 705, Leon, Gto, Mexico.

thing that is forever imprinted on my heart." His Jesuit education also affected his worldview. "They teach you to serve your community and country; to work for— and be for—others," Fox told Reding.

Unlike many Mexican elites, many of whom come to study in the United States, Fox chose to attend Universidad Iberoamericana, a Jesuit institution located in Mexico City. After earning a business degree in 1964, he took a job with Coca-Cola de Mexico as a route supervisor. He worked in six different cities during the next seven years, and moved to the corporate headquarters in Mexico City in 1971.

"At the university, they taught me to reflect and to analyze," Fox recalled to Sam Dillon of the *New York Times.* "But working at Coca-Cola was my second university education. I learned that the heart of a business is out in the field, not in the office. I learned strategy, marketing, financial management, optimization of resources. I learned not to accept anything but winning. I learned an iron discipline for getting results." He rose to marketing director, and in 1975, he was named chief executive of Coca-Cola de Mexico, a

position he held for four years. He also married Lillian de la Concha and they adopted four children: Ana Cristina, Paulina, Vicente, and Rodrigo; the couple divorced in 1991.

Challenged Mexico's Ruling Party

In 1979 Fox was faced with a difficult choice: he was offered the lead position of the Latin American division of Coca-Cola. Accepting the position, however, required relocating to the corporate headquarters in Miami. He opted to leave Coco-Cola and help his brothers manage Grupo Fox, the family farm. The farm exported frozen broccoli and cauliflower to the United States and cowboy boots to Europe.

The brothers, however, discovered that building a profitable business in a volatile economy was difficult. The North American Free Trade Agreement (NAFTA) went into effect on January 1, 1994, and Mexico experienced a banking crisis the same year. These changes, along with currency devaluations, opened a gulf between large corporations and small businesses: corporations were able to avoid economic fluctuations by trading in U.S. dollars while small businesses were tied to the unstable peso. "Every micro, small and medium sized entrepeneur (sic) in this country is a hero for surviving, growing and exporting under these circumstances," Fox told Dillon. "I' m not embarrassed to say the businesses of the [Grupo Fox] are still highly leveraged, because that's the situation of all Mexican businesses."

Fox did not plan on going into politics. In fact, many in Mexico consider politicians corrupt and dishonorable. "I never, ever, thought I'd be in politics, " he told Dillon. "My father told us that nothing would offend him more, because only thieves and crooks go into politics here." But his many frustrations over the negative impact government policy had on small businesses led Fox to change his mind, and in 1988 he joined the National Action Party (PAN), a conservative party that was pro-Catholic and pro-business. That same year, Fox won a seat on the legislature, but was defeated in a disputed 1991 bid for the governorship of the Guanajuato district.

Fox ran for the governorship again in 1995 and won. "... [T]he voters of Guanajuato elected Vincente Fox governor by a two-to-one landslide," wrote Reding, "the greatest margin ever for an opposition politician in a Mexican gubernatorial election." Fox made no secret of his plans to run for the office of president in 2000. "I am going to hire a governor," he told Tim Golden of the *New York Times.* "I'm going to be a politician."

Launched Presidential Campaign

In 1997 Fox launched his campaign for the presidency, and announced that he would be seeking the PAN nomination. "Ending 70 years of dictatorship will be a great heroic exploit for Mexico," Fox told Dillon, "something like when you Americans put a man on the moon. Reaching the moon took a decade of work. Defeating the PRI is also going to take lots of time, talent and money." Standing six feet, six inches, wearing black leather boots and a large belt buckle with his name emblazed upon it, Fox campaigned by keeping his distance from the pro-Catholic, right-of-center positions of his own party and broadening his message to include the minorities and poor of Mexico.

He also gained a reputation for "rough" language that included slang and profanities on the campaign trail. *Texas Monthly* noted, " Profanity fits into a strategy to attract the attention of smog-eyed and sweaty Jose Six-Pack, a strategy that had carded Fox to the governorship of Guanajuato in 1995." During one appearance, Fox deflected Catholic criticism of his language by announcing, "Ladies, please cover your ears and take the children outside," quoted Dillon. " Your Governor is about to give a speech."

Fox's primary opponent in the 2000 election was Francisco Labastida Ochoa, the PRI candidate. The race, however, became more complicated because a third candidate, Cuauhtémoc Cárdenas, ran on the Democratic Revolution Party (DRP) ticket. Fox worried that DRP would split the progressive vote, leading to a PRI victory, but Cárdenas' poll numbers dropped into the single digits months before the election. "So the real decision will have to be made by the voters themselves ...," wrote Paul Berman of the *New York Times Magazine,* "by many thousands of ordinary Mexicans who might normally prefer to vote for Cárdenas and the left but who will now have to consider voting, in the name of democracy, for Fox, the right-wing cowboy."

Attempted to Enact Reforms

Fox's victory in 2000 signaled an important change in the Mexican political system, and he began to set priorities for his administration even before assuming office on December 1, 2000. He promised to fight corruption and build a crime fighting force, the Federal Agency of Investigation, based on the FBI. He expressed a desire to expand NAFTA to reduce wage discrepancies and to allow a free flow of people between Mexico, the United States, and Canada. Opposition to change, however, remained entrenched. The PRI continued to hold the greatest number of governorships, and no party held a majority in the lower legislature. "Fox succeeded beyond almost anyone's expectations," wrote *Maclean's.* " Now, he faces a host of problems and pent-up demand for change."

In office Fox attempted to enact a number of reforms with mixed results. Some measures expanded educational subsidies and health benefits, while others enacted financial market reforms. He also helped convince President George W. Bush to grant amnesty to three million Mexicans living and working in the United States. In 2001, however, Mexico sank into recession, making new job creation difficult. "It is painful not to have generated jobs as we wanted," Fox told Lucy Conger of *Institutional Investor.* "These realities have brought a more demanding citizenry that asks when will there be accelerated development in Mexico." On July 2, 2001, a year after Fox's victory, on his 59th birthday, he married press secretary Martha Sahagun.

Sources

Periodicals

Institutional Investor, December 2001, p. 43.
Maclean's, July 17, 2000, p. 30.
New York Times, May 22, 1995, A7; May 11, 1998, A4; May 9, 1999, BU1; July 4, 2000, A12.
New York Times Magazine, July 2, 2000, p. 37.
Texas Monthly, December 2000, p126.
Time, September 3, 2001, p. 38.
World Policy Journal, Fall 1996, pp. 61-70.

On-line

Biography Resource Center, Gale, 2002, http://www.galenet.com/servlet/BioRC

—Ronnie D. Lankford, Jr.

Carlos Fuentes

1928—

Novelist , essayist

"The novelist takes it upon himself to reinvent in depth a world that must come alive again, for the future only exists if the past does also," Mexican novelist Carlos Fuentes told the *UNESCO Courier* in 1992. That statement might serve as a credo for the complex, challenging works of this master of the modern Latin American novel, the first Mexican writer to appear on U.S. bestseller lists and one of the key figures in the ascent of Latin American fiction to international significance. Fuentes creates a fictional world showing Mexican society in the throes of intense change—yet at the same time in the grip of forces unleashed at many different points of its long history. Primary among those forces has been Mexico's troubled relationship with its colossal neighbor to the north.

It was in the United States, in fact, that Fuentes began to write. He was the son of Rafael Fuentes Boettiger, a top member of Mexico's diplomatic corps. Fuentes was born in Panama City, Panama, on November 11, 1928, but attended school in Washington, D.C., after his father was assigned to a post at the Mexican embassy there. As a boy this later rather nationalistic novelist was a lover of American culture, but he saw its less tolerant side when he was taunted and called a Communist by schoolmates who had heard about the Mexican government's nationalization of American-owned oil facilities.

First Writings in English

In the early 1940s Fuentes lived in Argentina and Chile; he first took up residence in Mexico only at the age of 16. His first attempts at writing had been in English (at age 13 he was already a published short story writer), but in the process of reconnecting with Mexican culture he switched to Spanish. "I wasn't adding anything to the English language," he explained to *Publishers Weekly.* "I thought I could struggle more with the Spanish language and be on the edge of the precipice. My dreams were certainly in Spanish, my insults were in Spanish, my lovemaking was in Spanish, so I had to write in Spanish finally."

Fuentes wrote for a Mexican weekly called *Siempre* in the 1940s, but then resolved to follow in the professional path his father had laid down. He enrolled in law school at the National University of Mexico, graduating in 1948 and going on for further study in international law in Geneva, Switzerland. There he was sidetracked by his literary interests. He had already taught himself

At a Glance . . .

Born November 11, 1928, in Panama City, Panama; Mexican citizen; son of Rafael Fuentes Boettiger and Berta Macias Rivas; married Rita Macedo, 1959 (divorced, 1969); married Sylvia Lemus, 1973; children: (first marriage) Cecilia; (second marriage) Carlos Rafael, Natasha. *Education:* National University of Mexico, LL.B., 1948; graduate study, Institute des Hautes Etudes, Geneva, Switzerland.

Career: International Labor Organization, Geneva, Switzerland, secretary of the Mexican delegation, 1950-52; Ministry of Foreign Affairs, Mexico City, assistant chief of press section, 1954; National University of Mexico, secretary and assistant director of cultural dissemination, 1955-56, head of department of cultural relations, 1957-59; published debut novel, *La región más transparente,* 1958; Mexican ambassador to France, 1975-77; Cambridge University, Norman Maccoll Lecturer, 1977, Simon Bolivar professor, 1986-87; Barnard Coll., New York City, Virginia Gildersleeve Professor, 1977; Columbia Univ., New York City, Henry L. Tinker Lecturer, 1978; appointed Harvard Univ., Cambridge, MA, Robert F. Kennedy Professor of Latin American studies, 1987; fellow at Woodrow Wilson International Center for Scholars, fellow, 1974; lecturer or visiting professor.

Awards: Romulo Gallegos Prize (Venezuela), 1977, for *Terra Nostra;* Medal of Honor for Literature, National Arts Club, 1988; French Legion of Honor, 1992; honorary degrees from Bard College, Cambridge University, Columbia College, Chicago State University, Dartmouth College, Essex University, Georgetown University, Harvard University, and Washington University.

Memberships: American Academy and Institute of Arts and Letters (honorary).

Addresses: *Office*—401 Boylston Hall, Harvard University, Cambridge, MA 02138.

mas Mann, the experimental French poet Arthur Rimbaud, and the expatriate Irish tradition-breaker James Joyce. These influences gave him the tools to express the complexities of his country's cultural background—and of his own.

From his first novel, *Where the Air is Clear (La Región más transparente,* 1958), Fuentes experimented with complex narrative techniques: flashbacks, multiple perspectives that suggested the transplantation of cinematic techniques into the novel, fragmentation of the action into small episodes, and other devices. Fuentes has always faced his share of unfriendly literary critics, both in Mexico and the United States, his often critical stances toward both societies and the frequent difficulty of his works have put off some observers. But Fuentes, who has often said that novelists must create new audiences rather than simply giving the public what it wants, has done just that, gaining greater and greater repute over a five-decade career.

He first came to international attention with *The Death of Artemio Cruz (La muerte de Artemio Cruz,* 1962), a novel that seems cut from the fabric of modern Mexican life and that remains one of the best known works in the Fuentes canon. The book depicts the life of a ruthless Mexican millionaire; told from the perspective of his deathbed, it shifts between first-person, second-person (an unusual device cultivated by Fuentes), and third-person narration. The 1967 Fuentes novel *A Change of Skin (Cambio de piel,* 1967) featured another common trait in the author's output: an intense eroticism that sometimes put him at odds with his predominantly Catholic surroundings in Hispanic countries.

Fuentes showed a new level of literary ambition in the 1975 novel *Terra Nostra,* an 800-page tome that spans three continents and ranges temporally from the creation scenes of the biblical book of Genesis to the 21st century. "My chief stylistic device in 'Terra Nostra' is to follow *every* statement by a counter statement and *every* image by its opposite," Fuentes said in a *New York Times Book Review* interview quoted in *Contemporary Authors.* The result was a modern epic that matched the creations of the most stylistically challenging European writers, such as Joyce. Such devices posed readers considerable difficulties in understanding the book. Fuentes, however, believed that he had perfected his literary craft with the novel, and indeed his output since then has been both large and of a consistently high level.

Became Mexican Ambassador to France

Belatedly fulfilling his father's dream in the late 1970s, Fuentes went to Paris and served as Mexico's ambassador to France—writing novels in his head, he later recalled, as he attended to the bureaucratic details of

to read French by sitting down with a dictionary and the novels of Honoré de Balzac, and now he encountered the iconic works of European modernism in several languages—the Austrian epic-intellectual novelist Thothe daily embassy routine. A slew of novels appeared when Fuentes returned to full-time writing. The most significant Fuentes novel of this period was probably *The Old Gringo* (*El gringo viejo,* 1985), which became the first Mexican work to appear on the *New York Times* bestseller list and was made into a successful film. That novel, as well as *The Crystal Frontier* (*La frontera de cristal,* 1995) took up as subject matter the border and the wider relationship between Mexico and the United States.

The author of more than 60 books—fiction, nonfiction, and even several plays—Fuentes hardly slowed down as he approached and then surpassed his 80th year. His notable works of the 1990s included the semi-autobiographical novel *Diana, The Goddess Who Hunts Alone,* depicting a romance between a Mexican writer and an American film star; Fuentes was at one time romantically linked with American actress Jean Seberg. Married twice, he made his home in the United States for much of the 1990s but was in reality a globetrotter. In 2001 Fuentes published the novel *Inez's Instinct* (*Instinto de Inez*), a work that returned to a poetic-romantic strain in his writing that had been partially submerged by his series of historical masterpieces.

Selected writings

La región más transparente, Fondo de Cultura Económica, 1958, translation as *Where the Air Is Clear,* Ivan Obolensky, 1960.

Las buenas consciencias, Fondo de Cultura Económica, 1959, translation as *The Good Conscience,* Ivan Oblensky, 1961.

La muerte de Artemio Cruz, Fondo de Cultura Económica, 1962, translation as *The Death of Artemio Cruz,* Farrar, Straus, 1964.

Aura (novella), Era, 1962, reprinted, 1982, translation by Lysander Kemp, Farrar, Straus, 1965.

Zona sagrada, Siglo XXI, 1967, translation as *Holy Place* (also see below), Dutton, 1972.

Cambio de piel, Mortiz, 1967, translation as *A Change of Skin,* Farrar, Straus, 1968.

Cumpleaños, Mortiz, 1969, translation as *Birthday.*

Terra Nostra, Seix Barral, 1975, translation by Levine, Farrar, Straus, 1976.

La cabeza de hidra, Mortiz, 1978, translation as *Hydra Head,* Farrar, Straus, 1978.

Una familia lejana, Era, 1980, translation as *Distant Relations,* Farrar, Straus, 1982.

El gringo viejo, Fondo de Cultura Economica, 1985, translation as *The Old Gringo,* Farrar, Straus, 1985.

The Buried Mirror: Reflections on Spain in the New World (essays), Houghton Mifflin, 1992.

La naranja, translation as *The Orange Tree,* Farrar, Straus & Giroux, 1994.

Diana: The Goddess Who Hunts Alone, Farrar, Straus, 1995.

La frontera de cristal, Alfaguara, Mexico City, 1995, translation as *The Crystal Frontier,* 1997.

Los años con Laura Díaz, translation as *The Years with Laura Diaz,* Farrar, Straus & Giroux, 1999.

Instinto de Inez, Alfaguara, Mexico City, translation as *Inez's Instinct,* 2001.

Sources

Books

Contemporary Literary Criticism, Gale, vol. 3, 1975; vol. 8, 1978; vol. 13, 1980,; vol. 22, 1982; vol 41., 1987.

Dictionary of Hispanic Biography, Gale, 1996.

Periodicals

America, May 11, 1996, p. 25.

Library Journal, August, 1997, p. 137; August 2001, p. S33.

New Statesman, July 17, 1998, p. 46.

Publishers Weekly, October 25, 1991, p. 42; March 23, 1992, p. 58; February 14, 1994, p. 58; September 18, 2000, p. 85.

UNESCO Courier, January 1992, p. 8.

On-line

Contemporary Authors Online. The Gale Group, 2001. Reproduced in *Biography Resource Center.* Farmington Hills, MI: The Gale Group. 2001. (http://www.galenet.com/servlet/BioRC).

—James M. Manheim

Luis González Macchi

1947—

Paraguayan leader

Dubbed an "accidental president" by one diplomat and "the wrong man in the wrong place at the wrong time" by a Paraguayan radio talk-show host (both characterizations were quoted in the *New York Times,* Paraguayan president Luis González Macchi faced a series of extraordinarily difficult tasks when he ascended to his country's highest office in 1999. Although he succeeded in preserving Paraguay's nascent democratic institutions, his experiences in office demonstrated with unusual clarity that pitfalls that have awaited Latin American countries as they have struggled toward democracy and representative government. Chief among those pitfalls in Paraguay was the country's endemic corruption, vividly demonstrated in the year 2001 when it was revealed that González Macchi's presidential limousine, a symbol of any leader's office, was in fact a stolen car.

The recent political history of Paraguay, a poor, landlocked South American country largely dependent on agriculture, is dominated by the shadow of a single individual—General Alfredo Stroessner, who ruled the country for 45 years beginning in 1954. One of the continent's most notorious military strongmen, Stroessner ruthlessly stamped out political opposition and infringed on human rights during his long reign.

González Macchi's father Saul González was a justice and labor minister under the umbrella of Stroessner's Colorado Party, for many years the only road to advancement in Paraguayan civil society and still the country's ruling party.

Luis González Macchi, born on December 13, 1947, was a tall youth who initially seemed destined for a career as a professional basketball player. In his rare moments of free time as president, he still enjoys participating in an occasional basketball game. By the time he was 19, however, he had joined the Colorado Party. He studied labor law at the National University in the Paraguayan capital of Asunción and, then, like his father, took up a series of positions in the Stroessner government's labor and justice departments. The most significant of these was the post of president of the National Service of Professional Promotion (Servicio Nacional de Promoción Profesional), a division of the labor ministry.

In 1989 Stroessner was overthrown by a fellow military officer who represented a more moderate faction of the Colorado Party, one to which González Macchi was drawn by temperament and experience. The outlines of a democratic system took shape over the next several years in Paraguay, with a bicameral legislature

At a Glance . . .

Born December 13, 1947; son of Saul González, a Paraguayan government official; married twice; second wife Susana Galli, a former Miss Paraguay; one child. *Education:* Studied labor law at the National University of Paraguay.

Career: Joined Colorado Party at age 19; was a professional basketball player in Paraguay before entering politics; served in labor and judicial departments of Paraguayan dictator Alfredo Stroessner, 1970s and 1980s; elected to Paraguayan Chamber of Deputies, 1993; elected to Paraguayan senate and became its president, 1998; ascended to Paraguayan presidency in constitutional line of succession after resignation of President Raúl Cubas, 1999-.

Addresses: *Office—* Oficina del Presidente, Palacio del Gobierno, Asunción, Paraguay.

of 45 senators and 80 deputies modeled to some degree on that of the United States, and González Macchi was tapped to take part in the new government. He was elected to the chamber of deputies in 1993, the same year that Juan Carlos Wasmosy became the country's first democratically elected president in a half century. In the Chamber of Deputies, González Macchi was appointed to various committees and served as the body's vice-president in 1993 and 1994.

Married to a former Miss Paraguay, Susana Galli, González Macchi enjoyed a degree of popularity that transcended the political infighting that had characterized the years since the end of Stroessner's rule. González Macchi was elected to the Paraguayan senate in 1998 and was named president of that body, putting him third in line for the country's presidency. After Wasmosy was succeeded as president of Paraguay by Raúl Cubas, a political conflagration ensued when Cubas pardoned General Lino Oviedo, who had led an unsuccessful military coup. The subsequent assassination of the country's vice-president, Luis Maria Argaña, was widely thought to be the work of Cubas and Oviedo, and soon rioting and sniper fire rocked the streets of Asunción, killing six people and injuring 200. Under international pressure and the threat of impeachment, Cubas resigned.

It was in these unpromising circumstances that González Macchi, next in line for the presidency, became Paraguay's leader. He immediately embraced Paraguay's young democratic institutions, telling the audience at his inauguration that "the democratic process has passed the hardest test of all. The people of Paraguay have triumphed!"according to cnn.com. In his first months in office, González Macchi enjoyed wide popular support. He announced plans to cut taxes, to privatize moribund state industries, and to put in place a power-sharing arrangement, the first in Paraguay in decades, between the Colorado Party and several smaller parties. Riding high, González Macchi declared his intention to serve out the rest of Cubas's term, which was slated to end in 2003.

Within a year, however, his ability to reach that goal had begun to seem questionable. In May of 2000, six tanks rolled into Asunción and fired on Paraguay's senate building, blasting a hole in its side. The coup attempt, blamed on supporters of the now-exiled Oviedo, was squashed, and González Macchi gave a televised address reassuring Paraguayans. "Rest easy, countrymen!" he was quoted as saying by the *New York Times.* "Public order has been restored. The destabilizing and antidemocratic forces have been disbanded, the crisis brought under control and the mutineers detained." González Macchi pushed a measure through the legislature giving him expanded security powers.

But the situation did not stabilize. "The problem for the current government," noted an Argentine journalist quoted in the *World Press Review,* "is that, after the success [in crushing the coup] that in theory strengthens it, now the criticisms, doubts, and suspicions are raining down." Oviedo supporters suggested that the government might have staged the coup in order to shore up its own position. One pro-Oviedo journalist wrote (quoted again in the *World Press Review*) that making Oviedo "'public enemy number one' is an excellent excuse for concentrating on him all [the regime's] artillery, and thus avoiding engagement in the decisions that citizens require" on financial matters. One of those was an investigation of the finances of González Macchi's friend Wasmosy, who by one estimate had embezzled a sum equal to 60 percent of Paraguay's annual gross national product.

The following months brought González Macchi more problems, although he continued to hold on to power. Oviedo, now living in Brazil, continued to angle for power by peaceful means. In August of 2000 a special vice-presidential election held to replace Argaña resulted in the election of the pro-Oviedo Julio Cesar Franco of the Authentic Liberal Radical party, leaving the government with a president and vice-president of different parties. González Macchi's popularity plummeted, and the top candidate for Colorado Party leader even criticized González Macchi in his campaign platform.

Worse still, it was revealed in April of 2001 that González Macchi's armored 1999 BMW, his official car, had been smuggled into Paraguay from Brazil after being stolen from an office of the Johnson & Johnson pharmaceutical firm there. "The president's use of a stolen car has become the symbol of the degree to which corruption pervades things here and of the government's unwillingness to confront it," the Paraguayan academic and journalist Victor Jacinto Flecha was quoted as saying by the *New York Times*. The social ills Flecha described, it seemed, were well enough entrenched to drag down the fortunes of even a popular sports-hero national leader.

Sources

Periodicals

Baltimore Sun, June 24, 2001, p. C5.
Houston Chronicle, May 20, 2000, p. A25.
Irish Times, April 5, 1999, p. 13.
New York Times, April 8, 2001, Section 1, p. 4.
World Press Review, June 1999, p. 23; August 2000, p. 27.

On-line

Current Leaders of Nations, Gale Group, 1999. Reproduced in *Biography Resource Center,* Gale, 2001 (http://www.galenet.com/servlet/BioRC).
BBC News Online Country Profiles, http://news.bbc.co.uk/hi/english/world/americas/country_pro files/newsid_1222000/1222081.htm
CNN News, http://www.cnn.com/WORLD/ameri cas/9903/29/paraguay.01/
El Mundo, Spain, http://www.el-mundo.es/1999/03 /30/internacional/30N0068.html

—James M. Manheim

Christy Haubegger

1968—

Publisher

Founder of *Latina*, the first bilingual magazine for Hispanic women, Christy Haubegger had noted the visible lack of Hispanic role models in the media even as a child. As an adult she was determined to change this. Rather than pursue a career in law, Haubegger decided to pursue her dream of creating a women's magazine that dealt with health, beauty, political, and lifestyle issues from a Hispanic woman's perspective.

Christy Haubegger was born on August 15, 1968 in Houston, Texas to a Mexican-American woman, and then adopted by an Anglo couple, David and Ann Haubegger. Haubegger was raised in Bellaire, a middle-class suburb of Houston. Although her parents did not speak Spanish, they strongly encouraged her to learn the language and to explore Mexican culture, and Haubegger was enrolled in a bilingual preschool, continuing to learn Spanish in primary and secondary schools.

She graduated from St. John's High School in 1986 and then went to college at the University of Texas at Austin. After she received her bachelor of arts degree in philosophy in 1989, Haubegger attended Stanford Law School where she was class president and also served as the senior editor of the *Stanford Law Review*. Haubegger graduated with a juris doctor degree in 1992.

Searched for Role Model

As a young child, Haubegger noticed that magazines in the grocery stores did not show women who looked like her. In fact, she soon realized that all of the role models around her, in the movies, media, or even her own family, were tall, Caucasian, and blond. As a chubby girl of Mexican-American heritage, with dark hair and brown eyes, Haubegger could not relate to these images. Magazines were particularly problematic for Haubegger because they defined what teenagers considered to be beautiful. As Haubegger wrote in *Essence*, "I remember being in high school and noticing that none of the magazines showed models in bathing suits with bodies like mine." Haubegger believed that the fact that she had Anglo parents strengthened her desire to connect with her Hispanic heritage. As Haubegger explained to the *Texas Monthly*, "Other Hispanic kids were frustrated by a lack of popular images in the media, but at least when they went home, they found people who looked like they did."

Rather than be discouraged, Haubegger instead decided to find an outlet that would celebrate the beauty

At a Glance . . .

Born Christy Haubegger on August 15, 1968, in Houston, TX. *Education:* University of Texas at Austin, B.A., 1989; Stanford University, J.D., 1992.

Career: Freelance legal researcher, 1992-1995; *Latina* magazine, president and publisher, 1996-2001; *Latina* magazine, founder and board member, 2001-.

Awards: Most Inspiring Woman, *NBC Nightly News with Tom Brokaw,* 1996; 100 Most Influential Businesswomen, *Crain's New York Business,* 1999; Advertising Hall of Achievement, American Advertising Federation, 1999; Woman of the New Century, *Newsweek;* Top 10 Role Models of the Year, *Ms.* Foundation, 2001.

Addresses: *Latina* Magazine, 1500 Broadway, Suite 600, New York, NY 10036.

of Hispanic women. While still in law school, she came up with the idea of a magazine dedicated to Hispanic women as part of an assignment for a marketing class. Upon graduation she and a friend decided to try to turn that idea into reality. Her friend quit the project after only three months, but Haubegger continued to pursue it on her own, working as a freelance legal researcher to support herself financially.

Turned Dream into Reality

Haubegger formed her own company, Alegre Enterprises Incorporated, and turned her marketing class project into a 200-page business plan that outlined the need for a magazine that catered to Hispanic women. Next she began to look for investors who would back the project, searching in Palo Alto and Menlo Park, California, the home of several venture-capital firms. When this plan did not succeed, Haubegger expanded her search nationwide. As she told Folio magazine, "I knocked on 105 doors and got 5 yeses." Haubegger not only found a venture capitalist willing to fund her project, but she also sparked the interest of Edward Lewis, founder and owner of *Essence,* the leading magazine for Black women.

With some of the initial investment money, Haubegger developed a prototype of the magazine and mailed out 75,000 test copies. In addition, she conducted 21 focus groups in cities with large Hispanic populations. This initial research helped her refine the look and content of the magazine. In June of 1996 the first issue

of *Latina* hit the newsstands. The premiere issue featured Jennifer Lopez on the cover and sold over 200,000 copies.

Targeted Bicultural Hispanic Women

According to *Latina Online,* the result of Haubegger's efforts "was a bilingual lifestyle magazine that addressed the needs and concerns of an untapped Hispanic population," Hispanic Americans who were bilingual and bicultural. Haubegger explained her target audience in an interview with the *Los Angeles Times.* "They are also *Latina* like me—with one foot in each culture." She went on to describe this target audience as upwardly-mobile, educated, between the ages of 20 and 40, and employed with an average annual income above $30,000.

Latina was launched at a time when other publishers were also trying to tap into the Hispanic market. The death of Mexican singer Selena in 1995 resulted in a surge of purchases of magazines about the young star, demonstrating the purchasing power of the Hispanic population. In response, both *People* and *Newsweek* began to publish Spanish versions of their magazines. In addition, other Latino publications grew in popularity, such as *Moderna,* which targeted a fairly young audience, and *Si,* which was written only in English. However, as an article in the *Seattle Times* explained, "... selling to a Hispanic audience means more than simply translating words from English to Spanish or replacing thin models with curvaceous ones. The industry can be insensitive to minority groups, often exoticizing or dehumanizing them."

In contrast Haubegger envisioned *Latina* as a magazine for a population of Hispanic women who were bilingual and bicultural. Her readers were often second-generation citizens who flowed easily between the two cultures. In an article in *USA Today* Haubegger described the average reader of *Latina.* "She wants to make enchiladas, but she doesn't want to use lard. Her mother didn't work out, but she wants to. Their mothers don't speak English, their kids don't speak Spanish." To reach such an audience *Latina* features a wide range of articles, including a focus on health problems that disproportionately affect Hispanic women, highlighting promising careers for bilinguals, or health-conscious tips for making traditional Spanish meals.

The fact that the magazine was bilingual was important to Haubegger. Each issue is approximately 60 percent English and 40 percent Spanish. Editor-in-chief Patricia Duarte explained the reasons for having a bilingual magazine to *Folio.* "One is that there are several levels of language proficiency in Hispanic households, and another is that there is a community tradition of using periodicals as learning tools." Not only was *Latina* bilingual, but it also used some Spanglish, a slang hybrid of English and Spanish that is commonly spoken among Latinos. As Haubegger explained to the *New York Times,* "If we were an English magazine, we would just be general market. If we were a Spanish-language magazine, we would be Latin American. We are the intersection of the two, and we reflect a life between two languages and two cultures that our readers live in."

Established Powerful Business

Latina's biggest challenge has been attracting advertising dollars. Haubegger has worked hard at convincing major companies to create ads targeting the female Hispanic population and she succeeded in persuading several high-end advertisers to do their first Hispanic advertising in *Latina,* including Chanel, Ann Taylor, Polo Jeans, Timex, Gap, and Liz Claiborne. Haubegger used basic demographics to sell her magazine to advertisers, arguing that Hispanic households were larger than the U.S. median and Latinos had more than $5 billion of purchasing power. In addition, since Hispanic women were younger than the U.S. average, they accounted for a larger percentage of cosmetics sales. Her argument has been persuasive since advertising grew from 17 pages in the first issue to 114 pages by the end of 2001. As Haubegger explained to *Mediaweek,* "Anybody who ignores the Hispanic market in this country at this point is downright foolish."

Haubegger's instincts about the focus of her magazine have proven to be correct. Published quarterly when it was launched in 1996, the magazine increased its frequency to monthly issues only a year later, in July of 1997. By 2000 the circulation figures were about 225,000 issues, 80 percent of which were subscriptions. In 1997 Haubegger served as the president and publisher of the New York based company. She oversaw a staff of 20 and focused on the business management of the magazine. Since then the staff has grown to over 50, many of whom are Hispanic women. In 2000 *Latina* was named Best Magazine by *Advertising Age.* And both in 2000 and 2001 it was featured on the *Adweek* Hot List. In 2002 the magazine was awarded the Society of Publication Designer's Merit Award in design for a feature story on coffee that ran in the July 2001 issue.

In 1998 *Latina* expanded to the web with *Latina Online.* Two years later *Latina* received a $20 million equity investment by Solera capital to create Latina Media Ventures, a parent company to the magazine that aimed to expand the publication to the internet, broadcast, and other print media. In October of 2000 Haubegger published the book *Latina Beauty* (Hyperion), the country's first comprehensive beauty and wellness guide for Hispanic women. In the same year Time Inc. bought a 49 percent stake in *Essence,* but it did not include *Latina* as part of the deal. In July of 2001 Haubegger was replaced as the publisher of the magazine and no longer oversaw the daily operations. A *Latina* spokesperson told the *New York Post* that Haubegger "has assumed the role of founder, where she remains on the company's board and continues to focus on strategic initiatives, advertising and brand development." She has also served on the board of Latina Media Adventures.

In addition to her work at *Latina,* Haubegger has done numerous speaking engagements promoting both the magazine and her vision of how Hispanics should be portrayed in the media in particular and in American culture in general. As Haubegger told *Newsweek,* "At the dawn of the new millenium, America knows Latinos as entertainers and athletes. But, someday very soon, all American children can dream of growing up to be writers like Sandra Cisneros, astronauts like Ellen Ochoa, or judges like Jose Cabranes of the Second Circuit Court of Appeals." Haubegger has received numerous awards and recognition for her achievements. In particular, she was named one of the Most Inspiring Women of 1996 by *NBC Nightly News with Tom Brokaw; Crain's New York Business* selected her as one of the 100 Most Influential Businesswomen of 1999; *Newsweek* named her one of the Women of the New Century; and the *Ms.* Foundation chose her as one of the Top 10 Role Models of the Year in 2001. In addition, Haubegger was one of the youngest women to be inducted into the Advertising Hall of Achievement.

Sources

Periodicals

Advertising Age, February 7, 2000.
Business and Management Practices, 1998, pp. 199-201.
Essence, December 1994, p. 48.
Fleet Owner, May 1999.
Folio, February 1, 1995, p. 20; September 1, 1996, pp. 23-24; October 1, 1996, p. 29; April 15, 1999, p. 54.
Fresno Bee, October 16, 2000, p. E1; November 30, 2000, p. C1.
Grand Rapids Press (Grand Rapids, MI), October 10, 2001, p. A14.
Houston Chronicle, July 19, 2001.
Los Angeles Times, November 19, 1996; August 7, 1997, p. E1; June 19, 1998, p. E2; July 6, 1998; July 23, 1998; May 3, 2000, p. C6; November 15, 2000, p. C8.
Media International, February 1999, p. 27.
Mediaweek, June 10, 1996, p. 34; April 13, 1998; February 28, 2000, p. 79.
Milwaukee Journal Sentinel, November 10, 1996, p. Q1.
Ms., September/October 1997.
Newsday, April 5, 1998; November 4, 2000.
Newsweek, July 12, 1999.
New York Post, July 18, 2001.

New York Times, December 25, 1996, p. C3; March 25, 1997, p. A1; March 1, 1998; September 15, 1999, p. C6.
Pittsburgh Post-Gazette, August 25, 1999, p. S2.
Plain Dealer, March 19, 1998, p. 2C; September 28, 1999, p. 5F.
San Francisco Chronicle, August 14, 1996, p. E4.
Seattle Times, July 7, 1996, p. A8; November 30, 1997.
St. Petersburg Times, August 6, 1999, p. 1D.
Tampa Tribune, July 5, 1999; July 25, 1999.
Texas Monthly, 1997.
USA Today, March 18, 1998, p. 9D.

On-line

Business 2.0, www.business2.com/articles/mag/0,16 40,72,FF.html
Girls Can Do, www.girlscando.com
Las Mujeres, www.lasmujeres.com/christyhaubegger/ freshface.shtml
Latina Magazine Online, www.latina.com

Other

Additional information for this profile was obtained from Carolina Miranda, publicist for *Latina* magazine.

—Janet P. Stamatel

Rita Hayworth

1918–1987

Actor, dancer, producer

Called "the fiery epitome of screen sensuality," by *People* magazine, Rita Hayworth became one of America's most popular and famous actresses of the 1940s and beyond, known for her grace, her beauty, and her amazing dancing ability. Born Margarita Cansino on October 17, 1918 in Brooklyn, NY, Hayworth was part of a family descending from a long line of performers. When she was nine years old and the Vaudevillian scene was breaking up, Hayworth's family moved to Los Angeles. There her parents—Eduardo, a vaudevillian performer, dance instructor, and director, and Volga Haworth, a Ziegfield Follies showgirl—encouraged her to follow in the family line and started her in acting and dancing lessons. Hayworth's father at this time moved from Vaudeville performing to being a dancer and director for several Hollywood movie dance scenes.

While Hayworth was busy learning the family business, she also went to the Carthay School where she had parts in a few school plays, including a stage prologue for the movie *Back Street* at the Carthay Circle Theater. She then spent one year at Hamilton High before, in ninth grade, her schooling was halted when she became her dad's dancing partner. Called the

"Dancing Cansinos," they performed up to 20 times per week. The show traveled throughout Mexico and California until Fox Film Corporation spotted Hayworth in Agua Caliente, Mexico. Because of her grace and beauty she was invited by Fox Films, at age 16, to begin her career in film, acting in B-grade movies. Although her screen debut was with her family in *La Fiesta* in 1932, her first film by herself was *Dante's Inferno.* Hayworth was billed on the film as Rita Cansino. The movie wasn't popular, but it brought her to the attention of Fox Film bigwigs and Hayworth was given a year-long contract. For this one year Hayworth held small, ethnic parts in movies such as *Charlie Chan in Egypt,* 1935, *Under the Pampas Moon,* 1935, *Paddy O'Day,* 1935, and *Human Cargo,* 1936. Her contract was not renewed, and Hayworth was forced to take a line of small parts playing Mexican and Indian girls for very little money.

When Hayworth was 18 she married Edward C. Judson, a man who was a car salesman and businessman and soon became Hayworth's manager. Judson is said by the *Encyclopedia of World Biography* to have transformed Hayworth, changing her from a dark Latin girl into a red-headed sophisticate. Hayworth altered her hairline and eyebrows with electrolysis and changed her name to Rita Hayworth (This was a variation on her mother's maiden name, with the 'y' added to help pronunciation). Her new look brought her speedily into the public eye and garnered her a seven-year contract with Columbia Pictures. After a string of small parts in low-budget movies, Hayworth was finally given a leading role, portraying an unfaithful wife in *Only Angels Have Wings*, 1939, alongside Cary Grant. After that she was seen in movies such as *Strawberry Blonde*, 1941, with James Cagney, and *Blood and Sand*, 1941, with Tyrone Power.

It was, however, in 1941's *You'll Never Get Rich* in which Hayworth starred with Fred Astaire, that Hayworth began her ascent into the heights of stardom. It has even been said that Fred Astaire called Rita Hayworth his favorite dancing partner, not his more popularly known partner Ginger Rogers. For this part she appeared on the cover of *Time* magazine and was labeled "The Great American Love Goddess" by *Life*. The next year she made three hit movies, *My Gal Sal*, 1942, *Tales of Manhattan*, 1942, and *You Were Never Lovelier*, 1942, her only other movie with Fred Astaire. Although her career was becoming more and more successful, her marriage was not—she divorced Edward Judson in 1942.

Also in 1942 Hayworth married Orson Welles, the famous actor, director, and screenwriter. With him she had a daughter, Rebecca, and life was looking up for the new mother and increasingly popular lead actress. In 1944 she starred alongside Gene Kelly in *Cover Girl*. As a promotion *Life* had an article about the actress along with a seductive picture of her wearing black lace and satin which was infamous in World War II as an American servicemen's pinup picture. *American Decades* quoted *Times* magazine as having noted that "intended ... as the ultimate compliment, the picture was even pasted to a test atomic bomb that was dropped on Bikini atoll in 1946." As her celebrity rose, she started acting in better films. In 1945 she was seen in *Tonight and Every Night*, and in 1946 she took the leading role in the movie *Gilda*, the part that scandalized more conservative viewers because of a seductive strip scene, and the part which eventually became Hayworth's best known. According to *The Daily Mail*, it was Hayworth's part in *Gilda* that sealed her "screen goddess reputation." Another movie of hers done around this time, *Down to Earth*, was even included in a 20th century time capsule even though it received mixed reviews.

In 1948 Hayworth starred in *The Lady From Shanghai* alongside her husband Orson Welles who was also the director of the film. Although that seems rather nice, this was actually the end of Hayworth's relationship with Welles, she was in the process of divorcing him as they made the film. After making *The Loves of Carmen*, 1948, Hayworth married her third husband, Prince Aly Kahn in 1949. This marriage shocked the nation and brought Hayworth a little ways out of her popularity. Hayworth and Prince Aly Kahn had been having an affair even though they were both married, and she was already pregnant with their daughter Princess Yasmin Aga Kahn when they were married. Unfortunately this marriage ended, and the two were divorced in 1953.

At this point her career was beginning to fade. She never quite recovered from the scandal of her affair and marriage. She made the movies *Affair in Trinidad,* 1952, *Salome,* 1953, and *Miss Sadie Thompson,* 1953 and then was married again in 1953 to the singer Dick Haymes. The marriage was doomed to failure as Haymes beat Hayworth and was said to have tried capitalizing on her fame to bring back his failing career. The marriage ended in 1955. After her divorce she made the film *Fire Down Below,* 1957 and had a supporting role in 1957's *Pal Joey,* with Frank Sinatra and Kim Novak playing the leads. In 1958 Hayworth, although acclaimed for her part in *Separate Tables,* 1958, faced a career that was definitely on a downward spiral. It was at this time that she married for the fifth time, marrying producer James Hill. This marriage too ended in divorce, with Hayworth leaving him in 1961. She was quoted in *People* as having said, "Most men fell in love with *Gilda* but they woke up with me." Hayworth began to doubt that she would ever have a happy and successful relationship and she thought that one of the biggest problems was the fact that men went to bed with the image of glamour and sophistication shown in parts like Gilda and then woke in the morning with the real her. According to Barbara Learning, Hayworth's biographer, however, Hayworth's troubles with men were caused by her abusive relationship with her father. Although unknown prior to his, it seems that her father "raped [Hayworth] in the afternoons and danced with her at night." Whatever the problem really was, Hayworth never married again.

Hayworth's last string of films included such films as *They Came to Cordura,* 1959, *The Story on Page One,* 1960, *The Poppy Is Also a Flower,* 1967, *I Bastardi,* 1968, *The Naked Zoo,* 1971, and *The Wrath of God,* 1972. She attempted, in 1971, to perform on stage but couldn't do so because she could not remember her lines. It was about this time that people started realizing that there was something seriously wrong with Hayworth. Alzheimer's disease wasn't well known at the time, and there were a myriad of different diagnoses for what was wrong with the once famous actress. In 1981 she was declared unable to take care of herself, and for the next 6 years, until her death on May 14, 1987, her daughter Princess Yasmin Aga Kahn took care of her. Although she had been missing from the public eye for almost two decades, the public felt Hayworth's death, and the once called "American Goddess" will not be forgotten anytime soon. In 2000, according to *PR Newswire,* Sony Pictures Consumer Products and Hayworth's

daughter Princess Yasmin unveiled the first Rita Hayworth as Gilda Collector Doll. As *Interview* magazine said about why modern movie stars don't reach the heights of actresses like Rita Hayworth, "Hayworth's skin glows, her eyes beam with pleasure, her hair spills around her face like a river of luxury—it is impossible not to look at her, or long to know her, or want to be like her."

Sources

Books

American Decades CD-ROM, Gale Research, 1998.
Contemporary Newsmakers 1987, Gale Research, 1988.
Dictionary of Hispanic Biography, Gale Research, 1996.
DISCovering Biography, Gale Research, 1997.
DISCovering Multicultural America, Gale Research, 1996.
Encyclopedia of World Biography, 2nd edition, Gale Research, 1998.
International Dictionary of Films and Filmmakers, Volume 3: Actors and Actresses, St. James Press, 1996.
Learning Barbara, If This Was Happiness, Viking, 1989.
Notable Hispanic American Women, Book 1, Gale Research, 1993.
The Scribner Encyclopedia of American Lives, Volume 2: 1986-1990, Charles Scribner's Sons, 1999.

Periodicals

The Daily Mail (London, England), November 19, 2001, p. 43.
Entertainment Weekly, Fall, 1996, p. 48.
Interview, September, 2001, p. 72.
Ladies Home Journal, January, 1983, p. 84.
The New York Times, February 8, 2002, p. E28.
People, June 1, 1987.
PR Newswire, September 26, 2000.

On-line

www.allsands.com
Internet Movie Database, www.imdb.com
www.tiac.net/users/mharncy/hayworth.html

—Catherine Victoria Donaldson

Oscar Hijuelos

1951—

Novelist

The novel of immigrant life is a durable and extremely significant tradition in American literature, and Cuban-American writer Oscar Hijuelos has emerged as one of its top recent practitioners. His 1989 novel *The Mambo Kings Play Songs of Love* was both a prizewinner and a bestseller; in that work and in several other substantial novels Hijuelos has explored the worlds of Cuban-born and Cuban-descended characters who live in the major cities of the U.S. eastern seaboard. "Oscar Hijuelos," noted the *National Review,* "forces the Hispanic immigrant experience close to the center of our cultural consciousness, where it very much deserves to be."

Born in New York on August 24, 1951, Hijuelos was the son of a Cuban-born hotel worker. In the years before the takeover by Communist strongman Fidel Castro the family occasionally returned to Cuba. On one of those trips Hijuelos became seriously ill and had to spend several months in a Connecticut children's hopsital upon his return. Hijuelos was a product of New York's public education system through the Master's degree level, graduating from the City University of New York in 1975 and gaining his M.A. in creative writing a year later. Among his early influences as a

writer were the novelist Henry Roth, who had chronicled the experiences of Jewish immigrants, and the minimalist short-story craftsman Donald Barthelme.

Worked in Advertising Firm

Hijuelos, however, evolved into a writer who was no minimalist, but rather has been noted for his rich, detailed descriptions of Cuban-American life. He honed his craft over a period seven years, from 1977 to 1984, during which he worked in an advertising office and wrote fiction by night. Working in the short story genre at first, Hijuelos found gradually increasing recognition for his works. He landed a group of stories in the 1978 anthology *Best of Pushcart Press III.* That led to a series of small grants that gave him more and more free time to write; one of them, in 1980, was a scholarship to the prestigious Breadloaf Writers Conference in Vermont.

The first fruit of Hijuelos's long apprenticeship was the novel *Our House in the Last World,* published in 1983. That book, which included an episode paralleling its author's own childhood hospitalization, depicts the lives of the members of a Cuban-American family in New York's Spanish Harlem neighborhood in the

At a Glance . . .

Born August 24, 1951, in New York City; son of Pascual (a hotel worker) and Magdalena Torrens Hijuelos); divorced. *Education:* City College of the City University of New York, B.A., 1975; City University of New York, M.A. in creative writing, 1976. *Religion:* Roman Catholic.

Career: Transportation Display, Inc., New York, advertising media traffic manager, 1977-84; published debut novel, *Our House in the Last World,* 1983; appointed professor of English, Hofstra University, Hempstead, NY, 1989; international acclaim for *The Mambo Kings Play Songs of Love,* published by Farrar, Straus, 1989; signed publishing contract with HarperCollins, 1995; published novel *Empress of the Splended Season,* 1999.

Memberships: PEN international writers' organization.

Selected awards: Creative writing fellowship, National Endowment for the Arts, 1985; Pulitzer Prize for fiction and numerous other prizes and nominations for *The Mambo Kings Play Songs of Love,* 1990.

Addresses: *Home*—211 W. 106th St., New York, NY 10025; *Office*—Department of English, Hofstra University, 1000 Fulton Ave., Hempstead, NY 11550.

tells the story of two Cuban brothers, Cesar and Nestor Castillo, who move to New York in the early 1950s and establish a mambo orchestra.

Novel Featured Desi Arnaz as Character

One technique Hijuelos used to add realism to his depiction of the heavily Latin-tinged musical world of the 1950s was the inclusion of real-life individuals as characters—most significantly Latin star Desi Arnaz (the brothers make an appearance on the *I Love Lucy* television program). Such realistic touches, and a prose style that itself evoked Cuban rhythms, contributed to the book's success but ironically landed Hijuelos in court: Gloria Parker, leader of a group called Glorious Gloria Parker and Her All-Girl Rumba Orchestra alleged that an unflattering character in the book was based on her own, and sued Hijuelos for defamation of character. Closely watched as the first case of its kind to involve a work of fiction, the lawsuit was dismissed in 1991.

Awarded the Pulitzer Prize for fiction in 1990, *The Mambo Kings Play Songs of Love* played in important part in kicking off the 1990s renaissance in Latin American fiction. "I remember being told, when the novel came out, 'Minority novels don't sell. Period.'" Hijuelos told *Publishers Weekly.* "That's what you hear if you're Hispanic. 'Punto. Forget it, baby.'" But *The Mambo Kings Play Songs of Love* enjoyed strong support from its publisher and by early 1991 had more than 200,000 copies in print. "The book is overcoming a very subtle kind of bias people have about what they'll find in a Latino book—more drudgery, death, and taxes." Hijuelos reflected in the same interview.

After the long years he spent mastering the writing craft, Hijuelos was in no danger of suffering the kind of post-smash slump that has sometimes affected other young writers. His novels of the 1990s were a varied group in both subject matter and technique. *The Fourteen Sisters of Emilio Montez O'Brien* (1993) was set in rural Pennsylvania in the early 20th century and depicted the large and predominatly female offspring of an Irish-American father and a Cuban-American mother. Though some reviewers complained that the large cast of characters reduced some of the characterizations to shorthand, it was becoming increasingly clear that Hijuelos was claiming for his own large swaths of the American experience that earlier Hispanic writers had not dealt with.

The lyrical and spiritual novel *Mr Ives' Christmas* (1995) strengthened that impression with its presentation of a main character who finds redemption after his son is randomly murdered during the holiday season. A successful executive who grew up in poverty, Ives, the novel suggests, comes from a Hispanic background. But the novel was aimed at general audiences and was

1940s. Told through the eyes of the youngest son, the story reflects issues common to American immigrants: the pull of assimilation versus the barriers of discrimination and separateness, and the ambivalent attitudes immigrants may have toward their home cultures. In *Our House in the Last World* (the "Last World" refers to Cuba), those ambivalent attitudes crystallize around the family's attitudes toward the alcoholic father, Alejo Santinio, whose errant ways leave them trapped in poverty.

Our House in the Last World brought Hijuelos few general readers but plenty of critical attention, and in 1985 he won a National Endowment for the Arts fellowship. The fellowship enabled him to devote full time to the research into 1950s Cuban music that would underlie his sophomore release, *The Mambo Kings Play Songs of Love.* Published in 1989, that book remains his best known work. Tailor-made for cinematic adapation (a film version starring Armand Assante brought the film's musical world to life in the early 1990s), *The Mambo Kings Play Songs of Love* reviewed from that perspective. In 1999 Hijuelos struck a balance between his Cuban roots and his interest in American society in general with the novel *Empress of the Splendid Season*; the book told the story of a Cuban-American housecleaner and the varied American lives into which her work has given her a window. Perhaps just reaching his prime in the early 21st century, despite all the success he had already achieved, Hijuelos seemed ready to say much more to the nation of immigrants that his family had adopted as home.

Selected writings

Our House in the Last World, Persea Books, 1983.
The Mambo Kings Play Songs of Love, Farrar, Straus, 1989.
The Fourteen Sisters of Emilio Montez O'Brien, Farrar, Straus, 1993.
Mr Ives' Christmas, HarperCollins, 1995.

Empress of the Splendid Season, HarperCollins, 1999.

Sources

Periodicals

Library Journal, April 15, 1999, p. 163.
National Review, February 22, 1999, p. 50.
New Republic, March 22, 1993, p. 38.
Publishers Weekly, February 1, 1991, p. 17.
Time, November 27, 1995, p. 98.

On-line

Contemporary Authors Online. The Gale Group, 2001. Reproduced in *Biography Resource Center.* Farmington Hills, MI: The Gale Group. 2001. (http://www.galenet.com/servlet/BioRC).

—James M. Manheim

Enrique Iglesias

1975—

Singer, Songwriter

Enrique Iglesias catapulted to fame in the 1990s, holding a leading place among a new generation of Spanish-speaking pop stars whose music combines romantic ballads, hot Latin dance rhythms, and American rock influences. The son of globally-famous Latin crooner Julio Iglesias, Enrique Iglesias has charted an independent course to his musical career, breaking into the recording industry by using a pseudonym to dispel any notions of riding on his father's coattails. In the course of his brief career, the Spanish-born, American-reared singer with the husky baritone and smoldering good looks has racked up a Grammy award, broken Latin music sales records, landed a role in a Hollywood movie, and evoked the sort of adulation among female fans once associated with a young Frank Sinatra or a hip-swiveling Elvis Presley.

Enrique Iglesias was born on May 8, 1975, in Madrid, Spain, to Julio Iglesias, the legendary singer, and Isabel Preysler, a Philippine-born journalist. Julio Iglesias, who recorded the classic 1984 duet with Willie Nelson "To All the Girls I've Loved Before" has sold more than 200 million albums worldwide, earning him a place in the *Guinness Book of World Records*.

When Enrique was four, his parents divorced. For the next five years, Enrique and his older siblings—sister Chabeli and brother Julio Jr., also a singer—lived in Spain with their mother. Then Preysler became concerned that her children were in danger of being kidnapped, so she sent them to Miami to live with their father. Julio, however, was frequently gone on business, leaving the children to the care of the nanny, Elvira Olivares. Enrique later dedicated his first album to Olivares.

Secretly Dreamed of Singing

From the time he was a child, Enrique Iglesias dreamed of being a singer but kept his ambitions a secret from his parents. "I never told them because writing was like my own little diary—it was so private, so personal, " he said in a *Rolling Stone* interview in 2000 with Jancee Dunn.

As a teenager in Miami, Enrique spent his time jet-skiing, windsurfing, and listening to American rock and pop music. He and his friends found inspiration in the likes of Foreigner, Journey, Dire Straits, John Mellencamp, Billy Joel, and Bruce Springsteen. While his father attracted hordes of female fans, the teenaged

At a Glance . . .

Born Enrique Iglesias Preysler on May 8, 1975, in Madrid, Spain; son of Julio Iglesias (a singer) and Isabel Preysler (a Philippine-born journalist). *Education*—University of Miami, attended.

Career: Singer and songwriter. Albums: *Enrique Iglesias* 1995; *Vivir*, 1997; *Cosas Del Amor*, 1998; *Bailamos* (*We Dance*) 1999; *Best Hits 1999*; *Enrique*, 1999; *Escape*, 2001; feature film debut, *OnceUpon a Time in Mexico*, 2002.

Awards: World Music Award, Hispanic Artist of the Year, 1996; Billboard Award, Artist of the Year, 1996-97; Grammy Award, Best Latin Pop Performance for *Enrique Iglesias*),1997; Billboard Award, Best Latin Pop Artist, 1998; *People Weekly*, Spanish-language edition, "Sexiest Man Alive.&rdquo, 1998; VH1 *Vogue* Fashion Award, Most Fashionable Artist, Male, 2000; CCTV-MTV Music Honors, Male International Artist of the Year, Beijing, China, 2000; American Music Award,, Favorite Latin Artist, 1999, 2001, 2002; numerous others.

Address: *Record company*—Interscope Records, 2220 Colorado Avenue, Santa Monica, CA 90404

Enrique had trouble getting dates. "In high school I probably got rejected 70 percent of the time, " he told *Rolling Stone*. " I was too skinny and small. I ended up going to the prom by myself."

Iglesias began writing songs and playing music in a friend's garage but enrolled in the University of Miami to study business administration. In 1994, his sophomore year, he dropped out of college to pursue his musical aspirations, keeping the news a secret from his parents. When Julio reportedly learned of his son's ambitions from an industry insider at a cocktail party, he was displeased. "I told him I was sorry," Iglesias recalled in *People Weekly*. "I said, 'Look, this is exactly what I've always wanted to do. Just let me do it my way, please.'"

Iglesias contacted Fernan Martinez, a music industry acquaintance, who, upon hearing the young singer perform, urged him to make a demo tape. Iglesias used the pseudonym of Enrique Martinez to keep his identity as Julio's son a secret. For the next few months, Fernan Martinez sent the tape to various labels but was unable to drum up any interest. "I felt bad, you know,"

Iglesias later recalled in an interview with *CD Now*, " but at the same time I said, 'Good, if I make it, it will be because of my music and not because of my last name.'"

Finally Fonovisa Records, a small Los Angeles independent known primarily as a regional Mexican imprint, expressed an interest. "The voice was very masculine and different," recalled Guillermo Santiso, Fonovisa's president/CEO in *Billboard*. Santiso also reportedly liked the enclosed photograph of the handsome singer. Upon being informed of Iglesias's true identity, Santiso signed him to a three-album deal worth $1 million and won financial support from Fonovisa's parent company, Mexican media giant Televisa, for a massive promotional campaign. The first batch of radio spots identified the young singer only as Enrique to keep his identity as Julio's son under wraps. A promotional blitz followed, with Iglesias granting hundreds of interviews in both English and Spanish.

The singer took great pains to distinguish himself from his famous father. "Please do not introduce me as the son of Julio Iglesias," he said in *People Weekly*. "I'm very proud of my father, but when you read *Billboard* now, you see Enrique Iglesias." The two appealed to different generations, he later explained in an interview with MTV.

Sold Millions

All the money and hard work paid off. Iglesias's first album—the Spanish-language *Enrique Iglesias* released in September of 1995—eventually sold almost five million copies worldwide, according to Rock on the Net. The album was certified gold, then platinum. In 1996 Iglesias won the *Billboard* Award for Album of the Year, New Artist, as well as a World Music Award. In January of 1997, Iglesias released his follow-up album, *Vivir* (*Living*), which scored two top 10 singles on the *Billboard* charts. The following month the young singer won a Grammy for his first album. In January of 1998, according to Rock on the Net, he was nominated for an American Music Award for Favorite Latin Artist but lost out to his father.

Iglesias released his third album, *Cosas Del Amor* (*Things of Love*), in 1998. *Newsmakers* reported that Iglesias was the only artist to simultaneously top the Hot 100 Dance/Club Play, Hot Latin Tracks, and Latin 50 album charts in 1998. In a mere three years, Iglesias had sold more than 17 million Spanish-language albums, more than anyone else during that period, according to allmusic.com. The United States was his biggest market. In January of 1999, Iglesias won an American Music Award for Favorite Latin Artist Performance. That summer, Iglesias scored a pop radio hit with "Bailamos"— translated as "We Dance"—a hypnotic dance song featured in the film *Wild, Wild West* starring Will Smith. The song hit number onr on the top 40 charts for three weeks in September of 1999. As Iglesias's records topped the charts, many of the studios that had rejected the singer early in his career tried to woo him. BMG and Warner ardently courted Iglesias, but the young artist chose Universal Music Group/Interscope Records instead. In 1999 Igesias left Fonovisa for a six-album with Interscope worth an estimated $44 million, according to *Billboard*.

In November of 1999 Iglesias released *Enrique*, his first album in English and his first with Interscope Records. Like many artists with cross-cultural appeal, Iglesias included Spanish-language versions of a few of his songs on the album. *Enrique* brought the singer's global sales to more than 23 million, according to allmusic.com. Several singles from the album joined "Bailamos" on the charts: "Rhythm Divine,&rrdquo; "Be With You," "Could I Have This Kiss Forever," and "Sad Eyes." *Enrique* achieved gold or platinum status in an extraordinary 32 countries.

Earned Recognition Through "Latin Explosion"

Like fellow pop stars Ricky Martin and Marc Anthony, Iglesias established himself in the Spanish-language market before releasing his first English-language album. Iglesias and other rising stars appealed to a new generation of Spanish-speaking youth. Many of these young people's parents had grown up listening to Julio Iglesias. "It had gotten to the point in the Latino music market where it wasn't cool for the young kids to listen to it, " Iglesias told Richard Harrington of *Newsday*. "We had a lot of great singers, but they were in their 40s and 50s. Suddenly you start getting a bunch of young Latino singers, and then the young listeners started getting into it." In an interview with MTV, he added, " I'd be in an American restaurant and suddenly the people that did the valet parking, the people in the kitchen, who were Spanish or Mexican or Puerto Rican would be like, 'Can I have your autograph? ' All the Americans would be like, 'Who the hell is that?'"

Then, in 1999, the commercial breakthrough year for Latin music, Iglesias and other Spanish-speaking artists soared to the top of the pop charts, prompting some observers to speak of a "Latin Explosion." Iglesias, however, disliked the term. "I'm proud of who I am and where I come from," he said in an interview with MTV. "The only word I don't like there is 'explosion,' because when there is an explosion it's not bound to last too long. I think it all comes down to the artist and the song"

The young pop star also disliked the term "crossover," widely used to describe Spanish-speaking singers who moved into the English-language market. "'Crossover' ....what does it mean?" he mused to Mercedes Garcia-Aguilar of *CD Now*. "I grew up listening to English pop and rock, and I feel comfortable singing in the English language."

Although sometimes compared to fellow Latin pop star Ricky Martin, Iglesias has become recognized for certain qualities of his own, including a "raspy baritone, " flamenco dance rhythms, and ballads bearing the influence of American rock bands such as Journey and Foreigner. One of those ballads, "Hero," was written as a love song but acquired special significance in the wake of the September 11th terrorist attacks. "I'm nothing like him!" Iglesias said about Ricky Martin in a *Sun* Newspaper Online chat posted on Abstracts.net in January of 2002. "Come on, 'Hero'? 'Hero' and the rest of my music is very different to anything by Ricky Martin."

Iglesias considered himself a pop singer who sometimes sang in Spanish rather than a " Latin singer." Latin music, he said, encompassed a variety of styles— salsa, flamenco, and meringue, among them. While some observers distinguished Iglesias's style from Ricky Martin's adrenaline-charged dance pop and Marc Anthony's salsa rhythms, others saw them as one group of Latin musicians. In an interview with *CD Now*, Iglesias said that grouping the three artists together—Marc Anthony and Ricky Martin, both from Puerto Rico, and himself from Spain—was like "saying there's three guys from Ohio who are singers, and they start doing well; is that an Ohio music trend?"

Dubbed Sexiest Man Alive

Like his father, Iglesias attracted throngs of adoring female fans. "He has the same appeal his father has, but to a younger audience," Tony Campos, an executive with Miami's radio station WAMR, said in *People Weekly*. "He stands onstage, and the girls go crazy."

The Spanish language edition of *People Weekly* dubbed Enrique Iglesias the "Sexiest Man Alive" in 1998. Two years later, *Vogue* awarded him its "Most Fashionable Artist, Male" award as a result of "his innate coolness rather than any interest in being a clotheshorse." Although repeatedly described as a "heartthrob, " the singer, himself, has eschewed the ethnic stereotyping of the "Latin lover" label. "The word 'lover' I just think is corny, " Iglesias told rolling-stone.com.

Still, female fans clearly viewed him as a pop idol, showering him with roses, stuffed animals, jewelry, cologne, and phone numbers. During one promotional appearance in Toronto mentioned in enrique-online.com, a teenaged girl bit a security guard's hand. In the United States, fans reportedly mobbed the singer during a *Tonight Show* taping. "They actually can pull very hard, " he told *Rolling Stone*. "One pulls one way, the other pulls another way, another pulls the other way. " But Iglesias, who repeatedly described his female fans as "great" seemed unfazed. When asked by *Rolling Stone* if he ever got frightened, he replied, "Nah. Give me a break. What are they gonna do?"

Rumors Persisted

Despite his spectacular popularity, Iglesias faced continuing rumors and controversies. Reporters continually asked about Iglesias's relationship with his father, sometimes implying friction between the two men. In addition, some observers questioned the extent of Iglesias's talent.

In June of 2000 radio show host Howard Stern, whose controversial style has earned him the epithet of "shock jock," suggested on the air that Iglesias could not sing after listening to a tape of Iglesias singing off-key. Although Iglesias said that he was probably just fooling around, he nevertheless booked himself on the Howard Stern's show to dispel the rumors.

On the show, Iglesias performed acoustic versions of two songs, "Rhythm Divine" and "Be With You, " prompting everyone in the studio to applaud, according to the transcript posted on enrique-online.com. The singer also responded to questions from the host about his relationship with his father, describing it as one of "healthy competition" rather than rancor. At the end of Iglesias's performance, Stern declared, "You can sing."

"Hero" Soothed Terrified Nation

Iglesias's second English-language album, Escape, released in September of 2001, marked a musical departure from his earlier work. Escape featured more of an American arena-rock influence, showing the singer's affection for ballads by such 1980s groups as Journey and Foreigner. "This is the album that is the most like me," he said, describing Escape on his official website.

In a move unusual by industry standards, Iglesias decided to release a ballad, "Hero," rather than an up-tempo song as the first single from Escape. "Hero," which was written as a love song, hit the airwaves in September of 2001, captured the imagination of a nation grappling with the terrorist attacks of September 11th. In response to the September 11th tragedy, some radio stations reportedly played "Hero," with news clips and excerpts of a speech by President George W. Bush's talking over it. "It kinda bothered me a little bit in the beginning because I never gave permission, and that wasn't the meaning of the song," Iglesias told Gary Graff of CD Now. "And then I came to think, 'You know what? It's a love song. It's a song about helping the one you love. It's completely logical at a time like this. '" On September 21, 2001 Iglesias performed "Hero," on America: A Tribute to Heroes, a two-hour star-studded telecast to raise money for the United Way's September 11 fund.

Critics, however, gave both "Hero," and Escape mixed reviews. " Nothing here is even irritatingly catchy like his breakthrough hit, ' Bailamos,' said a review in People Weekly. "Such up-tempo Latin-lite numbers as the title tune, 'Love to See You Cry, ' and 'I Will Survive' (no relation to the disco chestnut) are as bland as white bread. The whimpering ballad 'Hero' only magnifies his trembly vocals." A critic for Knight/Ridder/Tribune News Service was similarly negative, criticizing Iglesias for "those little cries he omits at the end of a line" to convey emotion. Nevertheless, Iglesias's popularity remained strong. He had the clout to attract such high-profile actresses as Jennifer Love Hewitt and Shannon Elizabeth and tennis star Anna Kournikova to roles in his music videos. In January of 2002, Iglesias won an American Music Award for Favorite Latin Artist.

Landed Role in Film

Iglesias also had the star power to land a role in the 2002 movie Once Upon a Time in Mexico, the third installment in Robert Rodriguez's story of El Mariachi, a wandering guitar playing vigilante, starring Antonio Banderas. In the movie, Iglesias plays one of three mariachis involved in a plot to rescue the president of Mexico.

Iglesias spoke to MTV about deciding to take the role, "I loved his [Robert Rodriguez's] movies and I'm not an actor, but he said, 'you don't have to be an actor. You can do it, '" Iglesias recalled. "I said, 'It can't be that hard to pick up a couple of guns and shoot.' "

Music, however, remained his primary passion. "Music is an addiction, " he told Vogue in 2000. "I'm so addicted that I keep on doing it." When Rolling Stone's Jancee Dunn asked Iglesias what he did to relax, he said, "Sleep." He toured tirelessly, often appearing in a different city daily. During one concert tour, a rotating crane reportedly carried Iglesias in a circular motion 40 feet above the crowd. The Latin pop star set lofty goals for himself. In January of 1996, Iglesias told the New York Times Magazine, "My dream is for my music to be heard in every corner of the world. I'd like to be in an elevator in Hong Kong and hear my songs." Six years later, after performing in countries around the world, he told the Sun in an online chat posted on Abstracts.net: "Right now I haven't even reached the climax of my musical career, so I still have a long way to go. I still feel like I have a lot of music in me that I want to do."

Selected discography

Enrique Iglesias, Fonovisa, 1995.
Vivir, Fonovisa, 1997.
Cosas Del Amor, Fonovisa, 1998.
Bailamos (includes "Bailamos"), Fonovisa,1999.
Best Hits, Enrique Iglesias, Fonovisa, 1999.
Enrique(includes "Bailamos," "Be With You," "Rhythm Divine," "Could I Have This Kiss Forever," and "Sad Eyes"), Interscope, 1999.
Escape (includes "Hero", "Escape"), Interscope 2001.

Sources

Books

Current Biography Yearbook, H.W. Wilson Co., 1999, p. 282-283.
Newsmakers 2000, Issue 1, Gale Group, 2001.

Periodicals

Billboard, July 19, 1997, p. 1 October 30, 2001, p. 4.
Knight-Ridder/Tribune News Service, June 2, 2001, p. K1432, Oct. 30, 2001, p. K6736.
*New York Times Magazine*January 21, 1996, p. 14
*Newsday*March 15, 1999, p. B6.
People Weekly, April 22, 1996, p. 144 May 11, 1998, p. 141 Nov. 5, 2001, p. 43+, p.
RollingStone, February 3, 2000, p. 28

*South Florida Sun Sentinel*February 22, 2002, "Showtime" p. 36
Vogue November 2000, p. 226

On-line

Abstracts.net, http://abstracts.net
AMG All Music Guide, http://allmusic.com
Biography Resource Center, http://galenet.galegroup.com
CDNow, http://cdnow.com
Enrique Iglesias, Official Website, http://enriqueiglesias.com
Enrique-Online.com, http://silverwing. net/enrique/press/
MTV.com, http://www.mtv.com
Rock on the Net, http://www.rockonthenet.com
RollingStone.com, http://www.rollingstone.com

—Joan Axelrod-Contrada

Frida Kahlo

1907—1954

Artist

One primary impetus behind modernist movements in art is masculine and impersonal: many artists of the 20th century sought to smash rules and stylistic barriers and to break through to new principles of composition and subject matter. In the work of the Mexican artist Frida Kahlo, however, modernist breakthroughs were placed at the service of artistic autobiography. Kahlo lived a short life that was dramatic in the extreme and found a new visual language to express her experiences on canvas. An artist of only moderate repute during her own lifetime, Kahlo gained new admirers at the century's end.

One of six sisters, Kahlo was born Magdalena Carmen Frieda Kahlo y Calderón in Coyoacán, Mexico, near Mexico City, on July 6, 1907. The complexities of her life began with her family background: her father was a photographer of German and Hungarian Jewish ancestry, and her mother, Matilde Calderón, was a Mexican native, of mixed Spanish and Indian background, with little formal education and a strong devotion to the Catholic religion that caused friction between mother and daughter. Kahlo was always closer to her father, who encouraged her artistic pursuits, but throughout her life she identified herself with Native American

culture; some scholars have interpreted her art in terms of an effort to reconcile the varied influences brought to bear during her childhood.

Affected by Mexican Revolution

Kahlo suffered a bout with polio that left her mildly disabled by age seven; she was left with a limp and a deformed spine. Nevertheless, her father urged her to participate in physical activities that were extraordinarily unusual for a Mexican girl at the time—soccer, swimming, and even wrestling and boxing. Another major formative event of Kahlo's youth was the Mexican Revolution of 1910, after which ideals of equality and a communitarian state became ingrained in Mexican culture. "The clear and precise emotions of the 'Mexican Revolution' were the reason why, at the age of 13, I joined the Communist youth," Kahlo wrote in her diary later in life.

Kahlo's father also encouraged her academically, and in 1922, held back by polio, she entered an elite Mexican high school, the National Preparatory School. That year, the rising Mexican artist Diego Rivera, still several years away from the epic leftist murals that would make him famous in the United States, was hired

At a Glance . . .

Born Magdalena Carmen Frieda Kahlo y Calderón in Coyoacán, Mexico, near Mexico City, Mexico, on July 6, 1907; daughter of a German-Hungarian Jewish photographer father and a Native Mexican mother; survived polio during childhood; married artist Diego Rivera, 1929; died in Mexico City, July 13, 1954.*Education:* Attended National Preparatory School, Mexico City, 1922-25.

Career: Painted extensively during recuperation from serious injuries sustained in bus accident, 1925-27; accompanied Rivera to U.S. and formed mature style of her own, early 1930s; solo exhibitions in New York and Paris, late 1930s; health declined as a result of numerous operations to correct problems resulting from bus accident, but remained prolific through 1940s; first solo exhibition in Mexico City, 1953; critical reputation began steady ascent soon after her death, accelerating in 1970s.

to paint a mural at the school. Smitten, Kahlo declared to friends that she wanted to have Rivera's child. Rivera spurned her romantic advances at first, but encouraged her as a painter.

Then, in 1925, Kahlo's leg was broken in 11 places when a bus she was riding in Mexico City was split in two by a streetcar; her pelvis and spine were also broken. For the rest of her life Kahlo was troubled by chronic pain. She would also be forced to undergo surgeries of increasing severity. The only positive outcome of the accident was that Kahlo had plenty of time to devote to painting during her long convalescence. Back on her feet some two years later, Kahlo sought out Rivera and asked him to critique her work. This time, although Rivera was more than 20 years older than Kahlo and outweighed her by 200 pounds, romance bloomed and the two were married in 1929.

Suffered A Miscarriage

Kahlo would later refer to the marriage as the second accident in her life, but her own talent grew during its early years. Accompanying her husband to Michigan as he worked on a giant set of murals depicting industry and its effects at the Detroit Institute of Arts, she painted such masterworks as *Henry Ford Hospital.* That painting, rooted in a miscarriage Kahlo suffered at the time, showed a woman in a hospital bed, crying an oversized tear; her fingers are connected by tendonlike ribbons to various surreal images including a fetus and

a metal vise. Such works announced Kahlo's mature style, at once fantastically imaginative and highly personal. Surrealism was a major part of that style; although Kahlo denied any connection between her and the Spanish-French surrealists led by Salvador Dalí, she sometimes allowed her works to be included in exhibitions of surrealist art.

Indeed, such Kahlo works as *My Birth,* in which an adult Kahlo is seen emerging from her mother's womb, seem imbued with the psychoanalytic concerns that provided surrealism's underpinnings, but Kahlo's own ideology was more public-spirited. Whatever ugly disagreements might flair between Kahlo and Rivera over the course of their 25-year marriage (interrupted by a one-year divorce in 1939 and 1940), they shared the conception that they were making art for the public good. As an art teacher in the1940s, Kahlo organized her students into mural-painting brigades. Kahlo was capable of sympathetic portraiture; her *Portrait of Luther Burbank* (1931) portrays its subject as the top half of a living tree. But overall her works, mostly painted during the 1930s and 1940s, were predominantly self-portraits of one kind or another.

Those self-portraits gained their intensity in part from the turbulence of Kahlo's married life, which was marked by extramarital liaisons on both sides. Rivera had an affair with Kahlo's sister Cristina, and Kahlo retaliated by becoming involved with, among others, American artist Georgia O'Keeffe and the exiled Soviet leader Leon Trotsky. Kahlo suffered several more miscarriages, which are thought to have been aftereffects of the 1925 bus accident. After more than 30 operations, Kahlo had also developed an addiction to painkillers.

Madonna Collected Kahlo Works

Kahlo had solo exhibitions in New York and Paris in the late 1930s and in Mexico City in 1953, by which time her health was in serious decline. Her right leg was amputated at the knee that year, sending her into a final downward spiral; her death on July 13, 1954 (in the same house she had lived in all her life, now a Kahlo museum) may have resulted from a blood clot in the lungs or from an intentional drug overdose, but in either case released her from extreme misery. With each decade after her death her work gained appreciation from young art enthusiasts—including pop superstar Madonna—and by the century's end she was arguably as well known as Rivera.

Mexican, shaped by disabilities, bisexual, inexhaustibly creative—all these ideas describe Frida Kahlo, but neither separately nor even together do they suffice to capture her spirit. Kahlo was very much a 20th-century woman in her determination to carry out her own artistic vision. But with the 2002 release of a major film biography of Kahlo, starring actress Salma Hayek, a fresh round of interest in Kahlo's life and career seemed ready to persist well into the 21st century.

Sources

Books

Dictionary of Hispanic Biography, Gale, 1996.
Herrera, Hayden, *Frida Kahlo: A Biography,* Harper & Row, 1983.
Kahlo, Frida, *The Diary of Frida Kahlo: An Intimate: Self-Portrait,* Abrams, 1996.

Periodicals

Art in America, January 1993, p. 35; March 1996, p. 31; September 2001, p. 168.
People, February 12, 1996, p. 83.
Variety, January 1, 2001, p. 6.

—James M. Manheim

Jennifer Lopez

1970—

Actor, singer, dancer

Jennifer Lopez is what is known in the entertainment business as a "triple threat"—she can dance, sing, and act. She was a dancing Fly Girl on the 1990s television show *In Living Color,* and got her break in her lead role as *Selena,* the 1997 film about the murdered Tejano pop star. She became the first Latina actress to have a lead role in a major Hollywood film since Rita Hayworth, and the highest-paid Latina actress ever. Her early films include *Anaconda, U Turn, Jack,* and *Out of Sight.*

While some actors endure embarrassing results when they try to make the leap from acting to singing, Lopez proved in 1999 that she was not one of them. Her debut album, *On the 6,* produced the hit "If You Had My Love" and sold over eight million copies. Lopez's name has become inescapable in the media. In 2001 Lopez became the first actress to have a film, the romantic comedy *The Wedding Planner,* and music album, her sophomore release, *J.Lo,* hit number one in the same week. Later that year, the success of the psychological thriller *The Cell* proved that Lopez's box-office power was worth her paycheck, valued in 2002 at over two million dollars per film. Not one to rest on her laurels, Lopez is constantly making progress toward her next goal. "I want everything. I want family. I want to do good work. I want love. I want to be comfortable," she said in a 1998 interview with *Entertainment Weekly.* "I think of people like Cher and Bette Midler and Diana Ross and Barbra Streisand. That's always been the kind of career I'd hoped to have. I want it all."

Lopez was born July 24, 1970 in the Bronx neighborhood of Castle Hill. She is the second of three daughters of David, a computer technician, and Guadalupe Lopez, a kindergarten teacher. Though Lopez's parents were born in the same Puerto Rican town, David and Guadalupe Lopez did not meet until they lived in Castle Hill. They were strict with their girls and instilled a strong work ethic in them—no one in the family was allowed to miss a day of school, work, or church. "Our parents had a strong work ethic—there wasn't really any other way," Lynda Lopez told *Rolling Stone.* Lopez's parents also stressed assimilation—the need to speak English, to fit into the mainstream, to succeed. "Spanish was not something we spoke a lot of in the house," David Lopez told *Rolling Stone.* "They got that from their grandmothers." Though he worked nights throughout her childhood, Lopez idolized her father for working hard to provide for his family. "I'm a

At a Glance . . .

Born Jennifer Lopez on July 24, 1970, in Bronx, NY to David (a computer technician) and Guadalupe Lopez (a teacher); married Ojani Noa, 1997 (divorced 1998); married Cris Judd (a dancer), 2001.

Career: Actress, dancer, singer. Film appearances include *My Family/Mi Familia,* 1995; *Money Train,* 1995; *Jack,* 1996; *Blood and Wine,* 1997; *Selena,* 1997; *Anaconda,* 1997; *U Turn,* 1997; *Out of Sight,* 1998; *Antz,* 1998; *The Cell,* 2000; *The Wedding Planner,* 2001; *Angel Eyes,* 2001*Enough,* 2002; *The Chambermaid,* 2002; *Gigli,* 2003. Television appearances include "El Show de Cristina," 1989; "In Living Color," 1990; *Nurses on the Line: The Crash of Flight 7,* 1993; "Second Chances," 1993; "Hotel Malibu," 1994; "South Central," 1994; *Janet Jackson: Design of a Decade 1986-1996,* 1996; "TFI Friday," 1999; *VH1/ Vogue Fashion Awards,* 2000; *MTV Video Music Awards 2000,* 2000; "Parkinson," 2001; "Rove Live," 2001; *MTV Video Music Awards 2001,* 2001; *Jennifer Lopez in Concert,* 2001; *Royal Variety Performance 2001,* 2001; *MTV Icon: Janet Jackson,* 2001; *73rd Annual Academy Awards,* 2001; *USO Special for the Troops,* 2002; *Hello, He Lied & Other Truths From the Hollywood Trenches,* 2002. Sound recordings include *On the 6,* and the single "If You Had My Love,"1999; *J.Lo,* and the singles "I'm Real" and "Love Don't Cost a Thing," 2001.

Addresses: *Agent*—International Creative Management, 8942 Wilshire Blvd., Beverly Hills, CA 90211.

daddy's girl; he's the love of my life," she said in a 2001 interview with *Rolling Stone*'s Anthony Bozza. In 1998, after their kids were grown and gone, the Lopezes divorced.

Grew Up In Musical Household

There was always some kind of music on in the Lopez household. Guadalupe Lopez was a fan of many genres, including the girl groups from her own childhood—the Supremes, the Shirelles, and the Ronettes. She spent Sundays while her daughters were growing up listening to disc jockey Casey Kasem's Top Forty countdown. She often would gather her daughters to

watch Barbra Streisand musicals and sing, or act out songs from *West Side Story* in their living room. David Lopez was a fan of doo-wop music, but salsa, meringue, and rock were also heard in the house. Lopez's sisters are also musical—Lynda, her younger sister, is a radio disc jockey, VH1 VJ, and entertainment reporter on a New York morning television show, while her older sister Leslie sings opera. Because her parents were strict, Lopez spent much of what she called "the boyfriend years" in *Rolling Stone* sneaking around to meet up with first-love David Cruz, whom she remained with from the time she was 16 until she was 25. "I was always climbing out windows, jumping off roofs, and he was sneaking up," she said. "It was crazy."

Though father David Lopez sees talent in all of his girls, he acknowledged in *Rolling Stone* that "Jennifer is the one with the drive to put it all together. She was always very competitive. She's had that drive since she was a baby." Dance and singing lessons began for her at age five. She spent her entire academic career in Catholic school, and admits she still prays regularly. She was a driven student and natural athlete in gymnastics, softball, and tennis. She went out for the track team, though she had no experience. Her father feared that, new to the sport, she would be outclassed, but Lopez rose to the challenge and ended up competing nationally. "Basically, anything she wants to do, she'll be as successful as you can at it," sister Lynda Lopez told *Rolling Stone.* "That's the kind of person she is."

After she graduated high school, Lopez pursued her talent for dance. She split her time between her job at a law office, taking dance classes, and dancing in Manhattan clubs at night. Though she did not—and still does not—drink alcohol, her parents disapproved of her working nights so far from home and feared she was associating with a potentially dangerous crowd. She moved out of the house and was able to pay her rent with occasional work as a dancer.

Landed Fly-Girl Gig

The aspiring dancer's first steady paycheck came when she landed a spot as a "Fly Girl" dancer on the Wayans brothers' sketch-comedy show *In Living Color* on the Fox television network. On the show, she and the other Fly Girls danced between comedy skits and when musical guests were featured. *In Living Color* was filmed in Los Angeles, so Lopez was uprooted from her New York home and forced to move to the West Coast, where she was "miserable," she told *Rolling Stone.* David Cruz moved there to be with her, and stayed for four years. With his support, Lopez was happy and better able to work, she told *Rolling Stone.* Lopez's stability during that time parlayed into the earliest successes of her career. She got television acting parts in the made-for-TV movie *Nurses on the Line: The Crash of Flight 7* and on the series *Second Chances* and *Hotel Malibu,* but both were flops. She danced for

Janet Jackson on tour and in Jackson's video for the popular song "That's the Way Loves Goes" in 1995.

Lopez broke onto the big screen in 1995, in the drama *My Family/Mi Familia* and opposite Wesley Snipes in the action film *Money Train.* She appeared in Francis Ford Coppola's 1996 comedy *Jack,* and the 1997 thriller *Blood and Wine.* However, the actress's first big break came when she secured the lead role in *Selena,* based on the true story of the slain Tejano pop singer's life. Lopez accepted the public marriage proposal of then-boyfriend Ojani Noa, a model-turned-restaurateur, at the wrap party for *Selena* in 1996 in San Antonio, Texas. The two were married in 1997, but divorced after just a year, unable to endure the pressures of Lopez's rapid rise to stardom. In two years, wrote Degen Pener in *Entertainment Weekly,* Lopez "rocketed from up-and-coming actress to Hollywood's super-diva of 1998."

After *Selena,* Lopez had a steady stream of work. She played a documentary film director in the horror film *Anaconda,* about the world's largest and deadliest snake. She took a steamy role in Oliver Stone's 1997 film noir, *U Turn,* as a young woman who seduces and hires a drifter, played by Sean Penn, to murder her husband, played by Nick Nolte. Lopez's two-million dollar paycheck for role opposite George Clooney in Steven Soderbergh's *Out of Sight* made Lopez the highest-paid Latina actress in Hollywood history. Lopez played Karen Sisco, a U.S. Marshal assigned to capture two escaped convicts, played by Clooney and Ving Rhames. She is first kidnapped by the duo, then is charged with tracking them to Detroit, where they are planning their next big heist. Her romantic notions ultimately interfere with her job as she becomes attracted to Clooney's character. Lopez's turn in the psychological drama *The Cell,* opposite Vince Vaughn, proved she could "open" a movie after the film became a box-office blockbuster.

Known for Curvaceous Physique

The word "callipygian" came into common usage as journalists struggled to describe Lopez's curvaceous backside—the word is used to describe one as having shapely buttocks. Though she laughs at rumors that she has her body insured for one-billion dollars, Lopez is as heralded for her physical beauty as she is for her talents as singer, dancer, or actor. Once called "La Guitarra," for her guitar-shaped body, Lopez is the only woman in the world to have twice been voted number one in *FHM* magazine's "100 Sexiest Women" list. She is a regular on *People* magazine's annual "50 Most Beautiful People In The World" list, and was voted to have the best female body in the British *Celebrity Bodies* magazine. At the 2000 Grammy Awards, jaws dropped when she showed up wearing a risqué, barely-there dress that "showed as much as a dress could possibly show without actually showing anything,"

according to *Vanity Fair.* Fans missed out on seeing Lopez's heavenly body in *Antz,* the 1998 animated film that featured only the actress's voice.

Once she had conquered Hollywood, Lopez—known as "J.Lo" and "La Lopez"—made moves to fulfill her lifelong dream of singing. Many an actor has suffered the indignity of trying to rebuild a film career after a failed turn in the music industry. Such was not the case with Lopez. She spent a full year in the studio, working diligently on her debut album, *On the 6,* named for the train she used to take from her Bronx home to Manhattan. Built on Latin soul, pop, R&B, pop, and dance influences, the album sold over eight million copies and launched the popular single "If You Had My Love."

At the start of her career, Lopez had a rocky relationship with the media. She was reputed to be a difficult interview. One Hollywood public-relations firm declined to represent her, so bad was her reputation. She often was irritated or angry in interviews, and used them as an opportunity to lambaste everyone from actress Gwyneth Paltrow to former co-star Wesley Snipes. Over time, she softened that image, and learned to discuss only what she felt comfortable talking about—which did not include her love life, the subject of much tabloid and media attention. "In this business," she told Anthony Bozza in *Rolling Stone,* "Your soul is so public and open and out there for everybody. There is no privacy. At the end of the day, you really have to fight to keep certain things sacred so that they survive."

Tangled With Law, Walked Down Aisle

Though she maintained for some time that she and hip-hop mogul Sean "P. Diddy" Combs were "just friends," she told *Entertainment Weekly* in 1998, the two went public with their romance in 1999. Her hard-earned good-girl image took some hits in December of 1999, when she was arrested with Combs after a shooting at a New York City nightclub. She was released after 14 hours, but Combs ultimately was tried for possession of a stolen gun. Combs's trial was scheduled to begin just a week before the release of Lopez's second album, *J.Lo.*

Lopez and Combs announced their breakup in 2001. At that time she was the first actress to have both a hit movie, *The Wedding Planner,* and album, *J.Lo,* at number one at the same time. The album was "far superior" to *On the 6,* according to Anthony Bozza in *Rolling Stone,* and its multi-platinum sales status was fueled by such singles as "Love Don't Cost a Thing," and "I'm Real." Lopez played a wedding planner in the romantic comedy *The Wedding Planner* opposite actor Matthew McConaughey. Lopez planned her own wedding in 2001, when she and dancer Cris Judd tied the knot in a small ceremony. Her third album, *J to tha L-O!: The Remixes*, released in 2002, also reached platinum.

Selected filmography

My Family/Mi Familia, 1995.
Money Train, 1995.
Jack, 1996.
Blood and Wine, 1997.
Selena, 1997.
Anaconda, 1997.
U Turn, 1997.
Out of Sight, 1998.
Antz, 1998.
The Cell, 2000.
The Wedding Planner, 2001.
Angel Eyes, 2001.
Enough, 2002.

Selected discography

On the 6, Work/Sony, 1999.
J.Lo, Sony, 2001.
J to tha L-O!: The Remixes, 2002.

Sources

Periodicals

Cosmopolitan, March 1999, p. 202.
Entertainment Weekly, October 9, 1998, p. 28; January 7, 2000, p. 8.
In Style, June 1, 1999, p. 276.
Newsweek, December 20, 1999, p. 84; January 10, 2000, p. 58; January 29, 2001, p. 63.
People, May 10, 1999, p. 187; September 13, 1999, p. 71; March 13, 2000, p. 146; May 14, 2001, p. 88.
Redbook, January 2002, p. 58.
Rolling Stone, February 15, 2001, p. 44.
Time, February 5, 2001, p. 87.
Vanity Fair, June 2001, p. 166.

On-line

All Music Guide, www.amg.com
Internet Movie Database, www.imdb.com
Rolling Stone, www.rollingstone.com

—Brenna Sanchez

Nancy Lopez

1957—

Golfer

Hall-of-Fame golfer Nancy Lopez, who began playing golf at an early age, has won numerous championships including the LPGA Championship. Lopez has received many awards and is known for her phenomenal early rise to fame. Her enduring skill on the course, and her open and friendly demeanor has garnered her many fans across the nation.

An Early Success

Lopez, who grew up in Roswell, New Mexico, began playing golf at the age of eight, with her father, Domingo Lopez, an avid golfer, as her coach. Four years later, when she was twelve, she won the New Mexico Women's Amateur tournament. Lopez told Richard Lemon in *People Weekly,* "I was so scared I always threw up. I carried a trash can with me. My dad told me, 'If you're going to play golf, you've got to get over being sick.' I didn't want to quit, so I decided to get over it."

Lopez also faced other obstacles to her progress. Because her family was of Mexican descent, her parents were not allowed to join the Roswell country club and she had to play in Albuquerque, 200 miles away.

A writer for *Latino Sports Legends* commented that her intense competitive drive and "the fact that she was a Mexican-American winning so many tournaments did not sit well with others, but that didn't discourage her."

In 1972 and 1974 Lopez won the USGA Junior Girls Championship. In 1975 she won the Western Junior three times, as well as the Mexican Amateur. Her high school did not have a girls' golf team, so she played on the boys' team and helped them win two state championships.

Lopez attended the University of Tulsa for two years in 1976 and 1977; during her time there, she won the Association of Intercollegiate Athletics for Women National Championship and was a member of the U.S. Curtis Cup and World Amateur teams. In 1976 she was named 1976 All-American and also won the university's Female Athlete of the Year award. After two years at the university, Lopez decided to leave to pursue a professional golf career. Although her career was an instant success, her mother died from a heart attack before ever seeing Lopez win a professional tournament. Lopez's father encouraged her to continue playing despite this tragedy.

Became Professional Golfer

In 1977 Lopez tied for second place at the U.S. Women's Open as an amateur; that same year, she was named LPGA Rookie of the Year. Although she turned pro later that year, her official LPGA rookie season was 1978. In that first season, Lopez won an astonishing five tournaments in a row and was the LPGA Champion. She told Mechelle Voepel in the *Knight-Ridder/ Tribune News Service,* "It just happened so easily; it seemed like everything I did was right. It was just a year that was magical for me." Lopez won against major players of the day, including Hall of Famers JoAnne Carner and Kathy Whitworth, veterans Jan Blalock and Donna Caponi, as well as younger players Pat Bradley, Hollis Stacy, Jan Stephenson and Amy Alcott. She told Voepel, "I did feel like I was in contention every week. I wasn't afraid to be aggressive; I wasn't really afraid of anything at that time." She also told Voepel, "I was just playing because I loved it. But I think now I can look back at that and say, 'Boy, did I have a great year and it was something that people will always remember.'"

In addition to being noted for her talent, Lopez quickly attracted the attention of fans, who appreciated her friendly demeanor. Lopez told Voepel that when she was fifteen, she had attended a men's pro tournament, where she hoped to get an autograph from a well-known player. She and another fan were waiting in line when the player snarled, "I don't have time for this," and walked away. Lopez vowed that if she ever became a pro, she would never act like that. It's a vow she has kept throughout her career.

Lopez met her first husband, sportscaster Tim Melton, in June of 1978, at the end of her phenomenal 1978

winning-streak. They married shortly afterwards and she continued to play well, winning eight of the nineteen tournaments she entered. However, her marriage to Melton was stressful, partly because of her long absences from home to play in tournaments and partly because, as she told Richard Lemon in *People Weekly,* "We just grew apart," and in 1981 they divorced. At the same time, her game had been also been deteriorating. Although she won a dozen championships from 1980 through 1984, Lopez felt flat. She told Frank Deford in *Sports Illustrated,* "Suddenly, I couldn't hit the ball where I wanted to, and I'd been able to do that since I was twelve. There were times when every day I'd go back to the hotel crying."

Won Her Third LPGA Championship

After her divorce, Lopez began dating baseball player Ray Knight, whom she married in October of 1982. Their harmonious relationship led her to tell Bruce Newman in *Sports Illustrated,* "I think if professional athletes were all married to other professional athletes, it would make for better marriages. Athletes are better suited to each other." Her second marriage was more harmonious than her first, and Lopez and Knight eventually had three daughters.

In 1985, the second year she won the LPGA Championship, Lopez was named *Golf Magazine*'s Player of the Year. Lopez told Deford that her new family life had contributed to the improvement in her game: "Maybe I'm playing so well again just because I'm happy. More than anything else, it's probably because now I have peace of mind, so I can just go off and play golf." In 1989 Lopez won the LPGA Championship for a third time and was inducted into the LPGA Hall of Fame.

The 1990s were difficult for Lopez, who did not win from 1994 to 1996. In April of 1997 she began playing well again again, and in that year she had her lowest stroke average (70.70) since 1989. At the U.S. Women's Open, Lopez came in as runner-up for the fourth time in her career. Typically, fans did not ask why she had come in second; Lopez told Voepel that instead, they said, "Oh, we loved watching you play!" and noted, "It sounded like I won, basically, because people were so supportive." Golf star Laura Davies commented, "Nancy is obviously the most popular player that's ever been in our game." In 1997 Lopez was given a Hispanic Heritage Award for her contributions to Hispanic culture.

Experienced Health Problems

In the late 1990s Lopez began experiencing severe pain in her knees, partly as a result of overuse, and partly from arthritis. She underwent surgery, physical therapy, and began using a knee brace during play, According to Leonard Shapiro in the *Washington Post,* Lopez said her knees were often stiff in the morning, but after she walked for a while, they loosened up. She played in a limited number of events in 1990 after undergoing knee surgery.

In 2000 her play was limited because she underwent gall bladder surgery. Her season-best finish was a tie for ninth place. In recent months, Lopez has worked to promote public awareness of arthritis, as well as cardiovascular disease, which runs in her family. She, and other golfers, play against each other to raise money for the American Stroke Association, a division of the American Heart Association. In addition, through changes in her own diet and exercise habits, she has reduced her own risk factors for cardiovascular disease. In 2001 Lopez and Knight opened Ashbrook Quail Preserve, a 600-acre tract of land in southwest Georgia that offers hunting and fishing tours for eight guests at a time. The preserve has a lodge, cabin, three stocked fishing ponds, hunting dogs, horses, and vehicles; Lopez, who loves to cook, plans to assist in the kitchen of the lodge.

Sources

Periodicals

Golf Magazine, December, 1985, p. 49.

Golf World, October 5, 2001, p. 36; November 9, 2001, p. NA.

Knight-Ridder/Tribune News Service, May 13, 1998, p. 513K6710.

People Weekly, April 25, 1983, p. 85.

Sports Illustrated, June 10, 1985, p. 56; August 5, 1985, p. 58; August 4, 1986, p. 34; February 9, 1987, p. 84.

Time for Kids, October 3, 1997, p. 8.

Washington Post, June 3, 1999, p. D06.

On-line

Latino Sports Legends, www.latinosportslegends.com

LPGA, www.lpga.com

—Kelly Winters

Diego Maradona

1961(?)—

Athlete

Diego Maradona is considered one of the greatest stars in the history of soccer, but his has been a career marred by controversy. The Argentine midfielder's statistical record is impressive: he has scored 255 goals in the 483 professional games he has played over a two-decade career, and was credited with leading an underdog Italian team twice to a national championship. Along the way he became a national folk hero in Argentina, and his rise from the slums of Buenos Aires to one of the most generously compensated players in the history of the sport has become an oft-told tale.

Maradona's fall from grace came after some well-publicized drug scandals hampered a career already beset by signs of physical deterioration. Still, the man deemed "one of soccer's most vivid, controversial figures" by *People* writer Ron Arias remains a living legend in his native Argentina. "Maradona has always been more than just a footballer," noted a profile in the *Economist,* which described him as "an icon for the country's poor" and a man whose celebrity "helped to liberate Argentine pride at a time when, under military rule, nationalism was a matter of some ambivalence."

Child Soccer Star

Diego Armando Maradona was born in the early 1960s in the impoverished Villa Fiorito area of Buenos Aires. His father, also called Diego, was a bricklayer, factory worker, and security guard. The family was of Indio heritage, and grew to include eight children in all. At the age of three, Maradona's cousin gave him a soccer ball, and he played with it constantly. He later claimed even to have slept with it. A clear talent for the sport emerged early, and after he joined a Buenos Aires youth team, Los Cebollitas ("Little Onions"). The team went on to achieve a 140-game winning streak. At the age of ten, Maradona was selected to take the field for a halftime performance at a Buenos Aires professional game. He kept the soccer ball aloft the entire time, to the cheers of the crowd, "by bouncing it off his feet, knees, chest, ankles, head and shoulders as if it were a balloon and his body a spring breeze," wrote Rick Terlander in *Sports Illustrated.* "When the two teams returned to the field to resume play, the crowd began chanting to the wonder boy, 'Stay! Stay!'"

Maradona left school at the age of 14, and joined the Argentinos Juniors of Buenos Aires. They won the world junior championship, and Maradona became

At a Glance . . .

Born October 30, 1960 (some sources say 1961), in Villa Fiorito, Buenos Aires, Argentina; son of Diego and Dalma Franco Maradona; married Claudia Villafane, 1989; children: Dalma Nerea, Gianinna Dinorah.

Career: Member of Argentine junior soccer team, Los Cebollitas, c. 1970-76; turned professional with Argentinos Juniors, 1976-80; Boca Juniors (Argentine League), 1980-81; also played for Barcelona team (Spanish League), 1982-84, Napoli (Italian League), 1984-91, Sevilla (Spanish League), 1992-93, Newell's Old Boys (Argentine League), 1993-94, and Boca Juniors, 1995-96.

Awards: Co-recipient, Player of the Century award, FIFA (by Internet vote), 2000.

Addresses: *Office*—c/o FIFA House, P.O. Box 85, 8030 Zurich, Switzerland.

a frequent subject in the sports pages of Argentine newspapers. He was called "Pibe de Oro," or "Golden Boy," and though he was diminutive for a world-class athlete, in the game of soccer, his 5'5" height was not a detriment. He possessed a powerful form that made him one of the ablest competitors in the sport. Others dubbed him the successor to Pelé, the great Brazilian star of the 1960s.

Still, Maradona's prowess and fame did earn him enmity: he was sometimes called "cabecita negra," or "black head," the derisive term that Argentina's largely European-heritage middle class sometimes used for those of Indio background. In 1978 Maradona was passed over for a spot on the Argentine national team for the all-important World Cup competition. The World Cup, soccer's most coveted trophy and a fervent expression of nationalism held every four years, took place in Argentina that year as well. The insult rankled, and likely colored his decision to play in Europe.

Maradona went on to have an impressive season with another Argentine team, Boca Juniors, in 1980, but two years later set an industry record when Barcelona, a team in the Spanish League, paid $;7.7 million for his contract. Maradona soon gained a reputation as a carouser in the city's nightclubs, but led the Barcelona team to a Spanish championship title. On the pitch, he was considered unstoppable. Maradona was both quick and elusive when running with the ball, and had a seemingly miraculous ability to slide between opposing players and still retain control of the ball. In a sport where 1-0 finishes were common, Maradona often scored nearly a dozen goals per season. His prowess was so legendary that hostile players fouled him and even attempted to injure his knees or ankles.

Maradona made sports headlines around the world once again in 1984 when he joined a failing Italian franchise in Naples, the Napoli team. His contract stipulated that he would earn $26 million over nine years. Neapolitans liked to chant, when their world-famous midfielder appeared on the pitch, "Maradona is better than Pelé. We practically killed ourselves to get him." The team won two Italian league championships by 1990, and Maradona became the inarguable superstar of the sport. *Sports Illustrated*'s Terlander commented on his physique, noting that Maradona's "squatness puts him at a disadvantage for knocking down balls and for heading, but it plants him badgerlike on the turf and gives him a rock-solid base from which to launch his explosive left-footed shots. Any time he crosses the center line, he is close enough to score."

The Infamous "Hand of God" Goal

Maradona's enshrinement as a national hero in Argentina came when he competed for its national team in the 1986 World Cup. In a quarterfinals match between Argentina and England, Maradona scored a goal that went into the net after his fist touched it—in prohibition of one of soccer's most steadfast rules. The judges failed to see it, however, and Maradona then scored the winning goal of the game by taking the ball single-handedly down 55 yards of the field, and faking out the English goaltender. Thus Argentina ousted England from the World Cup, and went on to beat West Germany in the finals.

At the time, Maradona claimed that it was not his fist but rather "the hand of God" that had made the first goal, and the loss was an especially bitter one for England. Four years earlier, Britain had gone to war with Argentina over the Malvinas, a group of islands off Argentina's coast and long a territorial possession of Britain known as the Falklands. Royal Navy battleships had steamed across the Atlantic in a show of force against Argentine claims to the islands. Maradona's goal was viewed as fitting revenge on Britain, and years later it still rankled for some soccer fans. *Independent Sunday* writer John Carlin called the athlete "the expression of the Argentine people as a whole, as the avenger of the nation's wounded pride. As the man who, with those two goals, gave the most refined expression to the two qualities which Argentines believe they possess in richest abundance, 'viveza' (a sly cunning) and talent."

Argentina's win in the 1986 World Cup in Mexico City—against a formidable West Germany team in the finals—launched massive celebrations in the streets ofBuenos Aires. He was tagged with yet another nickname, El Rey, or "the king." Back in Italy, he was also treated as a national hero; his face and winning No. 10 jersey were familiar images in the media and all over Naples. But Maradona, the highest-paid player in the sport at the time, often made boastful statements to the media, and he periodically ran afoul of Napoli's management for skipping training sessions. Rumors began to surface that claimed he used illegal drugs, and had links to the city's *camorra,* or organized-crime syndicate. Maradona was usually derided by sports journalists for letting himself get paunchy, or claiming that he had been threatened by the camorra, and a war with press was underway by 1990, the same year in which he led Napoli to its second national championship. "They can say what they want about me," he told *People*'s Arias at the time. "Fine me, withhold my salary, but I won't change. Remember, it's the players who bring 90,000 people to the stadium. I am Maradona, who makes goals, who makes mistakes. I can take it all, I have shoulders big enough to fight with everybody."

Maradona's fall from grace was as spectacular as his rise from the Villa Fiorito slum. In February of 1991 he was charged with possession of cocaine in Naples. That spring, he tested positive for the drug, and was suspended from international play for 15 months. He returned to Buenos Aires, and was arrested in a police raid there on a suspected drug house. The Napoli team then filed suit against Maradona's managers, refusing to honor the remainder of contract because of the negative publicity. In 1992 Maradona played for a season with Seville's team in the Spanish League, and the following year joined an Argentine team, Newell's Old Boys. He began to exhibit increasingly erratic behavior: in February of 1994 he fired a pellet gun at group of reporters outside his home in Buenos Aires, injuring five. He disappeared for days at a time. That summer, he was banned once again from international play when he tested positive for drugs, which effectively barred him from the Argentine World Cup team. He was tried in absentia in Italy for drug possession, and in Buenos Aires, despite a wife and family, still maintained his fondness for nightclubs and parties.

National Folk Hero

Argentines remained loyal to Maradona, however. He backed a lagging presidential candidate, Carlos Saúl Menem, in 1995, and Menem afterwards won by a landslide. Maradona the midfielder returned in the fall of that year when he rejoined his old team, Boca Juniors, but it would be his last season in professional soccer. He was suspended a third time, and returned in July of 1997 to the Boca team, but injuries forced the announcement of his official retirement. Characteristically, he claimed that he and family were under threat, and that powerful factions wanted him out of the sport.

In early 2000 Maradona was rushed to an emergency room in Uruguay after a suspected cocaine overdose. The incident was said to have weakened his already damaged heart. He left South America for Cuba to enter a treatment program there. (He sports tattoos of Cuban revolutionary hero Ché Guevara and long-time Cuban leader Fidel Castro.) That same year, he shared the FIFA (Fédération Internationale de Football Association) Player of the Century award with Pelé. The Italian government claims that Maradona owes $25 million in back taxes, but he claims that the burden belongs to the Napoli team because of its fiscal mismanagement. The team offered him a management position in 2001, which he declined.

Maradona's "hand of God" goal—which he admitted on Italian television four years later was indeed his own fist—is still considered a defining national moment for Argentina. The broadcast of the moment is still replayed. The announcer screams "Goooooooool!" (goal) as is customary, but then amends it to "Diegooooooool!" before breaking into sobs. Maradona has been the subject of biographies and other books assessing his relation to the Argentine national character. When he was invited to play in a Buenos Aires exhibition match in his honor in November of 2001 and took a lap around the field with his two daughters, spectators in the stands cried.

"Death Would Glorify Him"

After the country convulsed in riots over a looming economic crisis a month later, there was talk that new Argentine president Eduardo Duhalde would ask Maradona join the Sports Secretariat. It is said that Maradona ranks with two other tragic figures from Argentine cultural history: 1930s tango singer Carlos Gardel, who died in a plane crash, and former First Lady Eva Perón, still a revered national icon. At times, callers to Argentina's popular radio shows speak of his imminent death. One sociologist, Alberto Quevedo, struggled to explain to Carlin in the *Independent Sunday* why this is so. "We're all embarrassed by him now because he has been so important for the Argentine people," Quevedo observed. "And death would glorify him. Maradona can offer no more and, like Achilles, he should die young and glorious." An Argentine psychoanalyst and television host also discussed the matter with the journalist. "We are the greatest when Maradona is the greatest," asserted Jose Abadi, "but when he falls we fall with him. And we do not want that."

Sources

Books

Encyclopedia of World Biography Supplement, Volume 20, Gale, 2000.

Periodicals

Economist, January 15, 2000.
Financial Times, January 30, 2002.
Independent Sunday (London, England), March 19, 2000.
Maclean's, January 15, 1996.
Mirror (London, England), February 15, 2002.
New York Times, November 14, 2001.
People, June 18, 1990.
Sports Illustrated, June 16, 1986; July 7, 1986; May 14, 1990; April 8, 1991; June 10, 1991; September 30, 1991; January 20, 1992; February 28, 1994; October 16, 1995; June 30, 1997.
Time, July 11, 1994.
World Press Review, April 2000.
Xinhua News Agency, January 20, 2000; September 26, 2000; December 10, 2000; January 12, 2001.

—Carol Brennan

Mel Martínez

1947—

Cabinet secretary

In January of 2001 Mel R. Martínez became the first American of Cuban heritage to hold a Cabinet post. Martínez was named Secretary of the Department of Housing and Urban Development (HUD) by President George W. Bush, an appointment that signaled the emergence of Florida's strongly Republican Cuban-American community as a significant political force. Martínez, a well-liked county executive from Florida, was considered one of the wisest choices among the Bush Administration cabinet nominees. "In one fell swoop," observed *Los Angeles Times* writer Geraldine Baum, "Bush effectively paid a debt to Cuban Americans who supported him during the postelection debacle in Florida, was able to elevate a Latino with a dramatic immigrant story and succeeded in promoting someone who—although he lacks experience in the public housing arena—has been in the thick of governing the fastest-growing community in the country."

Cuban Refugee

Melquiades Martínez was born in 1947 in Sagua la Grande, Cuba. The son of a veterinarian, he was twelve when a 1959 coup brought Communist guerrilla leader

Fidel Castro to power on the island. The new government was not supported by all, and one teen in Sagua la Grande was taken before a firing squad after being accused of anti-government activities. Catholic schools were closed, and the atmosphere grew tense as Martínez entered his teens. He once played in a basketball game wearing a religious symbol around his neck, and was taunted for it. "The words 'Kill him, he is a Catholic' had a chilling ring for my desperate and frightened parents," Martínez told a Senate Judiciary committee many years later, according to *St. Petersburg Times* writer Curtis Krueger.

Uneasy with a Communist government—Latin America's only one for a time—and firm Soviet ally so close, the United States government attempted to subvert Cuban communism in several ways. One of them was helping Catholic service groups launch "Operation Pedro Pan," an airlift for Cuban youth who were then resettled with Florida families. Martínez, with the date of his compulsory service in the Cuban military nearing, became one of 14,000 to participate in Operation Pedro Pan. He was fifteen and spoke only Spanish when he arrived at a refugee center on Matecumbe Key in the Florida Keys. He moved in with an Orlando

At a Glance . . .

Born Melquiades Rafael Martínez, October 23, 1946, in Sagua la Grande, Cuba; emigrated to United States, 1962; naturalized citizen, 1971; son of Melquiades C. (a veterinarian) and Gladys V. (Ruiz) Martínez.; m. Kathryn Tindal, June 13, 1970; children: Lauren Elizabeth, John Melquiades, Andrew Tindal. *Education:* Florida State University, B.A., 1969, J.D., 1973. *Religion:* Roman Catholic. *Politics:* Republican.

Career: Began career as attorney in private practice, Florida, 1973; partner in Martínez, Dalton, Dellecker and Wilson, Orlando, FL until 1985; chair, Orlando Housing Authority, 1984-86; Martínez, Dalton, Dellecker, Wilson and King, partner and civil trial attorney, 1985-98; president, Orlando Utilities Commission, 1994-97; chair, Orange County, FL, 1998-01; named secretary for Housing and Urban Development, 2001, by President George W. Bush. Has also served on the board of directors for Catholic Social Services of Orlando, 1978-86; founder and chair of Mayor's Hispanic Advisory Committee, Orlando, 1981-82; chair of board of commissioners, Orlando Housing Authority, 1983-86; commissioner for Orlando Utilities Commission, 1992-94.

Memberships: Bar of the state of Florida (board of governors, young lawyers section, 1980-81); Academy of Florida Trial Lawyers (director, 1981-85, treasurer, 1986-87, president, 1988-89), Ninth Judicial Circuit (judicial nomination commission, 1986).

Addresses: *Home*— Orlando, FL. *Office*— Department of Housing and Urban Development, Room 10000, 451 Seventh Street, S.W., Washington, DC 20410.

with an excellent command of the English language, and enrolled at Florida State University. After graduating in 1969, he entered law school at the same institution. He earned his J.D. and passed the Florida bar in 1973, and began a career as a successful personal-injury lawyer. His first foray into politics came when a law partner was elected mayor of Orlando, and named him to chair the Orlando Housing Authority.

Martínez served in that post for two years in the mid-1980s, and continued to practice law in Orlando. In 1994 he was appointed head of the city's Utilities Commission, and decided to make a bid for the lieutenant governorship in Florida's primary race. He lost, but the experience introduced him to another Florida Republican, Jeb Bush, the son of former President George Bush. Martínez ran once again for office in 1998, and won the top executive post in Orange County, home to Orlando, its booming local economy, Walt Disney World, and a population of 820,000. Because of unchecked growth in recent years, however, the area was beset by traffic congestion and overcrowded schools. One of Martínez's first decisions was to temporarily ban new construction of homes in areas where school districts were being forced to hold classes in trailers. The decision angered housing developers in the region, but Martínez was adamant.

By making budget cuts, Martínez was able to reduce some of the property taxes in Orange County, and set a positive example as a leader when he fired a fire department chief who refused to promote women and minorities. He also became involved in the 1999 media storm over Elian Gonzalez, the six-year-old boy who was rescued after fleeing Cuba with his mother on a raft. She died, but the family in Florida offered to take him in; his father in Cuba, however, requested his return. Martínez backed the Florida relatives, and even took Elian on a well-publicized visit to Walt Disney World.

Helped Bush Win Florida

Martínez was also attracting attention in national Republican circles. When the brother of Governor Jeb Bush became the GOP frontrunner in the 2000 presidential race, Martínez was named as co-chair of the state campaign to elect Texas governor George W. Bush to the White House. Martínez also became a member of Florida's Electoral College, a 25-member panel that played a key role in the contested race. Democratic candidate Al Gore was initially declared the winner of the Florida electoral votes, but the media then retracted the projection. As a case for disputed ballots arose, several Florida counties began a manual recount, but a U.S. Supreme Court decision put an end to the recount, and Bush was declared the winner in December of 2000.

Martínez became one of Bush's first cabinet appointees a week later. At a press conference, the president-elect

family, Walter and Eileen Young, and his brother Rafael soon followed. "We looked at ourselves many times through those years and said: 'We may never see our parents again,'" Rafael Martínez recalled in the *St. Petersburg Times* interview.

The Martínez sons were thrilled to greet their parents and sister when they arrived in Florida in 1966. By then Martínez had worked and saved $400 to give to his father so the family might buy a car, and had also lined up a job for him in a local dairy. Meanwhile, Martínez was also continuing with his own plans. He finished high school at a local Roman Catholic school mistakenly referred to Martínez as his pick to head the department of "housing and human development," but did praise the Cuban American as the embodiment of the American dream. "He's got a wonderful story," Bush stated at that press conference, according to a report by *New York Times* journalist Christopher Marquis. "He was a refugee, as a young boy, from Cuba. He understands American values; he's grown to appreciate them." Martínez was equally pleased to find himself before reporters as a Cabinet nominee. "Today, for me, is a fulfillment of the promise of America," Martínez told reporters, according to Marquis, "the promise that regardless of where you come from, what language you speak, the color of your skin or your economic circumstances, if you share the dream of a brighter tomorrow, and you're willing to pursue it with respect for others and have an abiding faith in God, all things are possible."

Martínez was confirmed as HUD secretary on January 23, 2001 by a Senate vote of 100-0. The Florida Republican Party chair, Al Cardenas, told Baum in the *Los Angeles Times* that Martínez was a solid pick for the job, and the ease of his confirmation hearings were no surprise. "He has been managing a place with an exploding population and overseeing all the infrastructure problems that creates—in housing, in transportation, in education," said Cardenas.

Martínez took over a department with a $30 billion budget and 9,100 employees. HUD's function is to ensure that all Americans have equal access to housing. It provides loans for first-time home buyers, block grants for troubled neighborhoods, a rent voucher program for low-income families, and works to eradicate abandoned and dilapidated housing. It also maintains public housing complexes across the country and helps the elderly and disabled keep and maintain their homes. Martínez stressed in an interview with *Washington Post* writer Ellen Nakashima that he was not about to undertake any major overhaul. "One thing I don't want to do is reinvent HUD," he told the newspaper. "There's been too much of that over the last several years. We need some stability. I want to find those things that are working, encourage them; find those things that need improvement and try to change those around."

Pledged to Fulfill HUD Aims

One goal Martínez hoped to achieve during his tenure was to improve minority home-ownership statistics. When he became HUD Secretary, figures showed that 72 percent of white households in United States owned their own home, compared with figures in the mid-40s range for blacks and Hispanics. "I'm not sure we can improve a whole lot on that 72 percent, but in that 45 to 46 percent, we darn sure can do better," Martínez told Nakashima in the *Washington Post* interview. In the spring of 2001 he and Attorney General John Ashcroft pledged to ensure that the landmark Fair Housing Act, signed by President Lyndon B. Johnson in 1968 as part of the Civil Rights Act of same year, was being upheld. At a news event, they reminded builders of the need to comply with regulations specified by the Americans with Disabilities Act, and sounded a warning note to mortgage brokers who charge excessive fees to first-time, low income home buyers. The Bush Administration's two top officials in this realm stated that discrimination in any form would not be tolerated. Martínez said his own experience trying to settle Cuban refugees in the early 1980s in the Orlando area awakened him to discriminatory practices. At the time, he used his law background to help the refugees overcome the obstacles, and "fortunately we were able to get them a decent place to live," a writer for the *St. Louis Post-Dispatch* quoted Martínez as saying that day. "But I wonder how many powerless people are out there who may not have an advocate. That is who we need to serve."

Martínez also surprised some when he spoke at the annual convention of the Mortgage Bankers Association of America during his first year as HUD Secretary. He told his audience that consumers needed more protection regarding mortgage-industry fees, and urged the group to comply. "Too many home buyers are taken advantage of at closing," Knight-Ridder/Tribune Business News writer John Handley quoted Martínez as saying. "Too many American families sit down at the settlement table and discover unexpected fees that can add thousands of dollars to the cost of their loan." Martínez said that some of the mortgage paperwork should include an exact description of the mortgage broker's services, and how much the broker will earn on the deal. "When you are committing to the biggest financial expenditure of your life, you should know all the costs up front," he declared.

In early 2002 Martínez was instrumental in securing a $700 million grant for New York State from HUD's Community Development Block Grant program. The money was given to help in the rebuilding of Lower Manhattan, devastated by the attacks on the World Trade Center. "It's the largest single grant in the history of our department," Martínez told *New York Times* writer Robert Pear. "We worked hard to get it out as quick as we could. The focus is on economic development, with a particular emphasis on small business." Around the same time, the HUD Secretary also spoke before Budget Committee senators regarding the Bush administration's proposed fiscal 2003 budget. It included an increase for HUD's Section 8 program that would yield 34,000 new Section 8 rental-assistance vouchers, but there were an estimated one million families on a waiting list for them. The proposed budget would also earmark $150 million in federal funds for a program to help first-time low-income home buyers.

Martínez and his wife Kitty, whom he met in college, have three children and have become foster parents to

Cuban and Vietnamese refugee children. His brother Rafael is also an attorney. Martínez believes he brings a unique perspective to HUD, one of the cabinet departments created during the mid-1960s by a civil-rights-minded political leadership. "I will try to be someone who shows a very caring heart, for people that are hurting, for people who may be homeless or in a less than desirable housing situation," he told the *Washington Post*'s Nakashima. "I myself in my own life experienced what it's like not to have a lot, not to be in a position where you couldn't do without the help of others."

Sources

Bond Buyer, December 14, 2001, p. 5; January 23, 2002, p. 5; February 14, 2002, p. 5.
Knight-Ridder/Tribune Business News, October 28, 2001.
Los Angeles Times, December 21, 2000, p. A32.
Mortgage Banking, February 2001, p. 13.
Nation's Cities Weekly, March 12, 2001, p. 8.
New York Times, December 21, 2000; February 3, 2002, p. 32.
Orlando Business Journal, May 18, 2001, p. 1; October 5, 2001, p. 3.
St. Louis Post-Dispatch, April 12, 2001, p. A11.
St. Petersburg Times, January 17, 2001, p. 1A.
U.S. Newswire, September 17, 2001.
Washington Post, February 21, 2001, p. A21.

—Carol Brennan

Carlos Saul Menem

1930—

Political leader

Twice elected president of Argentina, Carlos Menem's terms in office represented a rare period of political stability in the country. Yet Menem himself was never very far from controversy, both for his vivid public persona and a number of decisions that raised accusations of corruption and deceit. Since leaving the presidency, Menem has continued to be one of Argentina's most recognizable politicians. He has continued to lead his party, the Perónist *Partido Justicialista,* and has been rumored to be planning a run for a third term in office. Given Argentina's economic troubles, some Menem supporters claim that he is the best person to return the country to relative stability; however, his detractors point to a number of ongoing investigations into Menem's presidential actions that may derail any future political plans of the former president.

Carlos Saul Menem was born in the northwestern Argentina town of Anillaco. One of four sons of immigrants from Syria, Menem was raised in a Sunni Muslim family by his parents, Saul and Mohiba Menem. Saul Menem had worked his way up from being a simple street vendor to owning his own retail store and was proud that all of his children eventually finished college. Carlos Menem entered Córdoba University, located in Argentina's second-largest city, and earned a law degree in 1958. While a student, Menem already demonstrated an active interest in politics. In 1955 he created a chapter of the *Juventud Perónista,* a youth group for supporters of then-president Juan Perón. Although Perón was overthrown in a military coup that same year and ousted from the country, his party remained a significant force in Argentine politics. Menem continued to support the party and ran as a Perónist candidate in his first bid for elective office as a provincial deputy in 1962. The elections were called off, however, during another one of Argentina's frequent military coups.

Longtime Perónist

Menem set up a law practice in La Rioja, a major city located not far from his birthplace of Anillaco, after his graduation; yet politics were never far from his mind. He worked as a legal advisor for a Perónist trade union group, the *Confederación General del Trabajo,* and after his first aborted bid for elected office ran again for the provincial leadership position of the *Partido Justicialista* (PJ) in 1963. As the party of the Perónists, the

At a Glance . . .

Born Carlos Saul Menem on July 2, 1930, in Anillaco, Argentina; married Zulema Fatimah Yoma in 1966; two children. *Education:* Completed law degree at Córdoba University, 1958. *Religion:* Roman Catholic. *Politics:* Justicialist Party

Career: Private law practice, 1958; Justicialist Party provincial head, 1963; Governor, La Rioja province, 1973-89; President of Argentina, 1989-99; head of Justicialist Party, 1999-.

Address: *Political party*—Partido Justicialista, Matheu 130 1082 Buenos Aires, Argentina.

PJ continued to articulate its founder's platform of nationalism, massive government spending on public programs, and significant subsidies to businesses. Menem would follow these Perónist programs once he finally won elective office as governor of La Rioja province in 1973.

Menem met Zulema Fatimah Yoma on a trip to Damascus, Syria, in 1964. Menen had long since previously converted to Roman Catholicism, yet the couple was married in a Muslim religious ceremony in 1966. The Menems had two children, yet the marriage was often the focus of unwelcome attention during the couple's many public spats. Menem deliberately cultivated the image of the successful playboy—typically wearing white suits and keeping his hair (later on, carefully positioned hair pieces) immaculately groomed—and regularly appeared with young models and actresses on his arm. Such antics may have endeared the politician to the Argentine public, but his wife routinely complained about her husband's behavior. The couple separated twice but decided to reconcile both times.

Served as Governor

After gaining the governor's seat for the province of La Rioja in 1973, Menem immediately implemented a Perónist agenda. He doubled the number of employees on the public payroll, even though the action meant that the province had to circulate state bonds in place of currency after the government ran out of money for its payroll. Menem added so many employees to the public sector that it soon became the largest employer in the province, even outnumbering the total number of private sector employees in La Rioja. By lowering the unemployment rate to just three percent, however, Menem's popularity surged. He also claimed to have brought several new employers into the province by

promoting tax abatement and investment credit schemes. Although the policies reduced the amount of funds coming into government coffers, they also showed Menem to be a man of action in contrast to the typical Argentine politician.

With Juan Perón's return to Argentina from his exile in Spain in 1973, it appeared that the Perónists would once again dominate the country's political arena. Perón's rule turned out to be brief, however, for he died in July of 1974. His wife and successor, Isabel Perón, was subsequently thrown out of office in a military coup in March of 1976, and another era of rule by various military regimes followed. For Menem, the cost of the political upheavals was high: jailed in 1976 for his Perónist association, he spent five years as a political prisoner before being released in 1981.

Known as the "Dirty War," the period from 1976 to 1982 was one of the darkest in Argentina's history. In addition to political prisoners such as Menem, approximately 9,000 *desaparecidos* (or "the disappeared ones") were taken into custody by the military government on the pretext of representing a subversive threat. Many were tortured and some were drugged and thrown off of airplanes into the sea. For all the repression, however, Argentina's military rulers could not dampen the unrest brought on by deteriorating economic conditions. After the government hastily entered and lost a war with Great Britain over possession of the Falkland (or Malvinas) Islands in 1982, the junta declared that it would step aside in the face of enormous public opposition and turn power over to a civilian government. Before the transfer of power, however, the military government passed a law that absolved all participants in the deeds of the Dirty War.

Ran for President

After his release from jail, Menem returned to office as governor of La Rioja in 1983. That same year, the first elected government in ten years took power when Raul Alfonsín was elected president. Alfonsín repealed the amnesty law enacted in the last months of military rule and began to investigate and prosecute some of the most serious crimes. Alfonsín's greatest challenge, however, was to bring the Argentine economy back to stability. In 1985 inflation hit more than 1,000% percent annually; as unreal as that figure seemed, it climbed even higher, with reports of 3,000 percent at one time.

Against this backdrop of social and economic unrest, Menem announced his candidacy for the presidential elections scheduled for May of 1989. Riding a wave of popularity, Menem had been reelected as La Rioja's governor in 1987, and he now pointed to his past record as evidence that he could solve the nation's problems. On May 14, 1989, Menem was duly elected—the first time in over sixty years that one elected government had been succeeded by another in Argentina—and the PJ gained control of both houses of Congress.

At the time of Menem's election, monthly inflation stood at almost seventy-nine percent, a rate that neared two-hundred percent by July. With strikes and riots breaking out all over the country, Alfonsín abruptly resigned from office in July of 1989 and Menem's administration took over a few months early. While it was expected that the new president would fill his cabinet with Perónists, he startled many by appointing free-market reformer Domingo Cavallo as his finance minister. Under Cavallo's insistence, the government began to sell off state-owned enterprises and limited inflation by linking the Argentine peso to the American dollar. Menem also attempted to impose spending limits on the government, although this strategy was much more difficult to implement. The most controversial move of Menem's first term, however, came with his decision in October of 1989 to pardon almost three hundred of those convicted or suspected of human rights violations during the Dirty War.

Menem was also criticized for allowing corruption to continue during his administration and for failing to rein in government spending, which doubled during his terms in office. With the peso tied to the dollar, the government resorted to borrowing to pay its way, and foreign debt ballooned to over $142 billion under Menem's rule. Menem remained popular enough, however, to win reelection to a second term in 1994. During his second and last consecutive term, Menem continued to increase government spending and privatize certain state-owned enterprises.

During Menem's last year in office, cracks began to appear in the Argentine economy that showed how little his reforms had reshaped the country's economy. With the peso pegged at an artificially high rate, exports of Argentine products were stifled and labor costs remained high. Menem's feeble attempts to impose austerity measures also meant that the government maintained a large foreign debt, an enormous liability once the global economy slowed down in the late 1990s. As Menem left office, Argentina's gross domestic product growth rate plunged into negative territory and unemployment climbed to over fourteen percent. By 2000 an estimated forty percent of Argentine' people lived below the official poverty line.

Continued Controversies

After leaving the presidency, Menem remained the head of the PJ, which ruled as the official opposition party in Congress after political rival Fernando de la Rúa came into office in 1999. Unfortunately, a period of economic chaos that rivaled the worst extremes of the 1980s unfolded during de la Rúa's term, and he was ousted from office in favor of a series of short-lived presidents at the end of 2001 and first months of 2002. Given the political and economic upheavals, Menem once again put himself forward as the only person capable of bringing stability back to Argentina.

In preparing his political comeback, however, Menem refused to answer questions about two major scandals that unfolded during his two terms in office. In one corruption and drug-trafficking probe, Menen was even placed under house arrest by a court order; however, he was subsequently freed and had maintained his innocence. In a more far-reaching probe, however, accusations surfaced that Menem had accepted a bribe of ten million dollars to cover up a 1994 bombing of a Jewish community center in Buenos Aires that killed eight-five people. The investigation centered around the testimony of a former Iranian spy who presented evidence to Swiss authorities that Menem's administration had ties to both Muslim extremist groups and to international organized crime syndicates as well. With the investigation taking place in Switzerland—far out of Menem's sphere of political influence—it appeared that the former president's bid for a third term in office would be put on hold.

Sources

Books

Castañeda, Jorge G., *Utopia Unarmed: The Latin American Left After the Cold War*, Alfred A. Knopf, 1993.
Crassweller, Robert, *Perón and the Enigmas of Argentina*, W.W. Norton & Company, 1987.
France, Miranda, *Bad Times in Buenos Aires: A Writer's Adventures in Argentina*, Ecco Press, 1998.
Guillermoprieto, Alma, *Looking for History: Dispatches from Latin America*, Pantheon Books, 2001.
Rock, David, *Argentina 1516-1987: From Spanish Colonization to Alfonsín*, University of California Press, 1987.

Periodicals

America, February 11, 2002.
Business Week, January 21, 2002.
Christian Science Monitor, February 11, 2002.
Economist, January 5, 2002; January 19, 2002.
Los Angeles Times, January 13, 2002; January 24, 2002.

—Timothy Borden

Rita Moreno

1931—

Actress, singer, dancer

Rita Moreno's versatility as a performer has led to decades of success on stage, screen, and television. She is the only female entertainer to have won all four of the most prestigious show business awards: the Oscar for the role of Anita in the 1962 film *West Side Story*, the Tony for the role of Googie Gomez in the 1975 production of *The Ritz*, Emmy awards in 1977 and 1978 for appearances on *The Muppet Show* and *The Rockford Files*, and a Grammy for her 1972 performance on *The Electric Company Album*. She has also received dozens of other show business awards, most notably, The Golden Globe Award and the Joseph Jefferson Award as best actress in Chicago's theatrical season in 1968 for her performance as Serafina in *The Rose Tattoo*. She received a star on the Hollywood Walk of Fame in 1995.

Along the way Puerto Rican-born Moreno has become a trailblazer and inspiration for aspiring Latino actors. Until she achieved acclaim for her performance in *West Side Story*, Moreno was plagued with roles that propagated ethnic stereotypes, including "Latin Spitfire" roles in such forgettable films as *Jivaro*, (1954) and *Seven Cities of Gold* (1955). After winning the Oscar she became one of a few Latinos to achieve international acclaim. That has changed with the success of performers such as Rosie Perez, Sonia Braga, and Elizabeth Pena. "The first time I met Rosie Perez, she started to cry," Moreno told the *Times Union Albany*. "I can't tell you how surprising and moving it is, and how astonished I am that I meant that much to my colleagues of Hispanic descent."

Moreno was born Rosa Dolores Alverio on December 11, 1932, in Humacao, Puerto Rico. Her mother, Rosa Maria Mercano, married Paco Alverio, a small independent farmer, when she was just a teenager, but the marriage ended in divorce. In the 1930s the pressures of the Depression and the side effects of the island's rapid industrialization forced Rosa to look toward the United States for sustenance. She left home to work as a seamstress in New York City, leaving young Moreno in the care of relatives. A year later, five-year-old Moreno joined her mother.

The following year she began taking dance lessons, and it wasn't long before she was performing in the children's theater at Macy's Department Store and at weddings and bar mitzvahs. At age 13, she had her Broadway debut in the role of Angelina in Harry Kleiner's *Skydrift* and dropped out of school a year

At a Glance . . .

Born Rosa Dolores Alverio on December 11, 1931, in Humacao, Puerto Rico; married Leonard Gordon; children: Fernanda Luisa.

Career: First appeared on Broadway at the age of thirteen, in *Skydrift*; appeared in numerous films; numerous television guest appearances, sitcoms, and drama series, including Showtime's *Resurrection Blvd* and HBO's *Oz*.

Awards: Best Supporting Actress, Academy of Motion Picture Arts and Sciences, 1962; Best Supporting Actress, Golden Globe Awards, 1962; Best Recording for Children, Grammy Award, 1972; Outstanding Continuing or Single Performance by a Supporting Actress in Variety or Music, Emmy Award, 1977; Outstanding Lead Actress for a Single Appearance in a Drama or Comedy Series, Emmy Award, 1978; Best Supporting Actress, Antoinette Perry Award (Tony), 1975; Best Actress, Joseph Jefferson Award, 1985; Star on the Hollywood Walk of Fame, 1995; Lifetime Achievement Award, Nosostros Golden Eagle Award, 1997; Outstanding Actress in a Drama Series, American Latin Media Arts Award (ALMA), 1999.

Addresses: *Agent*—William Morris Agency, 151 El Camino, Beverly Hills, CA, 90212.

later to concentrate on her show business career. Then, in the true Hollywood tradition, a talent scout arranged a meeting for Moreno with Louis B. Mayer and she signed a contract with Metro-Goldwyn-Mayer in 1949 at the age of seventeen. Moreno, now using the surname of her stepfather Edward Moreno, shortened her nickname Rosita to "Rita" at the request of MGM.

Career Hindered by Stereotypes

After joining MGM Moreno's career advanced steadily. In little more than ten years she had reinvented herself into a Hollywood starlet. However, the range of her talents were ignored and she found herself incessantly cast as a fiery Latin sex kitten or an Indian maiden in a succession of stereotypical, ethnic roles in such films as *The Fabulous Senorita* (1952), *Latin Lovers* (1953), and *The Yellow Tomahawk* (1954). "There was no such animal as a Spanish-American actress. Lupi Valez and Dolores Del Rio, that was it," Moreno told the *Worcester Telegram & Gazette.* "What happened

was, in those days they did a lot of westerns and there was always a part for a senorita, singing and dancing my little bum off and, tock-eeng lahk deez. When that period was over, there was nothing left but gang movies." Still, when her contract with MGM was canceled early, Moreno was devastated.

After MGM she signed on with Twentieth Century-Fox. The roles she played were no different—she was typecast as the dumb, sexy characters moviemakers thought she was suited for, including a poor, barefooted Native American in *Seven Cities of Gold* (1955) and Tuptim, a slave girl, in the classic *The King and I* (1956). In 1957 she made *The Deerslayer* and then, without reason, Fox let her contract lapse. It would be three years before she would make another movie.

Recognized as a Major Talent

Moreno spent the next few years working in stage productions, including Arthur Miller's *A View from the Bridge*. In April of 1961, when a nearly decade-long affair with Marlon Brando ended, she took an overdose of sleeping pills. The suicide attempt was a turning point in her life, reminding her that "life is really very precious." Later that year she appeared in the movie version of *West Side Story* (1961). It was only after she won an Academy Award—the first for a Hispanic actress—for her outstanding performance as strong-willed and independent Anita that she was finally recognized as a major talent.

Although the role of Anita showcased Moreno's talent for all the world to see, it continued to reinforce the Latino stereotypes. The Academy Award, however, gave her some leverage in the moviemaking industry. "I decided once I won the Oscar that I was not going to do those kinds of movies again. I'm not speaking of *West Side Story*, obviously … I didn't do a movie for seven years," Moreno stated in an interview with National Public Radio.

In 1962 she moved to London where she played Ilona Ritter in Hal Prince's production of *She Loves Me*. She then returned to New York to star in Lorraine Hansbury's, *The Sign In Sidney Brustein's Window*, playing the role of Iris Parodus Brustein. Moreno returned to film in 1967, portraying a drug-addict in *The Night of the Following Day* (1968), opposite Marlon Brando. This led to roles in films such as *Marlowe* (1969), opposite James Garner; *Popi* (1969), as Alan Arkin's girlfriend; and Mike Nichol's production of *Carnal Knowledge* (1971), in which she played a prostitute visited by Jack Nicholson. In 1970 she returned to theater as the female lead with Robert Shaw in *Gantry* on Broadway, and was cast opposite Jimmy Coco in Neil Simon's *Last of the Red Hot Lovers*.

It was during this prolific period in Moreno's career that she met Dr. Lenoard Gordon, a cardiologist and internist and Mount Sinai Hospital in New York City. They married in June of 1965. Moreno attributed the success of her marriage to Gordon, who is Jewish, as an example of personal enrichment to exposure to differences, according to an interview with National Public Radio. In 1967 she gave birth to their only child, Fernanda Luisa. Lenny continued his medical practice until he was forced to retire due to congenital heart disease. This gave him the opportunity to devote himself to his daughter and Moreno's career. He would eventually became her manager.

Awarded Top Prizes

In 1971 Moreno took a hiatus from film and theater to work in television. She had captured the attention of producers of such shows as *The Electric Company*, of which she became part of the cast for six seasons, and *Sesame Street*, both highly regarded educational programs. In 1972 she won a Grammy, along with the rest of the cast, for the soundtrack recording of *The Electric Company*.

In 1975 Moreno received a best supporting actress Tony Award for her portrayal of Googie Gomez in *The Ritz*. Playwright Terrence McNally based the character on Moreno's own comic portrayal of the stereotypical roles she had always been cast to play. "Googie Gomez was the ultimate send-up," she told National Public Radio. "I was thumbing my nose at all the people who wrote those kind of roles seriously. And I think that everybody understood that on the whole." She would go on to receive Emmy awards for a guest appearance on *The Muppet Show* in 1977 and the portrayal of a vulnerable prostitute on *The Rockford Files* in 1978. In 1979 she was entered into the *Guinness Book of World Records* as the only performer to win all four top entertainment awards.

Demonstrated Versatile Talents

Finally breaking the mold, Moreno went on to portray a Jewish mother in *The Boss's Son* (1979) and to develop a nightclub act as "insurance." "It simply means that when there's no TV around to speak of, or film, it's a wonderful way to earn a living," she told the *Worcester Telegram & Gazette*. "That's the good thing about being a performer who does many different things, which you don't find many of anymore. People specialize, like in medicine and law, so much that they box themselves into corners. But I always have a venue. Always." Her next film role did not come until 1980, when she played an Italian American mistress in *Happy Birthday, Gemini*.

In 1982 Moreno returned to television in the sitcom version of the hit film *9 to 5*. While it did relatively well from 1982 to 1983, the time-slot was changed and its rating fell. Despite the demise of the series, Moreno was nominated for an Emmy. She went on to do Alan

Alda's *The Four Seasons,* with Carol Burnett in 1993, and then in 1994, the highly acclaimed Columbia Pictures release *Like It Like That*. In 1995 Moreno was featured in Showtime's, *Wharf Rat,* opposite Lou Diamond Phillips and Judge Reinhold and in the feature film *Angus* with George C. Scott. Then she found herself on Broadway again in the short-lived gender-switched version of *The Odd Couple,* co-starring with Sally Struthers. In another return to television, she played opposite Burt Reynolds in *B.L Stryker* from 1989 to 1990, and in the 1991-1992 Fox Network series, *The Top of the Heap*. In 1994 Moreno returned to New York to appear as a series regular with Bill Cosby on the *Cosby Mystery Series* on NBC.

But Moreno's greatest love is the theater. In 1995 she returned to the New York stage in Anne Meara's *After Play* and in Circle Repertory's production of *Size Of the World*. In the fall of 1997 Moreno again won the acclaim of the London audiences when she returned to the London stage in the starring role of doomed screen goddess Norma Desmond in Andrew Lloyd Webbers' *Sunset Blvd*. Moreno performed in *The Vagina Monologues* early in 2001 in New York and San Francisco. Moreno has appeared in many regional theaters, often with her daughter Fernanda, also an actress. They have appeared together as mother and daughter in *The Glass Menagerie, Steel Magnolias,* and *Gypsy,* and as sisters in *The Taming of the Shrew*.

Moreno's work on the acclaimed HBO prison series *Oz,* in which she bucked the stereotype once again as the tough-talking nun and counselor, Sister Peter Marie, has won her accolades. She also guest starred on the Showtime series *Resurrection Blvd* and appeared in *Piñero* (2001) as the mother of Puerto Rican poet and playwright Manual Piñero, played by Benjamin Bratt.

In addition to her film, stage, television, and concert careers, Moreno filled her spare time by lecturing to various organizations as well as to university audiences. She has spoken on the history of film, television and theater and the importance of self-esteem and education. She is also involved with a number of civic and charitable organizations and events. She has served on the National Foundation for the Arts, as a commissioner on the Presidents White House Fellowships, and as a member of the Presidents Committee on the Arts and Humanities.

It may be said that Rita Moreno, who has portrayed Shakespearean characters, an Irish teacher, and Italian widow, a reformed prostitute, a lady evangelist, an English lady, and a southern belle, has broken the rigid role of Latino stereotyping. Still, Moreno feels that Hollywood has a long way to go in its portrayal of Hispanics. "The door for Latinos has opened just a crack, [but] you still have to push," she told *Hispanic Magazine*. "I'm still fighting the battle. Being a woman, and being Latino, and then, horror of horrors, a mature Latino woman, is very difficult."

Selected works

Plays

Skydrift.
A View From the Bridge.
The Sign In Sidney Brustein's Window.
The Rose Tattoo.
Gantry.
Last of the Red Hot Lovers.
The Ritz.
The Odd Couple.
Size of the World.
Sunset Blvd.
The Vagina Monolgues.
The Glass Menagerie.
Steel Magnolias.
Gypsy.

Films

The Fabulous Senorita, 1952.
Latin Lovers, 1953.
The Yellow Tomahawk, 1954.
Seven Cities of Gold, 1955.
The King and I, 1956.
The Deerslayer, 1957.
West Side Story, 1961.
She Loves Me, 1964.
Marlowe, 1969.
The Night of the Following Day, 1969.
Popi, 1969.
Carnal Knowledge, 1971.
The Boss' Son, 1979.
Happy Birthday, Gemini, 1980.
The Four Seasons, 1981.
I Like It Like That, 1994.
Angus, 1995.

The Wharf Rat, Showtime, 1995.
Piñero, 2001.

Television

The Electric Company.
Sesame Street.
9 to 5.
B.L. Stryker.
The Top of the Heap.
Cosby Mystery Series.
Oz, HBO.

(guest apperances)

The Muppet Show.
The Rockford Files.
Resurrection Blvd., Showtime.

Sources

Periodicals

Times Union (Albany), October 5, 2000. P. 22.
Baltimore Sun, September 9, 1993. 1F.
Contra Costa Times, August 18, 2001. C03.
Hispanic Magazine, December 2001.
People Magazine, September 28, 1998. P. 167.
South Bend Tribune, October 9, 2001.
Telegram & Gazette (Worcester), September 18, 1992. C1.

Other

National Public Radio, Weekend Edition, November 7, 1999

—Kelly M. Cross

Grace Napolitano

1936—

Politician, business executive

A political force from urban Southern California, Grace Flores Napolitano has made an impact on U. S. congressional legislation affecting water and soil clean-up, teen suicide prevention, worker training, and the protection of small businesses and jobs for minorities. A retired business executive and concerned parent and citizen, she acquired inside information on national, state, and local Latino and workers' problems from experience at the local level. From Norwalk city councilwoman to mayor and three-term state legislator, in 1998, she worked her way up to two consecutive terms in the U. S. House of Representatives and mounted a strong advocacy for families, health, and the environment.

Grassroots Beginning in Politics

Napolitano, who is California's two-term congressional representative from the 34th district, is well-versed in Latino culture and the needs of Hispanic citizens. Born in the Mexican border town Brownsville, Texas, on December 4, 1936, to Miguel and Maria Alicia Ledezma Flores, Napolitano was christened Graciela Flores. She completed high school, divorced her first husband, and raised their children as a single mom. In 1976 she married New York entrepreneur Frank Napolitano and assisted him in opening a restaurant. The couple settled in Norwalk, California and Napolitano established a thriving career there as an employee of Ford Motor Company. In retirement, she shared her husband's enthusiasm for the local Roman Catholic parish and for community activism.

To better her business career, Napolitano studied at Cerritos College, Los Angeles Trade Technical College, and Technical Southwest College. She expressed concern for the Norwalk community through volunteerism in community family guidance, parish work, and membership in the Lions Club. Her rise up the political ladder began in 1986, when she pursued a four-year term as councilwoman in Norwalk and, simultaneously, as mayor from 1989 to 1990. Because of her involvement in solving local problems and strengthening the economy, she won re-election to the city council by the highest vote margin in Norwalk history. Central to her platform were citizens' needs for more jobs, a diversified job base, downtown redevelopment, and improvements to inter-urban transportation.

Upon election to the California Assembly in 1992, Napolitano championed international trade, environmental protection, improved highway development, and the financial needs of beginning entrepreneurs. In addition, she supported economic expansion and local-based solutions to family issues like teen suicide and domestic violence in the Hispanic community. As a proponent of American small business, she advocated the expansion of foreign markets for American products and better-paying jobs linked with trade. In 1996 she joined California legislator Richard Katz in sponsoring a bill requiring the ports of Los Angeles and Long Beach to plan more efficient, competitive facilities. At the local level, she led annual sessions of the International Trade and Procurement Conference.

Spirited U. S. Congresswoman

Napolitano's election to the 106th U. S. Congress from the 34th California district coincided with a national political shift that brought four other Latinas into the U. S. Congress. Her success derived in part from a trend toward Hispanic prominence in political leadership. For instance, there was a rapid rise of 30.1% Latinas in the nation's elective offices as compared to only 17.2% of white women. In November of 1998, before she took the oath of office, she plunged into a prickly issues forum weighing the effectiveness of unilateral U.S. trade sanctions.

During her first term in a federal office, Napolitano demonstrated the intelligence and courage of a seasoned politician. She accepted appointments to the small business and resources commissions, chaired the women's caucus, and served as vice-chair of the Latino caucus. In addition, she became an ardent spokeswoman for Armenians, Greeks, Native Americans, and the business-oriented New Democrat Coalition, a centrist thinktank promoting mainstream and bipartisan action on national problems.

Campaigned for Health and the Environment

In Napolitano's second run for Congress, she won reelection with 71% of the vote and added to her list of duties membership on the international relations commission. She committed herself to securing job-training funds and new business for the urban constituents of Southern California. As a result of her work, the U. S. Labor Department granted the area $2.8 million for specialized high-tech training and $4 million toward the reuse and redevelopment of the Northrop Grumman B-2 facility in Pico Rivera as a potential key to job diversity.

Napolitano showed no reticence in campaigning for a better life for Latino citizens. In August of 1999 she sparked wellness initiatives by endorsing Los Angeles health advocate Cesar Portillo for the California state legislature. A month later she echoed the protests of hundreds of community activists and union members against racial discrimination and unfair labor practices that targeted Latino employees of the new Gigante Supermarket in Pico Rivera, California.

Napolitano's battle against Gigante involved neighbors and business advocates for consensus building. In partnership with Radio Shack and Office Depot, the retailer, Grupo Gigante, sold groceries and general merchandise through a superstore chain owned by the heirs of Angel Losada Moreno, based in Mexico City. The company had just built a store in the Los Angeles commercial district when Napolitano joined State Senator Joe Dunn, Assemblyman Tom Calderon, and Pico Rivera City Councilman Gregory Salcido in demanding dignity and a fair wage for grocery workers. She networked an alert to the public of the company's intent to break state labor laws by limiting Latino employees to substandard wages. In a crusade for fair treatment, she protested salaries that were half the norm for California grocery workers and denounced exorbitant premiums for company health care coverage.

Built a People-Friendly Reputation

Napolitano quickly aimed her activism at hot-button environmental issues. In September of 2000, she earned endorsement of the Sierra Club, supporters of a cleaner world and protection for the endangered ecosystem. She denounced the insidious practice of "contract bundling," the consolidation of two or more procurement requirements into a single contract, as a deterrent to the flow of business capital to new, miniority, and female entrepreneurs. In October of 2000, she joined backers of small business in applauding President Bill Clinton's executive order directing federal agencies to bolster business for minority and disadvantaged entrepreneurs by increasing opportunities for subcontracts.

In a partisan effort that included the Northern Ute Indian tribe, Napolitano mobilized political effort in February of 2000 to protect the Metropolitan Water District from a potential disaster triggered by an 11-story heap of uranium waste 600 feet north of the Colorado River near Moab, Utah. She condemned the refuse left by a bankrupt factory that daily leaked some 28,000 gallons of radioactive waste plus arsenic, lead, and ammonia into groundwater daily. According to her reasoning, the outflow of contaminants endangered the drinking water of seven states, including California. She and other Californians demanded immediate action to protect the Lake Havasu intake from the Colorado River Aqueduct.

The resulting pact focused on the quality and reliability of the primary drinking water supply to 17 million citizens, who comprised 25 percent of mostly urban Southern California. The initiative prefaced Napolitano's subsequent promotion of legislation forcing a cleanup of the 130 acres soiled by 10.5 million tons of radioactive mill tailings. In October of 2000, President Bill Clinton made the cleanup an element of the Floyd G. Spence National Defense Authorization Act, which he signed into law. Napolitano remarked that the year-long campaign to rid the area of a significant agrarian and human health hazard had produced joint action by leaders throughout the Southwest.

Spokeswoman for Citizen Well-Being

Napolitano deliberately avoided a one-issue political career. She spearheaded suicide prevention among teenaged Latinas, who had the highest rate of self-destruction of any ethnic or racial group in the country. In 2001 a Labor, Health and Human Services, and Education appropriations bill underwrote an expanded school-based mental health service that focused on the needs of young Latinas in Southeast Los Angeles County. Additional federal funding that Napolitano directed toward district problems included grants for a youth center and sheriff's department office in La Puente, funds to lower diesel emissions by replacing diesel vehicles with environment-friendly models burning compressed natural gas, water recycling in Rio Hondo, and drainage and sewage systems to prevent flood damage to Norwalk, Pico Rivera, and Whittier. To limit congestion on I-5 between Norwalk and Santa Fe Springs, she secured $500,000 toward improving roadways and installing a commercial vehicle advanced traveler information system. She also supported the spending of $7.5 million to equip a 35-mile eastern Los Angeles rail corridor with a light rail transit system. A bonus to her district was the rail project's creation of new jobs and protection of existing jobs throughout the San Gabriel Valley.

Napolitano's outreach continued to target needy venues. On June 29, 2000, she addressed the House Resources Subcommittee on Water and Power on behalf of CALFED, an alliance of state and federal agencies with management and regulatory responsibility in the Bay-Delta Estuary. In her address she called for substantial water storage, state and federal water regulation, and assurances of drinking water quality in urban areas. That same month, she promoted dozens of national Latino organizations at the First National Latino Policy Summit on Domestic Violence, which pooled the wisdom of community activists, advocates, practitioners, and researchers to improve the lives of Hispanic citizens. Despite heavy demands on her time, she returned weekly to her family and spent free time talking with voters about their needs and wishes.

Sources

Books

Carroll's Federal Directory, Carroll Publishing, 2001.
The Complete Marquis Who's Who, Marquis Who's Who, 2001.

Periodicals

Business Wire, September 1, 1999; September 15, 1999; February 11, 2000; June 20, 2000; October 16, 2000; October 31, 2000; June 21, 2001.
Jet, October 30, 2000.
Journal of Commerce and Commercial, April 18, 1996, p. 1B(2).
PRNewswire, November 4, 1998; August 11, 1999; June 20, 2000. August 11, 1999.
PS: Political Science & Politics, September, 2000.
Sierra, September, 2000.

On-line

http://resourcescommittee.house.gov/106cong/water/00jun29/napolitano.htm/
http://www.house.gov/napolitano/bio.htm
http://www.aaainc.org/record/Napolitano.htm

Other

Additional Information for this profile was obtained through personal telephone interviews with Kevin Su on the Washington, D. C. congressional staff and with Ray Cordova of the district office of U. S. Representative Grace Napolitano in Santa Fe Springs, California.

—Mary Ellen Snodgrass

Antonia Novello

1944—

Pediatrician

Antonia Novello overcame childhood poverty and illness to become one of the leading doctors in America. She was trained as a pediatrician and served in the United States Public Health Service. After spending several years at the National Institute of Health, Novello was appointed United States Surgeon General by President George Bush. She was the first woman and first Hispanic to hold this position. Novello used this role to bring national attention to important health issues, such as alcohol abuse, smoking, violence, and AIDS, as well as issues that especially affected women and Hispanics.

Childhood Illness Led to Medical Career

Antonia Novello was born on August 23, 1944 in Fajardo, Puerto Rico, a town 32 miles southeast of San Juan. She was the oldest of three children. When she was eight years old, Novello's father, Antonio Coello, died. Novello and her siblings were primarily raised by her mother, Ana Delia Coello, a schoolteacher and later a junior high school and high school principal, who later remarried. At birth Novello was diagnosed with congenital megacolon, an abnormality of the large intestine. This was a painful condition that plagued Novello throughout her childhood and required frequent trips to the hospital. Novello was told that she should have surgery to correct this problem when she was eight years old; however, it was ten more years before that would happen. As Novello explained to the *Saturday Evening Post,* "I do believe some people fall through the cracks. I was one of those. I thought, when I grow up, no other person is going to wait 18 years for surgery."

Despite her medical problems, Novello excelled academically. She was a well-adjusted child who had a good sense of humor and who was very active in school activities. Her mother stressed the importance of an education and personally taught her math and science. "I went through a system of care that was not very keen, in a diseased state that makes you realize that there are good people and bad people in medicine, with a mother who said, 'I'm not going to let your disease be used for you not to succeed.' All those three prepared me for the job that God eventually made me have," Novello told the Hall of Public Service in an interview on June 18, 1994.

At a Glance . . .

Born Antonia Coello on August 23, 1944 in Fajardo, PR; married Joseph Novello. *Education:* University of Puerto Rico, B.S., 1965, M.D., 1970; Johns Hopkins School of Hygiene, M.P.H., 1982. *Military Service:* U.S. Public Health Service, 1978.

Career: Univ. of MI Dept of Pediatrics, intern, 1970-73; Georgetown Univ. Dept of Pediatric Nephrology, fellow, 1973-76; private practice in pediatrics, 1976-78; U.S. Public Health Service, 1978; Natl Institutes of Health Inst. of Arthritis, metabolism, and digestive disease project officer, 1978-79; NIH , staff physician, 1979-1980; NIH Div. of Research Grants exe. sec, 1981-86; Labor and Human Resources Committee, Congressional fellow, 1982-83; NIH Natl. Inst. of Child Health and Human Devel., dep. director, 1986-90; U.S. Surgeon General, 1990-93; UNICEF, special rep. for health and nutrition, 1993-96; NY State Dept. of Health, commissioner, 1999-.

Memberships: AMA; Intl. Soc. of Nephrology; Amer. Soc. of Nephrology; Latin Amer. Soc. of Nephrology; Soc. for Pediatric Research; Amer. Pediatric Soc.; Assn of US Military Surgeons; Amer. Soc. of Pediatric Nephrology; Pan Amer. Medical and Dental Soc.; DC Medical Soc.; Johns Hopkins Univ Soc. of Scholars; Alpha Omega Alpha.

Awards: Public Health Service Commendation Medal, 1983; Public Health Service Citation, 1984; Certifi. of Recognition, NIH, 1985; Public Health Service Outstanding medal, 1988; Public Health Service Surgeon General's Exemplary Service Medal, 1989; Surgeon General Medallion Awd., 1990; Congressional Hispanic Caucus Medal, 1991; Order of Military Medical Merit Awd., 1992; Elizabeth Ann Seton Awd., 1993; Natl Women's Hall of Fame Inductee, 1994; Natl Council of Catholic Women Distinguished Service Awd., 1995; Miami Children's Hospital Intl Pediatric Hall of Fame, 1996; Hispanic Heritage Leadership Award, 1998; numerous other awards and honors.

Addresses: Commissioner, NY State Department of Health, 14th Floor, Corning Tower, Empire State Plaza, Albany, NY 12237.

Novello graduated from high school at age 15 and then went to study at the University of Puerto Rico at Rio Pedras. When she was 18 years old she finally had surgery to correct her medical condition. However, the initial surgery was not successful and Novello continued to suffer from complications for two more years. When she was 20 years old Novello traveled to the renowned Mayo Clinic for another operation that finally corrected the problem.

Novello graduated from the University of Puerto Rico in 1965 with a Bachelor of Science degree. She then went on to study medicine at the same university, graduating in 1970. That same year she married Joseph Novello, a navy flight surgeon who later became a psychiatrist and a radio talk show host. The young couple moved to Ann Arbor, Michigan so that Novello could begin a pediatrics internship at the University of Michigan Medical Center. A year later Novello became the first woman to receive the University of Michigan Pediatrics Department Intern of the Year Award.

Novello stayed in Michigan until 1973 and then moved to Washington, D.C. to begin her residency at Georgetown University Hospital. Novello became interested in studying the kidneys after her favorite aunt had died from kidney failure and Novello herself was hospitalized with kidney problems. She then decided to specialize in pediatric nephrology at Georgetown. When her fellowship ended in 1976 Novello went into private practice in Springfield, Virginia. However, she soon realized that she was too emotionally involved with her patients so she left her practice. As she explained to *People* magazine in December of 1990, "When the pediatrician cries as much as the parents do, then you know it's time to get out."

In 1978 Novello thought about joining the United States Navy. However, a male recruiter discouraged her because of her gender. A year later she decided to join the United States Public Health Service Commissioned Corps instead. This is a branch of the United States Uniformed Services dedicated to providing highly trained health care professionals to deliver health services across the country. Her first assignment was as a project officer for the Institute of Arthritis, Metabolism, and Digestive Disease at the National Institutes of Health (NIH) in Bethesda, Maryland. A year later she was promoted to a staff physician at NIH. From 1981 to 1986 Novello worked as the executive secretary for the Division of Research Grants. During this time she continued her education, graduating in 1982 with a Master of Public Health degree from Johns Hopkins University. From 1982 to 1983 Novello also served as a Congressional Fellow for the Labor and Human Resources Committee chaired by Senator Orrin Hatch. In this position she worked on the National Transplant Act of 1984 and also helped draft the labels on cigarette packages to warn smokers of the health dangers of smoking.

In 1986 Novello was promoted again as deputy director of the National Institute of Child Health and Human Development, a position that fully utilized her pediatrics training. During her four years in this position Novello was a strong advocate for AIDS research. She was passionate about her work and felt she had reached the height of her career at NIH. However, in 1990 she was asked to fill the most prestigious position in public health, United States Surgeon General.

Became Nation's Leading Doctor

The Surgeon General of the United States is the nation's leading spokesperson on matters of public health and the head of the United States Public Health Service. The duties of this position include educating the public about health concerns, advocating disease prevention and health promotion, and providing scientifically based health policy analysis to the President and the Secretary of Health and Human Services. From 1981 to 1989 this position was held by Dr. C. Everett Koop who was appointed by President Ronald Reagan. Koop was an outspoken advocate of public health who created much controversy during his tenure since some of his views opposed those of the President. When Novello first took over for Koop, she was constantly asked, "How do you feel in Dr. Koop's shoes?" With her characteristic sense of humor, Novello told the *Saturday Evening Post* that she was asked that question so often that she was " going to have to learn a new specialty in podiatry."

On October 17, 1989 President George Bush nominated Novello for the position of Surgeon General. One of the key factors in his decision was the fact that Novello was publicly opposed to abortion, which was consistent with the President's views. Unlike the controversial Dr. Koop, Novello's Congressional confirmation hearings went smoothly. Antonia Novello became the fourteenth United States Surgeon General and the first woman and first Hispanic to ever hold the position. While Novello was committed to addressing the health issues of both women and Hispanics, she understood that her new role encompassed more than those particular social groups. As the *Medical World News* reported, at Novello's Senate confirmation hearings she stated, "I do not come before you as the surgeon general for Hispanics, or the surgeon general for women, or the surgeon general for children," but for "every citizen, regardless of race, age, sex, creed, circumstance, or political belief." Novello was sworn into her position on March 9, 1990. During the swearing-in ceremony, she announced that, "The American dream is well and alive today the West Side Story comes to the West Wing."

Fought for America's Health

During her three-year tenure Novello focused her energy on a number of health topics, including alcohol, tobacco, violence, and AIDS. She told the *Saturday Evening Post* that she followed the motto of "good science and good sense." Her first major public health campaign as Surgeon General attacked the problem of underage drinking. Novello publicly asked the alcohol industry to voluntarily stop creating advertisements that targeted young people. As Novello explained to the *American Medical News,* "I have nothing against the advertising industry. But I do have something against alcohol advertising that misleads, misinforms and unabashedly targets American youth." Novello especially criticized the distributors of Cisco, a wine with 20 percent alcohol content that was being sold as a cheap dessert wine with advertising aimed toward teenagers and the poor. In addition, Novello launched a "Spring Break '91" campaign to bring awareness to the rising number of binge drinkers among college students.

Novello used a similar strategy to continue Dr. Koop's public campaign against smoking. Most notably she joined forces with the American Medical Association to ask R.J. Reynolds Tobacco Company to voluntarily withdraw its "Old Joe Camel" cartoon advertisements for Camel cigarettes because they were too attractive to teenagers. In an article in *Adweek's Marketing Week* in March of 1992, Novello proclaimed, "I don't care whether their actions were intentional or unintentional. Their advertising has reached children and it is going to stop." Novello's campaign paid off several years after she left her position. In 1998 federal law prohibited such imagery in tobacco advertisements. Novello also fought to stop cigarette advertisements that targeted women, citing her concern over the fact that lung cancer had become the leading cancer death among women. She was especially critical of brands such as Virginia Slims, Satin, Ritz, and Capri that associated women's smoking with images of physical fitness and independence. As Novello explained to the *American Medical News* in November of 1990, "It is time that the self-serving, death-dealing tobacco industry and their soldiers of fortune, advertising agencies, stop blowing smoke in the face of America's women and children."

Novello also brought national attention to health problems that were especially prevalent to the Hispanic community, such as smoking and diabetes. As Surgeon General she convened a workshop on such issues that led to the development of a National Hispanic/Latino Health Initiative. When she left her position as Surgeon General she produced two public service announcements for the American Diabetes Association encouraging Hispanic Americans to get tested for diabetes. In 1994 she also edited a book on Hispanic/Latino health issues.

Continued Public Service after Washington

While the term of Surgeon General is four years long, Novello stepped down in June of 1993 due to the change in administration. Democratic President Bill Clinton appointed Dr. Joycelyn Elders to the job, the first African-American woman to hold the position. Novello spent the next three years working at the Georgetown University Medical School and serving as the United Nations Children's Fund (UNICEF) Special Representative for Health and Nutrition. In 1996 she was a Visiting Professor of Health Policy and Management. In June of 1999 Novello was chosen to serve as the Health Commissioner for New York. The Secretary of the United States Department of Health and Human Services at that time, Donna Shalala, told the *U.S. Newswire,* "Governor Pataki has made a sound choice in reaching out to Antonia Novello. She will serve New Yorkers with the same vigor and talent that she employed in serving all Americans during her tenure in Washington." In her new role Novello has continued to tackle tough issues. Her latest challenge has been to try to raise the level of accountability for hospitals and doctors in New York.

Novello has received numerous awards and honorary degrees in recognition for her public service. For example, in 1983 she received the Public Health Service Commendation Medal. In 1989 she was awarded the Surgeon General's Exemplary Service Medal and in 1998 she was recognized for her leadership at the Hispanic Heritage Awards. Novello is proud of her success and sees herself as a role model for others. In an interview for *Executive Female* in 1991, Novello stated, "I know that I am one example of someone who has refused to be told that she couldn't achieve her goals. As a woman, as a Hispanic, and as the first female Surgeon General, I am a testament to pushing back barriers."

Selected writings

"Condom Use for Prevention of Sexual Transmission of HIV Infection," *Journal of the American Medical Association,* June 9, 1993.

"Healthy Children Ready to Learn," *Journal of the American Medical Association,* October 7, 1992.

"Healthy Children Ready to Learn—The Challenge to the Medical Community," *Journal of the American Medical Association,* March 20, 1991.

"Healthy Children Ready to Learn: The Surgeon General's Initiative for Children," *Journal of School Health,* October 1991.

"Increasing Organ Donation—A Report from the Surgeon General's Workshop," *Journal of the American Medical Association,* January 8, 1992.

"The Secretary's Work Group on Pediatric HIV Infection and Disease," August 1989.

"Surgeon General's Report on Health Benefits of Smoking Cessation," *Public Health Reports,* November/December 1990.

"Violence Is A Greater Killer of Children than Disease," *Public Health Reports* , May/June 1991.

"Women and HIV Infection," *Journal of the American Medical Association,* April 10, 1991.

Sources

Books

The Complete Marquis Who's Who. Marquis Who's Who, 2001.

Periodicals

Addiction Letter, March 1993.
Adweek Eastern Edition, November 18, 1991.
Adweek's Marketing Week, October 8, 1990; March 16, 1992.
American Medical News, April 27, 1990; June 15, 1990; October 5, 1990; October 19, 1990; June 24, 1991; November 18, 1991; March 23, 1992; April 6, 1992.
Broadcasting, December 2, 1991.
Diabetes Forecast, July 1993.
Economist, December 21, 1991.
Executive Female, March-April 1991.
Mediaweek, November 18, 1991.
Modern Healthcare, March 13, 2000; February 19, 2001; December 21, 1992; July 5, 1993.
New Republic, August 10, 1992.
People Weekly, December 17, 1990.
Public Health Reports, May-June 1991.
Saturday Evening Post, May-June 1991.
U.S. Newswire, June 4, 1999.
Vital Speeches, May 15, 1993; July 15, 1993; July 14, 1994.

On-line

Glass Ceiling Biographies, www.theglassceiling.com
Hall of Public Service, www.achievement.org
National Institutes of Health, www.nih.gov
National Women's Hall of Fame, www.greatwomen.org
New York State Department of Health, www.health.state.ny.us
Puerto Rico Herald, www.puertorico-herald.org/issues/vol4n12/ProfileANovello-en.shtml
Office of the Surgeon General, www.surgeongeneral.gov

—Janet P. Stamatel

Soledad O'Brien

1966—

Reporter

Television news anchor Soledad O'Brien generated a flurry of her own news stories after she began appearing on the cable network MSNBC in 1996. Hired as the host of its daily technology show, O'Brien and her dramatically exotic looks garnered a slew of fan mail and helped make her one of the news channel's rising stars. O'Brien eventually moved over to the NBC news division, and since 1999 has hosted the weekend edition of the *Today* show. Her fan base remains a dedicated one: Peter Brown, O'Brien's onetime boss at a Boston television station, praised her in an interview with *San Francisco Chronicle* writer Sylvia Rubin. "She's smart, a quick learner and proves that a really nice person can finish first," Brown effused.

Long Island Childhood

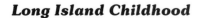

The future news star was born in 1966 and named Maria de la Soledad O'Brien. One of six children of her schoolteacher mother, a black Cuban, and Irish-Australian father, a college professor, she was called Solly by her family from an early age. "I consider myself black primarily, and Latina sort of secondarily," she

told *Washington Post* writer Lloyd Grove. Her parents had met in Baltimore, on the campus of Johns Hopkins University, but interracial marriage was illegal in the state of Maryland at the time, so they traveled to Washington, D.C. to wed in 1959. Her mixed ancestry distinguished O'Brien from her classmates in the community of St. James where she grew up, on Long Island's north shore, and she suffered the occasional racial slur. "I knew I was different from my early childhood," she told Grove. "I knew I would never date anybody in high school. Nobody wants to date somebody who looks different." Still, a strong sense of identity and membership in a family of overachievers helped her deal positively with the situation. "It would be incorrect to say I had a very traumatic experience," she said in the interview with Grove. "Once I went to college, where differences are more accepted, people didn't care much."

College for O'Brien was Harvard University, where she studied English literature, but also took courses in the pre-med curriculum. The science courses helped her win an internship at WBZ-TV, a Boston television station, and while still in college she was offered a full-time job at the CBS affiliate as a researcher for the

Born Maria de la Soledad O'Brien, September 19, 1966; daughter of a Edward (a college professor) and Estella (a public-school teacher) O'Brien; married Brad Raymond (an investment banker), c. 1995; children: Sofia Elizabeth. *Education:* Attended Harvard University, 1980s and 2000; earned degree, 2000.

Career: Reporter for KISS-FM (radio station), Boston, MA; WBZ-TV in Boston, associate producer and newswriter, late 1980s; NBC News, New York City, researcher and producer, 1991-93; KRON-TV, San Francisco, began as reporter, became East Bay bureau chief; *The Know Zone,* Discovery Channel, co-host. c. 1993-95; hired by MSNBC, 1996, as anchor of *The Site*; became host of *Morning Blend,* 1997; guest anchor of *Weekend Today,* NBC News, became permanent anchor, July 1999; contributing technology editor, *USA Weekend Magazine.*

Memberships: National Association of Hispanic Journalists; National Association of Black Journalists.

Awards: Emmy award, Northern California chapter of the Academy of Television Arts and Science, for *The Know Zone,* 1995; Hispanic Achievement Award in Communications, 1997.

Addresses: *Home*—New York City. *Office*—MSNBC, One MSNBC Plaza, Secaucus, NJ 07094.

station's medical reporter. She decided to leave school and pursue a career in journalism. She was hired by NBC News in New York City in 1991 as a researcher and producer for its science correspondent, Bob Bazell.

O'Brien headed west when she was hired as a reporter for San Francisco's KRON-TV. In 1993, she co-hosted a Discovery Channel program, *The Know Zone,* which earned her a local Emmy award. When she learned that Microsoft and NBC were planning a new cable venture to be called MSNBC, she lobbied for a job as host of its benchmark daily technology show, *The Site.* As she told the *San Francisco Chronicle*'s Rubin, "I just knew I was perfect for this job. My vision was that I didn't have to pretend to be a technologist; I could just be a lay person."

That Internet-novice status indeed won her the job, and O'Brien was commended for making the new technol-

ogy accessible to viewers. The show offered industry news, reviews of interesting Web sites, features on new software, and interviews with Silicon Valley executives. O'Brien even bantered with Dev, a virtual-reality character, for a viewer-mail segment. The taped show aired six nights a week, and O'Brien regularly worked 12-hour days. Some of that involved reviewing the broadcasts of the day before. "My mother sends e-mails telling me I'm so abrupt with the guests," she told the *San Francisco Chronicle.* "Am I too abrupt? I probably am, so I watch tapes to figure out how to do a more comfortable interview."

"Goddess to the Geeks"

By 1997 O'Brien and *The Site* had attracted somewhat of a cult following. The online magazine Salon.com named her "Goddess to the Geeks," and she was receiving up to 2,000 e-mails a week. Even *NBC Nightly News* anchor Tom Brokaw was a fan: Brokaw told the *Washington Post* that he found O'Brien "cute and so bright and so mature in her broadcasting skills. There she is, totally at ease, very articulate and commanding of the subject matter and the environment around her, and yet able to do all this in a user-friendly way." Inevitably, a programming shake-up at the fledgling network led to cancellation of *The Site,* and O'Brien was given the anchor slot of *Morning Blend,* a two-hour news talk show that aired Saturdays and Sundays. From there, MSNBC partner NBC invited her to guest-host on weekend edition of *Today* show, which was her first experience in live national television. She was named permanent co-anchor of the weekend show in July of 1999.

In 2000, O'Brien was named as one of *People* magazine's "50 Most Beautiful People In The World" annual list. She earned a more enduring honor that same year when she finished her Harvard degree, without taking any time off from her job at NBC. A resident of New York City, O'Brien finished her Harvard coursework by spending Monday through Wednesday at her sister's Boston-area home. Her semester also coincided with her first trimesters of pregnancy, and O'Brien told *Parents* magazine that she "underestimated how exhausting pregnancy can be. I'd walk around Harvard Yard thinking, I would pay one of these undergraduates $20 if I could just lie down in her bed for 20 minutes!"

Sofia Elizabeth, O'Brien's child with investment-banker husband Brad Raymond, was born in October of 2000. She still hosts *Weekend Today,* and files stories for NBC's *Nightly News.* Before *Today* co-anchor Katie Couric renewed her contract in 2001, O'Brien, who occasionally served as substitute anchor on the weekday show, was mentioned as a possible successor. She and her husband are committed to staying in New York City, in part to avoid for Sofia the kind of suburban isolation O'Brien experienced as a youth on Long

Island, as she told *Parents.* "I want to make sure she knows many different kinds of people."

Sources

Entertainment Weekly, January 10, 1997.
Parents, October 2001.
People, June 16, 1997; May 8, 2000.
*San Francisco Chronicle,*April 15, 1997.
St. Louis Post-Dispatch, March 16, 2001.
Washington Post, June 10, 1997.

On-Line

MSNBC, http://www.msnbc.com/onair/bios/s_obri en.asp (February 17, 2002).

—Carol Brennan

Ellen Ochoa

1958—

Astronaut

Ellen Ochoa became the first Latina in space in 1993 when she served as the sole female crew member of *Discovery* space shuttle. By 1999, with three missions behind her, Ochoa had logged 720 hours of space time. An accomplished engineer and scientist who has served at Mission Control for other shuttle flights, the native Californian also likes to speak to school groups and young audiences about her work at the National Aeronautics and Space Administration (NASA). Ochoa stresses that staying in school gives one many more career options, and though she herself had never considered becoming an astronaut as youngster, her educational background made it possible. "Getting to be an astronaut is tough for anybody," no matter what their background, she told Lydia Martin in a Knight-Ridder/Tribune News Service article. "[I]t's just a matter of working hard to have a very good education."

Twice Valedictorian

Ochoa was born 1958 in Los Angeles, but grew up in the San Diego area. Her Mexican heritage came to her through her father, but her parents had divorced by the time she was in her teens. Ochoa's mother struggled to raise five children as a single parent, but found time to take college courses in her spare time—setting an important example for Ochoa, her three brothers, and sister. All were achievers and award-winners in the La Mesa public schools, and Ochoa was valedictorian of her 1975 graduating class at Grossmont High. Offered a four-year scholarship to Stanford University in Palo Alto, near San Francisco, Ochoa chose to study at San Diego State University so that she could be near her two younger brothers, still in high school at the time.

Early on, Ochoa considered a career in journalism. She took writing, business, and computer science courses before settling on physics as her major. When she graduated in 1980, she was once again the valedictorian of her class. From there Ochoa entered Stanford University, where she earned both a master's degree in electrical engineering and a doctorate by 1985. While at Stanford, Ochoa met graduate students who were interested in NASA's astronaut training program, and realized that she might qualify for it as well. The candidates' program had only began accepting women in 1978, and the first Latino astronaut, Rodolfo Neri, flew his first space shuttle flight in 1985. Ochoa applied to the program that same year.

At a Glance . . .

Born May 10, 1958 in Los Angeles, CA; daughter of Joseph and Rosanne (Deardoff) Ochoa; married Coe Fulmer Miles; two children. *Education:* San Diego State University, B.S., 1980; Stanford University, M.S.E.E., 1981, Ph.D.E.E., 1985.

Career: Sandia National Laboratories, Livermore, CA, research engineer in Imaging Technology Branch, 1985-88; National Aeronautics and Space Administration (NASA)/Ames Research Center, Moffet Field Naval Air Station, Mountain View, CA, 1988-91; astronaut, NASA, Houston, TX, 1991-. Also member of the Presidential Commission on the Celebration of Women in American History.

Memberships: Optical Society of America; American Institute of Aeronautics and Astronautics; Phi Beta Kappa.

Awards: Women in Aerospace Outstanding Achievement Award; Hispanic Engineer Albert Baez Award for Outstanding Technical Contribution to Humanity, 1989; National Hispanic Quincentennial Commission, pride award, 1990; Hispanic Heritage Leadership Award; San Diego State University Alumna of the Year; Ochoa has also earned the following awards from the National Aeronautics and Space Administration (NASA): Space Act Tech Brief Awards, 1992; Space Flight Medal, 1993, 1994, 1999; Outstanding Leadership Medal, 1995; Exceptional Service Medal, 1997.

Addresses: *Office*—National Aeronautics and Space Administration, Lyndon B. Johnson Space Center, Houston, TX 77058.

After finishing her doctorate, Ochoa began her career as a research engineer at Sandia National Laboratories in Livermore, California. She found her niche in the Imaging Technology Branch and, with others, worked on optical inspection systems and other new technologies. In time she would share three patents for her research work. Meanwhile, Ochoa leaned she had become one of a hundred finalists for the NASA training program. The following year, in 1988, she was hired at the National Aeronautics and Space Administration (NASA) as chief of the Intelligent Systems Technology Branch at its Ames Research Center. Here Ochoa worked on computational systems for aerospace missions.

Ochoa won a highly coveted place in the astronaut training program in January of 1990. Over the next year, she underwent a series of physical and mental challenges. The trainees had to undergo rigorous courses and testing in the space sciences, astronomy, geology, oceanography, meteorology, first aid, survival techniques, and the complex systems of space shuttle design. They were expected to know every part of the shuttle and each part's function. In an interview with her *Stanford Department of Engineering Alumni Report*, Ochoa said that her diversified background helped. "If you are motivated to excel in one area, you are usually motivated to excel in others. NASA looks for that."

Loved the View

Ochoa began as a flight software specialist in robotics development, testing, and training in 1991, and was surprised when she was chosen for her first mission, scheduled for April of 1993. "Usually it takes quite a bit longer; I got lucky," Ochoa told Knight-Ridder/Tribune News Service journalist Martin a few months later. She was part of a five-member crew aboard the space shuttle *Discovery*, serving as a specialist the second ATLAS (Atmospheric Laboratory for Applications and Science) mission. Ochoa and hew crewmates conducted research on solar activity, and she used a Remote Manipulator System (RMS), a 50-foot robotic arm, to deploy and capture the Spartan satellite that retrieved data about the solar corona and solar winds. She recalled in the interview with Martin that she never tired of the view. "The most exciting thing was looking out at Earth from up there. It was beautiful."

Ochoa also took part in a November 1994 mission aboard the space shuttle *Atlantis* serving as payload commander for another data-collecting mission on solar energy. Her next flight was again on the *Discovery*, a ten-day space journey in the spring of 1999 for which she served as mission specialist and flight engineer. The *Discovery* mission was the first shuttle flight to dock to the International Space Station, which was expecting a resident permanent crew the following year. Ochoa and her team delivered several hundred pounds of supplies, again with the help of the RMS device. "There's no weight in space, so that's not the problem," *Contra Costa Times* reporter Elizabeth Zach quoted Ochoa as saying about this particular task. "What is a problem, though, is the mass. It's just so awkward." Ochoa was also scheduled for duty as a Mission Specialist on a planned Atlantis flight in April of 2002, which would be the thirteenth mission to the International Space Station.

Ochoa likens being an astronaut to being in school again, describing it as a constant learning process.

Back at NASA, she has also served as spacecraft communicator at Mission Control for other shuttle flights, and as assistant for the space station to Chief of the Astronaut Office. Married with two children, she flies her own single-engine plane for recreation, and still plays the flute, as she did in high school. Her status as America's first Latina astronaut has made her the recipient of many awards. She enjoys speaking to groups of students, and does not hesitate to encourage young women to explore science as a career. She has delivered more than 150 such talks, and as she told the *Stanford University School of Engineering Annual Report*, "I never thought about this aspect of the job when I was applying, but it's extremely rewarding. I'm not trying to make every kid an astronaut, but I want kids to think about a career and the preparation they'll need."

Sources

Books

Contemporary Heroes and Heroines, Book IV, Gale, 2000.
Dictionary of Hispanic Biography, Gale, 1996.
Notable Hispanic American Women, Book 1, Gale, 1993.

Periodicals

Contra Costa Times (Walnut Creek, CA), October 14, 1999.
Knight-Ridder/Tribune News Service, December 1, 1993.

On-line

Astronaut Ellen Ochoa, http://www.jsc.nasa.gov
"Crew Interview: Ochoa," http://spaceflight.nasa.gov /shuttle/archives/sts-96/crew/intochoa.html
Stanford University School of Engineering Annual Report, 1997-98, http://soe.stanford.edu/AR97-98/ochoa.html (February 23, 2002).
Impacto, Influencia, Cambio, http://educate.si.edu

—Carol Brennan

Arturo "Chico" O'Farrill

1921—2001

Composer, arranger, musician

One of the architects of Latin jazz, Arturo "Chico" O'Farrill made his mark by fusing jazz with Afro-Cuban music beginning in the late 1940s. Though he would write and arrange music for five more decades, he would receive the most recognition of his career in the last six years of his life. As the author of 1950's *Afro-Cuban Jazz Suite,* O'Farrill sealed his place in jazz history. Following a 30-year absence from recording his own material, O'Farrill re-emerged in 1995 with the Grammy nominated *Pure Emotion.* Two more acclaimed albums followed, as did a weekly gig at Manhattan's Birdland jazz club every Sunday night for three years, until illness prevented him from performing. He died of dysplastic anemia on June 27, 2001 in his adopted hometown of New York City, at the age of 79.

Arturo "Chico" O'Farrill was born in Havana, Cuba on October 28, 1921, the son of an Irish father and a Cuban mother of German descent. A bit of a troublemaker in his youth, O'Farrill's father sent him to a United States military school in Georgia in the hopes of instilling some discipline. The family had hoped that young Arturo would follow in the footsteps of his father and grandfather by becoming a lawyer upon returning to Cuba. Though that idea had already been abandoned by O'Farrill, it became a certainty when he discovered jazz. "In the States, I started listening to big bands on the radio — Benny Goodman, Artie Shaw, Glenn Miller, Tommy Dorsey," O'Farrill recalled in his Milestones Records biography. "And somewhere I got hold of a trumpet and joined the dance band in the school, and that sealed my fate."

Fused Jazz with Cuban Rhythms

Upon returning to Cuba, O'Farrill made a half-hearted attempt at law school, while simultaneously playing in a number of small jazz groups, such as Orquesta Bellemar, the Lecuona Cuban Boys, and with guitarist Isidro Perez. His father, irritated at his son's insistence on playing music, nevertheless arranged for O'Farrill to study composing and arrangement with the Cuban composer Felix Guerrero. Bored with the music of Cuba, O'Farrill decided the place he needed to be was New York.

In 1948 O'Farrill arrived in New York and immediately became aware of the possibilities of fusing jazz and Afro-Cuban rhythms. Witnessing the work the bandleader Machito was doing with the help of Rene Hernan-

At a Glance . . .

Born Arturo O'Farrill on October 28, 1921 in Havana, Cuba; died June 27, 2001 in New York, NY; married Lupe; children: Arturo, Jr., Georgina.

Career: Freelance arranger and composer in New York, 1948-; recording artist: *Chico O'Farrill Jazz*, Clef, 1951; *Jazz North of the Border*, Verve, 1951; *Chico O'Farrill*, Norgran, 1951; *The Second Afro-Cuban Jazz Suite*, Norgran, 1951; *Music from South America*, Verve, 1951; *Afro-Cuban*, Clef, 1951; *Mambo/Latino Dances*, Verve, 1951; *Mambo Dance Sessions*, Norgran, 1954; *Nine Flags*, Impulse, 1966; *Married Well*, Verve, 1968; *Pure Emotion*, Milestone, 1995; *Heart of a Legend*, Milestone, 1999; *Carambola*, Milestone, 2000; film composer, *Guaguasi*, 1979.

Awards: Grammy nomination, Best Latin Jazz Recording for *Pure Emotion*, 1995; Latin Grammy nomination, Best Jazz Recording, *Heart of a Legend*, 1999, and *Carambola*, 2000.

dez and Mario Bauza, of adding jazz concepts to big-band Cuban music, O'Farrill used his knowledge of arrangement to seamlessly blend Latin rhythms and jazz, placing himself at the forefront of Latin jazz. "I grew up in the 30s hearing typical danzon-style music," O'Farrill recalled to Don Heckman of the *Los Angeles Times*. "There were also a lot of sextets, with two trumpets and a lot more rhythm. But what I really loved was the big American-style bands, with trumpets, saxophones and trombones; I loved that kind of sound. And the one thing that I thought Cuban music needed at the time was the richness of the instrumentation of jazz, and of the harmonies. And since I understood jazz and Cuban music, I felt I could bring the two together."

O'Farrill made a name for himself in jazz circles almost as soon as he arrived in New York. Known as a competent arranger, most of his initial work was ghostwriting arrangements for arrangers such as Gil Fuller, Billy Byers and Quincy Jones, who had too much work on their hands. Still, he found time to pen songs under his own name, such as *Undercurrent Blues* which became a hit for Benny Goodman's bebop group.

Afro-Cuban Jazz Suite

In 1949 O'Farrill began a five year association with producer Norman Granz when he recorded *Gone City* with his friends Machito and Mario Bauza. The following year, O'Farrill brought another tune to a Machito recording session produced by Granz, that would become a Latin jazz classic and is considered O'Farrill's first masterpiece. *The Afro-Cuban Jazz Suite* was recorded on December 21, 1950 with guest soloists Charlie Parker, Flip Phillips and Buddy Rich. In his obituary of O'Farrill, Ben Ratliff of the *New York Times* called the tune, "an ambitious work that took the graduated crescendo of Latin big-band music and applied to it a classical sense of contrasting themes and sophisticated harmony."

O'Farrill then composed another classic, *The Manteca Suite*, for Dizzy Gillespie, before moving back to Havana to avoid legal and marital difficulties in New York. He spent two years in Havana and in 1957 moved to Mexico City where he would stay until returning to New York in 1965. "It was great, for a while," he told Heckman of the *Los Angeles Times*, about Mexico. "I had my own band, I had a TV show, I made some records, and we had a good life." Mexico City was also the place where he wrote *The Aztez Suite* for trumpeter Art Farmer.

Returning to New York in the mid-1960s, O'Farrill found work arranging for Gillespie, Count Basie, the Glenn Miller Orchestra and many others. He was also music director for the TV series, *Festival of the Lively Arts*, and began a long and lucrative career writing music for commercials. "I found out that they were paying more for a 60-second toothpaste commercial than for a full chart for Count Basie," he's quoted as saying in his DownBeat obituary. But O'Farrill still put great effort into his commercial endeavors. "I think one of the reasons he was so successful, though, is that he could never really be a hack," O'Farrill's son, Arturo, Jr., explained to Mark Holston of *Hispanic* magazine. "He always wrote from the heart. So even his commercials were good music."

Heart of a Legend

From the 1970s to 1995, O'Farrill's primary output was music for commercials although he would still do freelance arranging on occasion, including a few pieces for David Bowie's 1993 *Black Tie, White Noise* album. In 1995, however, he returned to the recording studio to record *Pure Emotion*, his first studio album in 20 years, which the *Los Angeles Times*, called "a brilliant assemblage of Latin jazz, rich with sly musical subtleties." The recording would go on to be nominated for a Grammy in the Best Latin Jazz category.

He followed *Pure Emotion* with *Heart of a Legend* in 1999 and *Carambola* in 2000. Both of those efforts were nominated for a Latin Grammy for Best Jazz Recording. Additionally, O'Farrill set up shop at the Birdland jazz club in New York, where he led the 18-piece Chico O'Farrill Afro-Cuban Jazz Orchestra every Sunday night for three years. He was also featured in Fernando Trueba's 2000 documentary on

Latin jazz, *Calle 54.* At the time of his death, he was working on the music for a Broadway adaptation of Oscar Hijuelo's novel, *The Mambo Kings Play Songs of Love.* A documentary was also being made about his life by filmmaker Jorge Ulla, which is to be called *Heart of a Legend.*

Sadly, though his career was still arcing higher, Chico O'Farrill died on June 27, 2001 of complications of dysplastic anemia. His music is permanent, however, and as Fernando Gonzalez wrote in *DownBeat:* "He wrote big and brilliantly…. In the process, he took the music from the ballroom to the concert hall and showed both doubters and believers the extraordinary possibilities of this music."

Selected recordings

Chico O'Farrill Jazz, Clef, 1951.
Jazz North of the Border, Verve, 1951.
Chico O'Farrill, Norgran, 1951.
The Second Afro-Cuban Jazz Suite, Norgran, 1951.
Music from South America, Verve, 1951.
Afro-Cuban, Clef, 1951.
Mambo/Latino Dances, Verve, 1951.
Mambo Dance Sessions, Norgran, 1954.
Nine Flags, Impulse, 1966.
Married Well, Verve, 1968.
Pure Emotion, Milestone, 1995.
Heart of a Legend, Milestone, 1999.
Carambola, Milestone, 2000.
Cuban Blues: The Chico O'Farrill Sessions, Verve, 2000.

Sources

Periodicals

DownBeat, September 1, 2001.
Hispanic, June 2000; July 2001.
Los Angeles Times, January 9, 2000.
Miami Herald, July 2, 2001; July 22, 2001.
New York Times, June 29, 2001.

On-line

All Music Guide, www.allmusic.com

Other

Additional information for this profile was obtained from Fantasy/Milestone Records.

—Brian Escamilla

Edward James Olmos

1947—

Actor

Edward James Olmos is one of the most influential voices of the Latino community in the United States. As an actor, he has produced a commendable body of work that has earned him numerous awards and unlimited accolades. But Olmos's life is more than a story of poor kid from the barrio who made it big in Hollywood. He is not only an actor but an activist, with a deep commitment to his community.

Grew Up in the Barrio

Olmos was born on February 24, 1947, in East Los Angeles to Pedro and Eleanor (Huizar) Olmos. Olmos credited his parents, who divorced in 1955, for being his lifelong inspiration. He told *Instyle*'s Kathryn Hart, "My mother is the reason I know God is a woman. She's worked for 20 years—from age 54 to 74—at County General Hospital in Los Angeles. She has worked from 11 o'clock at night to 7 in the morning in the AIDS ward, where she's held the hands of many, many people as they died. It's a gift."

Although diverse in culture and language, the East Los Angeles neighborhood in which Olmos grew up shared the common denominator of poverty. "Inside

this world, *everyone was the same*," he told Guy D. Garcia of *Time*. "We were all poor. And the only way to survive it was through a constant struggle of trying to be better today than you were yesterday." As a youngster, Olmos stayed out of trouble and out of the gangs that dominated much of life in the barrio. Instead of running with a gang, Olmos played baseball, which taught him discipline, patience, and determination—all traits that helped propel him out of the barrio. He excelled at the sport, winning the Golden State batting championship at the age of 14.

At the age of 15, Olmos's hopes of a career in baseball turned into dreams of singing and dancing, primarily because he believed that it held out more promise for getting him out of poverty. Despite lacking an overabundance of natural talent, Olmos committed himself to learning to play the piano and sing. By the time he graduated from high school, he had formed the band Pacific Ocean, which played frequently at clubs along Sunset Strip. It was during a Pacific Ocean gig that Olmos meet his first wife, Kaija Keel, daughter of actor Howard Keel. The two hit it off and married in 1971; by the time he was 25 years old, Olmos was married

At a Glance . . .

Born on February 24, 1947, in East Los Angeles; married Kaija Keel, 1971; divorced, 1994; children: two sons, Mico and Bodie (with Keel); married Lorraine Bracco, 1994; divorced, 2002. *Education:* studied at East Los Angeles City College.

Career: lead vocalist of Pacific Ocean, 1960s; owner of a furniture-moving business, 1970s; starred as El Pachuco in theatre production of *Zoot Suit,* 1978; *Blade Runner,* 1982; *The Ballad of Gregorio Cortez,* 1983; *Stand and Deliver,* 1988; *American Me,* 1992; *A Million to Juan,* 1994; *My Family/Mi Familia,* 1995;; *Selena,* 1997; *The Disappearance of Garcia Lorca,* 1997; *The Road to El Dorado,* 2000; *In the Time of the Butterflies,* 2001; tv series: *American Family,* 2002-.

Membership: Natl Goodwill Ambassador, UNICEF; Recruiting New Teachers; UCLA Mentoring Program; the Natl Council on Adoption; spokesperson: Diabetes Research Institute Foundation, Juvenile Diabetes Foundation, AIDS Awareness Foundation, Mothers Against Drunk Driving, Students Against Destructive Decisions, Parkinson's Disease Foundation, and Alzheimer's Foundation.

Awards: Best Actor, Los Angeles Drama Critics Circle, for *Zoot Suit,* 1978; *Theatre World* Award, for *Zoot Suit,*1979; Antoinette Perry Award, for *Zoot Suit,* 1979; Emmy Award, Golden Globe Award, Best Supporting Actor in a Drama Series, for *Miami Vice,* 1985; Golden Globe Award, for *The Burning Season,* 1994.

Address: *Agent*—Artists Agency, 10000 Santa Monica Boulevard, Suite 305, Los Angeles, CA 90067.

to provide for his family proved to be challenging initially. Undeterred, after Pacific Ocean broke up, Olmos bought the band's oversized van and started a business delivering antique furniture to supplement his income.

Hauling furniture during the day, Olmos spent his nights working in experimental theater. Eventually he began landing bit parts in television shows. Almost always playing a tough, bad-guy role, Olmos was awarded small parts in episodes of such television series as *Kojak, Hawaii Five-O, ChiPs, Medical Center, Magnum P.I.,* and *Police Woman.* He also had minor roles in several films, including *Alambrista* and *Aloha, Bobby and Rose.* Looking back, Olmos laughed at his acting abilities early in his career. As he told Elaine Dutka of *Time,* "I was the only person Jack Lord [of Hawaii Five-O] shot in the back, ever.... That's how bad I was."

Zoot Suit

Olmos's first major break came on the theatrical stage in 1978 when he landed a leading role of the Los Angeles production of Luis Valdez's *Zoot Suit.* The play, a musical drama, is a fictionalized account of the Sleepy Lagoon case, in which a group of young Hispanic men are falsely convicted of murder following what became known as the 1942 Los Angeles zoot suit riots. Olmos tried out for the part of "El Pachuco," the leader of the gang and the epitome of the angry, macho Hispanic man who acts as the narrator and conscience of the story. At the audition, Olmos told Garcia, "I spoke in *caló,* street jive from the streets of East L.A.—a mix of Spanish, English, and Gypsy. They asked me if I could dance, and I hit a perfect set of splits, turning the brim of my hat as I came up." Awarded the role, Olmos played the part to perfection and received rave reviews for his performance.

Zoot Suit was only scheduled for a ten-week run at the Mark Taper Forum in Los Angeles; however, after positive reviews, the production ran eight more weeks before relocating to the Aquarius Theater in Hollywood, where it ran for the next nine months. The production then moved to Broadway's Winter Garden theater, where it was not as well received and subsequently closed after only seven weeks. For his performance, he earned a Los Angeles Critics Circle Award, and his Broadway appearance garnered him the *Theatre World* Award for most outstanding new performer. He was also nominated for an Antoinette Perry Award. In 1982 *Zoot Suit* was released as a feature film, with Olmos retaining the role of El Pachuco. Despite the production's short run in New York City and a lukewarm reception of the film version, Olmos had clearly made his mark.

Following the success of *Zoot Suit,* Olmos no longer had to knock on doors for bit parts. During the early

with two children. The couple stayed together until their sons were grown, divorcing in 1994.

Despite his longhaired rocker appearance, Olmos maintained his industrious lifestyle. He attended East Los Angeles City College during the day and often studied at the clubs at night, pulling out his books during breaks between sets. At first he pursued psychology and criminology, until Olmos signed up for a drama course to help him with his stage presence as a singer. Much to his surprise, he discovered that he enjoyed acting, and soon he had fallen in love with the idea of becoming an actor. Making enough money as an actor

1980s he accepted supporting roles in the movies *Wolfen* (1981) and *Blade Runner* (1982). However, early in his career as a known and sought-after actor, Olmos decided to accept only projects that held meaning for him. For this reason, he turned down director Brian De Palma's offer to cast him in his movie *Scarface,* which told the story of a Cuban immigrant who is drawn into the violent world of drug-dealing. He also refused parts in *Red Dawn* and *Firestarter* and, although he made numerous appearances on the show, Olmos passed up an opportunity to join the permanent cast of the popular television drama *Hill Street Blues* because the required five-year contract was exclusive, thus denying him the ability to take on other, more meaningful, projects during that time.

Olmos's next major project was the 1982 Public Broadcasting Company's (PBS) *American Playhouse* production of *The Ballad of Gregorio Cortez,* in which Olmos played the title role. The film was based on the true tale of Gregorio Cortez, a Mexican folk hero who was traditionally held to be a fierce bandito. However, after researching the film, Olmos discovered that Cortez was, in fact, not an outlaw at all, but a poor rancher and honest family man. Only through misinterpretation and a misunderstanding between cultures was Cortez wrongly accused of murder in 1901 and pursued across Texas by a 600-man posse. After its run on television, *The Ballad of Gregorio Cortez* was slated for the big screen; however, no major studios could be persuaded to release it, perhaps in part because Olmos spoke Spanish throughout the film with no subtitles. Determined that the story of Cortez was too important to let fade, Olmos began a five-year personal crusade to distribute the film across the country.

In 1984 Olmos joined the cast of television series *Miami Vice* as Lieutenant Martin Castillo. The show, which centered on the careers of two undercover vice-squad cops, garnered a significant viewing audience even though the majority of critics were less than enthusiastic. Olmos, for his part, received commendable reviews, and although he did little promoting of the show and voiced concerns that it propagated stereotypes, he earned him an Emmy Award and a Golden Globe Award.

Stand and Deliver

The stand-out performance of Olmos's career thus far came in the 1988 release of *Stand and Deliver.* The film told the true story of Bolivian-born Jaime Escalante, a successful computer scientist who left his career to teach math to underprivileged Hispanic kids from the barrios of East Los Angeles. The inspirational story focused on Escalante's relationship with his students at Garfield High School as he challenged them to achieve more than expected and more than they believed they could. Then, in 1982 after scoring higher than expected on the Advanced Placement Calculus exam, they are launched into controversy when the Educational Testing Service suspected foul play and opened an investigation.

Olmos portrayed Escalante with intensity and exceptional accuracy. To prepare for the part, Olmos studied Escalante for hours, observing him both in and out of the classroom. He also gained 40 pounds and spent hours studying tapes of Escalante to perfect his speech and mannerisms. Olmos even considered moving in with Escalante for a time, but Escalante's wife vetoed that idea. The movie grossed more than nine times its modest production costs, and Olmos received an Academy Award nomination for his brilliant performance as Escalante. Hoping to bring the film to the largest possible audience, Olmos convinced several major corporations to sponsor his efforts to place a copy of the film in every school, library, and youth organization across the nation.

From *American Me* to *American Family*

Following *Stand and Deliver* Olmos appeared in numerous films, often in conjunction with director Robert M. Young, with whom he had formed the production company, YOY Productions. He played Gypsy in *Triumph of the Spirit* (1989) and a baseball talent scout in *Talent for the Game* (1991). In 1992 he delved into directing as he coproduced, directed, and starred in *American Me,* a graphic and realistic story of crime and violence in the United States as it moves from the streets into the prisons. Olmos portrayed a character named Santana, a gang member who lands in Folsom State Prison but continues to run his Mexican Mafia from his jail cell, operating drugs, gambling, prostitution, and extortion rings. Intense and accurate, the film served as a message of the dangerous, and often tragic, nature of gang and prison life.

Once again with something important to say, Olmos traveled the country promoting the film and attending special screenings for youth organizations and communities. "This film is not for one race, one subculture, one age range," Olmos explained to *Newsweek*'s Jack Kroll. "Gangs teach a distorted discipline, a distorted familial bonding, a distorted sense of pride and power. I made this movie to allow all society to take a journey into an uncharted land that they would never have the opportunity to go into." Olmos also took part in the production of *Lives in the Hazard.* Released in 1994 as a follow-up, the film was a documentary that revisited some of the real-life gang members that served as extras in *American Me.* For his involvement with *American Me* Olmos received death threats from the actual Mexican Mafia and for a time feared for life. In the same year Olmos married Lorraine Bracco, an actress and ex-wife of actor Harvey Keitel. In January of 2002 Bracco filed for divorce from Olmos.

Also notable on the list of Olmos's film work were his roles in *My Family/Mi Familia* (1995), a film in which he served as the narrator of a multigenerational Mexican-American family saga, and *Selena,* (1997) the story of the life and murder of Tejano music star Selena Quintanilla. Along with his film career, Olmos regularly appeared in television movies, series, and specials. He starred Home Box Office's film *The Burning Season* (1994), a film about the life of Brazilian activist Chico Mendes, for which Olmos received a Golden Globe Award and an Emmy Award nomination. Olmos also worked on *Dead Man's Walk* (1996), the prequel to the popular miniseries *Lonesome Dove,* and *12 Angry Men* (1997). In 2001 Olmos appeared in Steve Martini's *The Judge* and Showtime's production of *In the Time of the Butterflies,* a fictionalized account of three Dominican women martyred in 1960 during the last days of Dominican dictator Trujillo's rule. He has also narrated and contributed to numerous documentaries.

In 2002 Olmos joined the cast of a new television series, *American Family,* which airs on PBS. The episodes evolve around the lives of a Hispanic-American family in Los Angeles. Olmos plays Jess Gonzales, the conservative and old-fashioned father, something of a Latino Archie Bunker, who attempts with moderate success to deal with and understand his five grown children. It is the first Hispanic-dominated series to ever air on television.

Actor as Activist

Olmos is not only an actor, but also a tireless activist. Although sometimes the two roles blend together, as they did in his projects *The Ballad of Gregorio Cortez, Stand and Deliver,* and *American Me,* Olmos has spent a vast majority of his time over the course of his career simply working to make life better for others. By his own count, he spends 94 percent of his time working for free. Looking at his long resume of good deed doing, the number doesn't seem unrealistic. Besides his continually packed schedule on the speaker's circuit, Olmos offers his support to a wide range of social programs.

By living his life giving as much as possible and expecting little in return, Olmos hopes to leave a worthy legacy. As he told *Hispanic*'s Katherine Diaz, "I would hate to look back on my life and only see myself as a person who made lots of money and was a star and made *Rambo* and *Terminator* movies. I have made my body of work something that I am proud of and that in 100 years my great-great-grandchildren will go and see my work and say, 'Well, grandpa really did some extraordinarily different kinds of work.'"

Selected Films

Zoot Suit, 1981.
Wolfen, 1981.

Blade Runner, 1982.
The Ballad of Gregorio Cortez, 1983.
Miami Vice (television series), 1984—1989.
Saving Grace, 1986.
Stand and Deliver, 1987.
Triumph of the Spirit, 1989.
Talent for the Game, 1991.
American Me, 1992.
Roosters (television), 1993.
Menendez: A Killing in Beverly Hills (television miniseries), 1994.
The Burning Season—The Chico Mendes Story (television movie), 1994
A Million to Juan, 1994.
Mirage, 1995
My Family/Mia Familia, 1995.
Dead Man's Walk (television movie), 1996
Caught, 1996.
The Wonderful Ice Cream Suit, 1997.
The Disappearance of Garcia Lorca, 1997.
12 Angry Men (television movie), 1997.
Hollywood Confidential, 1997.
The Limbic Region, 1997.
Selena, 1997.
The Wall (television documentary), 1998.
Bonanno: A Godfather's Story, 1999.
The Princess and the Barrio Boy, 2000.
The Road to El Dorado, 2000.
In the Time of the Butterflies (television movie), 2001.
The Judge (television movie), 2001.
American Family (television series), 2002.

Sources

Books

Dictionary of Hispanic Biography. Farmington Hills, MI: Gale Research, 1996.
International Dictionary of Films and Filmmakers, Volume 3: Actors and Actresses. New York: St. James Press, 1996.
Newsmakers. Issue 1. Farmington Hills, MI: Gale Research, 1990.
Rooney, Terrie M., ed. *Contemporary Heroes and Heroines, Book III.* Farmington Hills: Gale Research, 1998.

Periodicals

Hispanic, December 2000.
Instyle, February 2002.
Los Angeles Magazine, April 1993.
The Los Angeles Times, May 10, 1992.
Newsweek, March 30, 1992.
People Weekly, January 21, 2002.
Star Tribune (Minneapolis, MN), January 30, 2002.
Time, April 4, 1988; July 11, 1988.
The Toronto Sun, January 24, 2002.
The Washington Times, January 21, 2002.

On-line

Behind the Scenes, Public Broadcasting System, www.pbs.org/americanfamily/
Sony Classics, www.sonyclassics.com/caught/crew/ olmos.html

—Kari Bethel

Derek Parra

1970—

Athlete

When Derek Parra set a new world record in the men's 1,500-meter speedskating competition at the 2002 Winter Olympics, he also became the first Mexican-American to win a gold medal at the Salt Lake City Games. Parra was an unlikely victor in the sport of long-track speedskating, having tried it for the first time just six years before. The Southern California native became a favorite subject for sports writers at the Salt Lake Games, who found the story of his rise from the barrio appealing. Parra himself was pleased with his success. "If I can challenge any kid—doesn't matter if they're Mexican or Asian or black or white—to challenge themselves and reach for their dreams," the 31-year-old told *San Bernardino Sun* reporter Paul Oberjuerge, "that's more important than anything else."

Raced for Food

Parra grew up in San Bernardino's West Side neighborhood. His mother had departed when he was a toddler, and Parra's father worked as a prison guard to support him and his brother. As a kid, Parra and his older brother, Gilbert, loved to skate at the Stardust Roller Rink. Having no money for snacks, they began racing as a way to win food tickets from others. "We used to race for hot dogs and Cokes," Gilbert Parra told *St. Petersburg Times* columnist John Romano. Parra began competing in races using the new inline skates, though his father disapproved; he sometimes refused to drive him to meets, but changed his mind when others began telling him that they had seen his son on television.

As a teen, Parra met a Florida roller-skating coach named Virgil Dooley at a U.S. Olympic Committee training camp. Parra told Dooley that he would like to train with him after he finished high school. He then graduated early and bought a ticket to Tampa, and phoned the coach. "He said, 'Could I stay with you for a couple of days until I find a place to live?,'" Dooley told Romano in the *St. Petersburg Times.* "I said, 'Yeah, I guess that'll be all right.' He lived with us for seven years." While Parra trained with Dooley, he held various jobs to pay his expenses. At times he was so poor that he sometimes took food destined for the dumpster at the fast-food restaurant where he worked.

That single-mindedness helped make Parra a champion. He dominated inline skating for nearly a decade, winning 18 titles and setting world records for speed.

He was also earning about $50,000 annually. At the 1995 Pan American Games, he was the most decorated athlete. He was keenly disappointed when inline skating was not chosen as a new Olympic sport for the 1996 Summer Olympic Games in Atlanta. Around this time, another inline skating champion, K.C. Boutiette, urged Parra to try ice skates. By switching to speedskating, Parra might have a shot at the Olympics.

Parra had worn ice skates only once before in life. He tried it, and decided to stick with it, despite some initial difficulties. "It was very frustrating coming to the ice and being a nobody, especially after being the best in the world," he told Knight-Ridder/Tribune News Service reporter Kamon Simpson. "I knew I could do it, but the results weren't coming as fast as I wanted them." By 1998 and the Nagano Winter Games, Parra had made the U.S. men's team, but did not get a chance to compete because a higher-ranking skater showed up. He considered quitting, but his wife, Tiffany, urged him not to give up yet.

Trained on World's Fastest Ice

Parra made the 2002 Winter Olympics his goal. He trained in Milwaukee, and worked at a Home Depot store there. In late 2000, he moved to Kearns, Utah, to train. Kearns's newly constructed Olympic Oval was situated more than 4,700 feet above sea level, making it the world's highest-altitude speedskating track. The high altitude also gave the ice a particularly dense quality, which made it a much faster surface. Again, Parra found a job at a local Home Depot store, which was the sole participating corporate member of a United States Olympic Committee sponsorship project. Athletes who met qualifications would work at the store 20 hours, but be paid for 40, in exchange for allowing themselves to be featured in commercials. In all, 140 Olympians were participating in the Home Depot program, and Parra appeared in a television ad

with Tristan Gale, the women's skeleton competitor. He was a favorite of customers and co-workers alike. "The way Derek runs around this place, it's no wonder he's a speedskater," supervisor Lara Berry told Knight-Ridder/Tribune News Service writer Mike Bianchi. "If a customer buys 12 bags of concrete, he's the guy who volunteers to load it in the car for them."

In March of 2001 the Utah Olympic Oval was host to the world speedskating single-distance championships. Parra came in second in the 1,500-meter race, the first medal finish for a U.S. men's team member in six years. His performance added to the anticipation surrounding the coming Salt Lake Games, and Parra continued to train intensely. He barely returned to Florida in time for the birth of his daughter, Mia Elizabeth, on December 14, 2001, and had to leave again a few days later. The situation was a stressful one. Parra's wife worked and was still in college, and there were some tearful phone conversations. "We get in arguments because I'm not there," Parra explained to a Madison, Wisconsin paper, the *Capital Times*. "I can't help out, and that just makes it worse. There's plenty of times during the year where you ask yourself, 'Is it really worth it?' Then you go out and skate and have a good day, and you say, 'Yeah, it is.'"

When the 2002 Winter Olympic Games opened in Salt Lake City, Parra was considered a long shot for the first men's speedskating event the next day, the 5,000-meter race. He had never done well in longer races, a sport usually dominated by the Dutch and Scandinavian-country teams. Moreover, Parra, who liked to snack on Fig Newton cookies as a night-before race ritual, was shorter than most in the sport at just 5 feet, 3 and a half inches; most champion speedskaters are tall and long-legged, which gives them a clear physical advantage. But on February 9, Parra clocked in a finish of 6:17.98 to huge cheers from crowd. The time set a new world record in the sport—the first broken in the 2002 Games—but just a half-hour later, Dutch skater Jochem Uytdehaage crossed the finish line on what had been deemed the world's fastest ice, beating Parra by just by three seconds to take the gold.

Sportswriters began predicting that silver-medal-winner Parra might become the second U.S. speedskater in Olympic history to win three medals; the feat had not happened since Eric Heiden's five gold medals at the 1980 Games in Lake Placid, New York. On February 19, before a crowd that included his wife, brother and father, King Harald V of Norway, and U.S. Secretary of Defense Donald Rumsfeld, Parra took to the ice in Kearns for the 1,500-meter men's speedskating competition. He set a new world record, 1:43:95 seconds, and took the gold medal. He and his coach, Bart Schouten, took a victory lap around the Oval with the American flag. Not even silver-medal winner Uytdehaage was surprised by the outcome, the Dutch athlete told the *Grand Rapids Press*. Uytdehaage remarked that Parra's performance at the world championships the year before had made him a skater to watch. "This is not really a big surprise, because I have seen Derek come up and up and up," Uytdehaage told the *Grand Rapids Press*. "I knew Derek would skate very fast, and this may sound strange, but I was happy for him to break the record. It was an awesome skate."

Landmark Win—Both National and Personal

Parra's gold that day was the 20th medal for the U.S. Olympic team at the Salt Lake Games, a number that the U.S. Olympic officials had deemed its goal (the U.S. team would eventually finish with 34 in all). Parra was thrilled that his wife could be there in the stands to see it. "I was hoping I would do well," he told *New York Times* writer Edward Wong. At the starting line, he continued, "I saw her up in the stands, and I told her before the race that I love her. Out of all the crowd, I could see her face there. It was really uplifting, because we've been away for so long. We see each other only every two months."

Parra surprised many a few days later on February 22, when he finished in twelfth place in the 10,000-meter men's speedskating contest. "I was hoping to have a good race and finish on a good note, but I'm tired," he said at a press conference afterward. "The 10K, it was just way out of reach, even going into this race, more than the 5K was…. I just didn't feel technically sound and was not too efficient in the first 5,000 (of the 10,000), and I started fatiguing and overheated." Uytdehaage took another gold medal for his first-place finish in this event. Still, Parra was pleased at his overall performance, noting that a gold and silver each "are just beyond what was probably possible," a Knight-Ridder/Tribune News Service report by Charean Williams quoted him as saying. "It was something I dreamed, but to actually have it in my hand and realize the dream is unbelievable." Even his older brother was impressed. As Gilbert Parra told Romano, the *St. Petersburg Times* columnist, "When he was little, he wanted to be like his older brother. Now I want to be like him."

Parra was upbeat about his future plans, and admitted to some realistic goals regarding his future in the sport. "My wife and I talked about it, and if it's not something I can't make a living off of, then I'll just go to Orlando and have a normal job and be a normal father and husband," Williams quoted him as saying. He was also looking forward to paying a visit to his former school, Roosevelt Elementary, in San Bernardino, and speaking to students who use roller- or inline skates on the same streets he did. "Mexican-Americans can reach for their goals," Parra asserted to Oberjuerge in a report that appeared in the *Daily News*. "Growing up in Southern California, I would have never even dreamed of being in a Winter Olympics sport, the sport of giants." He was also proud to have bested other world-class skaters who had the luxury of training full-time because of generous government support. His win, he told the *Grand Rapids Press*, "shows that a working-class man can be at the top of the podium, or on the podium."

Sources

Periodicals

Austin American-Statesman, February 10, 2002, p. C1.
Capital Times (Madison, WI), February 20, 2002, p. 1C.
Daily News (Los Angeles), February 10, 2002.
Grand Rapids Press (Grand Rapids, MI), February 20, 2002, p. C4.
Knight-Ridder/Tribune News Service, March 9, 2001; February 11, 2002; February 22, 2002.
New York Times, February 19, 2002; February 20, 2002; February 21, 2002.
St. Petersburg Times, February 20, 2002, p. 1C.

On-line

U.S. Speedskating, http://www.usspeedskating.org (February 27, 2002).

—Carol Brennan

Eddie Alberto Pérez

1957—

Political leader

In his first run for political office in 2001, Eddie Pérez made history as the first Hispanic–American to become mayor of a New England capital. A native of Puerto Rico, longtime Hartford, Connecticut resident Pérez also broke new political ground by forging a bipartisan coalition of community activists and corporate leaders that contributed to his landslide victory. Elected on a platform of administrative reform, educational improvement, and housing development, Pérez received seventy-five percent of the vote on election day. While he was helped by a $200,000 war chest in the election—the largest campaign fund in Hartford's history—Pérez credited grassroots support for giving him the victory. He also pointed to the reinvigorated sense of citizenship that his campaign had generated in Hartford's Hispanic community. "There was no sense of building social, economic, and cultural capital as Americans,"he told the *New York Times* shortly after his election, "We have to begin to rebuild that foundation."

Eddie Alberto Pérez was born in 1957 in Corozal, Puerto Rico, where he spent most of his childhood. In 1969 the Pérez family moved to Hartford, Connecticut, which had a growing number of Puerto Rican immigrants already living there. Puerto Ricans had first come to central Connecticut in significant numbers in the 1940s to work in the region's tobacco fields. Although many continued to work as seasonal agricultural help in the state, by the late 1960s many had settled permanently in Hartford, Waterbury, Bridgeport, and other cities throughout New England.

After their arrival, young Pérez, his mother, Felicita, and his two brothers, Nelson and Noel, settled into Hartford's north side. With a large Hispanic population, the life of the neighborhood was centered around the Roman Catholic Sacred Heart Parish. As a low—income area, however, Hartford's north side also had a reputation for being a tough and sometimes, dangerous place to live. Although he stayed out of trouble, the future mayor had some experience with the tougher side of the streets. As Pérez recalled in an interview with *El Extra News,* "My involvement with the youth gang the Ghetto Brothers responded in those times to a search for a peer group and personal protection in areas where there was a lot of violence. In those times the hold on drug trafficking by the gangs was minimal and in my case, my participation responded more to the sense of

At a Glance . . .

Born Eddie Alberto Pérez in 1958, in Corozal, Puerto Rico; married María Pérez; children: two. *Education:* Capital Community College, A.A.S. in liberal arts; Trinity University, B.A. in economics, 1996. *Religion:* Roman Catholic. *Politics:* Democrat.

Career: ONE/CHANE Community Development Corporation, director, 1978-88; Make Something Happen, director, 1988-90; Trinity College, associate vice president for Comunity and Government Relations; Southside Institutions Neighborhood Association, executive director, 1990-01; Mayor of Hartford, 2001-.

Address: *Office*—Mayor, City of Hartford, 550 Main Street, Hartford, Connecticut 06103.

control and territorial security, and I gained a sense of belonging."

After graduating from Hartford Public High School, Pérez worked in the Volunteers in Service to America (VISTA) program, part of a local community development effort sponsored by the federal government. His work with VISTA in 1978 marked the beginning of Pérez's more than twenty years in the non—profit sector before running for public office. After completing his term at VISTA, Pérez helped to found Organized Northeasterners/Clay Hill and North End (ONE/CHANE), a non–profit group that worked in the areas of housing development, community organizing, job training, and youth activities. He remained with ONE/CHANE for the next decade and retained the title of director. Based in Pérez's familiar north side neighborhood, ONE/CHANE gave the young activist the chance to develop his organizing, development, and community building skills while he completed his associate's degree at Hartford's Capital Community College.

In the late 1980s Pérez joined the Make Something Happen (MASH) project sponsored by the Urban League of Greater Hartford and the Connecticut Puerto Rican Forum. He stayed with MASH, a welfare-to-work program, for two years before taking a position with Trinity College around 1990. In the next decade, Pérez took on the role of associate vice president for community and government relations for the college while he chaired a non;profit group affiliated with Trinity, the Southside Institutions Neighborhood Association (SINA). Pérez also earned his B.A. in economics from Trinity College in 1996.

Pérez's work as an administrator made him the college's liason between the campus and the surrounding community. As the area around Trinity College deteriorated, however, the challenge to integrate the campus into the community seemed daunting. With the arrival of new president Evan Dobelle in 1995, Trinity College committed itself to a massive new program of community development to serve its Hartford neighborhood. Using SINA as its lead agency, Pérez, Dobelle, and the college put together a collaborative effort among local community development corporations (CDCs) and corporate sponsors, drawn largely from Hartford's major employers in the insurance and health care industries. Pooling their ideas and resources, the group envisioned a 16-acre Learning Corridor that would encompass four new public schools, recreational centers for children and families, and space for other public arts and recreation projects.

In addition to its focus on education, the SINA project also attempted to increase home ownership in the community by arranging federally subsidized down payments and lower interest rates. Working with the Hartford Areas Rally Together (HART) CDC, SINA also sponsored job training, housing redevelopment, and community policing efforts. By the time SINA's efforts came to fruition after six years of hard work, it was hailed as one of the most innovative and comprehensive urban renewal projects in the nation. Yet Pérez did not forget the challenges that SINA faced from the beginning. As he told *U.S. News and World Report*, "I've been part of the war for the last thirty years. And it *is* war." Early in 2001 Hartford Mayor Michael P. Peters announced that he would not seek another term in office. Pérez had been encouraged to run for a seat on Hartford's City Council in the past, and he once again declined the opportunity to enter the political arena. Eventually, however, Pérez decided that he stood a good chance of being elected to office. Although Hartford's Hispanic population was only about forty percent of the total, he quickly demonstrated his appeal beyond mere ethnic lines as he amassed a $200,000 campaign fund drawn mostly from Pérez's long standing contacts with the city's corporate leaders.

As a Democratic candidate, Pérez breezed through the primary with over seventy percent of the vote. During the final weeks of the campaign, Pérez pledged to follow a platform of housing redevelopment, educational initiatives, and administrative reform. To Pérez, each of these areas would play a crucial role in the city's future. As Hartford had lost about thirteen percent of its population between 1990 and 2000, Pérez believed that reviving the city's residential neighborhoods was the first step in ensuring its stability. He thus pledged to increase home ownership in Hartford by thirty percent in five years. Next, Pérez pointed to the success of the Learning Corridor in making Hartford an attractive place to raise a family. To encourage more families to move back from the suburbs, strengthening the city's public school system was a necessity. Finally, Pérez hoped to change the city's charter to give more power to the mayor's office. Because the city was run on a city council-manager plan, the mayor's post was something of a ceremonial one without any real political power to see projects through to completion.

Pérez made headlines as the first Hispanic mayor elected to lead a New England capital. He continued to forge new ground by shaking up Hartford's political establishment after taking office. In a showdown with the Democratic Party leadership on city council in his first months in office, the new mayor insisted upon appointing his own choices to the offices of deputy mayor and council majority leader. Crossing party lines for his new appointees, Pérez demonstrated that he would not be bound by tradition in carrying out his duties. As Pérez, the father of two with his wife, María, told the *Puerto Rico Herald* on election night, "It's a new beginning for my family. A new beginning for Hartford."

Sources

Periodicals

El Extra News, December 2001.
Hartford Courant, December 2, 2001.
New York Times, November 18, 2001.
Planning, April 2000.
U.S. News and World Report, April 2, 2001.

On-line

Puerto Rico Herald, November 7, 2001, http://www.puertorico-herald.org/issues/2001/vol5n45/SenorAlcalde-en.shtml
City of Hartford Web Site, http://www.ci.hartford.ct.us/government/mayor
Trinity College Web Site, http://www.trincoll.edu/depts/tcn/Community_Organizations/1chane.htm
American Planning Association Web Site, April 2000, http://www.planning.org/planningpractice/2000/apr200.htm

—Timothy Borden

Tony Pérez

1942—

Professional baseball player and manager

"If there's a runner on second base," former Cincinnati Reds manager Sparky Anderson told the National Baseball Hall of Fame on the occasion of Pérez's induction into that body, "there isn't anybody I'd rather see walk to the plate than Tony Pérez. He turns mean with men on base." Indeed, Pérez notched more runs batted in (RBIs) than any other Latin American player in history. One of a group of Hispanic players who dominated major-league play in the 1960s and 1970s, third baseman Pérez was a linchpin of the Reds' legendary offensive "Big Red Machine."

Pérez was born in Ciego de Ávila, Cuba, on May 14, 1942, and grew up in the small town of Central de Violeta. His father was a sugar-factory worker, and young Atanasio Pérez seemed destined to follow in his footsteps although he had been a baseball fan since early childhood and had particularly followed the career of the pioneering Latin American star Minnie Minoso. But he got his break when he attracted the attention of Reds' scout Tony Pacheco while playing with a factory baseball team. At the age of 17, Pérez was signed to the Reds. His only signing bonus was a $2.50 exit visa fee.

Pérez showed up in late winter to play for a Reds farm team in Geneva, New York in 1960. His dislike of cold northern winters was matched by his disorientation; he spoke little English, and the specialized jargon of baseball posed special challenges. Pérez spent six years in the minor leagues, moving to Rocky Mount, North Carolina, in 1962. Of Afro-Cuban background and identified as black, Pérez got a taste of southern segregation. "The black players and I could not stay with the rest of the team," he told *Sports Illustrated*. "We also couldn't eat with the white players, and sometimes we would wait in the bus outside a restaurant until the white players finished their meals and brought us hamburgers."

In 1963 Pérez moved up to the AAA level San Diego squad in the Pacific Coast League, leaving the South behind, and at the end of the next season was called up to join the Reds. For the 1965 and 1966 seasons he came off the bench frequently, playing in about 100 games each year and recording batting averages in the .260 range. In 1967 Pérez won the starting third-base slot and notched the first of an all-time record 11 seasons with over 90 RBIs. His celebrity in the baseball world got off to a spectacular start in the 1967

At a Glance . . .

Born Atanasio Pérez in Ciego de Ávila, Cuba, on May 14, 1942; son of a sugar-factory worker; married, Pituka; children: Orlando and Eduardo.

Career: Signed to Cincinnati Reds organization and joined minor-league team in Geneva, New York, 1960; moved to San Diego team, 1963; joined Reds' roster, 1964; became full-time starting third baseman, 1967; hit 15th-inning home run in 1967 All-Star Game; traded to Montreal Expos, 1976; traded to Boston Red Sox, 1980; traded to Philadelphia Phillies, 1983; traded back to Reds, 1984; retired, 1986; career totals of 379 home runs and 1,652 RBIs; worked in Reds organization, 1986-93; named Reds manager, 1993, but fired after 44 games; joined Florida Marlins organizaton; named Florida Marlins manager, 2001.

Awards: Named to National League All-Star team seven times.

Address: *Office:*—c/o Florida Marlins, 2267 Dan Marino Blvd., Miami, FL 33028.

All-StarGame, when he hit a home run in the 15th inning off Oakland Athletics pitching ace "Catfish" Hunter and was named the game's Most Valuable Player.

Over the next nine seasons with the Reds Pérez was remarkably consistent, the biggest variation in his year-to-year routine being a position switch from third to first base in 1972. Each year he batted close to .300, batted in about 100 runs, and hit over 20 home runs (except in 1968 when he hit only 18). Pérez's best year was 1970, when he hit 40 home runs, batted .317, and notched 129 RBIs—career-high totals in all three categories. As part of a power-hitting lineup that included Joe Morgan, Johnny Bench, and Pete Rose, Pérez helped the Reds dominate the National League and made numerous All-Star Game appearances. Another career high point came in 1975, when Perez hit three home runs in the Reds' World Series struggle against the Boston Red Sox, the last of them an ultimate clutch shot in the sixth inning of game seven.

Despite that contribution and another solid performance (19 home runs, 91 RBIs) the following year, Pérez was traded to the Montreal Expos at the end of the 1976 season. Shocked by the move, he had no desire to uproot himself for the still colder climes and foreign-language habitat of Quebec, and made his dissatisfaction known. In truth the trade had purely monetary motivations, as Reds general manager Bob Howsam hoped to elevate a young first baseman at the low end of the salary scale and unload the now well-paid Pérez. But it was at about this time that the Reds' fortunes began to crumble, and Howsam later admitted that the trade ranked as the worst move of his career.

Never one to let his feelings interfere with his performance on the field, Pérez continued to rank among the league leaders over three seasons with the Expos; he then was traded to the Boston Red Sox and played for three years there, topping 100 RBIs for the last time during the 1980 season. Pérez reunited with former teammates Morgan and Rose to play for the Philadelphia Phillies in 1983, landing in his fifth and final World Series. The Reds finally realized the error of their ways in 1984 and brought him back to finish his career in Cincinnati, where in 1985, at age 42, he hit a grand slam home run on May 13th, becoming the oldest player ever to do so. Pérez retired at the end of the 1986 season; his total of 379 home runs was tied for the lead among Hispanic players until the José Canseco years, and his 1,652 career RBIs are still tops among Latinos and in the top 25 of all players.

Pérez stayed in baseball after his retirement, working in the Reds' front office and getting an abortive shot as manager in 1993—because, some thought, Reds owner Marge Schott wanted to repair her standing with fans after some racially insensitive comments that were widely reported. Pérez lasted only 44 games. "The only thing I didn't like," Pérez told the *Sporting News,* "was the way I got fired—by a phone call." The Reds had a record of 20 wins and 24 losses at the time—not stellar, but perhaps not bad enough to disguise the fact that Pérez had suffered the fifth-quickest managerial firing in major-league history and had endured another indignity from a team to which he had given a great deal.

Moving to the Florida Marlins organization, Pérez prospered as a front-office executive. He was inducted into the Baseball Hall of Fame in the year 2000 and at the end of that year was hired as an interim manager by the Marlins. Things clicked with the Marlins squad, and Pérez was asked to stay on. The Marlins improved dramatically in 2001, winning 19 of its first 29 games and impressing observers with the bond between manager and team. "This team is young, with a lot of enthusiasm," first baseman Kevin Millar told *Sporting News.* "Everybody kind of feeds off Tony. We're all a bunch of loud, young idiots out there." At the end of the 2001 season, Pérez's future in his new career as manager seemed a promising one.

Sources

Periodicals

Ebony, May 1993, p. 110.
Jet, June 14, 1993, p. 48.

Sporting News, July 9, 2001, p. 27.
Sports Illustrated, June 30, 1986, p. 62.

On-line

*Baseball Hall of Fame,*http://www.baseballhallof
 fame.org
*Latino Legends in Sports,*http://www.latinolegends.
 com

—James M. Manheim

Eva "Evita" Perón

1919–1952

Political leader

Of all the figures of twentieth-century history, few have inspired as many passionate debates as the life and myth of Eva Perón. From her origins as an illegitimate girl in the Argentine provinces, she pursued a career as a film and radio actress in Buenos Aires before meeting, and subsequently marrying, the man who would make her the First Lady of Argentina, Juan Domingo Perón. Although she held no official government role during Perón's terms in office, Eva Perón became one of the most powerful political figures in the country and an influential ambassador for Argentina throughout the world. After her tragic, early death from cancer at the age of thirty-three, the woman whom millions called "Evita" had already made a lasting impact on her homeland. Few could have foreseen that a half-century later, her life would continue to inspire, provoke, and challenge those who live in the shadow of her memory.

Although she later claimed a birth date of 1922 under the name Eva Duarte, María Eva Ibarguren was actually born on May 7, 1919 near the provincial town of Los Toldos, Argentina, about one-hundred fifty miles west of the nation's capital, Buenos Aires. She was the last of five children born to Juana Ibarguren and Juan Duarte. Duarte, who worked as an agricultural estate manager near Los Toldos, kept his wife and three other children in a nearby town and never formalized his relationship with Ibarguren, who insisted on using the surname Duarte for herself and her children. In 1920 Juan Duarte returned to live with his wife. Juana Ibarguren Duarte, now in desperate financial straits, moved into a modest home in Los Toldos where she supported her family as a seamstress. When Juan Duarte died in a car accident in 1926, his "second family" was barred from the cemetery. It was a humiliation that young Eva Duarte would remember for the rest of her life.

Worked as an Actress

Juana Ibarguren Duarte moved her family to Junín, where one of her older daughters had secured a job in the post office, in 1930. Juana Duarte ran a small boardinghouse in Junín; despite the improved economic circumstances, however, young Eva Duarte felt stifled by life in the small town. From her weekly visits to the cinema, she dreamed of becoming an actress like her idol, Norma Shearer, who had also escaped a poverty-stricken childhood. After completing her sec-

At a Glance . . .

Born María Eva Ibarguren Duarte on May 7, 1919, in Los Toldos, Argentina; died July 16, 1952; married Juan Perón on October 22, 1945. *Education:* Completed secondary school in Junín, Argentina. *Religion:* Roman Catholic. *Politics:* Women's Peronist Party.

Career: Eva Franco theatrical company, 1935; José Franco theatrical company, 1936; film and radio work from 1937 onward; spokesperson, Association of Argentine Radio, 1943; unofficial representative, Department of Labor and Welfare, 1946; chair, María Eva Duarte de Perón Foundation, 1948; published *My Mission in Life*, 1951.

ondary studies in Junín, fifteen-year-old Eva Duarte traveled to Buenos Aires to look for work on one of the popular radio serials that dominated the airwaves. Although her enemies later claimed that the young woman had seduced a famous tango singer to make her way to the capital, it is more likely that her mother accompanied her on her initial foray into Buenos Aires. Either way, Eva Duarte was soon living on her own in the capital and within weeks had joined the theater company of Eva Franco. The following year she found more work with the traveling theater company of José Franco and in 1937 made her film debut in the movie *Segundos afuera* and her radio theater debut in the soap opera *Oro blanco*.

Although she acted in twenty plays and five movies, Duarte's work as a radio actress in at least two-dozen soap operas and historical dramas made her famous throughout Argentina by the late 1930s. She appeared regularly in the fan magazines and earned a considerable salary of five thousand pesos a month in 1943. When the Association of Argentine Radio was founded in August of 1943, Duarte was chosen to be its spokesperson. Yet her life took an abrupt turn on January 22, 1944, when she met Colonel Juan Domingo Perón at a benefit concert for earthquake victims that he had organized in his capacity as the country's secretary of labor and welfare.

Born in 1895, Perón had entered the Army in 1915 and slowly made his way through the ranks. Left a widower by his first wife's death of uterine cancer in 1938, Perón had traveled to Europe, where he became an admirer of the Italian Fascist government of Benito Mussolini. After a military coup in June of 1943, Perón used his political and propaganda skills to emerge as one of the leaders of the new government. One month after meeting Eva Duarte, Perón helped engineer the

removal of the sitting president and secured the position of minister of war, a crucial office given Argentina's declared neutrality during World War II.

The couple began sharing adjoining apartments almost immediately and Duarte continued her film and radio work. In September of 1945, however, Perón was forced out of office and eventually jailed in an attempted military coup. Conservative business interests, upset at the government's policies that included establishing a minimum wage, paid holidays, and medical care for workers, had organized the coup and remained hostile to Perón throughout his career. In the month after the attempted coup, however, Perón had rallied enough support from the military establishment and organized labor to make a triumphant return to Buenos Aires. His appearance at Casa Rosada, the president's official residence, on October 17, 1945 in front of a crowd of 200,000 supporters marked the beginning of Perón's domination of Argentine politics for the next ten years.

As Perón was immediately declared the front-runner for the presidential elections set for May of 1946, the couple sealed their relationship in a civil ceremony on October 22, 1945. The marriage was followed by a religious ceremony in December, and the Peróns set off together on the campaign trail. Eva Perón's appearances were the first time a candidate's wife had taken an active role in the political arena in the country. Abandoning her entertainment career, Perón quickly learned to use her performing skills as a passionate orator and striking public figure. While the upper classes derided her ostentatious style, she immediately became the country's biggest celebrity.

Became Political Leader

Although Eva Perón never held an official title in her husband's administration, her work through the Department of Labor and Welfare demonstrated her commitment to improving the lives of the poorest segments of Argentine society. Fueled in part by memories of her own mistreatment during her youth and a political shrewdness that capitalized on her husband's support by the country's working classes, Perón championed the cause of the "descamidados," (literally, "shirtless ones") in a number of ways. After setting up the María Eva Duarte de Perón Foundation in 1948, an estimated three billion pesos were spent on new houses, hospitals, clinics, and household items for the poor. The fact that the foundation's funds came from other government programs and in some cases, outright extortion of businesses, fueled charges that the Peronist government was corrupt. Indeed, to her critics Perón's actions were designed merely to increase support for her husband'regime at the expense of any sustainable long-term reforms.

Her goodwill trip to Europe in the summer of 1947 also demonstrated the conflicting images that Eva

Perón presented to the public. While she was greeted like a movie star in Spain, her expensive dresses and jewels—as well as the growing political repression in Argentina—caused a public uproar in Italy, where charges of fascism against her husband's government were revived. Her European tour, however, put the finishing touches on the First Lady's public persona. Simply dressed, her dyed-blond hair pulled back into two coiled braids, and rarely without jewels, Eva Perón was an original creation that combined aspects of the faithful political wife and independent social activist. For her part, Perón claimed that her work merely reflected her admiration of her husband—often speaking about him in Christ-like terms—and her dedication to the descamisados.

Death Moved a Nation

Despite pressure from some groups to run as the vice-presidential candidate in 1952, Perón eventually deflected such suggestions at her husband's insistence. In fact, the popularity of Eva Perón had greatly aided public support of the Perón government in a way that no elective office could compare. In addition, she was gravely ill and by the time her husband was sworn in to a second term as president in June of 1952, Eva Perón could barely stand unassisted. Debilitated by uterine cancer made worse by her initial refusal to undergo a hysterectomy, Perón's last public appearance came at her husband's inauguration.

While her illness had been reported in general terms in the media, Eva Perón's death on July 16, 1952 plunged Argentina into a period of unprecedented national mourning. It also initiated the gradual erosion of support for the Perón government, which had badly managed the country's finances while Argentina lost ground to its international trade rivals. In 1955 President Perón was ousted in another military coup and fled to Spain. He returned to Argentina in 1973 after another military coup installed him once again as president, and died while in office in July of 1974.

Since the time of her death, the myth of Eva Perón has continued to permeate Argentina's political, social, and historical landscapes. Viewed by some as a near-divine figure who died to redeem the country's sins, Perón has also been described as a corrupt, power-hungry, and egomaniacal figure by her detractors. While most observers agree that her commitment to social justice was genuine, her unyielding opposition to the slightest criticism of her husband's government made her motivations seem less than idealistic. Books on Perón's life continue to fill the bestseller lists in Argentina, and the 1997 movie adaptation of the play based loosely on her life, *Evita,* introduced the iconic Eva Perón as played by Madonna to a new generation around the world.

Sources

Crassweller, Robert, *Perón and the Enigmas of Argentina,* W.W. Norton & Company, 1987.

France, Miranda, *Bad Times in Buenos Aires: A Writer's Adventures in Argentina,* Ecco Press, 1998.

Fraser, Nicholas and Marysa Navarro, *Evita: The Real Life of Evita Perón,* W.W. Norton & Company, 1996.

Guillermoprieto, Alma, *Looking for History: Dispatches from Latin America,* Pantheon Books, 2001.

Ortiz, Alicia Dujovne, *Eva Perón: A Biography,* St. Martin's Press, 1995.

Page, Joseph, *Perón: A Biography,* Random House, 1983.

Perón, Eva, *In My Own Words,* reprint, New Press, 1996.

Rock, David, *Argentina 1516-1987: From Spanish Colonization to Alfonsín,* University of California Press, 1987.

—Timothy Borden

Tito Puente

1923-2000

Bandleader, arranger, percussionist

Tito Puente, legendary bandleader and percussionist, performed his unique blend of Latin music and American jazz for over sixty years. He recorded an astounding 118 albums and was a central figure in nearly every trend in Latin music in the 20th century. "He was the founding father of Latin music as we know it, the master of masters. He took all the hits in the beginning. Without Tito, who would have carried it on this long? Who would have helped generations make Latin music their own?," singer Marc Anthony wrote in *Time* following Puente's death in 2000. Though *Down Beat* noted that he once humbly dismissed himself as "just a street musician from the neighborhood," Puente was proud of his impact on Latin music and culture. "I'm very happy that Latin music is now getting the attention it deserves, both here and overseas," he told *Billboard*. "Especially in the last five years. They might not dig the language, but they dig the percussion, the excitement." It is the attention that Puente himself first stirred up when he moved his timbales—twin Cuban metal floor drums—from their traditional place behind the band to center stage, up front. From that moment he dazzled audiences with his showmanship and talent, playing wild-eyed and furious, stirring audience after audience to their feet and winning five Grammies and status as a

true musical icon along the way.

Showed Musical Talent at Young Age

Born Ernesto Antonio Puente, Jr., on April 20, 1923 in New York City's Harlem Hospital, Puente was one of three children of Puerto Rican immigrants Ernest and Ercilla Puente. His siblings both suffered untimely deaths while still children—brother Robert Anthony at the age of four from a fall from a fire escape and sister Anna in her teens. Raised in the Hispanic section of Manhattan known as Spanish Harlem or El Barrio, Puente gained the nickname Ernestito—Little Ernesto—because of his short stature. He soon became known simply as Tito. While his father worked as a foreman in a razor-blade factory, his mother stayed home to raise Puente. It was she that first noticed his musical leanings and enrolled him in piano classes at the New York School of Music when he was just seven. By ten, she had switched him to twenty-five cents-an-hour percussion lessons. "I was always banging on boxes, on the window sill," he recalled in with the *New York Post*. Though he originally wanted to be a dancer and even took lessons, a bicycle accident injured his ankle sidelining his dancing days. Though he later confidently

At a Glance . . .

Born Ernesto Antonio Puente, Jr., on April 20, 1923 in New York, NY; died May 31, 2000; son of Ernest (a factory foreman) and Ercilla (a homemaker); married Mirta Sanchez (divorced); married Margaret Acenio; children: (1st marriage) Ronald, (with Ida Carlini) Richard Anthony, (2nd marriage) one son, one daughter. *Education:* Julliard School of Perfoming Arts, 1945-47. *Military:* U.S. Navy, 1942-45.

Career: Percussionist, 1930s-48; band leader, percussionist, arranger, composer, recording artist, 1948- 00; recorded 118 albums; appeared on numerous other recordings; performed at major music festivals around the world; toured extensively for over fifty years; founded Tito Puente Scholarship Fund, 1979; appeared in *Radio Days, Armed and Dangerous,* 1986-87; appeared on *The Bill Cosby Show,* 1987; played self in the film adaptation of *The Mambo Kings,* 1992.

Awards: Recipient, Bronze Medallion City of N.Y., 1969; awarded, the Key to the City of Los Angeles, 1976; awarded the Key to the City of Chicago, 1985; awarded the Key to the City of Miami, 1986; named Musician of Month on several occasions by *Down Beat,,* American percussion magazine; named King of Latin Music, *La Prensa* newspaper, New York, NY, 1955; Best Latin American Orchestra, *New York Daily News,* 1977; received Grammy awards, 1978, 1983, 1985, 1990, and 1999; Awarded Honorary Doctorates from The College at Old Westbury, Hunter College in New York, and Long Island University; Eubie Blake Award, National Academy of Arts and Sciences, 1990; Percussionist of the Year in *Down Beat's* 56th Annual Readers Poll, 1992; Founders Award, American Society of Composers, Authors and Publishers, 1994; Hispanic Heritage Committee Award for the Arts, Washington D.C., 1994; El Premio Billboard Award, *Billboard,* 1995; National Medal of Arts, 1997; Named a "Living Legend", U.S. Library of Congress, 2000.

declared to *Americas,* " I pride myself as being one of the few bandleaders who really knows how to dance."

By the time he reached his teens, Puente was already something of a local celebrity having played as a child with local Latin bands at festivals and functions. By 16

he dropped out of Manhattan's Central Commercial High School to pursue music and was mentored by some of the most important names in Latin music at that time, flutist Anselmo Sacasas, pianist Noro Morales and band leader Frank "Machito" Grillo. In El Barrio traditional Latin music—boleros and rumbas—poured from open windows and street level clubs. But just blocks away in the swanky jazz clubs of Manhattan, big band, swing, and improvisational jazz were the norm. Puente, whose name means bridge in Spanish, was influenced by these two elements and he would spend his career building a bridge between them. "I was always trying to find a marriage between Latin music and jazz ... trying to play jazz but not lose the Latin-American authenticity," he would later tell *Down Beat.*

The next few years were instrumental in helping Puente to form that bridge. He began to develop his trademark showmanship when in 1941 he was called upon to fill in for the regular drummer of the Machito's famous Latin orchestra, the Afro-Cubans. Machito allowed the young prodigy to perform at the front of the stage. "For perhaps the first time in Latin music, the timbales were brought to the front of the bandstand, and Puente played the drums standing, not seated, as had been the custom. That simple change of routine liberated the rhythm section and opened the door for his extroverted style of performing," an article in *Americas* noted. Puente later was quoted in the *Miami Herald* as saying, "Once, I was strictly a musician with a long face and back to the audience. Now I'm a showman, selling what I'm doing, giving the people good vibes." A few years later Puente was drafted to serve in World War II. He found himself in the U.S. Navy stationed on the USS Santee along with a composer from a noted big band. The composer taught Puente the basics of big band composition. Despite participating in nine battles—for which he earned a presidential commendation—Puente also found time to teach himself saxophone. Finally, in 1945 Puente returned to New York and used his G.I. Bill money to study conducting, orchestration, and theory at the prestigious Julliard School of Music.

Formed His First Orchestra

Since his return from the South Pacific, Puente had become a sought-after arranger among the Latin orchestras. Then in 1948 he formed his own group, The Picadilly Boys, a ten-piece orchestra later renamed the Tito Puente Orchestra, and never looked back. The group became popular regulars at New York's Palladium Ballroom known as "Home of the Mambo," where audiences could not get enough of Puente's unique polyrhythmic sounds. He was soon tapped to record for Tico Records, the label of New York's Spanish Music Center. In 1949 his group recorded six songs one of which became the first mambo hit to crossover to mainstream audiences, "Abaniquito." Later that year, Tito signed with RCA Victor and recorded his classic song "Ran Kan Kan."

The 1950s and 1960s were exciting times for Puente. His music was becoming wildly popular and his trademark style was making him a bona fide star. In a 1956 poll conducted by the New York Hispanic daily *La Prensa,* Puente was voted "King of Latin Music," over older, more established musicians. Then in 1958, two years later, RCA released *Dance Mania,* which became his all-time best-selling album. His signature style of the era was to take Latin dance music such as the cha-cha, the pachanga, and of course, the mambo, and give them a Big Band twist. By the sixties he had begun to embrace jazz more and collaborated with many famed jazz musicians. He also was a regular fixture in recording studios and put out an immense body of work including titles such as *Top Percussion, Let's Cha-Cha with Puente, The Exciting Tito Puente Band in Hollywood, Pachanga Con Puente, Mucho Puente, Mambo Beat, Vaya Puente, El Rey Bravo,* and dozens more. Proof of his ability to appeal to Anglo audiences as well as Latin audiences was further demonstrated when he was invited in 1967 to perform a series of original compositions at New York's Metropolitan Opera, though he still catered to his Latin fans by hosting his own program, *The World of Tito Puente,* on Spanish-language television in 1968. That same year he served as the Grand Marshall of the New York's Puerto Rican Day Parade.

Puente found unprecedented fame outside Latin music circles when rock guitarist Carlos Santana recorded Puente's song "Oye Como Va" on the 1970 album *Abraxas.* The song became a top ten hit, opening up vast new audiences for Puente's music. About this time the music Puente was making became known as salsa. Puente rejected this term. "Salsa is a sauce. Something you put on a steak," he was quoted in *Down Beat.* "I don't play sauce. I play music." Whatever it was called, in 1979 it garnered Puente the first of five Grammy awards for his album, *Homenaje a Benny More.*

By this time Puente was well known as a musical virtuoso. In addition to his beloved timbales, he was a master at dozens of percussion instruments, from drums to cymbals. He was a skilled saxophonist, knew his way around a keyboard, and was a master of the vibraphone which is played with a mallet. In addition he had become renowned for his skills as a composer and arranger of music. However, it was for his over-the-top performance style that the general public knew him best. He acknowledged courting that image in an interview with *Down Beat* "I've even got my timbales painted different colors. It's what they see now, not what they hear. They've been hearing me for a hundred years already, so at least you see the drums. I put my cymbals around the timbales, three or four pairs of timbales—eight of them—and I put my sticks up in the air....I put them around my head, holding them, and the people like that. Because how much can you play?... They even talk about the instruments now, because they already know [I] can play." They also talked about his crazed facial gestures and mile-wide grin ever present as he played.

Became an Icon

Puente continued touring and recording throughout the 1980s and 1990s and was lauded with phenemonal success. He received four more Grammy Awards for the albums *Tito Puente and his Latin Ensemble on Broadway, Mambo Diablo, Goza mi Timbal,* and *Mambo Birdland.* In 1990 he was given a star on Hollywood's Walk of Fame. Then in 1991 he made music recording history when he recorded his 100th album, *The Mambo King: 100th LP.* He also moved from stage to screen during this period, making appearances on the television series *The Cosby Show* and in the movies *Radio Days* and *Armed and Dangerous.* In 1997 he was awarded the National Medal of Arts. Puente was edging into the status of icon. Oscar Hijuelos, who put Puente in his Pulitzer Prize-winning novel, *The Mambo Kings Play Songs of Love* acknowledged Puente's status, "If you grew up in the city, he was a fixture, like the mayor or Santa Claus," he told *U.S. News and World Report.* Puente later played himself in the film adaptation of Hijuelos's novel. Yet despite his fame, he was also known for being a regular guy. "Tito, he always made you laugh," producer Emilio Estefan told the *Miami Herald.* "The biggest stars are always the ones who are more down to earth, and Tito was a humble man. But he implemented new sounds and rhythms and he was one of the pioneers in bringing Latin music to the world at a time when doing such a thing was extremely difficult." Puente established The Tito Puente Scholarship fund in the hopes that future Latin musicians would not have to endure the same difficulties.

As his entire career had been, Puente's last year was a productive one. At the beginning of 2000 he completed a new CD, *Masterpiece/Obra Maestra: Tito Puente and Eddie Palmieri.* Then in April of 2000, he was declared a "Living Legend" by the U.S. Library of Congress. He was wrapping up a series of concerts in Puerto Rico with the island's Symphony Orchestra when breathing problems sent him to the hospital. Canceling his May and June concert dates, he returned to New York City for further treatment. On May 31, 2000, following heart valve replacement surgery, Tito Puente died. Though his passing was felt deeply by all who loved both the man and his music, Arturo Sandoval summed up his passing best. "That man spent 77 years spreading love and music throughout the world. He had a tremendous personality and extraordinary charisma. I think his music will be played forever," he told the *Miami Herald,* "and maintaining that legacy is the most important thing now."

Selected discography

Dance Mania, RCA, 1958.
Puente Now!, GNP Records/Crescendo, 1960.
El Rey Bravo, Tico Records, 1962.
Homenaje a Benny More, Tico Records, 1978.

Tito Puente and His Latin Ensemble on Broadway,
  Concord Picante, 1983.
Mambo Diablo, Concord Picante, 1985.
Un Poco Loco, Concord Picante, 1987.
Goza Mi Timbal, Concord Picante, 1990.
The Mambo King: 100th LP, RMM, 1991.
50 Years of Swing (Three CD Compilation), RMM,
  1997.
Mambo Birdland, RMM, 1999.

Sources

Americas (English Edition), Nov-Dec 1990, p56.
Billboard, June 10, 1995, pL12; April 5, 1997, p10.
Down Beat, January 1984, p27-29, 61; May 1991,
  p20-21; Nov 1995, p16; August 2000, p6, 12, 62.
Miami Herald, June 1, 2000.
New York Post, May 18, 1974, p. 15.
Time, June 12, 2000, p. 27.
U.S. News & World Report, June 12, 2000, p. 12.

—Candace LaBalle

Anthony Quinn

1915–2001

Actor , artist, writer

Anthony Quinn's robust portrayals of such characters as Zorba the Greek and the fierce Bedouin leader in *Lawrence of Arabia* (1962) made him larger than life to millions. Appearing in more than two hundred films during a career that spanned six decades, his image was defined by his charismatic performance as the lusty peasant Alexis Zorba in *Zorba the Greek* (1964), a role that seemed to reflect the sum and substance of his off-screen persona as someone proud, virile and passionate.

Early on the Mexican Irish actor was typecast as a Native American, a Latin villain, a Mafia don, and a Mexican bandito in mostly B-movies, but he resisted characterization. His successful stage performance of Stanley Kowalski in Tenessee Williams' *A Streetcar Named Desire* led to more challenging roles, such as the hot-tempered brother of Mexican revolutionary leader Emiliano Zapata in *Viva Zapata!* (1952) and the artist Paul Gauguin in *Lust for Life* (1956), winning Academy Awards for both performances.

Quinn also resisted being categorized as an actor. He considered running for governor of California, but was discouraged by labor leader Cesar Chavez, who told him he was more valuable as an actor than in politics.

He dedicated much of his time later in life to honing his artistic abilities, becoming an accomplished painter and sculptor, and designing houses in Italy and California.

Escaped the Mexican Revolution

Anthony Rudolph Oaxaca Quinn was born in Chihuahua, Mexico to Francisco Quinn of Irish-Mexican descent and Manuella Oaxaca of Mexican and Cherokee ancestry. His father was fighting in the Mexican Revolution with Pancho Villa's forces at the time of his birth until the family fled to El Paso, Texas to escape federal troops. The family, which had grown with the birth of Quinn's sister Stella, eventually moved to California where they worked as farm laborers, earning ten cents an hour picking fruit. After settling in East Los Angeles when Quinn was six, Frank found work at the Lincoln Park Zoo and then as a laborer at the burgeoning film studios. He was killed in a car accident when Quinn was just nine.

His father's death forced Quinn to support his mother with odd jobs, including shining shoes, digging ditches, and driving a taxi. He also worked as a professional boxer, racking up sixteen consecutive victories until he was knocked out in his seventeenth fight and gave up the sport for good. After taking up the saxophone and forming a small orchestra, he joined a band with the Foursquare Gospel Church of the evangelist Aimee Semple McPherson and did some preaching in Los Angeles' Mexican neighborhoods. During this time, Quinn was teaching himself literature, music and painting, and taking courses in art and architecture. After winning an architectural drawing contest, he met Frank Lloyd Wright, who advised him to get medical help to improve his speech impediment. His speech actually deteriorated after the surgery, so he sought the help of former actress Katherine Hamil to improve his stammer though acting lessons.

Debuted on Stage and Screen

In 1936 Quinn debuted on stage in Mae West's play *Clean Beds*, playing a role originally written for John Barrymore. The legendary actor made a surprise appearance on opening night, complimenting twenty-one-year-old Quinn on his performance. Over the years, Barrymore would become a friend and mentor. "Many people remember Jack Barrymore as either a wit or a drunk, but what impressed me was his courage

of conviction," Quinn told the *Los Angeles Times*. "He used to tell me that you can only be as right as you dare to be wrong. That you must be willing to take chances to achieve superiority in your craft. He gave me his armor from 'Richard III.' He was like a retiring matador, who gives his sword to the most promising newcomer he knows."

That same year, Quinn signed on with Paramount and made his film debut as a convict in *Parole!*. This would lead to a string of movies in which he appeared in the "ethnic" roles, including the Cheyenne chief in Cecil B. DeMille's *The Plainsman* (1936), starring Gary Cooper. It wasn't long before Quinn married DeMille's daughter Katherine, whom he met during the filming. Their first son, Christopher, drowned in 1941 after falling into a fishpond on the estate of W.C. Fields. They would go on to have four more children: Christina, born in 1941; Catalina in 1942; Duncan in 1945; and Valentina in 1952.

Quinn appeared in a number of B-movies between 1936 and 1947, including: *King of Alcatraz* (1938), *King of Chinatown*, (1939) and *Island of Lost Men* (1939), but he felt constrained by Hollywood. "I was the bad guy's bad guy," he told the *Guardian*. "I rarely made it to the final reel without being dispatched by a gun or knife or a length of twine, typically administered by a rival hood." He moved to New York City and made his debut on Broadway in 1947 in *Gentleman From Athens*, following it with a successful two-year run in Elia Kazan's production of *A Streetcar Named Desire*, replacing Marlon Brando, who had gone into films.

Part of the reason Quinn moved to New York in 1947 was due to the U.S. House Un-American Activities Committee investigating him along with other big names in Hollywood. Quinn was always a political man, sometimes taking stances considered radical at the time. He got involved in the 1942 "Sleepy Lagoon" trial, helping 22 Mexican youths from Los Angeles appeal a gang-related murder conviction. "Probably it's the Irish in me that makes me speak out," he told the *Los Angeles Times*. "But there are about 800 boys in my profession who have a political ideal and want to express it. How can an actor be real in his work if he hasn't some convictions regarding the problems in the world around him?"

Offered More Rewarding Roles

Quinn's multi-ethnic heritage had an acute effect on his sense of identity, which directly influenced his decision to become an actor and the various ethnic roles he played. "Those were rough times, right from the beginning," he said as he recalled his childhood in a 1981 interview with the *Los Angeles Times*. "With a name like Quinn, I wasn't totally accepted by the Mexican community in those days, and as a Mexican I wasn't accepted as an American. So as a kid I just decided, well, 'A plague on both your houses. I'll just become a world citizen.' So that's what I did. Acting is my nationality." Still, he was proud to portray Mexicans and Native American's in his films, seeing it as an opportunity to educate the audience. "I fought early to go beyond the stereotypes and demand Mexicans and Indians be treated with dignity in films."

After years of viewing his ethnicity as a disadvantage, Quinn began to realize its benefits. He returned to film in Robert Rosen's *The Brave Bulls* (1951). "The supporting cast was entirely Mexican, and I was thrilled to be in such company," he told the *Guardian*. "After so many years as the token Latin on the set, I found tremendous security in numbers. For the first time, I belonged." But it was his performance of the great Mexican revolutionary Emiliano Zapata in *Viva Zapata!* (1952) that won him fame and his first Academy Award.

Quinn spent much of his time in Italy, where he worked with several acclaimed Italian filmmakers, including Dino De Laurentiis, Carlo Ponti, and Giuseppe Amato. It was his next film, Federico Fellini's *La Strada* (1954), in which he played dim-witted circus strongman Zampano, that forever changed his career and demonstrated his capacity to play a leading role. He won his second Oscar in 1955 for his portrayal of Paul Gauguin in Vincente Minnelli's *Lust for Life* and was nominated again for his performance in *Wild is the Wind* (1957), with Anna Magnani. He even tried his hand at directing, taking over for his father-in-law when DeMille became ill during the making of *The Buccaneer* (1958). However, under Quinn's direction, the film would become more of a pirate epic than the intimate, political drama it was intended to be. It would also be his last stab at filmmaking.

Quinn's acting career reached its peak in the early sixties when he appeared on Broadway as Henry II, starred opposite Lawrence Olivier in Jean Anouilh's *Becket*, and starred with Margaret Leighton in Francois Billetdoux's *Tchin Tchin*. He had simultaneous box-office success with the WWII drama *The Guns of Navarone* (1961), in which he played a Greek colonel, and with David Lean's WWII epic *Lawrence of Arabia* (1962). This was followed by another acclaimed performance, and one of his personal favorites, as an over-the-hill prizefighter in *Requiem For a Heavyweight* (1962).

He went on to play what became his signature role— the ouzo-drinking and bouzouki-dancing peasant in Michael Cacoyannis's *Zorba the Greek* (1964), for which he earned another Oscar nomination. He would reprise the role on Broadway nearly twenty years later in what would become one of the most lucrative revivals in history, grossing $48 million over four years. He never found a part of the same caliber despite a busy career that produced such films as *A High Wind in Jamaica* (1965) and *The Secret of Santa Vittoria* (1969).

Quinn and DeMille's marriage ended in 1965 after he conceived a child with Iolanda Addolori, a wardrobe assistant on the set of *Barabbas* (1962). The marriage had lasted nearly thirty years, but Quinn had never been a faithful husband. He admitted to affairs with some of Hollywood's most glamorous women, including Carole Lombard, Rita Hayworth, Ingrid Bergman, and Maureen O'Hara. He married Addolori in 1966 when she was pregnant with their third child.

Focused on Other Talents

His success in acting allowed Quinn to exploit his artistic talents later in life, when he concentrated on painting, sculpting, and designing jewelry. He was known for cubist and pot-impressionist oils, showing his work at major international exhibitions, although he admitted to "stealing" from the masters. In an interview with the San Francisco Chronicle, he quoted Picasso: "A poor man borrows, a rich artist steals. I steal, of course." Nevertheless, he added, "I'm much more honest in my painting than I am as an actor. You can't do 240 films and do your best in each one." Quinn penned his memoirs, *The Original Sin: A Self Portrait* in 1972.

Quinn never stopped acting, but he slowed down quite a bit after 1975. "The parts dried up as I reached my sixtieth birthday, loosely coinciding with my growing disinclination to pursue them," he said to *The Guardian*. "Indeed, I could not see the point in playing old men on screen and I rejected the role for myself." However, he continued to make movies throughout the 1970s, appearing in such films as *The Greek Tycoon* (1978) and *The Children of Sanchez* (1978). Turning to television, he played Greek shipping magnate Aristotle Onassis in the 1988 movie *Onassis: The Richest Man in the World* and the tireless fisherman in Ernest Hemingway's *The Old Man and the Sea* (1990).

Quinn's second marriage lasted 31 years, but he was never a faithful husband. He had three children with two other women and carried on affairs with many more, including Ingrid Bergman's daughter Pia Lindstrom and the French actress Dominique Sanda. He and Addolori divorced in 1997 after he fathered two more children with his former secretary, Kathy Benvin, who was 50 years his junior. Their daughter, Antonia, was born in 1993 and a son, Ryan, was born in 1996.

Still active into his eighties, Quinn worked with Kevin Costner in *Revenge* (1990), director Spike Lee in *Jungle Fever* (1991) and Keanu Reeves in *A Walk in the Clouds* (1995). In 1995 he published *One Man Tango*, a second memoir in which he did some soul-searching and confessed to his womanizing ways. The title refers to a comment made by Orson Welles: "Tony, you're a one-man tango." He was working on the film *Avenging Angelo* with Sylvester Stallone at the time of his death from respiratory failure.

Selected works

Plays

Clean Beds.
A Streetcar Named Desire.
Gentlman from Athens.
Becket.
Tchin Tchin.

Films

Parole!, 1936.
The Plainsman, 1937.
King of Alcatraz, 1938.
King of Chinatown, 1939.
Islands of Lost Men, 1939.
The Brave Bulls, 1951.
Viva Zapata, 1952.
La Strada, 1954.
Lust for Life, 1956.
Wild Is the Wind, 1957.
(as director) *The Buccaneer,* 1958.
Guns of Navarone, 1961.
Becket, 1961.
Barabbas, 1962.
Requiem for a Heavyweight, 1962.
Lawrence of Arabia, 1962.
Zorba the Greek, 1964.
High Wind in Jamaica, (1965.
The Secret of Santa Vittoria, 1969.
Deaf Smith and Johnny Ears, 1973.

The Children of Sanchez, 1978.
The Greek Tycoon, 1978.
Revenge, 1990.
Jungle Fever, 1991.
A Walk in the Clouds, 1995.
Avenging Angelo, 2002.

Made-For-TV movies

Onassis: The Richest Man in the World.
The Old Man and the Sea.

Books

The Original Sin: A Self Portrait, 1972.
(with Michael Paisner) *One Man Tango,* 1995.

Sources

Periodicals

The Guardian (London), June 5, 2001.
Independent (London), June 5, 2001. B2.
Los Angeles Times, June 4, 2001. A1.
San Francisco Chronicle, June 5, 2001. B2.
The Scotsman, June 5, 2001. P. 14.
The Washington Post, June 4, 2001. B6.

On-line

Contemporary Authors Online, Gale, 2002.

—Kelly M. Cross

Denise Quiñones August

1980—

Miss Universe

"I feel like I am living a fantasy," Denise Quiñones August told *People en Español*. As the 50th Miss Universe, some would say she is. A rural girl from a mountain town, Quiñones had only been competing in pageants for three years before winning the title of Miss Universe. As the fourth Miss Universe to hail from this tiny Caribbean island of 3.9 million people, a U.S. territory, she is also living a fantasy for her people.

Denise Quiñones August (also known as Denise M. Quiñones) was born in Ponce, Puerto Rico and raised in Lares, a small town in the center of the island high in the mountains of Puerto Rico. Her father Hector Quiñones worked as an engineer while her mother Susanna August stayed home to care for Quiñones and her younger brother Hector. "I grew up around nature, nothing especially sophisticated," Quiñones told *People en Español*. Yet she found her own sophistication in performing. "Dance and song are my passions," she told *People en Español*. She was just eight years old when she enrolled in the dance school of Estela Velez. She hasn't stopped dancing or singing since. Quiñones first professional dance experience came while she was still a senior in high school. She was selected to dance on one of Puerto Rico's wildly popular variety shows, *El Super*

Show. This led to her being selected to co-host another show *Eso Vale*.

When not on stage wowing audiences, Quiñones was in school wowing teachers. She graduated from her high school, Colegio Nuestra Señora del Carmen located in Hatillo, Puerto Rico, with honors and was named in the *Who's Who Among American High School Students*. She had been a straight-A student and a former president of the school's honor society. Though her first language was Spanish, she had mastered English early on, becoming fully bilingual. Following graduation she enrolled as a journalism student in the Communications School of the University of Puerto Rico.

Unlike many pageant contestants who begin grooming for national titles at a very young age, Quiñones was already entering college when she decided to run for the title of Miss Puerto Rico. It fell to Magali Febles, an image consultant who had coached Dayanara Torres, another Puerto Rican Miss Universe, to prepare Quiñones for pageantry. "When Denise came to me she was a diamond in the rough," he told *People en Español*. He taught her to walk the catwalk, control her movements, and play up her features. Though she was originally adamant about winning the crown as naturally as possible, Febles convinced Quiñones to lighten her hair and have plastic surgery on her nose.

After becoming Miss Puerto Rico, excitement begun to build as it became known that the 2001 Miss Universe pageant would be held in Bayamon, Puerto Rico not far from the island's capital. Quiñones would compete with a home grown advantage. She courted local adoration from the opening ceremony of the 50th Miss Universe Pageant in May of 2001 when she arrived in a be-feathered bathing suit with wings representing a fighting cock. Cockfighting, though considered distasteful and even cruel in American culture, is a popular sport in Puerto Rico and many other Latin American countries. Over the week of the pageant, Quiñones was mobbed like a superstar much to the consternation of the other 76 contestants. Her dazzling smile was plastered across front pages and on television.

However, Quiñones garnered more than just the attention of her countrymen. Pageant officials awarded her the Miss Photogenic title and she won both the Bluepoint Swim Fitness Award and Clairol Herbal Essences Style Awards. Her ascension to the semi-finals seemed assured. However as hosts Naomi Campbell and Elle Macpherson read off the first nine names, Quiñones was not among them. "The crowd in Ruben Rodriguez Coliseum held their breath, fearing that perhaps Ms. Quiñones somehow had not made the cut. But then the tenth finalist was announced, and Ms. Quiñones traipsed down the grand staircase at the back of the set, beaming like the queen she would soon become.

Though all of the finalists were stunning, there was a star quality about Ms. Quiñones—buoyed as she was by the crowd's adoration—that set her apart from the rest," www.pageant.net noted.

During the pageant, Quiñones turned for inspiration to her grandmother who had died a few months before. She described to www.pageant.net how she spent a few moments speaking to her grandmother. "I was asking her to be with me in the competition, and I felt her in every part." This inspiration was with her when she was crowned Miss Universe. As her win was announced, the tiny island of Puerto Rico erupted in a cacophony of car horns, sirens, and cries of victory. Quiñones responded to her country's outpouring of joy, telling the assembled press after her victory, "I'm proud to have won this crown....I think I have left a great legacy for my beloved Puerto Rico."

Following her win, Quiñones relocated to New York City and a luxury apartment at Trump Tower which would become her home for the duration of her yearlong reign. The apartment, as well as $250,000 in prizes is part of her winnings. She is also allotted a clothing allowance. In return, Quiñones is expected to travel around the world as a representative of the Miss Universe organization, providing promotional support for pageant sponsors and charities. She has already taken up the struggle against AIDS and made a very public appearance at the AIDS Walk in New York. "By educating people about HIV/AIDS, I look forward to teaching tolerance of people with differences and doing my part to remove the stigma of HIV/AIDS," Quiñones was quoted on the UNAIDS website. "In my travels around the world, I've heard people speaking about AIDS in every language under the sun. If each one of us speaks out, we will overcome this epidemic together," she continued.

As her reign wound down in the earlier part of 2002, Quiñones began to long for her country. "Every day I awake and think of Puerto Rico, especially my family. I want to be with my people and spend time with my father, mother, and brother," she confessed to *Revista Vea,* a Puerto Rican magazine. When she does return she has great ambitions to pursue. "I would like to be a part of the entertainment and communication industry, becoming an acclaimed singer known worldwide and establishing my own television program. I plan to complete a Master's degree in communications and to continue training in the areas mentioned above," she was quoted on www.missuniverse.com.

During the Miss Universe pageant, Quiñones was asked what she thought the most important thing in life was. According to www.pageant.net she quickly answered, "to be the best I can be." Whether that is fighting AIDS, pursuing a career in showbiz, or inspiring a nation of young Puerto Ricans to love their country and reach for their dreams, there is no doubt Quiñones's best, will make a difference in many lives.

Sources

Periodicals

Latina, August 2001, p. 83.
People en Español, August 2001, p. 37.
The St. Petersburg Times (St. Petersburg, FL), May 12, 2001, p. 2B.

On-line

www.arabia.com
http://in.infocus.lycosasia.com/missuniverse
www.missuniverse.com
www.pageant.net/universe2001
*Revista Vea,*www.veavea.com

—Candace LaBalle

Alex Rodriguez

1975—

Baseball player

Baseball player Alex Rodriguez has been inspiring fans for years with his style of play. He became a household name when he signed a $252-million contract with the Texas Rangers in December of 2001. Rodriguez has won numerous awards and is known for his versatile talent on the field and his good conduct off it.

Rodriguez, known as "A-Rod" to his fans, was born in New York City and lived briefly in the Dominican Republic before his family moved to Kendall, Florida, a suburb of Miami. His father, Victor, had played professional baseball in the Dominican Republic and taught the game to Rodriguez. However, when Rodriguez was ten years old, his father left the family. Rodriguez told Ben Kaplan in *Sports Illustrated for Kids,* "It was hard. I did my best to help out around the house and bring home good grades to make my mom proud." He became an honor student and a star shortstop at Miami's Westminster Christian School. He did his best to play like his hero, baseball great Cal Ripken of the Baltimore Orioles; he kept a life-sized poster of Ripken on the wall in his bedroom.

Westminster's baseball coach, Rich Hoffman, became like a second father to Rodriguez when he made the varsity team in tenth grade. Hoffman encouraged Rodriguez to improve his hitting and to lift weights to become stronger. By his junior season, he was batting .450, helping Westminster to win the 1992 national high school championship. In his senior year, he batted .505 and stole 35 bases in 35 attempts.

His talent attracted attention, and in the 1993 draft, the Seattle Mariners chose him with the first pick. After playing in only 82 minor league games, in 1994 Rodriguez was called up to Seattle after lengthy contract negotiations. Although he expected to be the Mariners' starting shortstop, the Mariners were in contention for the pennant and didn't think Rodriguez could deal with the pressure. They called him up and sent him back to the minors three times, leaving him frustrated and wanting to quit and go home. According to Phillips, his mother, Lourdes, said, "I don't want you home with that attitude. Whether you have a month left or three, you go out and play hard. You better care."

The advice paid off. In 1996, his first year in the major leagues, Rodriguez had thirty-six home runs, led the league in doubles (54), grand slams (3), total bases (397), and runs scored (141). He also drove in 123 runs

At a Glance . . .

Born Alexander Emmanuel Rodriguez on July 27, 1975, in New York, New York.

Career: Baseball player, Seattle Mariners, 1993-00; Texas Rangers, 2001–.

Awards: *Sporting News*, Player of the Year, 1996; Silver Slugger Award, 1996, 1999, 2000, 2001; Rangers Player of the Year, 2001; American League,, Hank Aaron Award, 2001; American League, Player of the Year in Players Choice Award voting, 2001; Josh Gibson Legacy Award from the Negro Leagues Baseball Museum, 2001.

Address: *Team*—Texas Rangers, 1000 Ballpark Way, Arlington, TX 76011.

and batted .358, the best in the major leagues. In addition, that year, at age twenty, Rodriguez became the youngest shortstop to play in an All-Star Game. He was also named the *Sporting News* Player of the Year. Rodriguez's idol, Cal Ripken, told Mike Phillips in the *Knight-Ridder/Tribune News Service,* "I doubt that I had that much talent coming in. He has talent that flows with every action."

In 1997, according to Ben Kaplan in *Sports Illustrated for Kids,* Mariners' designated hitter Edgar Martinez said, "Alex has become a great player in a short time. He can run, throw, and field. He can hit for average and for power. He's also handled fame and attention well." In 1998 Rodriguez became the first "40-40" infielder in baseball—that is, the first to have 40 home runs and 40 stolen bases. He was only the third player in any position to achieve this. The following season a knee injury kept him on the disabled list for five weeks, but he still had a stellar year, with 42 home runs. According to Michael Knisley in *Sporting News,* baseball scout Rudy Terrasas praised Rodriguez's "power, his speed and his glove," and noted, "He's still young, with a tremendous upside.… For my money, if I was starting a club and needed a shortstop, considering his age and athleticism, he'd be my choice. If I had to take one, I'd take A-Rod."

Rodriguez's contract with the Mariners ended in 2000, and he was unsure whether he wanted to stay with the team. He told interviewer Mark Ribowsky in *Sport* that he would stay with the team if they went to the World Series. He agreed, however, that the team could have done better, saying, "We all could have done more to put us over the top. We did our best, but what we did wasn't good enough."

In December of 2000 Rodriguez became the best-paid ballplayer of all time when he signed a $252 million, ten-year free-agent contract with the Texas Rangers. Rangers owner Tom Hicks told *People Weekly* that Rodriguez "is the only person in baseball who would deserve this," but in *Texas Monthly,* Paul Burka objected, "The A-Rod contract is about business, not baseball," and noted that the expense of obtaining Rodriguez might hinder the Rangers from being able to attract and pay any other top players. In addition, *People Weekly* commented that the contract exemplified baseball officials' fears that baseball was becoming simply a financial contest between teams that could afford to hire top players and those that could not.

Although Rodriguez's good looks, personal charm, and clean lifestyle had made him a favorite of fans when he played for the Mariners, the expensive contract aroused anger and jealousy in fans. During the 2001 season, Rodriguez was booed by fans in cities around the United States, according to Ken Daley in *Knight-Ridder/Tribune News Service.* Daley noted that fans' anger might cost Rodriguez a place in the 72nd All-Star Game, set for July 10 in Seattle. Rodriguez told Daley, "All I can do is keep playing, be the same person I've always been on the field, and a solid citizen off it."

Rodriguez did make the 2001 All-Star team. He also led the American League with 52 home run, 133 runs scored, and 393 total bases, although the Rangers as a whole did not do well that year. He told Mark Kram in the *Knight-Ridder/Tribune News Service,* "I understand that it is a process to get where we want to be. We have a plan in place here." By the end of the 2001 season, he had accumulated four consecutive 40-home-run seasons and had also set a single-season record for home runs in one year by a shortstop, with 52 homeruns.

Rodriguez was also involved in giving something back to the community from which he came. As a boy, Rodriguez was a member of the Hank Kline Boys and Girls Club in Miami, and he continued his association with the club as a national spokesperson for the youth development organization. The advertisements for the club appeared in both English and Spanish, and were the club's first bilingual campaign. Speaking of his phenomenal success, Rodriguez told Kram, "In the long run, you can only be judged by how you treat people, what kind of teammate you are, or how you play baseball." And, he told Alan Schwarz in *Sports Illustrated for Kids,* "I don't think money really changes you. You have to remember that it doesn't make you who you are. I might make a lot of money, and people make a big deal about it. I still see myself as just a baseball player."

Sources

Baseball Digest, July, 2000, p. 40; December, 2000, p. 60; March, 2002, p. 24.

Knight-Ridder/Tribune News Service, July 8, 1994;
   July 13, 1996; May 8, 2001; July 21, 2002.
Newsweek, April 9, 2001, p. 54.
People Weekly, December 25, 2000, p. 75; May 14,
   2001, p. 131.
PR Newswire, January 30, 2002.
Sport, June, 1997, p. 65; July, 2000, p. 32.
Sporting News, October 14, 1996, p. 19; June 28,
   1999, p. 12.
Sports Illustrated, April 9, 2001, p. 56.
Sports Illustrated for Kids, July, 1997, p. 36; July 1,
   2002, p. 29.
Texas Monthly, February, 2001, p. 7.

—Kelly Winters

Loretta Sanchez

1960—

U.S. representative

An icon of the growing involvement in politics on the part of Hispanic Americans at the turn of the millennium, Loretta Sanchez is also very much an individualist who has stuck to her own beliefs even when they did not seem expedient. Sanchez came out of political obscurity to defeat an entrenched Anglo-American congressman in the 1996 national election. By the early 21st century, however, Sanchez was well entrenched in Congress herself, and she had become a figure of national renown.

Loretta Sanchez was born in Lynwood, California, on January 7, 1960, and has spent nearly all her life in southern California. When Sanchez was five the family moved to largely Anglo-American Anaheim. The daughter of two Mexican immigrants, a machinist father and a secretary mother, Sanchez spoke Spanish at home and first learned English in a Head Start education program. She had a strong personality from the start; her younger sister Linda fondly recalled her as a "bossy" presence (according to the *Los Angeles Times*) who would dress her younger sisters in new clothes.

The occasional discrimination the Sanchez children experienced dissolved in the face of their strong per-

formance in school; both her parents took an active hand in their children's education, and Sanchez as an adult credited her parents for her success. Sanchez attended Chapman University in Orange, California, graduating in 1982 with an economics major and winning a Business Student of the Year Award. She moved on for a Master of Business Administration degree at American University in Washington, D.C., receiving her degree in 1984 with a finance concentration after spending a year in Italy in a management program operated by the European Community.

Married to a stock trader named Stephen Brixey, Sanchez used her husband's last name until she entered politics in the 1990s. Her first job after receiving her Master's degree was with the Orange County Transportation Department, where she shepherded to completion a project to raise funds for and construct highway emergency-assistance call boxes on county freeways. Sanchez then took a position as assistant vice president with Fieldman, Rolapp & Associates, an Orange County financial-analysis company, and worked for several years in finance and investment firms that did business with county and municipal governments. Much of her work involved analyzing the finances of such institutions as schools and municipal government departments.

In 1993, Sanchez founded her own consulting firm, Amiga Associates. By that time, however, the seeds of her second career had already been sown. Although a registered Republican up to that point, Sanchez was troubled by the tone of the party's 1992 national convention. Though sympathetic to conservative Republican positions in fiscal matters, Sanchez, who generally favors abortion rights and gay rights, switched to the Democratic Party and plunged into the political arena in 1994 with a run for Anaheim's city council. Nearly unknown and running under the name Loretta Sanchez Brixey, she made an unimpressive showing.

Completely undeterred, Sanchez jumped two years later into a much bigger arena: she challenged nine-term incumbent Republican representative Robert Dornan for the U.S. House seat in California's 46th District. Angered by Dornan's support of the anti-immigrant Proposition 187 initiative passed by voters in 1994, Sanchez was given little chance at first. Upsetting a party-backed candidate in the primary, she enjoyed little support from the local Democratic party. And despite the district's shifting ethnic makeup— Mexican-Americans now consituted fully half its population—Dornan had always won comfortably by com-

bining conservative stands on social issues with a fierce anti-Communism that appealed to the district's substantial Vietnamese-American minority.

But, emboldened by a 29 percent rise in Latino voter registration in California between 1992 and 1996, Sanchez ran a vigorous grassroots campaign and benefited from financial support from entertainment-industry figures (Mexican-American Linda Ronstadt among them) outraged by Dornan's sharp anti-gay and anti-abortion rhetoric; the campaign turned ugly as he sought to tar Sanchez as a Catholic who repudiated church teachings on those issues. Sanchez herself emphasized immigrant rights and such bread-and-butter issues as education and Medicare funding, and shocked observers in November with a 984-vote victory.

Dornan, unsurprisingly, demanded a recount, but then further alienated himself from district voters by alleging that the results had been tainted by the votes of large numbers of non-citizens and illegal immigrants in the election. His charges were aired repeatedly during a year-long congressional investigation, which, though it found some merit in the complaint, ultimately decided that the numbers involved had been too small to make a difference in the outcome. That set the stage for a contentious 1998 rematch between Dornan and Sanchez. Again some obsevers gave Dornan the edge; as an unknown first-term representative, Sanchez seemed vulnerable to the midterm jinx that usually results in the party in control of the White House (in this case President Bill Clinton's Democrats) losing seats in Congress.

"Look, he's old, he's the past," Sanchez told *USA Today*. "We're talking about the future here." Dornan argued that he was "the real Latino" in the race due to his anti-abortion stance, but Sanchez had cultivated a centrist record during her first term, voting, among other things, for a resolution to permit the posting of the Ten Commandments in school classrooms. Sanchez won the 1998 election going away, with 57 percent of the vote, and increased that margin to 60 percent in the year 2000.

In Congress Sanchez served on the Armed Services and Education committees; she developed a close relationship with northern California Rep. Nancy Pelosi, who was emerging as a member of the Democratic House leadership. But Sanchez's rising political power derived as well from her status as, in the words of a 2000 Democratic National Convention delegate quoted in the *Los Angeles Times*, "a national Latino spokesperson." That status was underscored during the convention by the publicity that accompanied a controversy in which Sanchez became embroiled: she faced criticism for scheduling a fundraiser for a Hispanic political action committee at the Playboy Mansion and was dropped from her speaking slot at the convention as a result. The speaking slot was restored after

Sanchez backed down and moved the fundraiser, but she in turn refused to speak.

To those who had followed her career, the controversy showed a combative side of Sanchez's personality that was quite characteristic. A direct woman who connects with voters partly by virtue of not taking politics too seriously, Sanchez recalled a meeting she had held with then-President Bill Clinton. "I think, if you're going to bother to do Congress, then you should be willing to fight. And I do fight," she told the *Washington Post.* "We were discussing education, and I told the president, 'If you really feel what you're telling me, then get off your butt and get this sold. Get out and do this!' I think he stopped and looked around and said, 'Did you guys hear that? I think she used the word 'butt.'" In the spring of 2002, a Congress that had just finished adjusting to the energy of one Representative Sanchez looked toward a possible welcome for another: Loretta Sanchez's younger sister, Linda, won the Democratic nomination for California's 39th District seat in Los Angeles County.

Sources

Periodicals

Los Angeles Times, November 5, 1998, p. A1; August 15, 2000, p. B3; November 16, 2000, p. B5; March 7, 2002, p. B10.
The Nation, October 26, 1998, p. 21.
New Republic, October 27, 1997, p. 13.
New York Times, March 3, 2002, p. 25.
Newsweek, November 25, 1996, p. 35.
USA Today, November 2, 1998, p. 10A.
Washington Post, August 15, 2000, p. A14; November 4, 2001, p. W5.

On-line

Newsmakers, Issue 3, Gale Group, 2000. Reproduced in *Biography Resource Center,* Gale, 2001 (http://www.galenet.com/servlet/BioRC).
Notable Hispanic American Women, Book 2, Gale, 1998. Reproduced in *Biography Resource Center,* Gale, 2001 (http://www.galenet.com/servlet/Bio RC).
http://www.house.gov/sanchez/

—James M. Manheim

Carlos Santana

1947—

Rock guitarist

One of the great musical boundary crossers of the twentieth century, Mexican-American guitarist Carlos Santana was a central figure in the growth of rock music as a serious art form in the late 1960s and early 1970s. Santana blended rock and blues guitar styles with Latin rhythms, and later experimental jazz influences, to create a compelling hybrid that was both commercially and artistically successful. Both a major musical innovator and (at times) a musician motivated by spirituality, Santana nevertheless always kept close to the down-to-earth roots of his music. "These are the ingredients for being a complete communicator," he told *Guitar Player.* "Soul, heart, mind, body, cojones. One note."

Carlos Santana was born in the small Mexican town of Autlán de Navarro, in the state of Jalisco, on July 20, 1947. His father, José, was a violinist in a Mexican mariachi band and had a regional reputation. Even before the family's 1955 move to Tijuana, on the California border, Santana was sure of his place in the world. "I read books about how people in their thirties or forties are just beginning to find out what their purpose in life is," he told *Guitar Player.* "I found that out when I was five years old." Of course, living the musically rich borderlands focused his aims as he encountered a mix of American rock and roll sounds, from such artists as Little Richard, with traditional Mexican rhythms. Santana started out on the violin but soon switched to guitar.

Played Clubs in Tijuana

Santana's family moved to San Francisco in 1961, settling in the predominantly Mexican Mission District. Carlos joined them for good only in 1963, after putting in time as a club musician in Tijuana, and his arrival coincided with an explosion in creativity in San Francisco's music scene. In the Bay area psychedelic rock, then in its infancy, mixed with folk music, Latin jazz and dance music, and blues. All these forms made their mark on the young guitarist, who was working as a dishwasher and playing music wherever he could. But one influence stood out. Even after moving to San Francisco, Santana told *People,* he was slow to adopt a rock and roll lifestyle. But "that all changed after I saw B.B. King at the Fillmore," he recalled. In 1966 the Santana Blues Band, soon renamed simply Santana, was born.

Though they found work around the Bay area, Santana and his bandmates took their time developing their

At a Glance . . .

Born in Autlán de Navarro, Jalisco state, Mexico, on July 20, 1947; son of a mariachi violinist; married Deborah King, 1973. *Religion:* Studied with Indian mystic Sri Chinmoy, 1970s.

Career: Began performing c. 1961, Tijuana; formed Santana Blues Band, soon renamed Santana, San Francisco, 1966; appeared at Woodstock festival, 1969; signed to Columbia label, 1969; first four albums, *Santana,* Abraxas, *Santana III, Caravanserai,* 1969-72, considered classics of rock genre; performed in Live Aid concert, 1985; signed to Polydor label, 1991, creating own Guts and Grace label under Polygram aegis; signed to Arista label and released *Supernatural,* 1999; *Supernatural* sold over 10 million copies worldwide.

Awards: Eight Grammy awards for *Supernatural.*

Addresses: *Record Label*—Arista Records, 9975 Santa Monica Blvd., Beverly Hills, CA 90212.

distinctive sound. They turned down several offers of recording contracts, waiting for the perfect forum to announce their striking new music. In the 1969 Woodstock festival in upstate New York, they found that forum. Unknown to the crowd of 500,000, they produced one of the festival's highlights with their new number "Soul Sacrifice." They were quickly signed to the Columbia label and in three years released four of the undisputed classic albums of the rock genre, *Santana* (1969), *Abraxas,* (1970), *Santana III* (1971), and *Caravanserai* (1972). These albums spawned top ten hits such as "Evil Ways" and "Oye Como Va". The latter song, a rock treatment of a composition by salsa bandleader Tito Puente, exemplified the mixture of innovation and rhythmic earthiness that made Santana's music so compelling.

Caravanserai was a connected suite of pieces that showed a strong influence of jazz, a music that Santana had once derided as cocktail music. In the 1970s Santana's music took a new turn. Dismayed by the descent of many rock musicians into spirals of drug abuse he sought spiritual instruction from the Indian guru Sri Chinmoy, who rechristened him Devadip Carlos Santana; the name meant "the eye, the lamp, and the light of God." At the same time, Santana sought out new challenges musically. Learning to read music for the first time, Santana joined with fellow Chinmoy disciples John McLaughlin (for the album

Love Devotion Surrender, 1973), and with saxophonist John Coltrane's widow Alice Coltrane (for *Illuminations,* 1974). Since this period, Santana's public manner of speaking has had a certain mystical tinge.

Influenced by Fusion Jazz

From *Caravanserai* onward, Santana's music had shown marks of his acquaintance with the "fusion" jazz of trumpeter Miles Davis. Indeed Santana, coming from the rock world, might be regarded as having met Davis, coming from the other direction, in the center of the improvisatory space between jazz and rock. His albums of the 1970s and 1980s landed him less often on the pop charts than did his first releases, but they were no less influential and are still studied avidly by young guitarists. *The Swing of Delight* (1980) was a double LP featuring progressive jazzmen Herbie Hancock, Wayne Shorter, and Ron Carter. Sometimes he recorded under the Santana band name (which he owns), and sometimes as Carlos Santana, but the band's membership changed with each new release and the musical distinction between the two designations is slight.

The 1981 album *Zebop!* put Santana back on the charts with its hit single "Winning," and in 1986 Santana branched out into film music with a score for the film biography of the Mexican-American rock-and-roll vocal star Ritchie Valens. Santana's releases of the late 1980s and early 1990s each contained noteworthy elements, with *Blues for Salvador* (1987) bringing Santana a Grammy award for Best Rock Instrumental Performance. Santana was also always a reliable draw in concert. But the new albums were less successful commercially than his previous releases. A move to the Polydor label in 1990 did not improve matters, and after 1994's *Santana Brothers* (actually featuring Santana's brother Jorge and a nephew), Santana disappeared from the recording scene for five years.

Few could have predicted his spectacular re-emergence in 1999 with the release of the Arista-label CD *Supernatural*—but some hint of its success might have been garnered by gauging the enthusiastic reactions the 52-year-old Santana's youthful collaborators had to the project when it was hatched. "My God, he is one of the great influences of my life," hip-hop chart-topper Lauryn Hill was quoted as saying in *People,* and the other stars who cowrote songs with Santana and appeared in duets on the album, including Dave Matthews, Rob Thomas, and Wyclef Jean, were equally bowled over. *Supernatural* sold over ten million copies worldwide and swept up eight Grammy awards in the year 2000.

Some attributed the album's success to a boom in Latin American culture generally, but equally important was the way Santana's multifaceted musical personality had inspired his various collaborators in entirely different ways. *Supernatural* returned to and extended the kaleidoscopic musical patterns of Santana at his best. At the end of 2001 Santana projected the release of an album mostly in Spanish. But typically he planned to put his own fusion-making twist on it. "I'm looking for Persian melodies combined with Spanish lyrics," he told *Billboard*.

Selected discography

Santana, Columbia, 1969.
Abraxas, Columbia, 1970.
Santana III, Columbia, 1971.
Caravanserai, Columbia, 1972.
Carlos Santana & Buddy Miles Live, Columbia, 1972.
Welcome, Columbia, 1973.
Love, Devotion, Surrender, (with John McLaughlin), Columbia, 1973.
Borboletta, Columbia, 1974.
Illuminations, Columbia, 1974.
Lotus, Columbia, 1975.
Amigos, Columbia, 1976.
Festival, Columbia, 1976.
Moonflower, Columbia, 1977.
Inner Secrets, Columbia, 1978.
Marathon, Columbia, 1979
Oneness, Silver Dreams—Golden Reality, Columbia, 1979.
The Swing of Delight, Columbia,, 1980.
Zebop, Columbia, 1981.
Shango, Columbia,, 1982.
Havana Moon, Columbia, 1983.
Beyond Appearances, Columbia, 1985.
Freedom, Columbia, 1987.
Blues for Salvador, Columbia, 1987.
Viva Santana!, Columbia, 1988.
The Sound of Carlos Santana, Pair, 1989.
Spirits Dancing in the Flesh, CBS, 1990.
Milagro, Polydor, 1992.
Sacred Fire, Polydor, 1993.
Brothers, Polygram, 1994.
Supernatural, Arista, 1999.

Sources

Books

Contemporary Musicians, volume 19, Gale, 1997.
Stambler, Irwin, *Encyclopedia of Pop, Rock & Soul,* St. Martin's, 1989.

Periodicals

Billboard, March 4, 2000, p. 1; February 17, 2001, p. LM-3.
Entertainment Weekly, December 24, 1999, p. 36.
Guitar Player, January 1993, p. 58; August 1999, p. 74.
Interview, March 2000, p. 62.
Newsweek, February 14, 2000, p. 66.
People, February 28, 2000, p. 97.

On-line

All Music Guide, http://www.allmusic.com
http://music.lycos.com

—James M. Manheim

Shakira

1977—

Singer, songwriter

By the time Shakira released her first English language album, 2001's *Laundry Service,* she had long been an international star in the Spanish speaking world. With four records—the first recorded when she was just thirteen—the petite Colombian singer-songwriter was already established as an authentic rockera with a unique sound that hinged on a fusion of her Latin American and Middle Eastern roots and a childhood obsession with rock music. She had done this in culture where machismo ruled. "In Latin cultures historically, though not always, females are interpreters," Jose Tillan, vice president of music and talent at MTV Latin America, told *Time.* "For the most part, they don't make records. Shakira isn't like that. From the very beginning she has been involved with the songs and the recording." Could she maintain her success and individuality with a new record, in a new language? The numbers seem to say yes. *Laundry Service* sold 200,000 copies in its debut week. Suddenly a phenomenon in the United States, everybody wanted to know, who is Shakira? She answered the question in an radio interview quoted in the *Los Angeles Times,* "I think my music says it all."

Shakira Isabel Mebarak Ripoll was born on February 2, 1977 in the small town of Barranquilla on the coast of Columbia. Her father, William Mebarak Chadid was Lebanese and her mother, Nidia del Carmen Ripoll Torrado was Columbian with Italian roots. They worked as jewelers and provided Shakira and her seven older brothers and sisters with a decidedly middle class upbringing. Her father, who was also a writer, freely shared his love of Arabic music and culture with his children. In fact Shakira is an Arabic word meaning "woman full of grace." At age four Shakira was already belly dancing much to the delight of her father. Her mother, with a penchant for the practical, taught Shakira to read and write by the age of three. From her parents, whom she proudly proclaims as her heroes, Shakira inherited the trait that would propel her to stardom—the creativity and intelligence to weave her cultures into music for the masses.

Found Fame at an Early Age

She wrote her first song—a love song to her father—while in grade school. As a pre-teen she was winning local singing contests and performing in children's groups. Show business suited her. "I knew that I was going to be a public figure," she told *The Wall Street*

At a Glance . . .

Born on February 2, 1977, Barranquilla, Columbia; daughter of William Mebarak Chadid and Nidia del Carmen Ripoll Torrado. *Religion:* Catholic.

Career: Musician. Recorded *Magia,* 1991, *Peligro,* 1993, *Pies Descalzos,* 1996, *Dondé Están Los Ladrones?,* 1998, *Laundry Service,* 2001; spokesperson for Pepsi-Cola; Goodwill Ambassador for Colombia.

Memberships: Founded Pies Descalzos, an organization dedicated to helping Latin American orphans, 1997.

Awards: Latin Female Artist of the Year, World Music Awards, 1998; two Latin Grammy Awards, 2000.

Addresses: *Home*—Miami, FL; *Record Company*—Sony Discos Inc., 2190 N.W. 89 Place, Miami, FL 33172.

Journal. "It was like a prophecy." At thirteen a family friend arranged an impromptu audition with an executive from Sony Music Columbia. "I went to his hotel and sang a song—which I had written—a cappella for him," she told *CosmoGirl.* "A few days later I sang Madonna's 'Material Girl' in Spanish for more executives in Bogota. The next day I was signed by Sony." Shortly thereafter Shakira's debut album, *Magia (Magic)* was released in Columbia. She left music briefly to finish high school and then returned to release *Peligro (Danger)* at age 15. Both albums smacked of teen pop and neither generated much in the way of sales.

After a brief foray into acting on a Colombian soap opera, Shakira returned to music determined to make her next album a success. Just 17, she began to work on her third album. She wanted the album to reflect her voice and her vision. A self professed control freak, she went into the studio and insisted on being involved in the record's production. Her determination paid off. Released in 1996 *Pies Descalzos (Bare Feet)* sold over 3.6 million copies. During a two year tour in support of the album Shakira became one of Latin America's brightest stars.

In Brazil, where *Pies* had sold nearly a million copies, Shakira was moved to find her Portuguese-speaking fans singing her songs in Spanish. She promptly learned Portuguese and re-released many of her most popular songs in her new language as a gift for her Brazilian fans. On the album Shakira's unique sound—a fusion of rock, Latin, and Arabic rhythms—surfaced. "I was born and raised in Colombia, but I listened to bands like Led Zeppelin, the Cure, the Police, the Beatles and Nirvana," she was quoted on *www.shakira.com.* "I was so in love with that rock sound but at the same time because my father is of 100% Lebanese descent, I am devoted to Arabic tastes and sounds. Somehow I'm a fusion of all of those passions and my music is a fusion of elements that I can make coexist in the same place, in one song."

Her fame scorched through the Spanish-speaking world. She even gained the admiration of Nobel laureate Gabriel Garcia Marquez who devoted four pages to her in his magazine, *Hombre de Cambio.* "Shakira's music has a personal stamp that doesn't look like anyone else's and no one can sing or dance like her, at whatever age, with such an innocent sensuality, one that seems to be of her own invention," he gushed.

Achieved International Superstardom

1998's *Donde Están Los Ladrones? (Where are the Thieves?)* went multi-platinum throughout Latin America, Spain, and the United States where the Hispanic-market embraced Shakira as the new face of the Latin music invasion. The album reached the number one spot on Billboard's Latin 50, scored a Grammy nomination, and helped secure Shakira the title of Latin Female Artist of the Year at the 1998 World Music Awards. At the 2000 Latin Grammy Awards, two songs from the album won awards. However, it was her sizzling performance at the Latin Grammy's that mesmerized U.S. audiences. With her rock-hewn vocals, hip swirling moves, and indomitable Latin sex appeal Shakira seduced the American music scene. The fact that her sultry looks were as magnificent as her musical talent didn't hurt either. Shakira had become a bona fide international superstar. Shakira was suddenly everywhere. Her face appeared on the cover of countless magazines. She was signed to a lucrative Pepsi endorsement deal. MTV came calling and in 1999 she released an album recorded on "MTV Unplugged," the music channel's acoustic artist showcase. Colombia named her their Goodwill Ambassador. Even the pope took notice and granted Shakira an audience at the Vatican. At the same time she managed to provide support for Pies Descalzos a children's charity she had founded in 1997 to help Latin American orphans. And, much to the delight of the omnipresent Spanish-language tabloids, her high profile life didn't prevent her from finding true love with Antonio de la Rúa, the handsome son of then Argentinean president, Fernando de la Rúa.

With superstar status throughout the Spanish-speaking world, multi-platinum albums, a famous well-heeled boyfriend, and immense financial success, it seemed as if Shakira had it all. Yet, there was still something missing—cross-over success. She wanted to become an star in the English-speaking world too. "I want my music to transcend all the barriers," she explained to *Latina.* "The spirit of conquest is a trait that has survived in human beings from the beginning. I want if for the same reason the Spaniards wanted to come to America. To be able to sink my Colombian flag in this land, that is a motivation."

Having relocated to Miami with her parents, Shakira became close to Gloria and Emilio Estefan who treated her like a little sister. Their support helped Shakira believe that she could record an album in English. "Gloria injected me [with] so much confidence," Shakira told the *Los Angeles Times.* Originally, Estefan had offered to translate Shakira's songs and help her with the pronunciations during recording. However, for control freak Shakira, this wouldn't do. "I can't hire other people to write songs for me," Shakira told *Time.* "I have to write them myself." So with characteristic determination, Shakira set out to learn English. With well-worn copies of Walt Whitman poems and English rhyming dictionaries, she started to gain control of the language. Using it to express her deepest feelings through song was another problem altogether. "I didn't want to make anything that was not from the heart, that was not honest enough," she told the *Los Angeles Times.* "And it was quite a challenge, because I was born in Spanish and raised in Spanish. I live in Spanish. I love in Spanish." Finally, she wrote the first song, "Objection. " "I prayed and asked God to send me a good song today, and I remember I started writing the song a couple of hours after," she related on *www.Shakira.com.* That accomplishment gave her the confidence to finish the album.

Remained Committed to Her Roots

Released in 2000 *Laundry Service* shot straight to number three on the Billboard charts, selling more than 200,000 copies in its first week. It was an album of love songs inspired by her relationship with de la Rúa. With it, Shakira had succeeded in creating music in a new language while preserving her distinctive style. The album is peppered with bits of tango, a heavy dose of

rock guitar, brief flirtations with Andean flutes, and topped off with a decidedly Middle Eastern flair. "Yo soy una fusion," I'm a fusion she declared in *Teen People.* However, even as *Laundry Service* trumpeted her fame in the States and beyond, Shakira still knows who she is. Embracing both her roots and her future she declared to *Time,* "I plan to keep being the same artist, with the same musical language." She continued, "It's all still coming from my real feelings, my real-life experiences." And for her Hispanic fans who have supported her for so long, she told the *Los Angeles Times,* "I continue belonging to them. Forever." She has crossed over, but she hasn't turned away. That is something both her Anglo and her Latino fans can be thankful for.

Selected discography

Magia, 1991, Sony Music Columbia.
Peligro, 1993, Sony Music Columbia.
Pies Descalzos, 1996, Sony Music Columbia.
Dondé Están Los Ladrones, 1998, Sony Music Latin America.
Laundry Service, 2001, Sony Music.

Sources

Periodicals

CosmoGirl!, December 2001, p. 31.
Hombre de Cambio (Colombia), June 1999.
Latina, July 2001.
Los Angeles Times, November 4, 2001.
Teen People, March 1, 2002, p. 86.
Time, September 15, 2001, p. 16.
The Wall Street Journal, February 13, 2001.

On-line

www.donde-esta-shakira.com
www.shakira.com
www.shakiraheaven.com

—Candace LaBalle

Martin Sheen

1940—

Actor, activist

A powerful, versatile actor, Martin Sheen is equally convincing in roles as diverse as the rebel killer in *Badlands*, a homophobic father in *Consenting Adults*, and President Kennedy in the television miniseries *JFK*. In his film roles Sheen has often played the loner or outsider, whereas many of his television portrayals are of historical or political figures. His political activism is at least as important to him as his acting career; he is tireless in his appearance at rallies and protests for nuclear disarmament, homeless rights, opposition to the death penalty, and other causes.

Martin Sheen was born Ramon Estevez on August 3, 1940 in Dayton, Ohio, the seventh of ten children. His father, Francisco, was a Spanish emigre; his Irish-American mother, Mary Ann, died when he was 11. The family was quite poor and at times had to turn to local Catholic organizations for assistance.

Young Ramon decided to become an actor after a small role in *The Caine Mutiny* at Chaminade High School. This led to a prize-winning appearance on a local television talent show. His father wanted him to go to the University of Dayton rather than attempting to become an actor. To avoid directly defying his father's wishes, Ramon deliberately failed the college entrance exam.

Proud of Hispanic Heritage

Sheen's parish priest gave him bus fare to New York. He took the usual variety of low-income jobs such as clerking while pursuing his acting dream and going on casting calls. At this time he changed his name because jobs for Hispanic actors were almost nonexistent. He chose Sheen in honor of prominent televangelist Fulton Sheen. In an interview with *Horizon* Magazine, Sheen said, "I'm very proud of my Hispanic heritage ... I never changed my name. I never will. In the context of the business, I had to adapt to a way of nonconfrontation 40 years ago, so I invented myself. I invented Martin Sheen. Within my heart I'm still Ramon."

Sheen never took formal acting lessons. He began working with the experimental theater groups—The Actors' Co-op and The Living Theater—and did custodial work at the theater and sometimes was an understudy before moving up to appearing on stage. Early roles included ones in Yeat's *Purgatory* and the controversial *Connection*, a play about drug addiction. At

At a Glance . . .

Born Ramon Estevez on August 3, 1940, in Dayton, OH; married Janet Templeton, 1961; children: Charlie Sheen, Emilio Estevez, Ramon Estevez, Renée Estevez. *Religion:* Catholic. *Politics:* Democrat.

Career: Actor's Co-op/ Living Theatre, New York, 1961; numerous films, including: *The Incident,* 1967; *Catch-22,* 1972; *Badlands,* 1974; *Apocalypse Now,* 1979; *Gandhi,* 1982; *Firestarter,* 1984; *Wall Street,* 1987; *Cadence,* 1989; *The American President,* 1995; *Spawn,* 1997; *Not Another Teen Movie,* 2001; *Stockpile,* 2001; *The Apostle Paul,* 2001; *The Confidence Game,* 2002; *Catch Me If You Can,* 2002; *We the People,* 2002; tv series: *The West Wing, 1999-.*

Awards: Tony nomination, *Subject Was Roses,* 1964; Golden Globe Best Television Actor, *Blind Ambition,* 1979; Emmy, Best Guest Actor in a Comedy Series, *Murphy Brow,* 1993; Imagen Foundation Lifetime Achievement Award, 1998; Golden Satellite, Best Actor in a Television Series (Drama), *The West Wing, 1999;* TV Guide, Favorite Actor in a New Series, *The West Wing,* 2000; Golden Globe, Best Actor in a Television Series (Drama), *The West Wing,* 2000.

this time Sheen met Janet Templeton, an art student who became his wife in 1961.

In 1964 Sheen received critical acclaim on Broadway in *The Subject was Roses* in which he played a soldier returning home to his fractured family. He was nominated for a Tony award and also received a Golden Globe award nomination for his lead in the film adaptation. Throughout much of his career, Sheen has continued to work sporadically in theater.

Sheen first appeared in film as a teenage hoodlum who hijacked a subway in 1967's *The Incident.* He gave an arresting performance as the amoral teen killer in 1973's *Badlands,* but was less than stellar in the horror movies *Spawn, Firestarter,* and *The Dead Zone.* More recently, he has done excellent supporting work in respected films such as *Gandhi,* 1982 and *The American President,* 1995, in which he played the Chief of Staff. In the 1987 movie *Wall Street,* he played opposite his son Charlie.

Heart of Darkness

Of his film work, Sheen is best-known for his mesmerizing role in Francis Ford Coppola's *Apocalypse Now* (1979), even though he was not the actor Coppola wanted for the part. The story is based on Joseph Conrad's novel *Heart of Darkness.* The film takes place during the Vietnamese conflict and Sheen plays the pasrt of Captain Willard, a man leading a secret mission into Cambodia to assassinate a renegade officer, played by Marlon Brando. Sheen's character was often drunk, which was mirrored by the actor's growing problem with alcohol. His over consumption of alcohol, combined with extraordinarily difficult filming conditions in the Philippines (including a typhoon), may have contributed to the heart attack he suffered on location. He was stricken while alone in the wilds and had to drag himself almost a mile for help. Sheen prayed to Mary for strength and vowed to "change my life from this day forward." He has followed up on his vow. His strong religious beliefs as a Catholic have also contributed to many of his political convictions, including his anti-death penalty stance.

Sheen is also well-known for his television work. His early television work included playing a wife-beater in the series *East Side, West Side* and appearances in *The Outer Limits, The Defenders, Route 66,* and other dramatic series. In 1967 he was a regular on the soap opera *As The World Turns.* In 1974 he starred as Robert F. Kennedy in *The Missiles of October,* a show about the Cuban Missile Crisis. The same year, he was acclaimed for his work in *The Execution of Private Slovik.* In *Blind Ambition,* a 1979 miniseries, Sheen portrayed John Dean, special counsel to President Nixon, for which he won a Golden Globe Award for Best Television Actor. In 1993 he turned in another widely lauded performance as John F. Kennedy in the miniseries *JFK.*

Sheen's other notable television roles included the ground-breaking 1972 television movie *That Certain Summer,* in which he played the lover of a gay father revealing his homosexuality to his son. Ironically in 1985 Sheen gave a convincing rendition of a father unable to accept his son's homosexuality in *Consenting Adult.* He gave strong performances in *Samaritan: The Mitch Snyder Story,* about a champion of homeless rights, *The Andersonville Trial,* and *Gettysburg,* in which Sheen played General Robert E. Lee. Expanding outside the field of actor, Sheen won a daytime Emmy in 1986 for his directorial debut of *Babies Having Babies,* a CBS Schoolbreak Special.

Dedicated to Social Causes

In 1999 Sheen began his portrayal of another President on the very successful television show *The West Wing.* He plays New England Democrat President Josiah Bartlet, a role that has won him Emmy nominations. Although his character was a very decent, moral man, the role sometimes required Sheen to champion causes to which he was personally opposed.

Sheen, however, is able to separate his very strongly held beliefs from his acting career. His dedication to anti-nuclear weapons, anti-death penalty, workers' rights, and other causes have lead to his arrest on approximately 70 occasions.

Sheen didn't just show up at rallies, either. Sheen donated his income from the motion picture *Gandhi* to Mother Teresa. He helped pay for medical care for three young survivors of a massacre at a church in Mexico. Other favored causes included the United Farm Workers and the rights of the homeless.

Sheen was a strong supporter of the Democratic party. Despite his dedication to social causes and his frequent portrayals of political figures, Sheen says he has no interest in running for office himself. He is forthright about other conflicts between his acting career and his beliefs. In 1999 he stated his agreement with the views of Vice Presidential candidate Joseph Lieberman, who decried Hollywood's obsession with sex and violence. He will not accept roles that contain unnecessary sex or violence. Sheen believes that he has probably lost jobs because of his activism, but that he may have been hired for others by people who supported his views.

Sheen has been nominated for and has won awards in all fields of acting, from Tonys to Emmys. In 1998 Sheen received the prestigious Lifetime Achievement Award from the Imagen Foundation, an organization that honors positive portrayals of Latinos in film, television, and advertising. He received Golden Globe nominations for Best Performance by an Actor in a Miniseries or Motion Picture Made for Television for *Kennedy* and for Best TV Actor for the miniseries *Blind Ambition.* He won an Emmy for Outstanding Guest Actor in a Comedy Series on *Murphy Brown.* He has also received awards for his social activism, including the 2001 Peacemaker Award from the Physicians for Social Responsibility.

An Acting Dynasty

Unlike many celebrities, Sheen and his wife Janet have been happily married for four decades. Three of their children, Charlie Sheen, Emilio Estevez, and Renee Estevez, are actors; son Ramon is both an actor and a songwriter. Like his father, Charlie Sheen has had a much publicized struggle with alcohol and drugs. According to acquaintances, Martin felt a strong sense of responsibility for his son's problems, feeling that he was not there for his son growing up and gave Charlie too many material things. Martin has taken a "tough-love" approach to Charlie's problems. He called on Charlie's fellow actors Rob Lowe and Clint Eastwood to participate in a confrontation demanding that Charlie straighten up. Sheen stated in *The New York Times,* "Pray for my boy, he has appetites that get him into trouble." Finally he alerted authorities that Charlie had broken the terms of his probation by using drugs.

Charlie then attended a rehabilitation center, which has helped him stay sober.

Martin Sheen has appeared with his children in film and television. Most notably, Martin directed himself and sons Charlie and Ramon in the well-intentioned if heavy-handed *Cadence.* Charlie plays a young private thrown into the stockade. Martin plays the racist stockade commander. Martin Sheen both directed and acted in the television movie *Beverly Hill Brats* with son Ramon. His wife Janet was the producer. Martin had a small role parodying *Apocalypse Now* in *Hot Shots Part Deux,* which his son Charlie starred in. Martin also guest-starred on Charlie's hit series *Spin City.* Daughter Renee has a regular role on *The West Wing* with her father. The head of such a successful acting dynasty is certain to act in many more laudable roles, alone and with his family, and it is certain that his fans will follow him with the avid interest he deserves.

Selected filmography

The Incident, 1967.
The Subject Was Roses, 1968.
The Andersonville Trial, 1970.
Catch-22, 1972.
Badlands, 1974.
Apocalypse Now, 1979.
The Final Countdown, 1980.
Gandhi, 1982.
Firestarter, 1984.
Cadence, 1989.
JFK, 1991.
The American President, 1995.
Spawn, 1997.
Not Another Teen Movie, 2001.
The Confidence Game, 2002.
We the People, 2002.
Catch Me If You Can, 2002.

Sources

Books

Current Biography 1977, 38th edition, Moritz, Charles, ed., H.W. Wilson, 1977.
Gale Who's Who in the Theatre, 17th edition, Gale Research, 1981.
Hargrove, Jim, *Martin Sheen: Actor and Activist,* Children's Press, 1991.
Riley, Lee, and David Schumacher, *The Sheens: Martin, Charlie and Emilio Estevez,* New York, 1989.
International Dictionary of Films and Filmmakers, Volume 3: Actors and Actresses, St. James Press, 1996.
International Motion Picture Almanac 1996 edition, Quigley Publishing Co, 1996.
Sorkin, Aaron, Sheen, Martin, *The West Wing,* Pocket Books, 2002.

Periodicals

The American Feminist, Spring, 2001.
The Guardian (Manchester), November 2, 2001.
Horizon Magazine, December, 1999.
The New York Times, February 4, 2002.
People, January 5, 2001.
Toronto Sun, March 2, 1999; June 30, 1999.

On-line

About.com PrimeTime TV/The WestWing, http://
primetimetv.about.com/library/actors/
blmartinsheenbio.htm?terms=%22martin+sheen%22
http://members.tripod.com/vonne920/
martin_sheen/ms_dialogue.html
Fresh Air, NPR Interview Transcript, http://freshair.
npr.org/guestInfoFA.cfm?name=martinsheen

http://www.eonline.com/News/Items/
0,1,8480,00.html
http://www.nbc.com/The_West_Wing/bios/
Martin_Sheen.html
http://www.webactive.com/webactive/pacifica/
demnow/dn990810.html
http://www.celebrity1000.com/celebritysites/male/
martinsheen
http://www.hollywood.com/celebs/bio/celeb/
344674
Physicians for Social Responsibility, http://www.
psrla.org/sheen.html
http://news.bbc.co.uk/hi/english/entertainment/
newsid_941000/941165.stm
http://members.tripod.com/vonne920/
martin_sheen/order.html

—Ruth Savitz

Sammy Sosa

1968—

Professional baseball player

Chicago Cubs outfielder Sammy Sosa slugged his way to fame and revived flagging attendance at American baseball games by challenging the 1961 hitting record of New York Yankees slugger Roger Maris. In 1998 fans and newcomers to the game sat on edge anticipating Sosa's next swat of the bat. In addition to breaking the 37-year-old National League home-run record and resetting the bar at 66, he became a Latino hero as the first immigrant and first non-white player to gain 60 or more runs in a season.

From Poverty to Professional Athletics

Born on November 12, 1968, in San Pedro de Macoris on the southeastern shore of the Dominican Republic, Sosa is the son of farmer Juan Montero and housewife Lucrecia Sosa. After his father's sudden death from a brain aneurysm in 1975, Sammy, his two sisters and four brothers, and their mother lived in a two-bedroom apartment in an abandoned hospital. Sosa earned dimes by selling oranges on the street and shined shoes for a quarter a pair. He shifted to washing cars for cash and later found steady work as the janitor at a shoe factory.

Playtime found Sosa embroiled in neighborhood boxing matches and makeshift baseball games with a stick for a bat, a milk carton for a glove, and a rolled-up sock for a ball. At age 14, he was thin and gangly, but he demonstrated raw talent at baseball after his brother Juan encouraged him to learn the game and polish his skills. In 1983, Sosa signed with the Philadelphia Phillies, but had to vacate the contract because he was underage. At age 16, he cagily negotiated with scout Omar Minaya for a contract and a $3,500 signing bonus with the Texas Rangers. Sosa kept enough cash to buy his first bicycle and gave the remainder to his mother. His generosity to her and his siblings set a pattern over his extraordinarily lucrative career.

In 1986 Sosa traveled to winter training camp in Sarasota, Florida, his introduction to life and sports in the United States. Although he spoke no English, his career flourished immediately as he led the Gulf Coast League in doubles. He came to treasure American freedoms and prosperity enough to request formal immigration papers and to begin the long process of applying for U. S. citizenship.

At a Glance . . .

Born Samuel Sosa Peralta on November 12, 1968, in San Pedro de Macoris, Dominican Republic; married Sonia; children: Keysha, Kenia, Sammy Jr., and Michael.

Career: Drafted at age 16 by the Texas Rangers; began professional baseball career in the Gulf Coast League for rookies, 1986; traded from the Rangers to the Chicago White Sox, 1989-92; traded to the Chicago Cubs, 1992-.

Awards: South Atlantic League All-Star, 1987; Member of the National League All-Star team, 1995, 1998 ; named outfielder on the *Sporting News* National League Silver Slugger team, 1995; Commissioner's Historic Achievement Award, 1998; Roberto Clemente award for outstanding service to the community, 1998; Sporting News player of the year, 1998; Baseball Commissioner's Historic Achievement Award, 1998; named National League most valuable player by Baseball Writers Association of America, 1998; Gene Autry Courage Award, 1998; Sports Illustrated Co-Sportsman of the Year, 1998.

Addresses: *Home*—San Pedro de Macoris, Dominican Republic; *Office*—Chicago Cubs, Wrigley Field, 1060 W. Addison Street, Chicago, IL 60613-4397.

Stardom amid Frustrations

At age 19, while playing for a Class A team in Gastonia, North Carolina, Sosa was named South Atlantic League All-Star. The next year, he moved up to the Florida State League in Port Charlotte and advanced to the Rangers' Double A club in Tulsa, Oklahoma. More mature and less flighty at age 20, in 66 games, he averaged .297 at batting and racked up seven home runs and 31 runs batted in (RBIs). The unprecedented game-to-game surge in performance rocketed him to the major leagues.

Upon promotion to the Texas Rangers, on June 16, 1989, Sosa joined the team's regular lineup. As a rookie right-fielder against the New York Yankees, for snagging two hits, he generated headlines and predictions of future greatness. The hype accompanying his sudden emergence disappeared after the next 25 games, when his batting average sank to .238 with 20 strikeouts. Demoted to the Rangers' Triple A team

after one month's play, he passed to the Chicago White Sox in July, played the minors for three weeks, and surfaced on August 22 with the White Sox, grabbing attention once more with three hits and a homer.

Inconsistency continued to dog Sosa's playing. 1990 witnessed his debut as a potential major league star. With a .233 batting average, he surpassed other American League players by scoring 32 stolen bases, 26 doubles, 15 homers, and 10 triples. A slump marked by 98 strikeouts in 116 games caused management to doubt his staying power and to send him back to the minors on July 19, 1991.

Glory Days with the Cubs

Sosa began his long romance with fans of the Chicago Cubs after a trade in 1992. A broken right hand and ankle reduced his participation to 67 games. By 1993, his health restored, he managed 93 runs, 36 stolen bases, and 33 home runs and reached stardom as the first player in team history to chalk up 30 home runs and 30 stolen bases in the same season. To commemorate a personal victory and team milestone, he donated his bat to the National Baseball Hall of Fame in Cooperstown, New York. He also ordered a diamond-and-gold pendent spelling out 30-30 over crossed bats and displayed a license tag marked "SS 30-30." In his homeland, he bought a shopping mall and name it "30-30."

The next year Sosa continued his winning streak by topping the Cubs' batting average and leading in RBIs and home runs. By age 27 he earned a place on the National League All-Star team and won the Silver Slugger Award as one of the three best-hitting outfielders in the league. From the *Sporting News*, he received a commendation for power hitting.

Sosa ended the 1996 season on the bench after a pitch fractured his right hand. Despite unforeseen down time, he managed .273 batting average, 40 home runs, and a phenomenal 100 RBIs. In July, selection as the National League Player of the Month boosted his spirits. In the following season, he challenged the National League record with an amazing series of stats—642 at-bats, 303 total bases, 119 RBIs, 71 extra-base hits, 36 home runs, and 31 doubles. The stellar come-back primed him for international scrutiny as he achieved a 200th major league home run and his 1,000th major league hit. It was the beginning of a numbers game that threatened to swamp him.

A Spectacular Season

Sosa's name began to attach to controversy at the halfway point of 1997, when Cubs general manager Ed Lynch offered him $42.5 million for a four-year contract extension. An anti-Sosa rumble among fans and the press left doubt that "So-So" Sosa was worth the boost in pay. Some critics charged that he had become so self-absorbed with the quest to smash records that he placed the team's record far below personal gain. Scout Omar Minaya countered with a psychological explanation. He told *Sports Illustrated,* "You've got to understand something about Latin players whenthey're young—or really any players from low economic backgrounds. They know the only way to make money is by putting up offensive numbers." To Sosa playing for hits was more important that being a team player.

In 1998 Sosa reached a height of performance by settling down at the plate. He took sage advice from his coaches to discipline a hair-trigger response to the pitch, to control the speed of his swing, and to vary the direction of his hits over all the field. To interviewers, he summarized his growth from an untrained boy player to a seasoned athlete earning big money for the first time. The period of reflection worked to Sosa's advantage. In competition with St. Louis Cardinal hitter Mark McGwire that September, both "Slammin' Sammy" and "Big Mac" broke New York Yankee slugger Roger Maris's 1961 record of 61 home runs in a season.

The sizzling upshoot of the record to 63 found Sosa and McGwire tied for honors, but enjoying a friendly face-off. As the pair set and rebroke records, Latinos around the globe took notice. American fans boosted attendance at a game that had once been the national pastime. At season's end, Sosa attained 66 homers to McGwire's 70. According to *Jet,* Sosa said of McGwire, "He's still the man." Sosa shared *Sports Illustrated's* "Man of the Year" title with McGwire, whom he admired as a sports hero and role model. Sosa's soaring success at bat won him a second naming to the National League All-Star team plus a National League Most Valuable Player award and a Gene Autry Courage citation honoring him as an athlete displaying heroism in adversity.

Established Foundation

Immersed in family responsibilities at age 30, at a Chicago condo overlooking Lake Michigan and a luxury summer home at Santo Domingo, capital of the Dominican Republic, Sosa centered his hopes and activities on his wife, Sonia, and their children, Keysha, Kenia, Sammy, Jr., and Michael. Sosa treated his mother to a series of three upgrades in residence and rewarded himself with a fleet of expensive cars, SUVs, and a yacht he dubbed the "Sammy Jr." His ritual of touching his heart and kissing the index and middle fingers of his right hand as he approached the plate honored peace, love, and the two women in his life, his mother and wife. His jersey, number 21, celebrated Puerto Rican star athlete Roberto Clemente of the Pittsburgh Pirates, whom Sosa had admired from early childhood.

Athletic success did not spare Sosa from severe criticism of his actions and attitudes. With class and dignity, he weathered accusations of selfishness and cockiness and faced down boos from disgruntled Chicagoans at the annual Cubs fan convention in February of 2001. One of the league's highest-paid players, he began investing his earnings and time in others. In October of 1997, he established the Sammy Sosa Foundation to aid underprivileged young islanders in the Dominican Republic as well as Chicago's poorest children. To assure local children a chance to advance through sports, he treated them to free admission to Cubs games on "Sammy Sundays." His generosity to youngsters growing up in the type of poverty that he survived won him the Roberto Clemente award for outstanding service to the community.

Accolades continue to pour in to Sosa for his support of charities and for his influence on young fans to emulate his sportsmanship and great-heartedness. In the January of 1999 State of the Union address, President Bill Clinton recognized Sosa, who sat with First Lady Hillary Rodham Clinton in the chamber balcony. The President praised Sosa for aiding his homeland with shipments of beans, rice, and bottled water after Hurricane Georges slammed into the island in September of 1998. Clinton also thanked Sosa for purchasing school books, computers, hospital equipment and ambulances, and an office building to benefit fellow Dominicans. Quoted in *Jet,* Clinton told the nation, " ... sports records are made and sooner or later, they're broken. But making other peoples' lives better, and showing our children the true meaning of brotherhood—that lasts forever."

Sources

Books

Contemporary Black Biography, Volume 21. Gale Group, 1999.
Newsmakers 1999, Issue 1. Gale Group, 1999.
Sports Stars. Series 1-4. U*X*L, 1994-98.
World Almanac and Book of Facts, Annual 2001, p. 1043.

Periodicals

Jet, December 7, 1998; February 8, 1999.
Sporting News, February 12, 2001, p. 61; July 30, 2001, p. 8; September 3, 2001, p. 26.
Sports Illustrated, August 3, 1998, p. 40; June 26, 2000, p. 66.
U. S. News&World Report, September 28, 1998, p. 12.

On-line

Biography Resource Center. Farmington Hills, Mich.: The Gale Group. 2001.

http://www.latinosportslegends.com/sosa-martinez_
    dominators.htmhttp://baseball.espn.go.com/mlb/
    players/profile? statsId=4344
http://www.infoplease.com/ipsa/A0764413.html.

—Mary Ellen Snodgrass

Luis Tapia

1950—

Sculptor

Nobel Prize winner and Mexican poet Octavio Paz wrote, "No matter how terrible and powerful the reasons for leaving their countries, the Hispanics have not broken their ties with their places of origin." Like Los Angeles, Miami, and New York, New Mexico is an American center of Hispanic population. But unlike those booming metropolises, New Mexico is isolated from major cities and navigable waterways; the New Mexican landscape consists mainly of desert and mountain ranges. From the beginnings of Spanish settlement in New Mexico nearly 400 years ago until the turn of the twentieth century—which brought railways, hotels, and tourism to the state—New Mexico had largely been "ignored and virtually forgotten," according to writer Stephen Lewis in the magazine *American Craft.* This combination of isolation and Hispanic heritage has led to artisans and the production of traditional crafts that are unique to New Mexico. Sculptor and *santero* Luis Tapia is one of a number of Hispanic artists out of New Mexico who are "attempting to resolve issues of innovation and self-expression within a rigid framework of traditional forms," Lewis wrote.

Born July 6, 1950, and raised in Santa Fe, New Mexico, Luis Eligio Tapia grew up during an era that stressed cultural homogenization. It was typical for Hispanics to submerge their Latin identities. For example, growing up, Tapia was known as "Lou" or "Louie" to his friends, a more anglicized version of his Latin name. He graduated from St. Michael's High School in 1958 and studied briefly at New Mexico State University. In 1969, Tapia married a fellow artist, the former Star Rodriguez. Tapia worked a retail job at Cooper's Western Wear for five years—he was hired as a stock boy in 1969, and had been promoted to store manager by the time he left, in 1974. During the sixties and seventies, as many Hispanics of Tapia's generation grew older, they began to rediscover their heritage and Latin roots. Tapia was a founder of La Cofradia de Artes y Artesanos Hispanicos. The group helped revive Hispanic art in the Southwest in the early 1970s. Tapia and his wife had a son and a daughter before they divorced in 1980.

Tapia is a *santero,* or craftsman of holy images, called *santos,* which come in a variety of forms. *Retablos* are two-dimensional religious paintings on pine board coated with artist's gesso, *bultos* are three-dimensional sculptures of saints and the Holy Family carved out of aspen or cottonwood, and *reredos* are altar screens

At a Glance . . .

Born Luis Elegio Tapia on July 6, 1950, in Santa Fe, NM; divorced; two children.

Career: Cooper's Western Wear, stocker, store manager, 1969-74; opened own furniture and restoration business, 1974.

Memberships: Founder, La Cofradia de Artes y Artesanos Hispanicos.

Awards: Grant from National Endowment for the Arts, 1980.

Addresses: *Representative*—Owings-Dewey Fine Art, 76 E. San Francisco, Santa Fe, NM 87501.

which are ornately carved and painted. Because of New Mexico's isolation, early Catholic missionaries were left to create their own artwork to assist in worship—though some religious statues made it over from Spain, most were crafted by local artisans. Because religious stories were spread more by word-of-mouth than by visual instruction, they created their own images of religion. Theirs were not influenced by the provincial Baroque and Renaissance symbols and statues that were prevalent in priest-led and -organized Spanish Colonial form of religious worship. The artisans crafted simple but powerful and unique images of worship that reflected their skills as craftsmen.

Tapia was drawn to traditional Hispanic crafts during the civil rights movement of the 1960s. He was involved in the Chicano farm workers's struggles in California and with the militant land reform movement in the villages of northern New Mexico. The experiences compelled Tapia to discover his Hispanic heritage. Like many folk or craft artists, Tapia had no formal art training, but he pursued his interest by studying Hispanic carvings in the Museum of International Folk Art in Santa Fe, New Mexico. He got his start by restoring antique works, and used his retail experience to build a restoration and furniture business. Among his most important works is an early 19th-century altar screen that he repainted for the church at Rancho de Taos.

Tapia began carving his own santos in 1971, giving his first experiments away to older people. The response was so great that people began seeking him out. Tapia's best-known pieces are his carvings of Dona Sebastiana, a popular death figure. Part skeleton and part woman, the frightening Dona Sebastiana rides in her *carreto de muerte,* or death cart, as Tapia carves

her. He adorns his "Nuestra Senora de Guadalupe" with an aura made of painted lightening bolts. His works range in height from eight inches to seven feet tall. He has carved retablos and reredos for church altars that have measured up to 20-by-40 feet. Tapia has strayed from his more-traditional santeros work and has developed a more contemporary, cubist style. He also had built a collection of sleek and sensual carvings of nudes and guitar players, and some abstract works. His recent works include painted carvings of noble characters, including *Homage to Patrocino Barela,* a santero of the 1930s who broke into the New York art scene and became popular with the media, and *Immaculate Heart of Mary.* Both pieces illustrate Tapia's capability for refinement.

In 1987 Houston's Museum of Fine Arts and the Corcoran Gallery in Washington, D.C. organized a traveling art exhibit called *Hispanic Art in the United States.* Unlike Felix A. Lopez, the other santero represented in the show, Tapia sought to make a place for himself in the mainstream art world. While Lopez strove to devote himself full-time to being a santero, Tapia's goal always has been to represent his work among popular works of contemporary art. In 1980 Tapia received a very mainstream honor—he received a grant from the National Endowment for the Arts to fund his work. His work has been shown many times at the Museum of International Folk Art. It is a part of the permanent collections of the Smithsonian Institution, the National Museum of American Art, and the Los Angeles Craft and Folk Art Museum.

One of the greatest limitations on a santero is the need to adhere to tradition. Artists's style, form, and media are often constricted by some collector's and purist's need for the traditional. This can mean any deviation from the traditional aesthetic or craft. For some, this means that Tapia breaks tradition. If he does so, it is with no intention to disrespect or satirize the traditional forms. Rather, he considered his work to be in a constant dialogue with tradition, updating it so that it can remain a vital part of contemporary work. He "looks for the nourishment of blending tradition with contemporary culture so that the tradition may continue to grow and flourish," suggested his biography, located online at the Collector's Guide Website. At first glance, Tapia's work may look quite traditional, but in the seventies he was ridiculed for his use of modern paints that produce brighter colors. Tapia has said he imagines the old santeros would appreciate the bolder colors. He used a mix of both modern and antique chisels and rasps, while the authenticity of an artist's tools can be of great concern to a purist.

For a number of years Tapia participated in the Spanish Market and artisan's competition, which is held every July in Santa Fe. The Market is the most important venue for Hispanic artists in the Southwest, according to Stephen Lewis in *American Craft.* Like many artists trying to forge new ground with their work, Tapia is frustrated by what he considers the Market's "overly literal adherence to 'tradition,'" Lewis wrote. When the Spanish Colonial Arts Society insisted Tapia forgo showing his own new designs and copy the work of older santos, he declined. "I believe in the tradition," Tapia told Lewis in an interview. "I am the tradition."

Sources

Periodicals

American Craft, February/March 1991, p. 38.

On-line

Dictionary of Hispanic Biography, Gale Research, 1996. Reproduced in *Biography Resource Center,* The Gale Group, 2001 http://galenet.galegroup. com/servlet/BioRC (February 20, 2002).
The Collector's Guide, http://www.collectorsguide .com (February 21, 2002).

—Brenna Sanchez

Dara Torres

1967—

Olympic swimmer, model, TV reporter and announcer

Resilient Olympic sprinter Dara Torres brought home gold, silver, and bronze medals in swimming in 1984, 1988, and 1992 before entering a voluntary seven-year retirement. After defeating bulimia, which hampered her stamina, she began a career in modeling and TV sports commentary. At age 32, she returned to athletic fitness by following an intense regimen of workouts, diet, and treatment for chronic asthma. She re-entered Olympic competition and won five more medals—three bronze and two gold. Her career total reached four bronze, one silver, and three gold Olympic medals.

From Hyperactivity to Competition

Born on April 15, 1967 in Beverly Hills, California, Torres was born to former model Marylu Torres, a Miss Rheingold finalist, and real estate broker Edjward Torres. Dara Torres enjoyed a privileged childhood and displayed more than normal energy levels and heightened urges to best her siblings. She as well as her four older brothers—Mike, Kirk, Brad, and Rick —and little sister Lara learned swimming from their mom. Dara entered competitive swimming at age eight and quickly outpaced her elder brothers. After her mother's divorce and remarriage to tournament tennis player Edward Kauder in 1977, Dara rechanneled her hyperactivity, with Kauder's help, into athletic competition.

When she was 12 Torres set a national age-group swim record. On entering her teens at the prestigious Westlake School in Los Angeles, she received a "Most Likely to Break a Record in the Guinness Book" citation. At age 14, under the guidance of Tandem Swim Club coach Terry Palma of Culver City, California. Up, Torres started collecting a growing list of honors and won national acclaim. Upon entering Mission Viejo High School, to be near her coach and team for daily workouts, she boarded with Flo and Mike Stutzman and their 10-year-old daughter, Heather. Torres practiced regularly at the University of Southern California pool and followed strict house rules that allowed group activities, but no dating. In February 1983, an article in *Sports Illustrated* remarked on her breaking swim champ Jill Sterkel's world record at Amersfoort, Holland.

At a Glance . . .

Born on April 15, 1967, in Beverly Hills, CA. *Education:* University of Florida, degree in broadcasting and communication, 1989.

Career: Commentator TV sports, NBC, ESPN, TNT, Fox News, Fox Sports, and CNN; research assistant, NBC Sports; spokesperson Tae-Bo workout tapes; host, Discovery Channel; fashion model, 1992-99.

Awards: National age-group swim record, 1979; world speed record, Amersfoort, Holland, 1983; gold medal for the 400-meter freestyle relay, Los Angeles Olympic Games, 1984; three gold medals for 100-meter and 400-meter freestyle and 400-meter relay, Pan Pacific Championships, 1987; bronze medal for the 400-meter freestyle relay and silver medal for the 400-meter medley, 1988; 28 All-America honors, University of Florida, 1986-89; gold medal for the 400-meter free relay, Barcelona Olympics, 1992; 50-meter freestyle first place, U. S. Open, San Antonio, Texas, 1999; 100-meter freestyle, Phillips 66 Nationals in Federal Way, Washington, 2000; two gold medals for 400-meter freestyle and 400-meter medley, three bronze medals for 50-meter and 100-meter freestyle and 100-meter fly, Sydney Olympics, 2000; 12-time national swim champion; former world-record holder 50-meter freestyle, American record holder 50-meter freestyle and 100-meter fly, 2000.

Addresses: *Office*—USA Swimming, 1 Olympic Plaza, Colorado Springs, Colorado, 80909-5746. *Website*—http://www.dara-torres.com/

From Champion to Olympian

At 17 years old Torres was already 5' 10.5". She amazed Coach Marck Schubert of the Mission Viejo swim club with off-the-gun weight shifts, instant reflexes, and fast twitch muscle response, which biopsies the previous year compared with similar reactive tissue in Olympic diver Greg Louganis. She battled bulimia during regular swim meets and still took a first place in the Olympics 400-meter freestyle relay at the 1984 Los Angeles Games. Three years later, at the Pan Pacific Championships, she garnered a sweet reward for hard work—three golds in the 100-and 400-meter freestyle and the 400-meter relay. In 1988, she won bronze for the 400-meter freestyle relay and silver for the 400-meter medley.

While completing a bachelor's degree in broadcasting and communications at the University of Florida, Torres managed to garner 28 All-America honors for athletic achievement. In 1990 following several years of therapy she finally defeated her eating disorder. At the 1992 Barcelona Olympics she won gold once more in the 400-meter free relay and retired, contented with an additional first place, bringing her total of Olympic medals to six.

In 1993 Torres was diagnosed with chronic asthma, which she controlled with daily doses of inhalant drugs. Undeterred, she did not venture far from the sports realm. Work as sports commentator and reporter for ESPN, TNT, Fox News, and Fox Sports and as sports research assistant at NBC introduced her to different career goals. She branched out by hosting science and technology programs for the Discovery Channel, fashion modeling, and emceeing tae-bo workout tapes.

Training Again at 33

In March 1999 Torres resumed her athletic career after her boyfriend teased that just talking about swimming put a gleam in her eye. Her relationship with the boyfriend faded, but thoughts of a return to the lanes revived the natural competitiveness of the two-time Olympic gold medalist. Her first phone call to swim sprint specialist Richard Quick, the Stanford University and Olympic women's team coach, convinced him that she had reignited the competitive spark. With her savings, private donations, and sponsorship by Speedo and Computer Associates, she shucked a lucrative modeling contract and her work on the tae-bo infomercials and flew to Palo Alto, California. Despite the lapse of seven years and loss of muscle tone, she convinced Quick that she sincerely intended to qualify for the 2000 U.S. Olympic Team.

Torres also sought the support of 1992 swim teammate Jenny Thompson, a five-time gold medalist, who helped her locate temporary residence in Menlo Park, California. At age 32, Torres became the first American swimmer to train for a fourth try for Olympic gold. At Stanford University, she was surprised to feel old and underweight among the svelte, smooth-limbed teen-aged rivals, who dubbed her "granny," according to *Newsweek*.

Quick began retraining Torres in newer methods of stretching the body, rotating the hips, and gazing down while stroking out. To master the modern freestyle, she attended a youth swim camp and practiced among children who weren't even born when she retired in 1992. To compensate for lost breathing capacity from asthma, she forced a full exhale under water and drew a replacement breath when she surfaced. Workouts matched up to four hours of pool time with spinningand flexibility exercises, weight training, yoga, and Pilates.

Beat the Odds

Glorying in the rebuilding of flaccid limbs, Torres beefed up with 20 pounds of muscle while cross-training and stabilizing abdominal muscles, lower back, hips, thighs, and buttocks. Under the guidance of British strength trainer Robert Weir, an Olympic discus and hammer throw competitor, she increased bench-presses from 105 to 205 pounds. The workouts started her on the way to new challenges. In December of 1999 at the U. S. Open in San Antonio, Texas, she won the 50-meter freestyle against her friend Jenny Thompson. In March of 2000 Torres snagged a national title in the 100-meter freestyle at the Phillips 66 Nationals in Federal Way, Washington. She told *Newsweek*, "I am more competitive now than I've ever been in my life."

For 13 months Torres swam, trained, and lifted weights for six hours a day, specializing in kickboard workouts and the Gravitron, her favorite exercise machine. The program demanded one-on-one strength training, dry-land aerobics, flip turn maneuvers, and weekly circuit training by jumping rope, building abs, rope climbing, and doing hundreds of crunches and pullups daily. De-stressing muscles called for pummeling from two trainers who walked in sock feet on her back and legs. The added exertion required six meals per day comprised of 30 percent protein, 30 percent fat, and 40 percent carbohydrates supplemented with 25 pills, Gu carbohydrate powder, Zone bars, Runner's Advantage (liquid creatine), and hydration with Revenge sports drink.

In view of her fervor, fellow Olympic swimming medalist Donna de Varona surmised that Torres had quit before reaching the greatness she was capable of. The return was a means of completing "unfinished business." Torres warded off a spurious announcement by the *New York Post* that she was dating New York Senator Alphonse D'Amato. More serious were teammates' accusations of attention grabbing, which prompted Coach Quick to begin training Torres away from the other Olympic aspirants. She strongly rebutted the implication of *USA Today* columnist Christine Brennan that Torres might owe her rapid reduction of lane sprints to performance-enhancing drugs. Torres's mother credited her daughter's performance to a life-long pattern of overachieving. Quick told *USA Today*, "She's packed three years of training into one."

A Star with a Future

The records began to fall to Torres's intense energy and determination. In June of 2000 she set a U. S. record at the 50-meter freestyle trials. In early August of 2000 at the Olympic tryouts in Indianapolis, she thrashed out her fastest times to qualify for the Sydney events in the 50-meter and 100-meter freestyle, 100-meter butterfly, and 400-meter freestyle relay. Speculators immediately predicted that she would become the oldest U. S. female swimmer to win a medal and the first swimmer to medal at four separate Olympics. Their prophecies came true as she left Sydney with three bronze medals for the 50-meter and 100-meter freestyle and the 100-meter fly and two gold medals for the 400-meter freestyle and 400-meter medley.

While looking for ways to aid young swimmers and give something back to the sport that brought her fame, Torres savored stardom, yet stored her medals under her bed. In November *Women's Wear Daily* invited her along with gymnast Nadia Comaneci and track star Jackie Joyner-Kersee to the unveiling of a salute to female athletes at New York City's Madison Square Garden. In March of 2001 Torres published a brief memoir, "The Beauty of Dreams," in *Rodale's Fitness Swimmer*, in which she acknowledged a maturity that enabled her to select and attain worthy aims. Graciously, she recognized Coach Quick for building her cardiovascular endurance and core strength.

Torres showed no intention of abandoning sports. She considered applying her understanding of physiology and nutrition to coaching, sports commentary, and public relations. To keep the hunger for competition under control, she worked for Turner Sports, served *Self Magazine* as fitness expert, and began pursuing extreme sports, including high-speed race-car driving at the Toyota Grand Prix at Long Beach.

Sources

Books

The Complete Marquis Who's Who. Marquis Who's Who, 2001.

Periodicals

Newsweek, August 14, 2000.
New York Times, August 8, 2000; August 15, 2000; August 17, 2000.
People Weekly, September 18, 2000.
Rodale's Fitness Swimmer, November, 1999; July, 2000; November, 2000; March, 2001.
Sports Illustrated, February 28, 1983; June 18, 1984; August 28, 2000.
Sports Illustrated for Women, March 1, 2001.
Swimming, July 30, 1999.
WWD, November 17, 2000.

On-line

http://www.dara-torres.com/
http://sportsillustrated.cnn.com/ siforwomen/news/1999/07/30/spotlight/
http://www.swiminfo.com/ lane9/news/3106.asp

http://www.fina.org/bio_Torres.html
http://www.sportshollywood.com/ asktorres.html
http://uk.sports.yahoo.com/oly/oldgames/bio/
  14076.html

—Mary Ellen Snodgrass

Luis Valdez

1940—

Playwright, Director, Writer, Actor, Teacher

Acknowledged as the "godfather of Chicano theater," Luis Valdez is the founder and artistic director of El Teatro Campesino, which translates to *The Farmworkers Theater.* Started in 1965, Valdez has led the theater company to international acclaim and numerous awards. The author and director of numerous plays, Valdez has also written and directed two films: *Zoot Suit,* based on his play of the same name and *La Bamba,* the 1987 hit movie based on the life of the Mexican-American rock star, Ritchie Valens. It's his work with El Teatro Campesino, however, and his dedication to advancing the role of the arts in people's lives that sets Valdez apart from his contemporaries. "If you want to understand modern Latino theater, you have to know that Luis was the start," Sean San Jose of San Francicso's Campo Santo Theater Company told Karen D'Souza of the *San Jose Mercury News.* "Everything that came after him was informed by him."

Born Luis Miguel Valdez on June 26, 1940 in Delano, California, Valdez was raised in the agricultural labor camps around California where his parents worked in the fields, picking what ever crop was in season. It was a small role in an elementary school play and seeing his parents and those like them work the long, grueling hours for little pay that moved Valdez to use the theater to shed light on the Latino experience. "I took what I most feared, the thing I was most ashamed of, and turned it into something I could write about," he told students at San Diego State Universtiy in 2000.

El Teatro Campesino

Following graduation from high school, Valdez attended San Jose State University where he produced his first play, *The Shrunken Head of Pancho Villa,* in 1964. Following a short time with the famed San Francisco Mime Troupe, Valdez joined activist Cesar Chavez in 1965 and sought to raise funds for the grape boycott and farmworkers strike that Chavez had organized, and bring attention to the plight of migrant farmworkers. Thus begun El Teatro Campesino which performed short plays based on the struggles of the farmworkers and people of Mexican descent. "He addressed cultural and Chicano issues from the point of view of a migrant farmworker," Professor Arsenio Cordova of the University of New Mexico told the *Albuquerque Journal.* "He's been able to address those attitudes totally, of discrimination."

After four years the small theater company received national recognition by winning an Obie Award in New York and a Los Angeles Drama Critics Award in 1969, and then another L.A. Drama Critics Award in 1972. In 1977 Valdez co-wrote the screenplay for *Which Way is Up?,* a comedy starring Richard Pryor, and

received a Rockefeller Foundation Artists-In-Residence grant which enabled him to write the most famous play to come out of El Teatro Campesino in 1979, *Zoot Suit.*

Zoot Suit was based on the murder of a Mexican American and the subsequent unfair trial of Mexican Americans or *zoot suiters,* as they were termed by the press in Los Angeles in the early 1940s. A musical, Valdez's *Zoot Suit* become one of the most popular plays to have ever originated in Los Angeles and was the first play by a Chicano to be presented on Broadway. A movie version, also written and directed by Valdez and starring Edward James Olmos, was released in 1981 and was nominated for a Golden Globe Award for Best Musical Picture.

La Bamba

Valdez had his most mainstream success in 1987 with another film he wrote and directed, *La Bamba.* The story of Mexican American rock and roller Ritchie Valens, whose brief time in the spotlight ended when he was killed in the same plane crash as Buddy Holly, was one of that year's biggest box office successes. That same year, Valdez adapted his play, *Corridos: Tales of Passion and Revolution,* for PBS and won the prestigous Peabody Award. That play had previously won the San Francisco Bay Critics Circle Award for Best Musical, when it premiered in 1983.

In 1993 Valdez co-wrote and directed a made-for-TV movie of *The Cisco Kid* starring Jimmy Smits. Broadcast on the Turner Television Network, the entire production was filmed on location in Mexico. The following year, Valdez received the prestigious Aguila Azteca Award (Golden Eagle Award), which is the highest honor bestowed by the Mexican government for citizens of other countries.

In 2000 Valdez became a founding faculty tenured professor at the Center for Teledramatic Arts and Technology at California State University, Monterey Bay. In this role, the playwright works with students from a variety of backgrounds and encourages them to use technology in an effort to continue the tradition of raising social issues through art. "Today, the opportunity to distribute artistic work and share untold stories has never been greater," Valdez told Alejandra Navarro of the *Modesto Bee,* adding that he envisioned live theater going out over the Internet.

Back to "the Farmworker Question"

In 2001 Valdez returned to a play he began writing in 1976, and to a subject matter that's never left him: farmworkers. "It's been 25 years," Valdez confessed to the *San Jose Mercury News.* "It's time to come full circle, to come back to the farmworker question." *Mundo Mata* tells the story of two migrant worker brothers divided by their beliefs. One brother is ideal-istic and eager to join the United Farm Workers, while the other falls into drugs after a tour of duty in Vietnam, and begins working for the landowners.

In the title role of Mundo was one of Valdez's sons, Kinan, who shares his father's beliefs in the social significance of art and seeks to instill those ideas in El Teatro Campesino of the future. "We, the new genera-tion at the theater, really want to take the company back to its roots in agitational propaganda," Kinan Valdez told the *San Jose Mercury News.* "The farm-workers are still stuck in the same place. We want to remind people of the struggle."

In his work, Valdez attempts to illustrate, not just the plight of Latinos and the prejudices they face, but also the fact that there are differences among all people and that there is much to be learned from them. "What comes out in the final analysis," he told the students at San Diego State University, "is we are all more alike than we think, we're just from different tribes."

Selected Works

Plays

The Shrunken Head of Pancho Villa, 1964.
La Virgen de Tepeyac, 1971.
La Carpa de los Rasquachis, 1974.
El Fin del Mundo, 1976.
Zoot Suit, 1979.
Tibercio Vasquez, 1980.
Corridos: Tales of Passion and Revolution, 1983.
I Don't Have to Show You No Stinking Badges, 1986.
Bandido!, 1994.

The Mummified Deer, 2000.
Mundo Mata, 2001.

Screenplays

Which Way Is Up?, 1977.
Zoot Suit, (also director)1982.
La Bamba, (also director) 1987.

Television Plays and Movies

Corridos: Tales of Passion and Revolution, (also director) 1987.
La Pastorela: A Shepherd's Tale, 1991.
The Cisco Kid, (also director), 1993.

Books

Actos: Produced Between 1965-70, Cucaracha Press, 1971.
Aztlan: An Anthology of Mexican American Litera-ture, (with Stan Steiner), Knopf, 1972.
Pensamiento Serpentino: A Chicano Approach to the Theater of Reality, Cucaracha Press, 1973.

Sources

Albuquerque Journal, April 1, 2001.
Daily Aztec (San Diego State University), May 11, 2000.
Modesto Bee, April 29, 2000.
San Jose Mercury News, May 31, 2001.

Other

Additional information for this profile was obtained from El Teatro Campesino.

—Brian Escamilla

Mario Vargas Llosa

1936—

Writer

Already a profound chronicler of South America's political and social reality, Mario Vargas Llosa took an unusual step for a writer in the 1980s: he immersed himself in the political life of his native Peru rather than simply standing outside it as an observer. In the widest sense, Vargas Llosa has been a champion of freedom, a writer who spoke out against abuses of military and government power, who defied literary conventions, and who stood up for the cause of freedom of expression for writers worldwide. His more than 15 novels and numerous other writings have gained him international acclaim as one of Latin America's most significant writers of the 20th century.

Vargas Llosa was born in the Peruvian city of Arequipa on March 28, 1936. He spent part of his childhood in Bolivia and was a voracious reader from the start; with an inclination toward classic novels of adventure such as *The Three Musketeers,* he sometimes penned his own endings, if the ones supplied were not to his liking. Vargas Llosa moved back to Peru with his family in 1945. For a time they lived in the small city of Piura, whose desolate house of prostitution would figure heavily in Vargas Llosa's novel, The Green House (*La casa verde*). Vargas Llosa later attended parochial school in Lima, but after his father found out about his literary efforts he was sent for two years to a military school called Leoncio Prado.

Stayed On in France

From then on, Vargas Llosa resisted his parents' wishes. Attending law school in Lima with the intention of serving Peru's poor, he began to write in earnest and in 1958 won a trip to France as a prize for a short story he had submitted as a contest entry. The trip would be the beginning of a 15-year exile from Peru, during which Vargas Llosa ascended to literary fame. His first novel, *The Time of the Hero* (in Spanish *La ciudad y los perros,* 1962) drew on his experiences at the military school. Military personnel there gave Vargas Llosa invaluable publicity when they burned 1,000 copies of the novel in the school's courtyard.

With the highly acclaimed *The Green House* (1966) and *Conversation in the Cathedral* (*Conversación en la catedral,* 1969), Vargas Llosa adopted what became his characteristic mode of narrative in his more substantial works: a nonlinear approach to storytelling that alternated and juxtaposed, sometimes suddenly, the points of view of various characters. Vargas Llosa's intent was not literary experimentation, but rather an

At a Glance . . .

Born March 28, 1936, in Arequipa, Peru; married Julia Urquidi, 1955; married Patricia Llosa, 1965; three children. *Education:* Attended military school Peru; attended law school in Peru; University of San Marcos, Spain, Ph.D., 1959.

Career: Moved to Paris, France, after winning literary prize, 1958; worked as journalist with Agence France-Presse and with ORTF radio and television network; published debut novel *La ciudad y los perros* (trans. as *The Time of the Hero*), 1963; University of London, faculty member, 1966-68; visiting professorships in Americas and Europe; 1960s-1990s; Peruvian presidential candidate, 1990; has published over 50 books and five plays.

Memberships: PEN international writers' organization; servied as president, 1976-79.

Selected awards: Romulo Gallegos award, 1967, for *La casa verde;* Cervantes Prize for literature, 1994; National Book Critics Circle award for criticism, 1997.

Addresses: *Office*—Agencia Carmen Balcells, Diagonal 580, 08021 Barcelona, Spain; *Agent*—c/o PEN, 7 Duke St., London SW3, England.

ambitious effort to capture social formations in their totality. The 600-page *Conversation in the Cathedral,* set during the dictatorship of Peruvian strongman Manuel Odría in the 1940s and 1950s, presented a panoramic view of a society plagued by corruption at many levels.

Vargas Llosa's unease with military institutions showed through once again in the satirical novel *Captain Pantoja and the Special Service (Pantaleón y las visitadoras,* 1973), which depicted a military officer assigned to procure prostitutes for a jungle brigade of soldiers. In 1976 Vargas Llosa became president of the international writers' organization PEN, which works to help writers who have been persecuted for their political beliefs. The political cast of many of his novels sensitized him to the plight of writers imprisoned in repressive societies, but Aunt Julia and the Scriptwriter (*La tía Julia y el escribidor,* 1977) was an autobiographical work that juxtaposed the events leading to his own first marriage against a background of televison soap opera. Vargas Llosa has also written erotic novels on occasion.

Rejected Socialism

As a young man Vargas Llosa had admired Cuban Communist Party leader Fidel Castro, but he grew disillusioned with socialism. As a result his long friendship with Colombian novelist Gabriel García Marquez ended in 1976 in a slugfest in a Mexico City theater—Vargas Llosa knocked García Marquez out cold. Vargas Llosa's novel *The War of the End of the World (La guerra del fin del mundo,* 1981), set in 19th-century Brazil, took a more pacifist view of conflict in its depiction of a struggle between the Brazilian government and a group of religious fanatics holed up in a city they had established. The novel was interpreted as a symbolic representation of the ways in which struggles between right-wing governments and violent left-wing rebels were sapping the strength of Latin American societies.

He cast a jaundiced eye on European and American leftists who embraced a chic radicalism in the Third World while doing little about it at home; he wrote, as quoted in the *New Republic,* that such activists treated Latin America like "a plebian mistress with who all those secret fantasies and frightful excesses—prudently repressed in their relations with their wives (their native countries)—can be given free rein." Peruvian leftist intellectuals attacked Vargas Llosa for his role in a government commission that blamed members of a small Andean community for the killing of eight journalists, and the experience marked something of a crisis point for the novelist. Vargas Llosa became more and more involved in the political life of the homeland he had abandoned for so long.

After leading several mass protests against the left-wing Peruvian government's plan to nationalize key industries, Vargas Llosa ran for president of the country himself in 1990. Calling for an expansion of free enterprise, he surged to an early lead as his oratorical skills matched those he had shown with the pen. In one speech late in the campaign, according to the *National Review,* he compared Peru to "an ancient, beautiful, never-ending book." In the end, however, Vargas Llosa lost the election to Alberto Fujimori, who later ran into trouble because of allegations of civil rights abuses. Vargas Llosa has not run for elective office again, but has continued his involvement in Peru's civil life.

Some in the literary community actually welcomed Vargas Llosa's election loss, for the campaign had somewhat reduced his extraordinary fertility as a writer. Vargas Llosa looked back on his campaign in the memoir *A Fish in the Water (El pez en el agua,* 1993), and took up political questions in several new novels. *Death in the Andes (Lituma en los Andes,* 1993) dealt with the Shining Path (Sendero Luminso) Marxist guerrilla movement that had troubled Peru for many years, and *The Feast of the Goat (La fiesta del chivo,* 2001) was an epic of the long dictatorship of Rafael Trujillo, who ruled the Dominican Republic from 1930 until his 1961 assassination.

Vargas Llosa had lost none of his ability to provide masses of realistic detail; many of the true-life characters in The Feast of the Goat were so accurately drawn that the book caused a scandal in the Dominican Republic, even half a century after the events it depicted. Well into his seventh decade, Vargas Llosa showed no signs of slowing down. Many called him the conscience of Peru, but his substantial body of writing perhaps qualified him to serve as conscience and moral compass for a much wider area.

Selected writings

Los jefes (The Leaders; short stories), Rocas (Barcelona), 1959, translation by Ronald Christ and Gregory Kolovakos published in *The Cubs and Other Stories,*Harper, 1979.

La ciudad y los perros (novel), Seix Barral (Barcelona), 1963, translation by Lysander Kemp published as *The Time of the Hero,* Grove, 1966, 2nd edition, Alfaguara (Madrid, Spain), 1999.

La casa verde (novel), Seix Barral, 1966, translation by Gregory Rabassa published as *The Green House,* Harper, 1968.

Conversación en la catedral (novel), two volumes, Seix Barral, 1969, translation by Rabassa published as *Conversation in the Cathedral,* Harper, 1975.

Pantaleón y las visitadoras

(novel), Seix Barral, 1973, translation by Christ and Kolovakos published as *Captain Pantoja and the Special Service,* Harper, 1978.

La tia Julia y el escribidor (novel), Seix Barral, 1977, translation by Lane published as *Aunt Julia and the Scriptwriter,* Farrar, Straus, 1982.

La guerra del fin del mundo (novel), Seix Barral, 1981, translation by Lane published as *The War of the End of the World,* Farrar, Straus, 1984.

Historia de Mayta (novel), Seix Barral, 1985, translation by Alfred MacAdam published as *The Real Life of Alejandro Mayta,* Farrar, Straus, 1986.

Quien mató a Palomino Molero? (novel), Seix Barral, 1986, translation by MacAdam published as *Who Killed Palomino Molero?,* Farrar, Straus, 1987.

El hablador (novel), Seix Barral, 1987, translation by Lane published as *The Storyteller,* Farrar, Straus, 1989.

Elogio de la madrastra (novel), Tusquets (Barcelona), 1988, translation by Lane published as *In Praise of the Stepmother,* Farrar, Straus, 1990.

Lituma en los Andes (novel), Planeta (Barcelona), 1993, translation by Edith Grossman published as *Death in the Andes,* Farrar, Straus, 1996.

A Writer's Reality (nonfiction), Syracuse University Press, 1991.

El pez en el agua (memoir), Seix Barral, 1993, translated by Lane as *A Fish in the Water: A Memoir,* Farrar, Straus, 1994.

Los cuadernos de don Rigoberto, Alfaguara, 1997, published as *The Notebooks of Don Rigoberto,* translated by Edith Grossman, Farrar, Straus and Giroux, 1998.

La Fiesta del chivo, Alfaguara (Madrid, Spain), 2000, published as *The Feast of the Goat,* translated by Edith Grossman, Farrar, Straus, and Giroux, 2001.

Sources

Books

Dictionary of Hispanic Biography, Gale, 1996. Periodicals

Economist, January 20, 2001, p. 9.

Library Journal, April 1, 1998, p. 126.

National Review, May 14, 1990, p. 26; April 17, 1995, p. 53.

New Leader, November-December 2001, p. 30.

The New Republic, February 12, 1990, p. 20.

Publishers Weekly, April 11, 1994, p. 49; April 21, 1997, p. 49; July 30, 2001, p. 55.

Review of Contemporary Fiction, Spring 1997, p. 70.

Time, February 12, 1996, p. 75; December 10, 2001, p. 107.

U.S. News & World Report, May 9, 1988, p. 69; November 5, 1990, p. 15.

On-line

Contemporary Authors Online. The Gale Group, 2001. Reproduced in *Biography Resource Center.* Farmington Hills, MI: The Gale Group, 2001. (http://www.galenet.com/servlet/BioRC).

—James M. Manheim

Nydia Velázquez

1953—

U.S. Congressional representative

The first Puerto Rican-born woman elected to the U.S. Congress, Nydia Velázquez has served New York State's 12th District since winning election in 1992. She has also, however, served as an able advocate for the interests of her Puerto Rican homeland. In this mixed deployment of her energies Velázquez was perhaps an ideal reflection of her constituency, for New York's Puerto Rican population has long divided its time fluidly between island and mainland metropolis. A veteran of many years in New York's political trenches, Velázquez has never lost touch with her roots in rural Puerto Rico.

Velázquez was born on March 23, 1953, in the village of Yabucoa in Puerto Rico's sugar-cane country. Trying to support his nine children, her father worked variously as a cane-cutter, butcher, cockfighting promoter, and construction materials salesman. Velázquez's own later interest in the problems faced by small businesses came from her own observations of her father's experiences. "He didn't have the capital, the equity or the sophistication of information to be successful," she told *Crain's New York Business.* Her father was also a local political leader who instilled in his daughter a lifelong belief in social justice.

Earned Master's Degree

Though no one in her family had ever finished high school, much less college, Velázquez excelled in school from age five onward. She graduated early from high school and enrolled at the University of Puerto Rico's Río Piedras campus at 16, majoring in political science and graduating in 1974 with honors. Velázquez went to New York for a master's degree at New York University, but then returned to Puerto Rico for several years. In 1981 she took up residence in New York once again to become an adjunct professor of Puerto Rican studies at the City University of New York's Hunter College unit.

Part of the reason for her bipolar career was that Velázquez, like so many other Puerto Ricans in New York, maintained strong ties with her family members, who had been reluctant to see her leave in the first place. But Velázquez also had brushes with the conservative administration of Puerto Rico's New Progressive Party, which made it clear that her own brand of progressive politics was unwelcome. More and more her career became centered on New York, where she married and began to become involved in politics.

At a Glance . . .

Born March 28, 1953, in Yabucoa, Puerto Rico; married Paul Bader. *Education:* University of Puerto Rico, B.A., 1974; New York University, M.A., 1976. *Religion:* Roman Catholic. *Politics:* Democrat.

Career: University of Puerto Rico, instructor, 1976-81; Hunter College, New York, adjunct professor of Puerto Rican Studies, 1981-83; special assistant to New York U.S. Rep. Edolphus Towns, with responsibility for immigrantion and Hispanic affairs, 1983; served on New York city council, 1984-85; Migration Director, Puerto Rico Dept. of Labor & Human Resources, 1986-89; Secretary, Puerto Rico Dept. of Community Affairs in the U.S., 1989-92; U.S. Representative, New York 12th District, 1992-.

Address: *Office*—2241 Rayburn House Office Building, Washington, DC, 20515.

Served on New York City Council

Velázquez first entered the political arena in 1983 as a special assistant to Brooklyn U.S. Representative Edolphus Towns after her temporary position at Hunter College ended. She worked on immigration legislation and gained enough contacts that when a New York city council seat became available after its holder was convicted on attempted extortion charges, she was appointed to fill it. Velázquez lost the seat in the 1986 council election and worked in Puerto Rico as a divisional director in the commonwealth's Department of Labor and Human Resources from 1986 to 1989. Then she returned to New York once again to take a high-level liaison position representing the Puerto Rican government on the mainland United States. One of her first tasks was to direct aid dollars to Puerto Rican communities devastated by Hurricane Hugo. The job also stoked her political ambitions. Spearheading a voter-registration campaign financed by the commonwealth's government, Velázquez was able to place her name and face before New York's Hispanic voters.

In 1992 Velázquez was one of several candidates who angled for New York's new 12th District seat, created in the 1990 congressional redistricting to promote the election of a Hispanic candidate. The district encompassed parts of Brooklyn, Queens, and Lower Manhattan and was dubbed the "Bullwinkle" district in reference to its bizarre shape. Facing charges that she was too entwined with Puerto Rico to represent New Yorkers effectively, Velázquez's faced incumbent con-

gressman Stephen Solarz, who for his part insisted that a non-Hispanic was qualified to represent a predominantly Hispanic district. Velázquez defeated Solarz and another Latina candidate to win the fall primary election, tantamount to election in the largely poor and heavily Democratic district. Her victory was celebrated enthusiastically in her Puerto Rican hometown.

The fall campaign was marred by the anonymous release of medical records showing that Velázquez had attempted to take an overdose of sleeping pills in 1991, depressed over her mother's illness and a brother's drug abuse problems. "It was a painful time," she told *Time.* "But I've learned I can't be a robot trying to solve everybody's problems without paying attention to my own needs." Velázquez faced the issue head-on; it did her no damage and may even have helped her with district voters, who gave her 77 percent of the vote in the November 1992 election.

Re-Elected Despite Reduced Latino Percentage

Velázquez cruised to re-election in 1994 and 1996. The following year the boundary lines of her district were ruled to have been impermissibly based on racial categories (although Hispanics can be of any race), and the new district that resulted contained a sharply reduced Latino proportion of 49 percent. The sometimes outspoken Velázquez also wrangled with local Democratic party leaders, and she faced unfavorable demographic trends—by the late 1990s most of New York's Hispanics came from places other than Puerto Rico. For all these reasons, observers speculated that Velázquez might face a primary challenge in 1998. But by that time she had built a formidable grass-roots and fundraising organization, and the potential challenge evaporated.

In Congress Velázquez has continued to work on behalf of immigrants and to take an interest in Puerto Rican affairs. Velázquez supported the island's commonwealth status rather than statehood or independence from the United States. She was among those arrested during protests that eventually brought an end to military exercises at the U.S. Navy's Vieques bombing range in the year 2000. Her influence rose sharply when she became the ranking Democrat on the House's Small Business Committee in 1998. That post helped Velázquez grease the wheels for legislation aiding small business owners hurt by the terrorist attacks of September 11, 2001, and put her in line for a powerful committee chairmanship should the Democrats manage to regain their House majority in the 2002 elections.

Velázquez had lobbied former president Bill Clinton to increase Hispanic representation in his adminstration, but became a bigger thorn in the side of President George W. Bush. She pushed for tax relief for small business owners (including tax deductions for health insurance for the self-employed) as Congress debated Bush's tax cuts in 2001 and 2002, telling the *Boston Business Journal* that "Bush says the economy is in trouble and that tax cuts are the main solution to the problem. Yet he neglects the prime force in this economy—small business—instead favoring big business and the richest people in the country." Velázquez faced redistricting once again as a result of New York's loss of a congressional seat after the 2000 census, but seemed likely to emerge unscathed. She seemed a rising political star whose influence could only grow as Hispanic representation in the United States showed its inevitable increase.

Sources

Books

Barone, Michael, and Richard E. Cohen, *The Almanac of American Politics: 2002,* National Journal, 2001.

Periodicals

Boston Business Journal, February 16, 2001, p. 31.
Campaigns and Elections, April 2000, p. 18.
Crain's New York Business, November 15, 1999, p. 24; July 24, 2000, p. 4.
Time, November 2, 1992, p. 44.
US Newswire, October 3, 2001.
WWD, July 11, 1996, p. 2.

On-line

http://www.house.gov/velazquez

—James M. Manheim

Raquel Welch

1940—

Actress

After moving from Beverly Hills to New York City with her husband in 1985, Raquel Welch reflected in *Ladies Home Journal* that her big California home had been "a glossed-over paradise, a padded cell." The description might have been a metaphor for the first part of Welch's acting career, which trapped her in the role of sex symbol. Nearly universally known as a star, Welch has had few actual hits over her film career. Nevertheless, she has proven a durable figure in the ever-changing Hollywood scene and has carved out a niche for herself beyond the one afforded her by her natural allure.

The child of a Bolivian-born father and an American mother, Welch was born Raquel Tejada on September 5, 1940, in Chicago. While she was still a toddler her family moved to La Jolla, California, outside of San Diego, where her father worked as a General Dynamics Corporation engineer. She took dance lessons as a child and became a cheerleader in high school, while also performing in school plays. Thus blessed with the discipline to make the most of her natural good looks, she began to take home top prizes from California beauty pageants. In 1957 she won the title of Miss Fairest of the Fair, and graduated from La Jolla High

School the following year. Her IQ was once measured at 140, but scholarly pursuits were not on her mind.

Appeared in Elvis Presley Film

In the spring of 1959 Raquel married her high school boyfriend James Welch, and the couple quickly had a son and daughter (daughter Tahnee has gone on to an acting career of her own, appearing in 1985's *Cocoon,* among other films). She tried to break into films and television, enjoying little success but landing a shot on the weather segment of a San Diego television station for a time. The marriage fell apart in 1964, and Welch deposited her children with her parents and lit out for New York, dreaming of stardom. She got as far as Dallas, where she modeled and worked as a cocktail waitress. She returned to California discouraged, but now began to land bit parts in films such as Elvis Presley's *Roustabout.*

Welch rocketed to stardom as a result of meeting a male American entertainment entrepreneur who made a career out of developing and promoting the talents of young female stars. Welch and publicist Patrick Curtis formed a company primarily devoted to the promotion

At a Glance . . .

Born Raquel Tejada in Chicago, Illinois, September 5, 1940; daughter of a Bolivian-American engineer father and an Anglo-American mother; married James Welch, 1959 (divorced 1964); married Patrick Curtis, 1967 (divorced 1971); married André Weinfeld, 1980 (divorced); married Richard Palmer, 1999; children: Damon and Tahnee; two adopted children. *Education:* Attended San Diego State College.

Career: Weather reader on a television station in San Diego, early 1960s; film debut in *A House Is Not a Home,* 1964; signed to 20th Century Fox studio, 1966; roles in *Fantastic Voyage* and *One Million Years B.C.,* 1966-67; appeared on Broadway in *Woman of the Year,* 1982; many guest-star appearances on television, 1980s and 1990s.

Awards: Golden Globe award, 1974, *The Three Musketeers.*

Addresses: *Agent*—Cunninghame, Escott, Dipene & Associates, 10635 Santa Monica Blvd., Suite 130, Los Angeles, CA 90025.

of Welch's career; the pair married around 1967. Several more parts and a *Life* magazine photo spread brought Welch to the attention of the Twentieth-Century Fox studios; she was signed to a contract and was featured in the science-fiction film *Fantastic Voyage* (1966).

That film was widely acclaimed, but Welch's next few outings, mostly low-budget comedies made in Europe, were less prestigious. Still, Welch acquiesced in her growing image as sex symbol; she told *Hispanic* magazine that at the time she thought it was fun "to strut my stuff." That image grew into full flower with the 1966 British production *One Million Years B.C.,* a remake of a tale set in prehistoric times that allowed Welch to strut her stuff in a bikini made of animal fur pelts. As a result she landed on the cover of over 100 magazines, although the film itself had been only a modest success.

Featured in Interracial Love Scene

After Welch toured South Vietnam with comedian Bob Hope, producers were typecasting her mostly as a representation of physical beauty. She found film work mostly in Europe, appearing in the United States in *Bedazzled* (1968) as a character who embodied the

inspiration of Lust. Welch was in the news the following year because of the western *100 Rifles,* which featured her in an early interracial love scene with former football star Jim Brown. There was a good-natured quality even to Welch's least ambitious film outings that bespoke a greater talent than she had yet been allowed to show, but her first lead role, in 1970's *Myra Breckinridge,* was a disastrous flop all around.

Attempting to salvage something usable in the film, Welch gained a reputation for being difficult to work with—entirely undeserved in her view. "All I ever fought for was quality in my films," she was quoted as saying in *Ladies Home Journal.* "I really felt I was being penalized for being the sex symbol they had created, and that made my Spanish blood boil." Her appearance in *The Three Musketeers* (1973) and its sequel allowed her to show her considerable sense of humor. Nevertheless, her film roles of the 1970s were largely forgettable; they included the roller-derby drama *Kansas City Bomber* (1973). Welch had more luck with several television specials over which she could exercise more creative control. After divorcing Curtis in 1971, she married French producer André Weinfeld in 1977.

The year 1981 brought Welch serious disappointment, and then finally creative triumph and respect. She was dropped from the cast of the movie adaptation of John Steinbeck's *Cannery Row* in 1981 in favor of Debra Winger. The studio, Metro-Goldwyn-Mayer, claimed that Welch's behavior on the set had been unprofessional; Welch argued that the studio was merely trying to cut costs and sued for $20 million. After a long court battle she was awarded $10.8 million, but later even that award was overturned. The debacle did have a positive outcome, however: Welch fled Hollywood for New York and a starring role in the Broadway musical *Woman of the Year.* That appearance brought Welch the critical respect she craved, although its strenuous schedule may have caused her to suffer a miscarriage after she became pregnant with her third child.

In 1984 Welch marketed three successful fitness videos, and she increasingly found success with television projects. In the 1987 made-for-TV film *Right to Die,* she gave a widely praised and decidedly unglamorous performance as a woman suffering from a terminal disease. Welch occasionally appeared in movies, playing herself in the final installment of the *Naked Gun* spoof series, *The Naked Gun 33 1/3,* and found several guest star slots in both dramatic and comic television series through the 1990s. She often, as on one episode of *Seinfeld,* played herself and gently spoofed her image. She returned to the stage as a replacement for Julie Andrews in the comic musical *Victor/Victoria* in 1997. In 1999 she married pizza chain owner Richard Palmer, 14 years her junior. In 2002 Welch appeared in *American Family,* a television series featuring a Latino family.

Selected films

A House Is Not a Home, 1964.
Roustabout, 1964.
Do Not Disturb, 1965.
A Swingin' Summer, 1965.
Fantastic Voyage, 1966.
Fathom, 1966.
Shoot Loud, Louder, I Don't Understand!, 1966.
Bedazzled, 1967.
The Queens: The Oldest Profession, 1967.
One Million Years B.C., 1967.
Bandolero!, 1968.
The Biggest Bundle of Them All, 1968.
Lady in Cement, 1968.
Flare Ups, 1969.
100 Rifles, 1969.
The Magic Christian, 1970.
Myra Breckenridge,
1970.
Hannie Calder, 1971.
Bluebeard, 1972.
Fuzz, 1972.
Kansas City Bomber, 1972.
The Last of Sheila, 1973.
The Three Musketeers, 1974.
Wild Party, 1974.
The Four Musketeers, 1975.
Mother, Jugs and Speed, 1976.
L' Animal, 1977.
Crossed Swords, 1978.
The Prince and the Pauper, 1978.

Restless, 1978.
You and Me Together, 1979.
Stuntwoman, 1981.
The Legend of Walks Far Woman, 1982.
Right to Die, 1987.
Scandal in a Small Town, 1988.
Trouble in Paradise, 1988.
Hero for Hire, 1990.

Sources

Books

Dictionary of Hispanic Biography, Gale, 1996.
Haining, Peter, *Raquel Welch,* St. Martin's, 1984.
International Dictionary of Films and Filmmakers, Volume 3: Actors and Actresses, St. James, 1996.

Periodicals

Entertainment Weekly, June 20, 1997, p. 28.
Hispanic, April 1988, p. 20.
Ladies Home Journal, February 1985, p. 44; May 1989, p. 46.
People, August 2, 1999, p. 110.
Variety, June 30, 1997, p. 72.

On-line

Internet Movie Database http://us.imdb.com
All Movie Guide http://www.allmovie.com

—James M. Manheim

Cumulative Nationality Index

Page numbers appear in **bold**

Cumulative Occupation Index

Page numbers appear in **bold**

Actors
Diaz, Cameron, **73–75**
Hayworth, Rita, **102–104**
Lopez, Jennifer, **116–119**
Moreno, Rita, **134–137**
Olmos, Edward James, **155–159**
Quinn, Anthony, **176–179**
Sheen, Martin, **195–198**
Valdez, Luis, **210–212**
Welch, Raquel, **219–221**

Artists
Dalí, Salvador, **63–65**
Kahlo, Frida, **113–115**
See also Sculptors

Astronauts
Ochoa, Ellen, **149–151**

**Athletes. See Olympic athletes; specific
  sports occupations**

Attorneys. See Lawyers

**Authors. See Novelists; Playwrights; Po-
  ets; Writers**

Bandleaders
Puente, Tito, **172–175**
See also Conductors

Baseball players and managers
Pérez, Tony, **166–168**
Rodriquez, Alex, **183–185**
Sosa, Sammy, **199–202**

Basketball players
Arcain, Janeth, **19–21**

Boxers
De La Hoya, Oscar, **66–69**

Businesspersons
Fox, Vincente, **89–91**
Napolitano, Grace, **138–141**

Cabinet officials, U.S.
Cisneros, Henry, **50–52**
Martínez, Mel, **127–130**

Choreographers
Alonso, Alicia, **11–14**

Clergy
Flores, Patrick, **86–88**

Composers
O'Farrill, Arturo "Chico," **152–154**
See also Songwriters

Conductors
Domingo, Plácido, **76–78**
See also Bandleaders

Dancers
Alonso, Alicia, **11–14**
Hayworth, Rita, **102–104**
Lopez, Jennifer, **116–119**
Moreno, Rita, **134–137**

Doctors. See Physicians

Filmmakers. See Movie directors

Golfers
Lopez, Nancy, **120–122**

Government officials, U.S.
Castro, Ida, **40–42**

Journalists
O'Brien, Soledad, **146–148**
Torres, Dara, **206–209**

Labor activists
Chavez-Thompson, Linda, **47–49**
Corona, Bert, **57–59**

Lawyers
Castro, Ida, **40–42**
de la Rúa, Fernando, **70–72**

Mayors, U.S.
Cisneros, Henry, **50–52**
Pérez, Eddie Alberto, **163–165**

Ministers. See Clergy

Models
Diaz, Cameron, **73–75**
Torres, Dara, **206–209**

Movie directors
Almodóvar, Pedro, **7–10**
Valdez, Luis, **210–212**

Musicians
O'Farrill, Arturo "Chico," **152–154**
Puente, Tito, **172–175**
Santana, Carlos, **189–191**

Novelists
Allende, Isabel, **4–6**
Castillo, Ana, **33–35**
Esquivel, Laura, **79–81**
Fuentes, Carlos, **92–94**
Hijuelos, Oscaar, **105–107**

Olympic athletes
Arcain, Janeth, **19–21**
De La Hoya, Oscar, **66–69**
Parra, Derek, **160–162**
Torres, Dara, **206–209**

Opera singers
Domingo, Plácido, **76–78**

Pageant contestants
Quiñones August, Denise, **180–182**

Physicians
Novello, Antonia, **142–145**

Playwrights
Valdez, Luis, **210–212**

Poets
Castillo, Ana, **33–35**

Politicians, international
Aznar, José Maria, **22–24**
Bánzer Suárez, Hugo, **25–28**
Perón, Eva "Evita," **169–171**
See also Presidents and heads of state

Politicians, U.S.
Napolitano, Grace, **138–141**
Pérez, Eddie Alberto, **163–165**
Sanchez, Loretta, **186–188**
Velázquez, Nydia, **216–218**

Cumulative Subject Index

Page numbers appear in **bold**

Cumulative Name Index

Page numbers appear in **bold**